Classical Literature

BLACKWELL INTRODUCTIONS TO THE CLASSICAL WORLD

This series provides concise introductions to classical culture in the broadest sense. Written by the most distinguished scholars in the field, these books survey key authors, periods and topics for students and scholars alike.

PUBLISHED

Classical Literature
Richard Rutherford

Homer
Barry B. Powell

IN PREPARATION

Sophocles
William Allan

Cicero
Robert Cape

Ancient Comedy
Eric Csapo

Catullus
Julia Haig Gaisser

Ancient Rhetoric and Oratory
Thomas Habinek

Ancient History
Charles Hedrick

Roman Satire
Daniel Hooley

Roman Historiography
Andreas Mehl

Greek Tragedy
Nancy Rabinowitz

Ancient Fiction
Gareth Schmeling

Euripides
Scott Scullion

Classical Mythology
Jon Solomon

Augustan Poetry
Richard Thomas

Classical Literature

A Concise History

Richard Rutherford

Blackwell
Publishing

350 Main Street, Malden, MA 02148–5 020, USA
108 Cowley Road, Oxford OX4 1JF, UK
550 Swanston Street, Carlton, Victoria 3053, Australia

The right of Richard Rutherford to be identified as the Author of this Work has
been asserted in accordance with the UK Copyright, Designs, and Patents Act 1988.

First published 2005 by Blackwell Publishing Ltd

Library of Congress Cataloging-in-Publication Data

Rutherford, R. B.
Classical literature : a concise history / Richard Rutherford.
p. cm. – (Blackwell introductions to the classical world)
Includes bibliographical references and index.
ISBN 0-631-23132-3 (alk. paper) – ISBN 0-631-23133-1 (alk. paper)
1. Classical literature – History and criticism.   I. Title.   II. Series.

PA3001.R88 2004
880′.09–dc22   2003024528

A catalogue record for this title is available from the British Library.

Set in 10/12.5pt Galliard
by Graphicraft Limited, Hong Kong
Printed and bound in the United Kingdom
by MPG Books Ltd, Bodmin, Cornwall

For further information on
Blackwell Publishing, visit our website:
http://www.blackwellpublishing.com

Contents

To Peter
who knows it all already

Preface

My aim in this volume is to provide a short, accurate and readable guide to the works of Greek and Latin literature which have generally been found most important and interesting. In addition, I have tried to say something about a number of works which have either been only recently discovered or for other reasons have been undervalued in earlier criticism. The chronological limits are from approximately 750 BC to AD 400, from the emergence of literacy in Greece to the decline of the Western Empire, from Homer to Augustine.

There are many histories of classical literature, some of them encyclopaedic and unreadable, or at least unread. Two points (other than brevity) make this book unusual. First, there are several good one-author accounts of Greek literature, and likewise of Latin; there are also several large histories of both with chapters by multiple authors. I know of no other book by a single author which attempts to survey the whole field, both Greek and Latin. Second, the arrangement of the book is not straightforwardly chronological, but generic and thematic: in each chapter a particular area of literature is surveyed, with discussion of both Greek and Roman examples. This book aims at a synoptic view, while also trying to make it easier to see the wood surrounding the trees.

There are obvious objections to this project. One is to declare that the book is simply too short to do the job. This may be true, but it is a complaint that can be made about any work of this kind, of whatever length: there will always be more to say and other passages to quote. I have judged it more important to produce a book which the reader has a realistic chance of reading end to end. Second, the author's competence may be questioned. One of the shorter histories of Greek literature, by Gilbert Murray (1897), contains a preface that opens with the words: 'To read and re-read the scanty remains now left to us of the Literature of Ancient Greece, is a pleasant and not a laborious task.' This book was published

when the author was 31. A much older scholar, it is reported, scrawled in
the margin of his copy 'Insolent puppy!'[1] Puppy or prodigy, Murray obviously
wrote the book he wanted to write, and I have done the same, though
without claiming to be a scholar of his stature. This is a partial, subjective and
highly selective survey. A third objection would be that the arrangement is
unhelpful, and that I should have stuck to a more orthodox chronological
sequence. But although chronological discussion may be valuable for some
purposes, I have concluded that this more experimental ordering has advantages for my own purposes, and that it is (for example) more helpful to move
from Euripides to Menander to Plautus and Terence in the same chapter
rather than having to look back over a bulky section on diverse genres of
the Hellenistic period. It is true that this does mean that discussion of (say)
Horace is spread across several different chapters. This does not seem to me
a serious difficulty when a book has an index; and chronological arrangement carries its own problems. Indeed, there are many important works of
classical literature that are of uncertain date, sometimes within a range of
years, sometimes even within a given century. Horace's *Ars Poetica* is
probably a late work, but nobody can prove it. Five of Sophocles' seven
plays cannot be dated within his long career; experts dispute whether the
lyric poet Corinna belongs in the fifth or the third century.

A fourth objection might be to the whole notion of literary history as an
attempt to impose structure on an ocean or a quagmire. However, while
I have taken account of the cautionary words of David Perkins in his
stimulating *Is Literary History Possible?* (1992), I hope that the form chosen
for the present volume avoids some of the more obvious traps. Readers will
find little about 'periods' or 'movements' or 'circles'. We must always
remember how much classical literature we have lost: we have, for instance,
massive amounts of prose from the fourth century BC but virtually no verse
(making it hard to assess the originality of the poets of the third century).
We possess no complete epic between Homer and Apollonius. We have no
early Latin tragedy and no late Latin comedy. Key figures such as Archilochus
and Simonides, Ennius and Gallus survive only in scrappy fragments. The
reader should supply in most sentences the tediously cautious phrase 'in the
present state of our evidence'. I have avoided endless repetition of 'possibly'
and 'perhaps', but I believe that most of the sentences in this book are at
least more likely to be true than their opposites (including this one). The
notes, which are intended mainly for students or scholars, give access to
works which will help those wishing to test my assertions to find the evidence on which they are based.

Literary history has been compared with aerial photography: one sees the
geographical contours, but not the detail. In this age of satellite cameras we
may perhaps be bolder, and I have done my best to include a fair number of

quotations, though fewer and shorter than I would have wished because of the limitations of space. I hope at least that they may whet the appetite of the reader to track down these authors in anthologies or complete versions. Translations are usually my own unless otherwise stated.

The scope of the book is restricted to classical *literature*. It is not a history of the ancient world, or of classical scholarship, or of the transmission or reception of ancient literature, though all of these are adjacent and indispensably relevant topics (a few words on these topics, intended only to provide the most basic framework, are included in the Introduction). Philosophy and religion figure where they are embodied in literary form: hence Plato bulks large but Aristotle is marginal. Politics play a small role, political theory still smaller, while art, architecture and archaeology do not appear. None of this is to deny the fascination and the importance of all these disciplines.

In the spelling of ancient names, a matter which evidently excites many people more than it does me, I have followed the formations which seem to me most natural in modern English, in the conviction that readers unfamiliar with the ancient languages are not helped by such spellings as Akhilleus for Achilles.

As for the intended audience of this book: scholars will find little that is new in it, though they may be glad to be reminded of certain points. I shall be very pleased if undergraduate and graduate students find it helpful. But my chief hope is that it may lead the non-classical reader, or simply the reader, to discover how much there is that still lives and delights and provokes in the literature of the ancient world, so often misrepresented as dead or dry-as-dust. I have done my best to give at least a glimpse of what these authors have to offer.

A further word is perhaps necessary about the term 'classical', which appears in the title. My use of it to cover the authors who fall within this fairly extensive period follows fairly common usage today. Many older works use 'classical' in a more restricted sense and with strongly evaluative implications: the 'classical' authors are the best ones, those who most deserve to be read. The term derives from the Latin word *classis*, which originally designated one of the divisions of the people of Rome into six classes for taxation, that is, on the basis of their wealth. Citizens of the first class were called *classici*. Cicero uses the term metaphorically, in ranking philosophers; Gellius a century later uses it in a literary context; Pope appears to have introduced it into English. For many the whole concept of 'classics' is long discredited. In an egalitarian age any elite, even of writers, seems suspect. Modern critics are hostile to the very idea of a canon of 'great books', whatever the criteria for choosing them. Moreover, we no longer assume that Greek and Latin literature or civilization have a special status, above all else and immune from adverse criticism. Even if all these points are accepted, however, it does not follow that the literature of Greece and Rome should be seen as irrelevant or out-of-date. Obviously there is much that is strange to us, and some things that are objectionable, in classical literature, but that is not a reason for ceasing to study it. This book, in other words, assumes that the reader is willing to give classical literature a chance to prove its continuing worth.

One of the objections that will immediately strike the reader is the fact that almost all the authors discussed are men. Of course this is regrettable, but there is no getting round the evidence. Only a tiny proportion of what survives comes from female writers; how many female readers there were is an important question, but virtually impossible to answer. Hence in speaking of authors in an ancient context I have normally used the masculine pronoun, despite modern convention.

In a work of this kind it is inevitable that there will be errors, but they would have been more numerous without the help of many friends. The project was originally proposed to me by Al Bertrand, who has encouraged my work at all stages with good humour and intelligence, as well as showing a generous tolerance of the gradual expansion of the original scale of the book. No one could have been a more supportive and tactful editor. Initiated in 2000, the work was completed during a sabbatical year (2002–3): I am deeply grateful to my college, Christ Church, for granting me this leave, and to Dirk Obbink and Bruno Currie for shouldering my burdens during that time. My warmest thanks go to two colleagues who have read the whole book in draft, Peter Brown and Robert Parker: their painstaking comments drew my attention to many important new points. They have also done much to remove factual errors, expel ambiguities, and chasten my prose style. Catherine Whistler has, as always, given constant moral support as well as taking a keen interest in the content of the book. I owe much also to those who have commented on specific chapters: Kathleen Coleman, Bruno Currie, Belinda Jack, Chris and Margaret Pelling, Nancy Rutherford, Jacqueline Thalmann, and Carolinne White. The text was copy-edited by Helen Gray, whose meticulous work did much to clarify a complex typescript. I alone am responsible for all surviving blemishes. Others who have advised me on bibliography and the like will, I hope, accept a general expression of thanks. I am also aware of a long-standing and continuing debt to many colleagues in Oxford and elsewhere, who through their publications and the stimulus of their conversations have made me see things afresh or admire a work more. At a time when government and administrative bodies seem to do little but place obstacles in the way of research, it is all the more important to acknowledge the unselfish generosity of countless individual scholars.

This quality of scholarly generosity of spirit has been evident in Peter Parsons throughout his academic career, and I count myself fortunate indeed to have had him as a friend and colleague for over twenty years. In the year of his retirement it gives me special pleasure to dedicate this book to him with much admiration and affection.

RBR
October 2003

Acknowledgements

The author and publishers would like to thank the following for permission to use copyrighted material:

Quotation from Andrew Miller, *Greek Lyric: An Anthology in Translation* (Hackett 1996), Copyright © 1996 by Hackett Publishing Company: Reprinted by permission of Hackett Publishing Company, Inc. All rights reserved.

Quotation from James Michie, *The Poems of Catullus* (originally published by Rupert Hart Davis, London 1969; reprinted by Wordsworth Editions 1998). Reprinted by permission of Wordsworth Editions Ltd. All rights reserved.

Quotation from James Michie, *The Odes of Horace* (originally published by Rupert Hart Davies, London 1964, reprinted by Random House 2002). Reprinted by permission of David Higham Associates.

Every effort has been made to trace the copyright holders, but if any have been inadvertently overlooked, the publishers will be pleased to make the necessary arrangements at the first opportunity.

Abbreviations

Abbreviations for authors and their works follow a regular and, I hope, easily understood pattern (e.g. 'Virg. *Aen.*' for Virgil, *Aeneid*): often the full title is used shortly before. Doubtful cases may usually be clarified from the list of abbreviations in the *Oxford Classical Dictionary*.

In addition the following are used, mainly in the notes:

F or fr. = 'fragment number'
fl. = 'floruit' (i.e. an author was active at the period mentioned)

AP	*Anthologia Palatina*, the collection of epigrams which constitutes the bulk of the so-called Greek Anthology.
BNP	M. Beard, J. North, S. Price, *Religions at Rome i, A History* (1998): all references to this work are to the first volume.
CHCL	*Cambridge History of Classical Literature* (see Further Reading, p. 334).
CQ	*Classical Quarterly.*
FGH	*Fragmente der griechischen Historiker*, ed. F. Jacoby (1923–).
G&R	*Greece and Rome.*
GLP	*Greek Literary Papyri*, ed. D. L. Page (Loeb series, 1942).
HSCP	*Harvard Studies in Classical Philology.*
JHS	*Journal of Hellenic Studies.*
JRS	*Journal of Roman Studies.*
PCPS	*Proceedings of the Cambridge Philological Society.*
PMG	*Poetae Melici Graeci*, ed. D. L. Page (1962).
SH	*Supplementum Hellenisticum*, ed. H. Lloyd-Jones and P. J. Parsons (1982).
SIG	*Sylloge Inscriptionum Graecarum*, ed. W. Dittenberger (3rd edn, 1915–24).
TAPA	*Transactions of the American Philological Association.*

TGF   *Tragicorum Graecorum Fragmenta*, ed. B. Snell and others
           (1971–1985, 2nd edn of vol.1, 1986).
W   attached to a fragment-reference, indicates a citation from
           M. L. West, *Iambi et Elegi Graeci* (2nd edn, 1989).
ZPE   *Zeitschrift für Papyrologie und Epigraphik.*

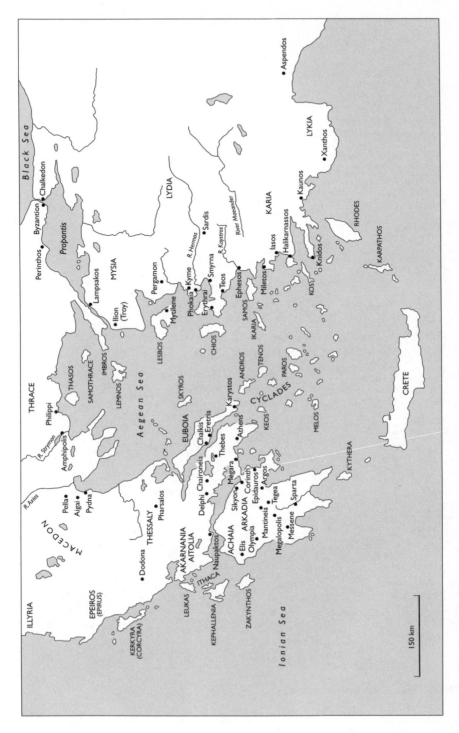

Map 1   The Greek world

Map 2   Italy in the first century BC

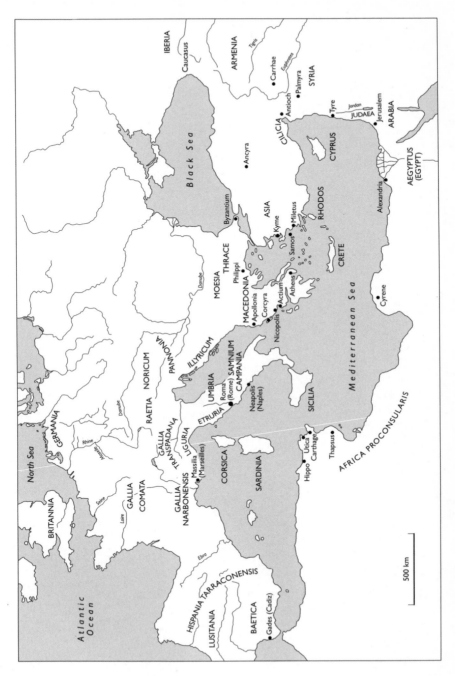

Map 3   The Roman Empire in the time of Augustus

Introduction

In this introduction I deal with three topics. First, I give a brief outline of the history of ancient Greece and Rome, to help the reader see the literature of these societies against the background of political developments; second, I discuss the important topic of genre; third, I summarize some of the problems that arise from the way in which these texts have come down to us over the centuries.

I

The time span of this book extends from the late eighth century BC to the early fifth century AD, a period of some 1,100 years. In the study of ancient literature and history, as in most study of past times, it is conventional to speak of certain subdivisions or 'periods' of both literary history and socio-political history: thus in English literature we refer to the Romantic movement, the Victorian age, and so on. In Greek history a common modern division is into the archaic period (up to the end of the sixth century BC), the classical period (from about 500 BC to the death of Alexander), and the Hellenistic age (from Alexander to the beginning of the Roman Empire); in Roman history, the obvious division is between the Republic and the Empire, and lesser subdivisions also reflect political change, for instance the Augustan age, the Julio-Claudian or Flavian periods, the 'High' and 'Low' Empire. Such divisions are convenient, but can often be misleading. In literary history, one division which, for all its popularity, has hampered criticism in the past is between the so-called golden and silver eras of Latin literature. The metaphor of metals, as in Hesiod's myth of ages, reflects an evaluative judgement, a traditional assumption that Cicero and Virgil belong to a golden age of literature, while Lucan and Tacitus do not. All period-divisions of this kind are suspect, for there are many writers who bridge the divisions, many kinds of literature that are not affected by political change, and many aspects of the arts which are more fruitfully examined in a long perspective. However, it is obvious that literary forms do not remain static over a period of centuries, and some attempt to define phases in literary history is inevitable; what matters is that we should remain aware of their partial validity and artificial construction.

Greek literature begins for us with Homer and Hesiod, authors of extensive poetic works dealing mainly with myths of man and god. The chronology is murky, but we are probably dealing with compositions from around 720–680 BC. At this date the Greeks had already begun to travel more widely. They inhabited not only the mainland region we still call Greece but Asia Minor, and were also settling permanently all around the Mediterranean: 'colonies' soon existed in Sicily, South Italy, North Africa and the Black Sea. What most strikes the modern reader, especially in contrast with Rome, is the separation of Greeks into independent political units: the *polis* (plural *poleis*), the small city-state, was tiny by modern standards, but throughout their history the Greeks resisted unification into larger leagues or kingdoms.

Greek travellers and traders regularly encountered the large monarchies of Egypt, Lydia and later Persia. Contact with the Near East not only fertilized the mythic imagination but gave the Greeks access to more prosperous cultures and (very importantly) an alphabet. The Homeric poems were preserved because someone, probably in the seventh century, thought them important enough to write down. After Homer and Hesiod there is a large gap of time before we reach the next writers to survive in bulk, namely Pindar and Aeschylus in the fifth centuries. In between we have the tantalizing remains of lyric poetry, composed by poets of scattered date and origin – Archilochus from Paros, Alcaeus and Sappho from Lesbos, others from other Greek islands, from Rhegium in Italy, from Ephesus and Smyrna in Asia Minor. Continuous historical narrative has to be reconstructed from later accounts, making detailed study of most *poleis* an impossibility. The exceptions tend to be those which were politically or culturally important, or both, so that in later times readers wanted to know about these places and authors were able to supply the information. Hence the bulk of our evidence concerns Athens and Sparta: in particular, they figure prominently in the *History* of Herodotus.

The authors of *1066 and All That* concluded that in English history only two dates were truly memorable. In describing the classical world I shall allow myself five (emboldened in what follows to distinguish them from other dates mentioned more in passing). The first is **479** BC, the conclusion of the Persian King Xerxes' unsuccessful invasion of Greece (following up the earlier attempt by his father Darius). The paradoxical success of the Greeks in repelling the far larger forces of the Persians was a key moment in their development: not only did it seem to vindicate their own way of life, one of freedom and self-sufficiency as opposed to enslavement to a monarch, but it also stimulated their cultural self-confidence. The rest of the century is the heyday of Athens, which eventually assumed leadership of an anti-Persian alliance, one that gradually developed into an empire run in Athens' own interests. Athenian literature of the fifth century included the great tragedies and comedies; many other writers and thinkers (including Herodotus) were drawn to Athens because of her wealth and power. Socrates talked and taught there, visiting sophists such as Gorgias performed there. This was also the period of the radical democracy, which made Athens famous for its constitutional structures as well as for its literary achievement. In the end Athens fought a long war against Sparta and her allies rather than be deprived of her empire; defeated, she lost it anyway. Thucydides (writing from 431 onwards) chronicled the conflict in a work which became a paradigm of political and military history. In the fourth century our evidence shifts from verse to prose: instead of tragedy and comedy, oratory and philosophy become especially important. Plato and Aristotle taught in Athens, though the former grew steadily more disillusioned with his city, and the latter (not a native Athenian) migrated to Macedonia, where he gave instruction to the young Prince Alexander.

Political independence ended for the Greek states when Philip II of Macedon, Alexander's father, conquered their armies at the battle of Chaeronea: the orator Demosthenes' long efforts to nurture resistance to Philip ended in disaster. From that time on Greece was dependent on the will of larger and far more powerful states, first Macedon and ultimately Rome. But Greek horizons were now hugely expanded. The conquests of Alexander, extending as far as the northern regions of India, created with astonishing speed an empire larger than that of Persia, but he seems to have given little thought to the preservation of his conquests, and after his death in **323** (my second memorable date) they became the object of jealous conflict among his heirs and generals. Alexander's death marks the start of the Hellenistic age (so-called because of the theory that he and his successors 'Hellenized' or educated their conquered peoples into civilized Greek ways, a proposition now viewed as neither factually nor politically correct). One of the more notable effects of Greek expansion was the development of a more universal form of the Greek language, the so-called *koine* or 'common speech': the various regional dialects became less important for literature, though sometimes utilized for recherché effect. A persistent counter-tendency to ignore the *koine* and mimic the old Attic classics even in vocabulary and syntax reached its height in the second century AD.

Alexander's empire eventually split into three vast kingdoms, Macedonia itself, the Seleucid empire (Asia and the East) and the Ptolemaic kingdom

(Egypt), the last two being named after two of Alexander's marshals. Greece itself became a political backwater, though Athens long retained its intellectual glamour as a university city. In due course Romans such as Cicero and the poet Horace would go there for education, especially in philosophy. But other major centres of culture now emerged, especially Alexandria, the capital of Egypt, where under royal patronage major poets composed in old genres and new (Apollonius in epic, Theocritus in short and exquisite poems on country life, Herodas in deliberately coarse verse on city lowlife). Minor poets above all cultivated the epigram. Prose flourished too, including much scientific and speculative writing: Alexandria with its great library was a centre of learning. The scholar-poet Callimachus, who had a powerful influence on Roman literature, supremely merged poetry and arcane learning.

Inevitably we think that Greece comes first, then Rome. This is true in terms of literature but entirely false if we think of history. One traditional date for the 'beginnings' of Greek history is the supposed date of the first Olympic Games, 776 BC; this is little more than 20 years away from the legendary foundation date for Rome, 753 BC. More substantially, Greeks had been resident in parts of Sicily and Italy since at least 700; Aristotle and others knew about Rome. More militaristic than the Greeks, the Romans determinedly extended their domain throughout Italy, then to Sardinia, Sicily and beyond. Firm discipline and organization, strong, sometimes ruthless leadership, and a refusal to accept defeat, eventually made theirs one of the most formidable empires in history. Their attitude to the Greeks and their culture was always complex: on the one hand Quintilian could claim that 'the Greeks excel in teaching, but the Romans in examples of doing – and that is greater'. On the other hand, Horace memorably commented that 'vanquished Greece captivated her savage conqueror' – that is, Romans succumbed to the spell of Greek culture.[1] The earliest major figure known to us is Livius Andronicus, who may have been part-Greek and who translated the *Odyssey* into Latin, wrote both comedies and tragedies on Greek mythic themes, and transplanted a number of Greek metres. But our first complete works in Latin, the comedies of Plautus, do not much predate 200 BC, by which time virtually all the most famous Greek writers were dead. Roman literature is strongly indebted to Greek, yet is never merely imitative.

As for politics, Rome increasingly showed interest in the nations to the East and by the second century BC was expanding her conquests across the Mediterranean. The kingdoms established by Alexander's successors were gradually overthrown. Rome's conquest ('liberation') of Greece, together with her other achievements from 220–146, were chronicled by the Greek historian Polybius, the first of a long line of Greek writers who came to Rome and celebrated or at least sought to record, explain or justify her successes. The last of the Hellenistic kingdoms, Egypt, fell to Rome with the defeat of Mark Antony and Cleopatra (a descendant of Ptolemy) in **31** BC. This is our third key date, marking not only the end of the Hellenistic era but the beginning of the Roman empire, with the ascendancy of Octavian, shortly to take the solemn title of Augustus. His establishment of one-man dynastic rule changed the nature of Roman politics, after an eventful half-century dominated by civil wars (the period which witnessed the careers of Caesar and Cicero, the poetry of Lucretius and Catullus, and the early works of Virgil and Horace). The 'Augustan' era (31 BC to AD 14) was distinguished by some of the most gifted writers Rome ever produced, especially Virgil, Horace, Propertius, Tibullus and Livy. Ovid, a younger author, straddled the reigns of Augustus and Tiberius; exile was the punishment for his subversively frivolous poetry. The last years of Augustus saw not only exiled writers but burning of books. Autocracy was on the increase.

The Republic was never restored, despite emperors' proclamations and the efforts of conspirators. Much literature of the first century AD is over-shadowed by the expectations of the emperor and the fears of the authors. Writers could be executed for their politics (Lucan, Seneca), and it is hardly fair for us to condemn some of them for playing it safe (Pliny, Martial). Imperial literature of this period often has a dark and sinister flavour (Seneca's tragedies, Lucan's and Statius' epic, Juvenal's satires); philosophy emphasizes personal morality and the need to preserve the inner integrity of the indi-vidual (Seneca, Epictetus); the historical works of Tacitus, with their damning presentation of royal family, court and senate, are the high empire's most lasting memorial. Yet in many ways the stability of the empire improved government and even benefited the citizens: our perspective is skewed because so much of the Latin literature of this period comes from the disenchanted aristocratic class.

Bad emperors could not go on forever. The period from Nerva's accession to the death of Marcus Aurelius was famously singled out by Gibbon as a time of supreme human prosperity. Roman literature becomes less viciously intense and more refined: archaism becomes the fashion, led by the Emperor Hadrian. Greece re-enters the picture with a change in the balance of our evidence in the second century, from which the most attractive figures are the moralist-biographer Plutarch, and Lucian, the immortal writer of satiric dialogues, essays and fantasies. Though politically powerless, the Greeks had not lost their capacity to devise new genres and pour old wine into new bottles.

Modern studies of later antiquity are naturally much concerned with the rise of Christianity. Its gradual encroachment on the literature of the pagan world makes a fascinating study: we see both antagonism and interaction.

Pagan thinkers sometimes dismiss the new faith as trivial, but are in due course obliged to argue in detail against it, only to be countered by more skilful polemicists (Origen against Celsus). Christians sometimes reject all pagan culture, but sometimes present Christian beliefs in attractively classical dress (Minucius Felix). By any standards a key date (the fourth in our series) is the adoption of the Christian faith by the Emperor Constantine, who then gave it his endorsement throughout the empire (AD 312). It would be exaggerating to claim that henceforth paganism was on the defensive, but there was now no doubt that Christianity would survive and prosper. Julian the Apostate's attempt to turn the clock back came too late, even if he had not swiftly died on campaign.

Late antiquity sees the split of the Roman empire into two halves. By the fourth century Rome had lost its prominence in the West, and emperors often ruled from Milan or Trier. In the East power was firmly established in Constantinople (formerly known as Byzantium, but established as a new capital by Constantine). The business of ruling, defending and administering the empire had become too vast. But the potential for a complete division was accelerated when invaders from northern Europe assailed the frontiers of Italy over the period from the late fourth century to the end of the fifth. The sack of Rome by the Visigoths in AD 410 (the last of my five key years) has a claim to be the end of the classical era: this was the first time that foreign invaders had taken Rome in more than 800 years. This sack stimulated the writing of Augustine's late masterpiece, *The City of God*, a meditation on the transience of the worldly city in contrast with the kingdom of heaven. Rome did not fall in a day: there were further emperors of the West after 410, and classical culture lived on in the Eastern empire, but Augustine's enormous epitaph on Rome provides a terminus to the present book.

II

In the chapters which follow we will be surveying a very wide range of different kinds of literature, in both poetry and prose. The term genre means just that – a kind, a *genus* or type. It is indeed obvious that literature falls into different types or categories: even today, we distinguish between poetry and prose, sometimes separating drama as a third category, and further subdivisions are possible, for instance between tragedy and comedy, or novel and short-story. Other categorizations depend on strictly formal features: most of us can identify a sonnet or a limerick by the arrangement of rhymes and lines. In the ancient world genre-distinctions were numerous. They were made on various principles: a genre might be characterized by its metre, its typical subject matter, the occasion with which it was associated, and its stylistic level. In practice these were usually correlated: thus the typical epic would be composed in hexameter verse, would describe the deeds of a hero or heroes, often belonging to the mythical age, might be recited at a festival or some other formal event, and would be phrased in an elevated poetic style, remote from everyday speech, as suited the dignified subject.

Some but not all of the genres identified by modern critics were also recognized by the ancient writers themselves. The terms tragedy and comedy, for example, are already in use in the age of Sophocles and Aristophanes. Lyric, elegy, epigram and other terms are all derived from Greek words, though their nuances have altered. Similarly Herodotus used the term *historia* in his opening paragraph, though referring to the process of inquiry: we may doubt whether he had a fully developed concept of his genre. Other generic terms are of later origin: there is for instance no ancient word for 'novel'. Also, some of the forms which we would regard as distinct were not regularly segregated by ancient critics: epic could embrace the didactic poetry of Hesiod and others, and perhaps even the hexameter poetry of Theocritus, as a result of a classification based on metre, when we might see differences of subject matter as more significant. However, the fact that the ancient critics lacked a fixed term for pastoral poetry does not mean that they were unable to see that some of Theocritus' poems about shepherds had a clear family resemblance. Propertius and Tibullus could write amatory poems in imitation of Gallus without distinguishing the subclass of love elegy from the larger category of elegy as a whole. In the same way, we learn to swim, wrestle, or make love without necessarily knowing all the technical terms. Writers could compose grammatical sentences long before the terminology of tenses and participles had been codified.

Terminology matters less than mind-set. In ancient times authors were much more aware of literary forms and conventions than they are today. Whereas nowadays a writer may sit down intending to write a poem on a specific topic, in antiquity writers thought more in terms of composing in a particular genre. In earlier times they might also be composing for a specific occasion, religious or celebratory or convivial. Already in Homer we find references to other literary forms: the wedding song, or the paean, a type of hymn in praise of Apollo. Precedent and tradition provided inspiration and promptings, a framework within which the poet found his individual voice. Often a poet might be the pupil of his predecessor; in any case, he would learn by heart and study closely older poets' work. The interest in tradition is demonstrated by the special importance attached to the founder or originator of each genre – Homer for epic, Archilochus for iambic, and so on; but as time went on similar prestige would be attached to later writers who acquired classic status. It was common practice to imitate, quote from or echo the words of one's predecessors: often the author would choose a particularly famous passage for emulation. Thus conventions develop in each genre: besides the regular correlation of subject and metre, there are certain subsidiary features which become typical – the epic simile, for example, or the messenger's speech in tragedy. These recurring typical features are sometimes referred to as *topoi*, a Greek term meaning commonplaces. They form part of the poetic stock in-trade. In a tradition founded on respect for and imitation of older models, originality is demonstrated not by a rejection of older works, but by reshaping or giving a new freshness to an older poet's plot, imagery or language. This respect for tradition should not be seen as a straitjacket: admiration for the great models of the past could be combined with a spirit of rivalry and competitiveness.[2] This is particularly clear when we turn to Roman writers. Their imitation of the Greek masters, already established as classics, involves a clear and sometimes aggressive determination to colonize a particular literary territory, to import a new genre to Roman literature. The same motive is discernible in the eagerness of Roman writers to identify a Latin equivalent to a Greek author: Varro probably named Ennius the Latin Homer, and Propertius styles himself the Roman Callimachus.[3]

The very notion of a founder implies that there was a time when each genre was invented, and this was indeed the normal ancient assumption. Clearly this is often an over-simplification: there was epic poetry long before Homer, and even the ancients were vague on the origins of some types of poetry which they knew to be older than the practitioners familiar to them. Commenting on the question 'who first composed elegy?', Horace quips: 'the schoolmasters are in dispute, and the case is still under scrutiny' (*Art of Poetry* 78). In some cases, particularly later ones, it does seem justifiable to identify the prime mover. The philosophic prose dialogue is an example: whether or not it was first invented by Plato, it surely originates in the Socratic circle. Similarly Theocritus is either the inventor of pastoral or close in time to that invention. Both these cases, however, also show the advantages of a more evolutionary approach. These genres did not spring from nowhere: we can identify some of the ingredients of each in earlier, related forms, though in each case the authors named contributed something crucial and transformed the compound. So too with a genre like elegy, vaguely defined and accommodating poetry of very different subject, length and tone. In such cases it is better to explore the ways in which the form develops, and the prominence of different themes at different times, than to regard it as a rigidly consistent type of verse.

As more genres emerged, both poets and critics began to view them in relation to one another. We can detect a kind of hierarchy emerging, in which some literary forms have greater prestige and their authors are more highly regarded than others. This hierarchy is neither defined in detail nor set in stone, but certain assumptions can be deduced from a variety of ancient texts and still more from practice. An epigram of Martial lists a series of genres in descending order of merit and difficulty: epic, tragedy, lyric, satire, elegy, epigram (12.94). Broadly speaking, 'high' forms are those which deal in elevated language with serious subject matter presented in a consistently dignified way (epic, tragedy, some history); 'low' genres tend in the opposite direction (comedy, epigram, mime). Related oppositions are those between the mythical and the contemporary, and between public or sacred subject matter and private, personal, more trivial material. There is also some tendency to look down on shorter works – satire, epigram, short lyrics like those of Catullus, epistles, pastorals, some elegy. Longer works, it could be felt, demand greater ambition and more sustained effort. Language is also important: writers were expected to select a vocabulary and style suited to the type of work they were writing, and the artificial but magnificent language of epic could be seen as superior to the conversational and colloquial manner of satire. Horace makes this point while protesting that his satires cannot be taken seriously as poetry (needless to say, he has his tongue in his cheek here): as he puts it, if you rearranged the words of his own poem and disrupted the metre, there would be no sign that it had been poetry before, whereas the lofty diction of Ennius is such that, 'even when he is dismembered, you would still discover the limbs of a poet' (*Satires* 1.4.56–62).

Something more should be said about the relationship of poetry and prose. Poetry was older and in some ways more prestigious: the poet had the advantage of elevated and sensuous language, variety of metrical forms, greater freedom in vocabulary and syntax. But it is a mistake to group all prose authors together, still more to brand them prosaic. Prose-writing too called for a highly developed sense of style and decorum: an historian, an orator, even a philosopher, would write not only to persuade but to move, arouse, excite and inspire. Formal prose deployed many stylistic devices to heighten and enrich the information conveyed: figures of speech, many of them shared with poetry, are the most obvious. Although prose was not metrical, most writers paid attention to the rhythms and cadences of their work (oratory was meant to be declaimed, and although silent reading, contrary to a common assumption, was recognized as usual in antiquity, it remains true that readers were keenly alert to the auditory effect of a work).[4] Not all prose genres would be considered inferior to verse: Dionysius declares that the power and pathos of Thucydides' history are such as to outclass any historians and any poets (*On Thucydides* 15). Horace the lyricist pays respectful tribute to Pollio the great historian (*Odes* ii.1). The philosophic

myths of Plato or Plutarch, the inspirational opening of the fifth book of
Cicero's *Tusculan Disputations*, reach a level of eloquence that rivals the
most sublime passages of Lucretius. Polemic by prose against poetry was
also possible: Seneca the moralist can pour scorn upon the fabulous tales of
the *Odyssey*: 'do you ask where Ulysses' wanderings took him rather than
ensuring that we are not ourselves forever astray?' (*Letters* 88.7)

The conception of a hierarchy is important and widespread, but it must
be emphasized that we are not dealing with a fixed rule book, that genre
relationships vary as the different forms develop, and that different oppositions are handled in different ways for polemical purposes. Comedy can
make fun of grandiose tragedy. Satire can represent itself as closer to real life
than bombastic epic (Juvenal 1.1ff.). Plato in his dialogues includes parody
of rhetoric and satirical portraits of its practitioners. Plutarch declares that
biography, with its attention to small-scale detail and personal idiosyncrasy,
can often provide illumination in a way that history cannot (*Alexander* 1).
Writers in the higher genres generally abstain from comment on lesser
forms (and impersonal genres like epic and tragedy have little room for such
comment in any case); as a result we tend to see more examples of low
authors parodying or sniping at high than the reverse. But the principle
works both ways, and in each case partly serves as a form of self-assertion,
or, better, an indication of what the author and his own style of writing is
capable of. Tacitus in his account of Nero's reign remarks that a particular
year was of little note, 'unless one were to take pleasure in filling volumes
with praise of the foundations and timber work on which the emperor piled
the immense amphitheatre on the field of Mars. But we have learnt that it
suits the dignity of the Roman people to reserve history for great achievements, and to leave such details to the city's daily register' (*Annals* 13.31).
Ranking, like evaluation generally, depends on your point of view. Cicero
disparagingly declared that if he had his lifetime over again, he still would
not consider he had time to waste reading Greek lyric poets (Seneca, *Letters*
49.5); Julian dismisses the immoral trivialities of the erotic novel (p. 145).
In both cases this is not mere philistinism but says something about the
writers' own literary and educational priorities. Comments on literature,
ancient and modern, spring from an individual reader and reflect that
person's priorities. For example, a famous reading list in Quintilian (x.1) is
not intended to be a total picture of ancient literature, but a selection
angled towards the needs of the aspiring orator, and his judgements need to
be weighed with that principle in mind: thus Sappho passes unmentioned,
while apart from the orators Homer, Euripides and Menander get extended
treatment.

Neither the hierarchy nor generic boundaries are absolute. In the
first place, new genres emerge out of and are derived from old, or from

particular elements of the old (pastoral poetry, for example, had some precedent in the descriptions of landscape in epic and early lyric). Second, they complement, influence, interact with each other (e.g. Greek tragedy in relation to comedy, or history to biography); they take up positions in relation to one another which shift and develop in response to changing literary trends and sometimes in reaction to historical constraints (thus political oratory and poetic invective become tamer under the Roman Empire). Genres could change and adapt. Callimachus did something entirely new with elegy in his poem the *Aetia*; still further potentials in the same genre were tapped by Gallus. Genres not only influenced one another but blended, producing a hybrid. Ovid in his *Art of Love* composed a didactic poem in the 'wrong' metre, elegiac couplets, so parodying and deflating the lofty didactic aspirations of Lucretius and Virgil. Older critics spoke of 'mixing' genres (aetiological elegy; tragic history; epistolary novel); moderns prefer to use terms like 'inclusion', 'incorporation', 'appropriation'; perhaps even 'invasion' may sometimes be suitable. Thus Virgil introduces his friend and predecessor, the love-elegist Gallus, as the leading character in one of Virgil's own pastoral poems: pastoral mounts a kind of takeover bid on elegiac territory, though the tone is humorous and parodic. Much more ambitious is the way in which the mature Virgil includes a great range of non-epic material, themes, characters and ideas from other genres within the *Aeneid*. The epic of Roman imperialism is itself a document of generic colonization.

This kind of generic fluidity, and the frequency with which generic rules seem to be bent or broken, has persuaded some scholars that the concept of genre is irrelevant or of limited value. Nothing could be further from the truth. Classical authors, in both poetry and prose, are always conscious of what they are writing, and what kind of work it is. It is true that some forms are more precisely defined than others: sometimes, indeed, a poet may deliberately choose to write in a stricter mode than the genre requires (Pindar in his victory odes is perhaps an example). Some genres affected a loose and anarchic manner: Latin satire comes to mind, but it would be a mistake to take this affectation of informality too literally. Conventions varied in importance and evolved over time; if a rule had been breached once, that too established itself as a precedent (Virgil followed Apollonius in including a love affair in epic). Both the artists and the critics regularly refer to generic rules and expectations: the fact that the system was flexible, that the boundaries could be breached, does not prove that the system did not exist but rather that the creative writers were constantly engaging with and stimulated by it. Any reader who wishes to appreciate classical literature needs to recognize that a system of this kind can offer positive advantages which total freedom could not.

III

It is all too easy for a modern reader to forget that every copy of every work of classical literature had to be produced by hand, whether by the author or by scribes. Only the invention of the printing press in the fifteenth century changed this situation. These facts are of central importance for our understanding of the place of literature in ancient society, its distribution, and its transmission to modern times. To produce even one copy of a work involved time and skilled labour. To distribute multiple copies of any work was a major undertaking. The concept of publication itself is difficult, as the procedure was a less formal one than it is today. An author would often begin by reciting extracts, or circulating drafts among close friends for criticism. Detailed revision might follow, but occasionally works were passed on and copied, even distributed without the author's knowledge before he was ready to pronounce the work 'finished'.[5] Special considerations arise with particular genres: dramas were composed for performance in the theatre, speeches for oral delivery. The decision to circulate a written text might depend on the success or failure of the performed version.

The principal medium in the Greek world, and under Rome until about the third century AD, was the papyrus roll, on one side of which the text was written out in a series of columns. The reader had to unwind the roll as he read, using one hand to hold and roll up again the part he had already seen. The awkwardness of the unrolling process was considerable; to judge by surviving examples, some of the papyrus rolls were as much as 10 metres long. The material was by no means strong, and could easily be damaged. As a rule writers would use only one side of the roll, as the outside would be handled and easily smudged or worse. As for the text itself, punctuation was often absent or minimal. Texts were frequently written without spaces between words; it was not until the Middle Ages that an effort was made to systematize word-division, though in some Latin texts around the time of Augustus there is a step towards it in putting small dots between words. In texts of plays, not much was done to identify the names of speakers, and this has led to many problems and doubtful attributions. On papyri of drama, we can see that a change of speaker was often indicated only by a dash. Considering how appallingly difficult this must have made the reading and interpretation of texts, it is surprising that more was not done to improve practice; but often, we may suspect, a quick cheap job was preferred to an expensive de luxe copy.

There are many unanswerable questions related to the production and use of books in the ancient world. We know much less than we would like about levels of literacy, the degree to which different types of text were used in education, the relative importance of public performance and private reading, the development of the book trade, the growth of libraries, and other equally important topics. The nature of our evidence varies according to time and place, and often we do not know whether an anecdote or a particular datum is typical or extraordinary. It is clear that in both Greece and Rome the poets were used as study texts in schools, and at any rate by the late fifth century in Athens there was an active book trade. Books certainly existed in private hands: a character in Xenophon owns a complete text of Homer.[6] Much poetry was learned by heart; prose authors may have depended more on the written word and on readers. Heraclitus is said to have dedicated his philosophical work in the temple of Artemis at Ephesus, perhaps to ensure its preservation. Herodotus allegedly gave recitations, but it is less easy to imagine audiences listening avidly to Thucydides' complex speeches and analyses. By the latter part of the fifth century books were becoming more common, although associated with intellectuals and other eccentrics. ('Either a book or Prodicus has corrupted the man', remarks a character in Aristophanes.) In earlier periods, it is often maintained, performance was primary and readers rare or non-existent. This may be true, although it is usually taken far too much for granted. We can accept that oral performance, whether to small or large audiences, may have been the norm without denying that writers would also have been concerned that their work should be preserved in writing and continued to be read. The lyric poets hope that their works and their subjects will outlive them: Theognis includes his own name as a 'seal' to guarantee to later readers that this is his authentic work. We can also argue from the knowledge of these writers in later times. The scholars of Alexandria were able to assemble most of the oeuvre of Sappho and Alcaeus, Aeschylus and Sophocles. Sappho's work alone occupied nine books, the first of which included 330 stanzas. These texts could not have survived so long had they not been treated as important in themselves, independent of performance.

Evidence is more abundant in Hellenistic and Roman times: in particular, the letters of Cicero give us many insights into the writer's life and the process of publication (his friend Atticus regularly organized the copying and distribution of Cicero's numerous works). Cicero had a considerable library of his own, and also borrowed extensively from those of others. The first public library in Rome was established by Asinius Pollio (39 BC), and others, including one founded by Augustus, soon followed.[7] Writers became more self-conscious about their books as artefacts: Catullus and others dwell on the physical appearance of the finished product. A fine book could be a luxury object, a book of love poetry should itself be sleek and seductive; by contrast, the despised output of the poet's enemy is suited only to be wrapping for cheap mackerel.[8]

Turning to the problems of transmission, we must again remember the crucial fact that each copy is hand-produced, not a replica but a new version. The major writers of antiquity do not survive in versions from their own hands. In all cases we are dealing with a tradition that transmits the ancient text through many stages of recopying, and often by several different routes. We may draw the analogy of a family tree that begins from a single ancestor, the original authorial text. First let us assume that there are three copies made, but these are then split up, sent off to different places, and subsequently more copies are made from each. Fresh mistakes will be introduced at each stage, and if these manuscripts are never brought together again they cannot be rechecked against one another. The family analogy works, in that each separate branch of the tradition will tend to multiply, though of course one of the manuscripts might get destroyed and a branch of the family might die out. Or it might be partially destroyed, and only the surviving part could be copied in that particular line of descent (here the family-tree analogy breaks down). If this happens at an early enough stage then all subsequent copies may be deficient. Thus we have lost substantial parts of Tacitus' *Annals* and *Histories*.

A huge amount of ancient literature has been lost. It is quite rare for us to possess the complete works of an author: Plato, Virgil, Horace, are among the few major examples. More often we have only a small portion of a writer's work: seven complete plays by Sophocles from a total of over a hundred. The reasons for loss over the centuries are various: not only fire, flood and other accidents, but deliberate selection, changes of fashion which caused certain authors to fall out of favour, inertia, limited resources (papyrus and parchment were expensive) and occasionally bowdlerization. Canonization of the great authors has its negative aspect: those excluded from the central core of classics will tend to disappear. Some authors were found too difficult: the more straightforward Euripides was read more often in schools than Aeschylus. Others were too long for comfort. The critic Dionysius lists a number of Greek historians whom (he says) no one has ever read through to the end: Polybius is among them, and it is true that only the first six books, out of 40, survive complete. Livy was already available in an abridged version by the time of Martial, less than a century after the historian's death. Abridgements of the *Reader's Digest* variety became common; popular also were anthologies, often concentrating on morally uplifting passages. Another contributing factor was technological, in the change (itself highly beneficial) from roll to codex: that is, from the use of a lengthy papyrus roll as described above to a bound volume of sheets, glued together within a protective binding, something much more like our 'book'. This format is first attested in the first century AD and the shift from one format to the other seems to have substantially taken place during the third and fourth centuries. It is likely that not all works found in papyrus would have been thought worth transcribing laboriously into this new format.[9] The rise of Christianity, with its ambiguous attitude to 'pagan' writings, must have played an important part: scribes concentrated on transcribing Scripture and sermons rather than texts containing false mythology or misguided philosophy. But more important than any of these causes were the political unrest and destructive wars which marked the end of the Roman Empire in the West and the beginning of medieval Europe. Literature and scholarship fell into abeyance, learned readers were fewer, new books were not being produced, and, more damagingly, old books were not being re-copied. Even if wanton destruction was not as widespread as has sometimes been supposed, neglect could be just as damaging.

Political changes have cultural consequences. A cultural gulf widened between East and West. The Empire had been divided administratively since Diocletian (AD 293), and linguistic separation followed. By the fourth century few Latin writers knew Greek. Although Neoplatonic teachings were so important to Augustine, in his formative years he could hardly read Plato or Plotinus in the original. By 700 Greek was virtually unknown in the West. It was hundreds of years before detailed knowledge of Greek language and literature returned to Europe, and in the meantime much was lost, for instance in the sack of Constantinople by the Crusaders (1204). Callimachus' *Hecale* was probably one of the many casualties of Christian zeal (lost when the Crusaders took Athens).[10] Some authors were sufficiently well known and continuously used for their future never to be in doubt. The tradition of Virgil is one of the strongest, and he is fully preserved in several fine manuscripts which go back as far as the fifth and sixth centuries. Few were so fortunate.

The gradual disappearance of so much classical literature is partly compensated for by the excitement of gradual rediscovery, first in the period of Charlemagne (*c.*800) and later in the Renaissance. Many texts survived in monasteries or other refuges, and were eventually identified. Others are known to have existed surprisingly late, but eventually perished. A complete text of Ennius' *Annals*, the first great epic of Latin literature, may have been extant as late as the fifth century AD.[11] There were narrow escapes and miraculous strokes of good fortune: the process by which the Renaissance recovered the classics is a memorable story, a tale of survival against great odds. In each phase of revival fresh texts were found and copied, but some came through by the skin of their teeth. Parts of Aeschylus, almost all of Catullus, the Tiberian books of Tacitus (*Annals* 1–6), are among the treasures preserved only through the survival of a single manuscript. The delight and excitement of recovery can still be felt in the writings of the scholars chiefly involved, as in the triumphant epigram added to the text of Catullus by an Italian notary, celebrating the survival of the unique manuscript of the poet, unknown for over three centuries (*c*.1320).[12] Pleasure is mingled with touching disillusionment in Petrarch's famous 'letter' to Cicero, in which he expresses his amazement at what he has found in the orator's *Letters to Atticus*: we see him coming to terms with the realization that his idol has, if not feet of clay, at any rate human weaknesses.[13]

Once found, a text had to be deciphered, copied, explained. Interpretation of classical texts has traditionally been done in the form of an edition with commentary (often longer than the text and full of tangentially interesting information). Older editions tended to concentrate almost exclusively on linguistic phenomena, identification of historical or mythological references, and above all exegesis and correction ('emendation') of the text. Over the last few centuries editorial technique has become more systematic: our texts of the central authors have been greatly improved, by comparison of different manuscripts, through a better understanding of language, dialect and metre, and by the insight of particularly gifted critics. The importance of textual criticism is unquestionable, though sometimes exaggerated: the followers of A. E. Housman, admittedly a master of his craft whom few could equal, have sometimes almost deified their hero. A more ambitious conception of classical scholarship was propounded and practised by the great German classicist Wilamowitz, a towering figure of immense influence, who urged that all departments of knowledge (linguistic, historical, religious, philosophical, archaeological . . .) should combine in order to illuminate an author or a text or a period – a kind of total ancient history. Modern studies have gone still further in an effort to bridge disciplines: anthropology, ethnography, psychology, discourse analysis, even determinist biology are among the approaches which have been applied, not to mention the endless varieties of structuralism. Commentaries on texts are still written, but more numerous now are monographs on authors or on broader synthesizing topics. In 1902 Gilbert Murray declared that Euripides was more in need of interpretation than of emendation, and this has been the keynote of the century since then; but scholars with exact linguistic knowledge are still needed, to edit new texts and improve old.

New texts do in fact come to light, though this may surprise those who assume that classicists continue to chew the same old cud forever. The sands of Egypt, where the absence of rain makes it possible for written documents to survive for centuries, have yielded up many treasures in fragmentary form, most of them far older than the manuscripts we now have for the main authors. For over a century scholars have been publishing the massive hoard of papyri dug up by the pioneers at Oxyrhynchus and elsewhere. There have been many cases where these papyri have provided earlier versions of texts we have, and enabled scholars to improve on the versions which the manuscript tradition gave us. More excitingly, there have been many discoveries of new texts: lyrics by Sappho and Alcaeus, invectives by Archilochus, poems by Pindar and his contemporary Bacchylides, Aristotle's analysis of the Constitution of Athens, significant parts of lost plays by Sophocles and Euripides and still more substantial portions of Menander's comedies, have been among the new finds. Study of the Hellenistic age has been transformed: we now know much more about both Callimachus and his context. Roman literature has benefited less from these discoveries, but the poet Cornelius Gallus, founder of Latin erotic elegy and friend of Virgil, has become more than a great name, with the publication of the papyrus of a few lines of his elegies in 1979:[14] this is the earliest known Latin papyrus, not later than AD 25, perhaps from the reign of Augustus himself. Since Gallus died in 27 BC, this brings us excitingly close to the poet's own copy. Sometimes these discoveries confirm old guesses; as often they refute them. Above all they open new perspectives, raise new questions. I shall often have reason to quote some of these new finds in the pages which follow.

Finally, something should be said about the terminology of 'book' and 'fragment'. Readers are often puzzled to find references to 'the sixth book of the *Aeneid*' and the like. A book in ancient times is normally much shorter than an average modern book. Essentially this is because of the original format, the papyrus roll. The longer the roll, the more unwieldy it becomes. Lengths vary in different periods, but a 'book' of verse is often not longer than 1,000 lines and almost never as high as 2,000. (All of Virgil's books are less than 1,000 lines). Similar considerations apply in prose: Plato's *Republic* is divided into 10 books (i.e. rolls), Herodotus' History into nine, but we might think of these as more like long chapters. Once the codex was introduced, several books might be combined into one volume, and we are a step or two closer to the modern format. Practical considerations of length, however, are not the whole story: the variation in length is quite considerable, and aesthetic concerns evidently enter into play. Each book of Lucretius' poem begins with an impressive prologue, making a fresh start and heralding the themes of a new phase in the argument: he is not simply continuing from where he left off. The Augustan poets in particular clearly plan the arrangement of their books very carefully, cultivating effects of variety and significant juxtaposition (as in Virgil's *Eclogues* and Horace's *Odes*). On the larger scale, groupings of books could provide a structuring principle in a very lengthy work. Livy seems to have planned his *History* in terms of 'pentads' (5-book sections) and 'decades' (10 books); Augustine took pains to ensure that the *City of God* was bound up in codices in such a way as to make the structure of the argument as clear as possible.[15]

As for 'fragment', this term arises from the losses of much ancient literature already described. Providence has not been kind enough to ensure that everything of high quality has survived: chance and prejudice have played too great a part. In any case, we want to know about the background as well as the masterpieces. Hence the interest in what we can discover about lost works by a major author, and about authors by whom no complete works survive. Surviving texts often quote from older writers, sometimes by name. A quotation, for instance, from a lost play of Aeschylus by Plato counts as a 'fragment' of Aeschylus and is included in standard collections of that poet's remains. The other common use of the term is to refer to a papyrus find, since we are seldom lucky enough to discover complete works in this form. Sometimes quotations already known from a surviving source ('book-fragments', as they are often called) may be supplemented by a papyrus find. An example is a short citation from Aeschylus' lost play *Niobe*, quoted by Plato as an example of the immoral ideas about the gods which are to be found in the tragic poets, and which require them to be expelled from the ideal society. Plato quotes only two lines: 'God plants a fault in mortals, when he wishes utterly to ravage a household.' A papyrus fragment, some 20 lines long, has put the extract in a context (and incidentally shown that Plato's treatment of the Aeschylean religious conception is unduly harsh). A find like this has important consequences for students of both Aeschylus and Plato.[16]

Besides fragments, ancient comments or 'testimonies' about a lost work can be just as important. A summary of a lost play or poem may be as valuable as brief quotations devoid of context. Sometimes we are lucky enough to have both: the fragments of Callimachus' poem the *Aetia* would be largely unintelligible without the concise résumé of its contents which survives for much of the work. Even briefer, more impressionistic comment or evaluation may give us a clearer notion of the characteristics of an author, as with Demetrius' enthusiastic praise of Sappho: 'This is why when Sappho sings of beauty her words are beautiful and sweet; so too when she sings of loves and spring and the halcyon; every type of beautiful word is woven into her poetry, and some of them are her own creation.' (Demetrius, *On Style* 166 = Sappho F 195) Such comments also form a part of the history of taste.

The obstacles which make a full understanding of ancient literature difficult for the modern reader, some of which have been outlined above, are considerable: the remoteness in time, the differences in their ways of life and ways of thought, the different assumptions they brought to literature and the conventions by which they composed it, the linguistic barriers, and the damage to the textual tradition. I hope that the following chapters will demonstrate that despite these obstacles, the encounter with Greek and Latin literature also offers rich rewards.

I

Epic

Thus they held funeral rites for Hector, tamer of horses.
Iliad 24.804

I

In the modern world epic as a genre of poetry is no more: in lamenting its passing we can mimic one of the most characteristic activities of the form, grieving for what is lost, whether it be a dead hero or a vanished age. Yet we all feel we know what 'epic' means. Hardly a week goes by without some claim that a new Hollywood blockbuster is epic in scope. Here we need to distinguish between epic form and epic spirit. The ancient poems grouped under this title (though the title is of surprisingly late origin) follow certain rules and conventions: notably, they are almost universally composed in the metre which Homer used, a long and swiftly moving line known as the dactylic hexameter, and in a dignified, self-consciously elevated style. Certain formal features are particularly frequent in epic: an invocation of the inspiring Muse is one; others are the extended simile and the use of elaborate speeches. Even more obvious, an epic is a lengthy work, often extending to many thousands of lines. But we can also see that epic regularly addresses certain kinds of theme. Epic does not restrict itself to the adventures of an individual, nor to the private lives of its characters: the scope of the genre often embraces major events, events of historical or even cosmic import (the destruction of Troy, the foundation of Rome, the fall of the Roman Republic; in Milton, the Fall of Man). Both the length of the work and a large cast of characters make the reader conscious of the narrative as significant, an effect often reinforced by the involvement of supernatural powers. Epic records great events or great achievements, often involving great suffering: the characters are noble or at least exceptional. Thus *War and Peace* or *The Lord of the Rings* can be said to have something of the epic scope or spirit, although their medium is narrative prose.

Already these generalizations evoke objections. The *Odyssey* is more the tale of the individual Odysseus than of any larger theme: the world would not be changed if the hero failed to return to tiny, marginal Ithaca. The high seriousness and public dimension of epic are at least severely compromised in Ovid. The characters in Statius, and still more in Lucan, may be larger than life, but they would be hard to call noble. And so on. As in all genres, the later writers reshape or rethink the tradition, reacting to and often fighting against the work of their predecessors. This is inevitable in any literary tradition but is perhaps especially conspicuous in epic, and from the beginning: the *Odyssey* is a reaction to, almost a critique of, the *Iliad*; Ovid's *Metamorphoses* has been seen as an anti-*Aeneid*; Lucan defies many of the conventions of his models, not least in the expulsion of the gods from his cast of characters. This reaction is partly a form of self-assertion against impossibly great predecessors: Harold Bloom's theories of poets engaged in an Oedipal struggle with their 'fathers' work better with epic than with most genres.[1] Humility and tributes are combined with 'going one better' than the model. The imitator aspires to recreate the qualities of the model but also to surpass them. Readers shared these expectations: Propertius eagerly awaited the completion of the *Aeneid*, writing that 'a work *greater than* the *Iliad* is in the making' (2.34.66).

The special prestige of epic derives from its prominence at the earliest stages of the classical tradition. It is an astonishing fact that Greek literature begins with the *Iliad* and *Odyssey*, by any standards among the greatest works of any age. (Obviously there was poetry before Homer, and the epics themselves make reference to other types of song; but these do not survive.) The Homeric poems stand at the fountain-head of classical literature, and although parodists or pedagogues might find fault with some aspects, in antiquity their rank was never seriously questioned. Aristophanes called Homer 'divine'; others simply refer to him as 'the poet' – no confusion was possible. These poems were often compared with the Ocean surrounding the whole world, the source on which, in early geographic conceptions, all lesser rivers were dependent.[2] Similarly epic could be seen as the source for other later genres, notably tragedy, comedy, and historiography: the last in particular shared the concern to commemorate glorious deeds. In turn, later epic extended its scope and absorbed or incorporated material from other genres which had developed independently: oratory, ethnography, aetiology. Virgil drew on Cato and Varro for his picture of early Italy; Lucan quarried Nicander on horrific snake-bites.

But epic remained central and stood at the peak of the generic hierarchy. In the Roman period it became an expectation that a poet would not attempt this form until he had reached full maturity. Thus Virgil began with the brief but exquisite pastoral *Eclogues*, progressed through the didactic *Georgics*, and only in his fifth decade embarked on his climactic work, a pattern which was noted and imitated by Ovid and later by Spenser and Milton (Lucan, who died at 26, broke this rule along with many others). This special prestige made epic the natural form in which to compose the National Poem: the *Aeneid*, whatever else it embraces, is clearly conceived as a patriotic poem that celebrates the history and character of Rome, composed at a time which was perhaps already perceived as a key moment in her history. Although few poems have been enjoyed more for their sheer storytelling than the *Odyssey*, for serious-minded readers, to be entertaining was not enough. Didactic import was soon attached to Homer's poems: they showed examples of virtue and vice, illustrated the perils of the passions. Ingenious reading could interpret monsters as symbols. Horace was familiar with moralizing readings of Homer; they may well have influenced Virgil's conception of the *Aeneid*, and certainly influenced later readers who saw Virgil as a philosophic mystic and the *Aeneid* as an allegorical 'voyage of life'. The history of epic is of a constantly adapting and expanding form, in which traditional elements are put to new uses, new elements boldly imported, and in which the epic poet's own voice, barely audible in Homer, becomes more conspicuous, sometimes mischievously intrusive (Ovid), sometimes polemically strident (Lucan).

One feature which has not so far been mentioned explicitly is the role of myth. But although the most famous ancient epics use plots set in the mythical past, there was also a strong tradition of historical epic. Our surviving examples are Roman (Lucan, Silius), but it is clear that the line went back to the Greek world. A few early Greek poets seem to have written in epic form about their communities and about the weird places they travelled to in the colonizing period. Later, the panegyrical epics composed for Alexander and his successors became notorious. Interestingly, the line between myth and history was not always firmly drawn. Ennius told of the sack of Troy, of Aeneas and Romulus, but went on to bring his *Annales* down to the historical wars of Rome and his own day, including praise of individual leaders. Virgil's technique in the *Aeneid* was more subtle: while treating the relatively brief episode of Aeneas' journey and victory in war, he celebrated the future history of Rome through explicit prophecy and by complex techniques of foreshadowing. Aeneas prefigures Augustus in a number of ways: myth provides the paradigm for history. The influence of myth on history in antiquity was potent: passages from the Homeric catalogue of forces could be invoked (some said forged) to back up claims to territory, and Alexander the Great seems to have seen himself as a new Achilles.[3] The influence worked both ways: myths were naturally reshaped or even invented to reflect historical developments. The conquest of India by Dionysus, described at gargantuan length in the epic of Nonnus, seems to have been invented as a mythic analogue to the historical campaigns of Alexander in 326.

II

It is time to give a fuller idea of the most important ancient epics one by one: other general considerations will be noted en route, but what follows is intended to bring out more clearly the diversity of the genre.

'Homer' is the name traditionally given to the poet who composed the *Iliad* and the *Odyssey*. In fact other poems were ascribed to him in the classical period, including the surviving parody *Battle of Frogs and Mice*, which is certainly a much later work, and various other epics which do not survive. It is in any case clear that nothing was known about Homer in later times: his date and place of origin were disputed, and he never refers to himself or his career in the poems themselves. Moderns tend to place him in the period around 700, but the dating and much else are affected by the so-called 'Homeric question', an expression which refers to the disputes over the authorship and composition of the two epics.[4] This debate is too complex to treat in detail here: briefly, it is well established that the *Iliad* and the *Odyssey* draw on and probably form part of a long tradition of oral poetry, an inherited body of material repeatedly reworked and reperformed over many generations, so that the precise date of 'composition' is theoretically difficult and practically impossible to define. (The proof is partly linguistic, partly based on the references to archaeological or other material evidence of diverse periods.) We cannot identify 'Homer's' own contribution: for some, he is the master poet who drew together a variety of legends and created a massive super-epic (the stimulus of writing may have played a part here, encouraging a more ambitious work because the means now existed to preserve it); others have held that the name of Homer should be attached to the author of the core narrative of the work, to be distinguished from later additions (though the different strata are not easily identified). Some ancient scholars already wondered whether the *Odyssey* was by the same poet as the *Iliad*, and the 'separatist' view which sees it as a work by a later hand has much support today. It remains convenient to use the name 'Homer' as shorthand for the *Iliad* and the *Odyssey*. Even if their composers were different, they belong to the same tradition and are most unlikely to be independent of each other: the *Odyssey* is surely conceived with a view to completing or complementing the *Iliad*. Indeed, in many ways the poems are thematic opposites: war versus peace, glorious death versus hard-won survival, heroic individual versus father, husband and ruler.

Two major plots dominate virtually all the ancient epics, war and the quest or journey: the *Iliad* provides the prototype for the former, the *Odyssey* for the latter. Often they are combined, though one may predominate: the *Aeneid* uses the journey-theme in the first half, war in the second. The *Iliad* describes an episode near the end of the Greeks' 10-year war against Troy. Its hero, Achilles, slighted by the arrogant King Agamemnon, withdraws from the conflict with disastrous results for his fellow Greeks. In the end, having rejected the desperate appeals of his comrades, he concedes to Patroclus, his closest friend, that he may take the field in his place, wearing his armour, and so drive off the Trojans. But Patroclus, advancing too far, is slain by the Trojan champion Hector, and Achilles' anger, far fiercer than before, is turned against the slayer of his friend. In the climactic combat Achilles kills Hector, and maltreats his body: in the days which follow, he persists in his awe-inspiring grief and wrath. But in the final book of the poem Hector's father, the aged Priam, travels to the Greek camp by night and throws himself at Achilles' feet, begging the hero to return his son's body for burial.

> 'Reverence the gods, Achilles, and pity me,
> remembering your own father; yet I am still more pitiable.
> I have endured such things as no mortal on this earth has endured,
> Drawing to my lips the hands of the man who has slain my son.'
> These were his words, and in Achilles he roused a deep longing to
> weep for his own father . . .   (24.503–7: see Appendix 1.1)

Achilles' anger gives way to pity, and he makes this concession, although both men know that death is hanging over them and that this moment of magnanimity will achieve nothing permanent. The poem ends with the burial of Hector: the Trojans mourn their lost defender and are left waiting for the imminent destruction of their city and society, which Hector had already foreseen. 'For I know this well, in my mind and my heart: there will come a day when holy Ilium will perish, and with it Priam and the host of Priam of the good ashen spear' (6.447–9).

This summary cannot give any adequate idea of the richness of texture with which the *Iliad* presents the narrative and characters. Even minor characters are unforgettably portrayed: Helen, the adulteress who caused the war, appears only rarely, but every occasion is memorable. The handling of Helen, indeed, is representative of the poem's humane spirit. She is not villainous or shameless, but in some ways a victim herself – while partly responsible for the war, she never ceases to blame herself and long for her former husband, watching the combat that she cannot halt, and despising the adulterer Paris, her Trojan spouse. She mentions more than once the hostility of the Trojans, especially the women; but their king Priam treats her with generous affection, and Hector too, she recalls, has always shown her kindness and courtesy. Although later ages took the *Iliad* as a panhellenic poem, commemorating the victory of Western heroes over Eastern barbarians,[5] this is not Homer's perspective. The Trojans may be inferior in numbers and prowess, but they are sympathetically treated throughout. We are left in no doubt that the fall of Troy is a tragic and horrific event. This perception that victory can be terrible, that one's enemy deserves compassion in art even if not receiving it in life, is a crucial part of Homer's legacy. These lessons were not lost on Euripides (*Hecuba*, *Trojan Women*).

No less remarkable is the construction of the poem. Rather than recounting the Trojan war from start to finish, Homer narrates a short episode, a matter of days, but deepens our understanding by extensive forward and backward glances. Minor sub-plots and lesser characters are also frequent. This highlights an important feature of epic narrative technique. The focus on a central plot and a few key personalities calls for intensity of emotion, whereas the sheer length of most epics encourages diversity and variety. There is a constant fluctuation between linear development of the main plot and a more episodic structure. While in general there is a firm control over the epic's coherence and development, inset stories and subordinate episodes are sometimes loosely connected with the whole. (In Ovid, diversity and centrifugal structures are the norm.) The same technique is used in the *Odyssey*.

The action of the *Iliad* is overseen by the Olympian gods, as vividly characterized as the human principals. The opening lines of the poem anticipate the action to come, declaring 'and so the plan of Zeus was brought to fulfilment'. The first event of the poem, Agamemnon's insult to the priest Chryses, brings down divine wrath in the form of Apollo's plague. The war of Troy must continue, so that the anger of Hera and Athena may be appeased. The slow progress of the war is partly explained by the fact that powerful gods are involved as supporters of each side, and the most powerful of all, Zeus, is slow to impose his will. The heroes are formidable warriors, but still more deadly when they are inspired and given added strength by divine allies, as Diomedes and Achilles are inspired by Athena. The divine involvement raises the stakes and increases the significance of the action. The gods can often foresee but seldom avert the tragic outcome: Zeus weeps tears of blood for his beloved son Sarpedon, who must die despite his father's longing to save him. Yet although the gods give grandeur and dignity to the heroic conflict, Homer can also use them as foils to the human action. Gods, being immortal, cannot die or suffer lasting pain; their lives of eternal feasting and security are contrasted with the misery and death of their human favourites. Both the seriousness and the frivolity of the Homeric gods serve to bring out in different ways the human cost of the Trojan war. Describing Apollo's attack on the Greek defensive wall, Homer uses a simile, as he often does in order to make divine intervention comprehensible: between them narrative and simile show both the awesome power and the light-heartedness of the god's assault.

> He hurled down the wall of the Achaeans
> With great ease, just like a child with sand by the sea shore,
> A child who has made a plaything of sand in his childish way
> And then, still playing, confounds it with his hands and feet.
> Just so did you, Phoebus whom we invoke,
> confound the work of the Argives, their long toil and pain,
> and in them you stirred up panicking fear.   (15.361–6)

What was 'long toil and pain' for the Greeks to construct is shattered by the god at a stroke, 'with great ease'.[6]

Even one who is favoured by the gods does not find happiness as a result. Although Achilles is the 'hero' of the *Iliad*, heroism is made problematic, to himself as well as to the audience. By insisting on his own honour as all-important, he brings about the deaths of many other Greeks, culminating in that of Patroclus, his dearest friend and in later versions his lover. The other Greeks find him hard to understand or to live with. Achilles is special because he is close to the gods (son of the sea-nymph Thetis) but denied immortality: instead he has foreknowledge of his own mortality. This awareness of his early death overshadows all that he does: it drives him to insist on his rightful recognition while he lives; it drives him, in his lonely brooding, to question the purpose of the war and perhaps even the value of heroic prowess. A greater fighter than the other Greeks, he is also a more eloquent orator. In book 9 he makes an unforgettable speech in which denunciation of Agamemnon is combined with a powerful though confusing statement of his own dilemma;[7] in book 24 he transcends his former selfishness and speaks gently to Priam of the fragility of the human lot. Knowing that he himself will not live to see the doom of Troy, he regards that goal with greater detachment than Agamemnon and the rest. The *Iliad* is not a poem of pacifism: it constantly celebrates the zest and excitement of the battlefield, and the glory won through fighting is no mere illusion. But the poem also repeatedly stresses the losses and the fate of the losers. For every dead warrior there is a grieving father: Hector's father Priam is the mirror image of Achilles' own.

The *Iliad* is the poem of Ilium, another name for Troy. The *Odyssey*, set in the aftermath of the war, is much more focused on the experience of the hero who gives the poem its name. It narrates his homecoming after ten years of wandering in strange lands, and his reunion with his wife, son and household, his reassertion of authority in his kingdom. Whereas the *Iliad* is a poem of disintegration, the *Odyssey* tells of reintegration. In other ways too it seems to be intended as a response, perhaps even a sequel. Several of the heroes of the *Iliad* reappear in cameo roles; the events since the end of the earlier poem are filled in, often narrated by participants. Even the dead may reappear: Odysseus' wanderings take him to the underworld, where he converses with the ghosts of Agamemnon and Achilles. Although Odysseus speaks admiringly to Achilles, the dead hero's response is one of bleak disillusion: 'I would rather be a serf on the land, in service to another, to a poor man of no great substance, than be king among all the corpses of the dead.' (11.489–91) Odysseus the canny survivor is contrasted with the younger Achilles, whose passionate temper led him to throw away his life in battle. The *Odyssey* gives much more space to the things that make life worth living – home, family, friends, affection. Odysseus is 'much-enduring', but his suffering is for a purpose. Though Dante and Tennyson cast Ulysses as the eternal wanderer, in Homer he does not lose sight of the ultimate goal of homecoming.[8]

The adventures of Odysseus overseas, told by the hero himself, have always been the most popular part of the poem. Later pedants tried to plot them on the map, but the hero is wandering in a fantasy world, at a time when even the Mediterranean was not well known. The Sirens, the bag of winds, the enchantress Circe who turns his men into pigs, the Lotus-eaters, are all deliciously exotic and perilous. Best of all is the encounter with Polyphemus, the monstrous Cyclops, a giant with one eye who devours several of Odysseus' companions raw. The episode highlights the creature's barbarism and Odysseus' cunning. Trapped in the monster's cave, he be-fuddles his captor with strong wine and then puts out his eye with a stake. Earlier the Cyclops has asked him his name, and Odysseus answered 'No-body'. When the other Cyclopes hear their friend screaming with pain, they run to his cave and call out, asking him what is the matter. He replies: 'Friends, Nobody is killing me by guile not /nor by force.' Misunderstand-ing, they depart in annoyance at being disturbed. 'And my heart laughed within me,' says Odysseus, 'as my name and my excellent wit had deceived them' (9.413–4). There is cunning in the expression here too, as the word for 'wit' in Greek also punningly means 'nobody', alluding to the pseudo-nym Odysseus has used. This fast-moving adventure has deeper implica-tions: names and identity are important in the *Odyssey*, in which the hero and others are often disguised or concealing the truth. The open conflicts of the *Iliad* have given way to a more subtle and ironic narrative of deception and delayed revelation.

These themes are especially prominent once Odysseus returns to Ithaca, where he adopts the guise of an aged beggar and tests the loyalty and mettle of his swineherd, his other servants, his son and even his wife Penelope (she is being wooed by aristocratic suitors who believe he is dead). Intense pathos is achieved by the device of having Odysseus questioned by his wife, who wishes to know if he can give her any news of her husband. Despite their proximity and the opportunity for self-revelation, Odysseus maintains his self-discipline.

> Thus her lovely cheeks were wasted as she shed tears, weeping for her husband who sat there beside her. As for Odysseus, in his heart he pitied his wife as she wept, but his own eyes remained steady, as though made of horn or iron. Through guile he masked his distress. (19.208–12)

Penelope is a deeply sympathetic figure, but also an intelligent woman, a wife worthy of Odysseus. It is a satisfying moment in book 23 when she tests him, and he falls into her trap, losing his self-control at last and confirming his own identity. In the *Iliad* the archetypal marriage of Hector and Andromache is doomed: he is killed by Achilles, she foresees slavery for herself and death for her infant son. The *Odyssey* allows a happier outcome, though achieved after many struggles and after deadly slaughter (the killing of the suitors):

> He wept as he held the true-hearted wife so dear to him. As land is welcome to shipwrecked sailors swimming, when out at sea Poseidon has struck their well-built vessel, as it was driven by wind and massed waves, and only a few have escaped to land from the grey sea by swimming, their bodies encrusted with thick brine – and gratefully they welcome their first step on the land, after escaping from misfortune – so welcome to her was the husband she kept gazing upon, and even now her white arms around his neck would not let him go. (23.232–40)

The extended simile here begins as a comparison applying to Odysseus, but ends with Penelope; it also alludes to the experiences of Odysseus himself in his voyages. Now that husband and wife are reunited, we see that their sufferings have been parallel, and both are now rewarded for their years of endurance.

'Compare and contrast' is a stock formula in examination papers. It was already a recognized method in ancient scholarship, and we often find critics comparing Homer and Virgil, Demosthenes and Cicero. In one distinguished work of ancient criticism the procedure soars above pedantry: in chapter 9 of *On the Sublime*, the enthusiasm of Longinus for Homer leads him to set out a finely worded argument for the superiority of the

Iliad over the *Odyssey*. He does not escape the lure of biographical explanation, assuming that the *Odyssey* is the product of Homer's later and less
creative old age. He stresses the greater amount of dramatic action and
greater intensity of emotions in the *Iliad*, as opposed to the predominance
of romance, reminiscence and storytelling in the *Odyssey*. He also criticizes
the impossible or magical tales, such as Aeolus imprisoning the winds in a
bag: these almost naive fantasies offended later readers. Most important is
his observation that 'with the decline of their emotional power (*pathos*)
great writers and poets give way to character study (*ethos*).[9] His character-
sketches of daily life in Odysseus' household are like a kind of comedy of
manners.' One may dissent from Longinus' verdict, but his comments have
been hugely influential, and much that he says is extremely suggestive, both
for Homer's poems and by implication for other works which draw on
one or the other of them or which gravitate to one end or the other of this
comparative scale.

Hesiod is regularly paired with Homer as one of the foundational figures
of Greek poetry. The poems certainly his are the *Theogony* ('birth of the
gods'), an account of the creation and the genealogies of the gods, focusing
especially on the rise of Zeus as supreme ruler, and the *Works and Days*,
which also has sections on the mythological origins of the world (here
viewed from the perspective of man), but passes on to advice on morality
and on the life of the hard-working farmer. Central to the *Works and Days*
are the necessity of labour and of a prudential piety: the gods reward the
work ethic. Both poems are labelled 'didactic' poetry by modern critics, but
in ancient times Hesiod was usually classed as epic, and he is close to
Homer in date and language, though both poems are much shorter than
the Homeric epics, and his poetic style is less fluent ('hobnailed hexameters',
in M. L. West's phrase) The pairing with Homer is partly explained in a
famous comment by Herodotus: 'It is they [Hesiod and Homer] who by
their poetry gave the Greeks a theogony and gave the gods their titles, who
assigned to them their statuses and skills, and gave an idea of their appearance' (2.53). It is not literally true that Homer and Hesiod invented the
whole elaborate pantheon of Olympus, but it is likely that they both made
a substantial contribution. Homer anthropomorphizes the gods and presents
them in action; Hesiod makes sense of their relationships, setting out for
instance the succession myth by which the kingship of heaven passes from
Uranus to Cronos to Zeus. The 1,000 lines of the *Theogony* include hundreds of names (50 daughters of the sea-god Nereus), many of which were
doubtless Hesiod's invention. In some of his genealogies we can see a kind
of mythical logic: Sleep and Death are the offspring of Night, while Themis
('Order') is the mother of Lawfulness, Justice and Peace. Neither allegory
nor personification, these family structures associate related abstract ideas

and indicate their divine origin and authorization. Although he often seems artless to us, the solemnity and self-righteousness of Hesiod charmed more sophisticated generations of readers.

Hesiod also fascinates as a poet who tells us something of himself, even his name. Homer is anonymous and withdrawn, unless we choose to see hints about his way of life in the bards who figure in the *Odyssey*. Hesiod by contrast tells us where he lives (Ascra in Boeotia – 'bad in winter, sultry in summer, and no good at any time' is his grumpy verdict), a little about his father and a good deal, much of it negative, about his brother. Some see the dispute between them as a fiction, used as a springboard to introduce the moral rebukes and exhortations of the *Works and Days*. This may be right, but Hesiod still gives us a vivid sense of the vindictiveness that could arise from small-time inheritance quarrels in small-town communities. More influential is the opening of the *Theogony*, in which he describes his poetic initiation – an encounter on the mountainside with the Muses, who gave him a staff of laurel and 'breathed wondrous song into me'. Poets in many early societies conceive their talent as the gods' gift (Homer also refers to these ideas), and this belief in inspiration brings them respect from society, as the poetic craft comes close to that of prophet or priest. The Muses' words as quoted are enigmatic enough: 'Rustic shepherds, vile disgraces, mere bellies as you are, we know how to tell many lies that are like the truth, but we also know, when we wish, how to tell the truth.' (*Th.* 26–8) Hesiod presumably wants us to accept his own poetry as truth, but the lines show an awareness that poetry is sometimes fiction, and point the way toward many a later criticism of poetic and mythical 'lies'. Hesiod's meeting with the Muses was much imitated, eventually becoming a literary cliché. In the *Theogony* it still has something of the freshness and mystery of a time when the hills were lonely places and a god might not be far away.

Hesiod was also believed to be the author of the *Catalogue of Women*, a poem which survives only in short fragments. In fact it was probably composed rather later than Hesiod, but shared some of his interests. This poem seems to have presented genealogies of human families, tracing the mythical heroes' descent from divine ancestry and to some extent relating descent-lines to one another. Founders of cities and of larger communities were prominent: the poem reflects political concerns of the author's own time without bringing the genealogies all the way down to the present day.[10] Whereas the *Theogony* gave order to the generations of the gods, the *Catalogue* performed a similar service for the generations of heroic humanity.

There were many other early poems, some on the wars of Thebes and the Argonautic expedition, others filling out the parts of the Trojan war which Homer had ignored; all are lost, though we know something of them from later summaries.[11] What matters is that a rich and varied range of myths and characters, divine and human, was established, though not without variations in detail, and that this entire range was available to later poets for development and ingenious modification. The myths were common property, and poets could embark on them at almost any point with the confidence that audiences would know where they were. Even in Homer the characters appeal to earlier events for illustration, as Phoenix reminds Achilles of the tale of Meleager ('it is not a new story' (*Iliad* 9.527)). In that specific case, however, there is good reason to suppose that Homer is introducing a new version: inspiration does not rule out (perhaps indeed it authorizes) invention. As the accumulated literature became more bulky and poets became scholars, the audience might be in doubt whether a particular version had prior authority: Callimachus knowingly comments 'I sing nothing that is not attested' (fr.612), but the game is to spot the out-of-the-way source.

These considerations become relevant when we turn to the later period (for between Homer and Apollonius, a gap of over 400 years, we have no complete epic). Much had changed by the third century BC, when Apollonius was writing in Hellenistic Alexandria; but the modern idea that epic had become unfashionable or obsolescent is not well-founded in the evidence. Apollonius' *Argonautica* is in four books, totalling less than 6,000 lines (less than half the length of the *Odyssey*). It narrates the expedition of Jason and his followers in quest of the Golden Fleece, the precious relic of a magical ram, which is guarded by a monstrous serpent at the court of the sinister King Aeetes in Colchis, at the far end of the Black Sea. Jason achieves his goal with the aid of the king's daughter Medea, who falls in love with him and joins him on the homeward voyage. Books 1 and 2 describe the journey to Colchis, book 3 focuses on Jason and Medea, and in book 4, having accomplished the task, the *Argo* returns to the West by a very different route, even travelling through Italian waters and transported by the crew across the Libyan desert. The *Odyssey* is the prime model, and above all the books describing Odysseus' travels and the supernatural adventures. Apollonius sets none of the poem in Greece: throughout, his heroes are involved with the exotic and the unknown. The Argonauts encounter many new dangers (such as the Harpies, who do not figure in Homer), but also find themselves facing Odyssean characters: Circe, the Sirens, the king and queen of Phaeacia. In all these cases, however, Apollonius changes mood and alters characterization or relationships. In the *Odyssey* Circe is an amoral witch-woman; in the *Argonautica*, a severe moral authority who must purify Jason and Medea of their crimes but still condemns their actions. This reworking with variation and innovation of Homer's model is Apollonius' regular practice on every level, including the verbal texture of the poem.[12]

From the start the poem is a mythographic paradise. The opening catalogue of Jason's companions gives the poet opportunity to allude to many
strands of legend, either naming their origins, their ancestors or their prior
exploits, in some cases anticipating their deaths (1.77ff.). Throughout the
poem he is ready to allude, by passing reference or full digression, to tales
which are tangentially connected to the main narrative, or to other stories
associated with the regions through which the *Argo* passes. Sometimes
these allusions are eerie and haunting, as when they pass the Caucasus and
observe in mid-flight the great eagle that perpetually torments the Titan
Prometheus: moments later they hear the dreadful screams of the victim
(2.1242–59). At another stage they are granted a brief but majestic epiphany
of the god Apollo, far away, journeying to the realm of the Hyperboreans
(2.674–82). Other references have more the quality of learned footnotes
(Apollonius was a scholar-poet, at one stage the head of the great Alexandrian
Library). A good example comes when the poet gives a mythical explanation for the drops of amber that seep from poplar trees. He even offers
variant versions: some say these are the tears of the sisters of Phaethon,
others those of Apollo at a time when he was in exile from heaven (4.603–
18, attributing the second story to 'the Celts'). His learning extends
beyond mythology to ethnography and (sometimes fanciful) geography,
drawing on a wide range of prose and poetic sources (e.g. 2.1002–29).
Above all we find repeated aetiologies (explanations for why things came
about, whether features of nature or human rituals and customs): the
influence of his contemporary Callimachus, author of the *Aetia*, is evident.[13]

The most popular part of the poem has always been the sequence in
Colchis, involving Medea's gradual succumbing to love for Jason. For the
history of epic this is a major novelty: the erotic had played no such major
role in Homer and is unlikely to have been as prominent in his successors;
but Apollonius' narrative powerfully influenced Virgil's Dido. Magic and
the supernatural are conspicuous. In a delightful opening, Hera and Athena
persuade Aphrodite to bribe her disobedient son Eros to shoot an arrow at
Medea, making her fall in love: the whole episode is witty and charming,
carrying to an extreme the Homeric divine comedy (3.6–166, 275–98).
The light-heartedness of this introduction contrasts with the agonies
of Medea throughout much of the book, expressed through similes,
soliloquies, wish-fulfilment dreams and tearful colloquy with her sister (above
all 3.449–71, 616–824). The meeting of Jason and Medea is a subtle scene
in which successive exchanges show each testing the ground, neither speaking their full mind at first. Jason, initially prepared to make use of Medea,
himself falls in love with her (1078). But deception and half-truths characterize their dialogue, and we have already seen in book 1 that Jason, an
adaptable lover, is prepared to leave his women. When he appeals for Medea's

help invoking the example of Ariadne, who readily assisted Theseus (a mythical anachronism of the kind that delights the poets of this period), Jason wisely omits the crucial point that Theseus later abandoned her, and maintains his discretion on this point even when Medea presses to know more of the story (3.997ff., 1074–6). No reader would have been unaware of the eventual disastrous end of Jason and Medea's relationship: the classic tragedy of Euripides is a major forerunner of Apollonius' poem, and although he does not take the tale that far, there are signs enough that their union is imperfect and ill-starred (4.1161–9).

One other major contribution of Apollonius deserves emphasis: his readiness to intervene as commentator in his own poem. Traditionally the epic narrator had been invisible, detached though not impersonal. In Homer the exceptions are rare and hence particularly powerful: most notable is the device of 'apostrophe' by which the poet addresses a character, normally a sympathetic or favourite figure at a turning-point in the action. In the *Iliad* this is used with special force in the case of Patroclus, whom the poet addresses several times (esp. 16.692–3: 'now whom first, whom last, Patroclus, did you slay at that time when the gods called you to your death?', 787). But Apollonius thrusts himself and his poetic activity on the audience's attention far more frequently, sometimes with boldly bizarre effect. At times he expresses his astonishment, bafflement or dismay at the turn the story is taking, or draws back with mannered piety from uttering something blasphemous (1.919–21, 4.984–6). Elsewhere he expresses foreboding or anticipates subsequent events (in this too he has Homeric precedent, but carries the device further). Sombre moralizing strikes an appropriate note at the night when, under unhappy circumstances, Medea and Jason become man and wife: 'so we tribes of suffering men never tread firmly on the path of delight, but always there is some bitter pain accompanying our joy' (4.1165–7). Most striking is the famous denunication of Love itself – a darker and more potent figure, now, than the whimsical child of the scene that opens book 3. As Jason and Medea prepare to ambush and murder her brother Apsyrtus, the poet suspends the action and declares:

> Ruthless Love, great hurt, great curse to mankind, from you come deadly strifes and laments and groans, and countless pains as well have their stormy birth from you. Arise, power divine, and arm yourself against the sons of our foes after the same fashion as when you filled Medea's heart with deadly madness. How then, by evil doom, did she slay Apsyrtus when he came to meet her? For this is what comes next in my song. (4.445–51)

The involvement of the poet in his poem produces a complex effect: emotional heightening, certainly, but this is also countered by the editorial glossing and self-conscious reference to the sequence of his own epic; and given the overt criticism of Medea's killing, the appeal to Eros to strike down the poet's own enemies' sons is morally disorienting. The *Argonautica* sets a precedent which will be followed with caution by Virgil, and carried to still more startling extremes by Ovid and above all by Lucan, whose comments on the action often threaten to displace the narrative proper. Though often disparaged or patronized (Longinus damned it as a work of the second rank – too perfect, as opposed to the bolder spirit of sublime Homer), Apollonius' poem is a key work in the epic succession.

Epic was always long, but it was possible to tell shorter tales in hexameters and using many of the customary devices of epic style. Moderns use the term 'epyllion' or 'mini-epic' to describe a group of poems, not all surviving, of which the best known is Catullus' *Peleus and Thetis*, a work of 400-odd lines.[14] The form seems to have originated in Hellenistic times: Moschus' *Europa*, a short but delightful work, survives from that period, as do fragments of Callimachus' *Hecale*. Though myth provided the material, the emphasis was often significantly different from that of full-scale epic: more emphasis on personal emotions, and especially on the erotic; sometimes greater inter-est in rural life or unheroic activities; always intense refinement of style and exquisite composition. Narrative technique was often boldly unconventional, avoiding the apparent core of the tale: thus Callimachus seems to have made Theseus' visit to the humble home of an old countrywoman Hecale the main focus of his epyllion (he stayed there en route to kill the Marathonian bull). Homely detail and personal reminiscence were more prominent than heroic action. This example and others show that epyllion is almost epic turned inside out. Moschus' poem lingers on Europa's dream, her visit to the seaside, her games with her maidens: the model is the Princess Nausicaa in book 6 of the *Odyssey*, but what was a brief episode in Homer's massive epic becomes the main focus in Moschus.

Catullus' epyllion is at least as bizarre: it begins with the Argo but swiftly moves to the marriage of Peleus and Thetis, then spends half the poem describing the scenes on a coverlet adorning their marriage-couch, scenes from the independent tale of Theseus and Ariadne. Theseus deserted Ariadne, Thetis will in due course abandon Peleus; other correspondences and resonances have been sought, and the whole poem, its verbal texture as rich as its structure is complex, seems to be devised as an entrancing riddle. This device of including a separate but subtly related tale (also used on a smaller scale in Moschus) seems to have become fashionable, and is developed in larger works: thus the end of Virgil's *Georgics* tells the story of Aristaeus, which encloses the story of Orpheus and Eurydice, with which it was surely not previously linked. These Russian-doll structures particularly delighted Ovid, who in one passage achieves a four-level *tour de force* (*Met.* 5.577ff.), with direct speech in the innermost tale by Arethusa, as narrated by Calliope, herself being quoted by another Muse, and the poet's own narrative voice embracing all of these. The other feature which Catullus' poem highlights is the so-called *ecphrasis*, a word signifying digression, but frequently applied to a special type, the description of a work of art (here, the coverlet's images). Achilles' shield in the *Iliad* is the ultimate model: Jason's cloak, Europa's beach-bag, and the images on Juno's temple in *Aeneid* 1 are other famous instances. The image always has more than decorative purpose, but the interpretation is rarely straightforward, thus cautioning the critic against complacency in 'reading' the larger meaning of the poem as a whole.

III

Roman culture was more militaristic than Greek: the very name of Rome was sometimes etymologized as meaning 'Might', and the image of a she-wolf suckling the twins Romulus and Remus suggests a certain pride in the primitive violence with which their society had begun. Roman epic is more concerned with concepts of empire and conquest than with exploration and adventure for its own sake. We also see a deep fascination with *civil* wars: Virgil represents the war in Italy as a civil war, as Aeneas is returning to his ancestral roots, and Lucan constantly brings kinsmen, even fathers and sons, into conflict. The climax of Statius' *Thebaid* is fratricide: again, we remember the founding fathers and how Romulus killed his brother Remus for daring to cross the civic boundary. Prowess leads to excess, and excess to self-destruction.

As in Greek, so in Latin we find epic at the very origins of the nation's literary tradition, with Livius Andronicus' version of the *Odyssey* in Latin. Although often referred to as a translation, the scanty fragments do show some adjustments and an effort to give the Homeric language a Latin flavouring. This went further than alterations of names to their Latin forms. A clever instance of creative adaptation is the line 'when the day arrives which Morta has foretold' (F 10 Morel), in which Morta, an Italian god of death, replaces the similar but unrelated word *moira* ('fate') in the Greek (*Odyssey* 3.238), and 'foretold' is an addition. Livius used the saturnian metre, a shorter line than the hexameter: so did Naevius, another figure of the third century, in his seven-book epic about the first Carthaginian war. Naevius seems to have dealt with the origins of Rome: he certainly included the tale of Aeneas in a long digression and probably also covered the origins of Carthage. This makes him an intriguing predecessor of Virgil, who evidently knew his work. But Naevius' work was overshadowed by that of a greater poet, Ennius, who adopted the hexameter. He was a poet of immense range and diversity – not only epic but tragedy, satire, epigram, even a Latin version of the comical poem about the pleasures of the table by Archestratus of Gela, the doyen of Greek foodies.

But his epic, the 18-book *Annals*, was clearly his masterpiece.[15] We have some 600 lines, but many of these are short phrases or single verses. This was a chronological account of Roman history beginning in mythic times and coming down to his own day (like Ovid in the *Metamorphoses*, but in grander and more patriotic vein). Its structure is not wholly beyond reconstruction. By the end of book 3 he had reached the founding of the Republic; the wars against the Greek states bulked large from book 7 onwards. Originally the poem (again like Ovid's) consisted of 15 books, the last three being added later: book 15 reached a climax with the events of 189 BC and the successes of his patron Fulvius Nobilior. Some books (1, 7 and 16) included prologues in which he stated his poetic programme: in one important passage he describes himself as initiated by the Muses in a dream (the Hesiodic allusion is patent; Ennius evidently also knew Callimachus' imitation). In another he declares himself the first true scholar writing in Latin: the phrasing, 'dicti studiosus', echoes the Greek word *philologos*. Ennius thus proclaims himself the successor of the Greek masters, even the reincarnation of Homer. The overall quality of the *Annals* is hard to judge. On the one hand we find lumpy Latin and thumping metre, on the other passages of remarkable energy and beauty (notably a 10-line passage concerning Ilia, the mother of Romulus and Remus, describing a dream which prefigures her rape by the god Mars). His impact on later poetry was immense, though sophisticates such as Ovid might dismiss him as artless.[16]

With the *Aeneid* of Virgil, left unfinished at the poet's death in 19 BC, we reach one of the real landmarks of ancient literature. Virgil clearly conceived it as *the* Roman national epic, an attempt to match Homer. In his earlier works he refers to his own poetic ambitions, and he is conscious of composing it at a key period in his country's history. The triumph of Octavian over Antony in 31 had brought the civil wars to (as it proved) a lasting conclusion, and the victor, styling himself as a benevolent constitutional ruler or first citizen, was bringing peace, prosperity and order to a war-weary nation. Whatever he may at one time have contemplated, however, Virgil did not compose an epic about Octavian/Augustus. The *Aeneid* views recent history through a mythical perspective. In 12 books it narrates the fall of Troy (book 2, one of the finest parts of the poem) and the journey of Trojan refugees to the west, where they are destined to settle in Italy and where the descendants of Aeneas, their leader, will found Rome and build a worldwide empire. The opening words, 'arma virumque cano' ('my song is of arms [warfare] and of a man') echo the themes of the *Iliad* and *Odyssey* (*andra*, 'a man', being the first word of the *Odyssey*). In a single poem Virgil imitates both the canonical Homeric epics, though reversing the order. The first half of the *Aeneid* (describing the wanderings of Aeneas and his followers) owes more to the *Odyssey*, the second (focusing on war in Italy) to the *Iliad*. Major episodes are reworked with complex variations: the funeral games, the visit to the underworld, the catalogues of forces and the forging of divine armour for the hero. The compression of the material is evident, with 48 Homeric books being transformed into 12. Although imitation of Homeric scenes, language and personalities is constantly visible, the process involves a rethinking of the model, not mere reproduction. Above all, the heroic vision is adapted to Roman contexts and values.

Most important, Virgil's very theme involves a long historical perspective. This is absent from Homer, who does not attempt to relate his narrative to the world of his own time: at most, there is an occasional statement that one of the heroes can achieve feats of strength 'such as two men on the earth today could not perform'. Virgil by contrast is constantly seeing the future (his own present) in the past: the actions of Aeneas will determine the destiny of generations yet unborn. The Hellenistic interest in *aetia* or origins is influential: mythical origins are given for many place names, cults, institutions (the Gates of War, the recently revived 'Trojan games'); Aeneas' son Iulus will be the ancestor of the Julian dynasty, to which both Julius Caesar and Augustus belonged, and other Roman families are also traced to Trojan prototypes (as was fashionable in the period). The origins of future conflicts are shown, with Greece and above all with Carthage, which Rome will eventually destroy. The whole poem is, indeed, the foundation-myth or *aetion* of Rome, although we do not reach that actual point. The Romans had two conflicting foundation-myths, that which concerned Aeneas and the story of Romulus and Remus; various ways of reconciling them were found. Ennius had made Romulus Aeneas' grandson, but Virgil, influenced by contemporary research in early chronology, extends the time-line drastically. Aeneas will reign in Italy for three years, his son for 30 (founding Alba Longa), and another 300 years must pass before the founding of Rome itself. (The number 3 has semi-magical resonances.) But Aeneas is granted glimpses of the distant future, and even visits the site of Rome, still a mere village of primitive huts, but fraught with a mighty destiny.

> The fiery sun had mounted the middle of the sky's curve when they observed walls, a citadel and scattered houses: now the power of Rome has raised them to heaven's height, but in those days Evander inhabited them, a paltry domain. (8.97–100)

The expansion of historical perspective is one way in which Virgil develops the Homeric forms in new directions: another is the Romanizing of the genre. Ennius in a much-quoted line had said that 'the Roman state stands upon its ancient customs and men' (467 W). Following Ennius, Virgil set

Roman virtues and values at the centre of the work. The first extended simile of the poem is a fine example. It was conventional for similes to reflect a more everyday world than the main narrative (thus making it more intelligible); anachronisms sometimes also figured. Virgil inverts the normal simile-narrative pattern: instead of using nature to illuminate man, he does the opposite. The calming of the storm at sea by Neptune and his entourage is compared with a civic riot which is pacified by the moral authority of a virtuous statesman – a simile which has no precedent in Homer.

> Just as has often happened among a great people, when a rebellious spirit emerges, and the ignoble mob grows savage at heart: now they fling fire and stones, as madness supplies them with weapons; but then, should they catch sight of some figure who claims authority through his sense of duty and his past good deeds, they fall silent and stand attentive; he governs their hearts with his words and soothes their passions. Even so the clamour of the sea subsided . . . (1.148–54)

The hero of the *Aeneid* must be a governor and a lawgiver, not an egocentric warrior.

The divine pantheon is also modified. Homer had presented the Olympian gods as a family of quick-tempered individualists, frequently ordered or bullied into line by Zeus. Although fate and foreknowledge play a part in reinforcing suspense, there is little suggestion in the *Iliad* that 'the plan of Zeus' involves more than fulfilling Thetis' request: at most, it extends to the destruction of Troy. In the *Aeneid* the stakes are higher, and the gods more formidable. It is the will of Jupiter that Rome shall be founded and conquer the world: by a bold stride of imagination, Virgil makes the Roman dominion analogous to, and a central part of, the cosmic world order.[17] Fate, seemingly identical with Jupiter's ordinance, can be delayed but not averted. The opponents of fate are formidable, however: whereas in the *Iliad* Hera in some scenes was hardly more than an indignant wife, in the *Aeneid* Juno, her Roman equivalent, is a vengeful and daemonic figure, ready to defy the will of fate and prepared to call on forces of chaos and disorder, even to unleash the powers of the underworld ('If I cannot sway heaven, I shall let hell loose', 7.312). It is naturally tempting to see the poem in polar terms of good versus evil, fate versus counter-fate, but Virgil denies us any such simplicity. At the end of the poem Jupiter and Juno come to terms, but only (it seems) temporarily: Juno will oppose Rome again in the future, by supporting Carthage in her wars, and Jupiter settles the combat between Aeneas and Turnus by unleashing a Fury, a horrific creature disturbingly reminiscent of Allecto, Juno's emissary earlier in the poem.[18]

The structure of the *Aeneid* is designed to emphasize the progress of Aeneas and his followers. From the nadir of their fortunes, homeless and

wretched, they must make their way to a new land and re-establish themselves. At first constantly looking backward to the home they have lost, they
gradually become more conscious of the purpose of their journey: Aeneas in
particular gains in maturity and confidence to face the further obstacles and
achieve his mission. It is made clear that there must be no compromises
with destiny: the new city cannot be a mere recreation of Troy, nor can
Aeneas be allowed to divert to the promising new foundation of Carthage,
where Dido welcomes them and offers them a partnership in her city.
Aeneas' affair with Dido, and his subsequent desertion of her, has outraged
countless readers (book 4). Many Romans would have read it differently:
although Dido is an attractive and sympathetic figure, her role as queen of
Carthage makes her an ancestral enemy, and her passionate emotions must
be rejected by the resolute hero. Uncontrolled passion leads to violence,
and is always suspect in Virgil. The equally emotional Turnus, Aeneas' chief
foe and foil in the second half, shows this still more clearly. Although
humanly sympathetic, these opponents of Rome must be resisted; but the
poet does not deny that their deaths are cause for sorrow. The development
of Aeneas involves self-sacrifice, even a kind of dehumanization. That the
hero seems less accessible, less of a 'well-rounded character', in the second
half of the poem is surely part of Virgil's design: Aeneas has made the
transition from being an individual to his true role as leader of a people.
Characterization is here shaped by ideology.

The *Aeneid* foretells the future triumphs of Rome and foreshadows the
achievements of Augustus in numerous ways. Aeneas holds funeral games
in memory of his father, not only because Homer's Achilles held them in
honour of Patroclus, but because Augustus similarly commemorated his
adopted father Julius Caesar: the *Aeneid* looks both ways, to the epic past
and the historical future. Most obvious are the prophetic passages in which
Jupiter and Anchises predict later events; on the same scale is the description of Aeneas' shield, forged by Vulcan, on which are set images of future
Roman victories. Central is the battle of Actium, glorified as a divinely
ordained victory of Western civilization over the barbaric gods and deadly
queen of Egypt. The reign of Augustus is envisaged as a golden age of
peace and civilizing government. The patriotic note, however, is less strident
than this sounds. Virgil often hints at suffering and loss, even failure, along
the path to greatness. Even Aeneas is a figure who performs his duty rather
than achieving contentment. He has lost his former home, his father, wife
and lover; he will live only three years after the poem ends, wedded to
a wife whose mother has just hung herself in despair at the impending
triumph of the Trojans, and whose suitor, Turnus, he has violently killed;
he will not see the greatness that is to come. Although he admires the
images on the shield, he does not grasp their meaning as Virgil's reader

can: 'ignorant of the matter, he delights in the image, as he hoists on his shoulder the renown and the destiny of his grandchildren' (8.730–1). The symbolism is unmistakable: Aeneas is the vehicle of destiny, but its full interpretation is beyond his reach.

Long critical wars have raged over the degree to which Virgil was or was not an 'Augustan' poet, whether he did or did not wholeheartedly support the new regime. The debate has often been insufficiently nuanced: talk of Virgil as 'anti-Augustan' or 'subversive' is crude and implausible. But the *Aeneid* does not present a simple picture, and its narrative allows for conflicts that end in loss and tragedy.[19] The arrival of the Trojans brings war to a land of seemingly pastoral tranquillity (7.46). The pet deer of the Italian girl Silvia is slain in a hunting expedition by Iulus (7.475–510). Aeneas performs human sacrifice, executing eight Italian youths in recompense for a dead friend (11.81). The Trojans hack down indiscriminately a tree sacred to the Italian country god Faunus, 'so that they might fight on an open plain' (12.771). Perhaps most memorable, together with the abrupt and disturbing close of the poem (where Aeneas kills Turnus in a vengeful fit of rage), is the earlier scene in which the hero faces the youthful Lausus. This young warrior is fighting in defence of his father, but in a frenzy of battle-rage Aeneas sneers at his pious devotion ('it will be your undoing' 10.812) and runs the boy through without hesitation. Yet piety is Aeneas' own supreme quality: his most famous mythical act is to rescue his aged father from the destruction of Troy, bearing him to safety on his shoulders. In this scene his mood alters in the moment after the killing:

> when the son of Anchises saw the visage of the dying lad, saw the face, that face growing miraculously pale, he moaned deeply with pity, stretching forth his hand, and the picture of devotion to a father filled his thoughts. 'Pitiable boy, what shall the pious Aeneas give you now, a fitting reward for your praiseworthy acts, for so noble a character?' (10.821–6)

Too late he sees that the piety which he mocked should have created a bond between them. The winning side does not have a monopoly on Roman virtues.

The *Aeneid* celebrates the greatness of Rome and her people, but that does not exclude compassion for those who have been swept aside or annihilated in her imperial advance. The public achievement outshines but does not wholly mask personal griefs. In general the poem seems to endorse imperialism but deplore the tragedies of war, a difficult position to sustain. Subsequent epic, above all Lucan, widens the faultlines in the *Aeneid*'s outlook.

Virgil was a famous figure in his own lifetime and the *Aeneid* became immediately established as a classic, a position it has never lost, though occasionally overshadowed by the periodic rediscovery of Homer. The beauty of his style and his mastery of language made him central to the Latin curriculum; because he was prescribed as the standard to emulate, it has not always been clear to readers how individual and startling his style actually is (it was not admired by all contemporaries). His reputation was raised further by the belief that he was in some sense a Christian poet before his time, a notion partly supported by the spiritual vision of *Aeneid* 6, in which the Homeric underworld is enriched with Platonic and mystical doctrines of reincarnation, but still more by the so-called 'Messianic' *Eclogue* 4 of around 40 BC, a poem which predicts a new era associated with the birth of a marvellous child (possibly the expected son of Antony and Octavia). This was read as signifying that Virgil, best of the pagans, had been granted a vision of the coming Christ (the idea is first found in a speech ascribed to the Emperor Constantine).[20] Hence the medieval idea of Virgil as a magician or sage, and the role of the poet as Dante's guide through the Inferno and Purgatory. Because Virgil was not himself a Christian, he cannot go further, and Dante's beloved Beatrice must take over the task in Paradise. The idea of Virgil as in some way a proto-Christian was given a fresh lease on life in two puzzling but influential essays by Eliot;[21] Pound and Graves vigorously dissented from his high evaluation of the Roman poet. But whatever value is set on his work and whatever the upshot of the perpetual comparison with Homer (a topic which already bored Juvenal in the salons of learned ladies), Virgil is one of the indispensable figures in European literary history.

IV

In a famous autobiographical poem written late in life, Ovid tells us that he knew and heard Horace and Propertius, but 'Virgil I only saw' (*Tristia* 4.10). He was nearly 30 years Virgil's junior, and would have been in his early 20s when the *Aeneid* was published. His own poetry was profoundly influenced by Virgil from the start, but in his epic he deliberately produced a work as unlike the *Aeneid* as possible. The *Metamorphoses*, an extravaganza of mythology in 15 books, is his only hexameter work, and shows the mentality of an elegist (which at this date meant principally a love poet). Well over 200 mythical tales are narrated, and there are allusions to many more. Some are told at considerable length – the story of Phaethon is one of the longest, at over 400 lines – but many others are disposed of more swiftly (the grim tale of Marsyas is over in less than 20 lines). Ovid does not allow us to become too preoccupied with a single situation: there is no 'hero' to the *Metamorphoses*. No poem is so readily anthologized. The structure is ostensibly chronological: he claims that he will bring his continuous verse from the origins of the cosmos down to his own day, and indeed the last three books do bring us from the Greek world to Italy. The last book culminates in the deification of Caesar and (anticipated) Augustus, with Ovid's own immortality providing the coping-stone. This design is however frequently disrupted by devices such as digression or the narration of unrelated events by a character, or a series of characters: dinner-party conversation in book 8 produces several narratives, and the whole of book 10 consists of Orpheus' lament for his dead wife, in which he recounts numerous other erotic tales, mostly tragic.

The tone of the *Metamorphoses* is no less erratic. Only gradually is the novelty of the poem revealed, for the opening lines give little away other than referring to the theme of transformation and the broad time scheme. The first episodes describe the initial forming of the world from chaos, the creation of living things, the early history of the gods: these sections have a more traditional epic flavour, mingled with Lucretian language. A council of the gods introduces Jupiter in judgemental mood, calling for the punishment of the evil King Lycaon: his metamorphosis into a wolf is deserved and appropriate (233ff.), and this creates an expectation of moral deities and punishment that will suit the crime. Similarly the story of the flood, from which the virtuous Deucalion and Pyrrha are saved, shows righteousness rewarded. But after Apollo has slain the monstrous Python, we are told that 'the first love of Phoebus was Daphne, daughter of the river god' (452), and the poet embarks on a more light-hearted erotic tale of pursuit and loss through metamorphosis (a recurring story-type in the poem); a lively narrative style, a more indulgent moral outlook, and a more extensive and ingenious use of speeches appear. The lighter treatment of the Olympians is also characteristic. A great German critic has remarked that Homer's gods display 'sublime frivolity':[22] Virgil chose to enhance the sublime side, while Ovid puts the emphasis on frivolity. The gods cannot serve as moral authorities in this epic. Nor can the poet. Ovid declines to allow us either moral or narrative stability: the shifting subject and tone of the *Metamorphoses* are as fluid as the physical forms the poem transmogrifies.

The subject of metamorphosis has some background in Hellenistic literature. For Ovid, it provided a convenient way of combining a variety of colourful and vividly imagined tales from countless sources. For many of these, his is the best or most famous version: Daphne, Phaethon, Actaeon, Callisto, Cephalus and Procris, Midas' golden touch, Perseus and Andromeda. Shakespeare is only his most distinguished debtor.[23] Metamorphosis offers ample scope for humorous grotesquerie, and Ovid relishes the opportunity to describe human flesh and limbs morphing into wings and feathers, branches and leaves, flower and stem. His hapless characters may become spiders, magpies, frogs, ants, bats, snakes or streams, while mischievous aetiologies are provided for the hyacinth and the partridge. In most cases the story ends with the alteration of form. Few recover their former shape, although they may continue to perform their characteristic functions (as Arachne, punished for rivalling Minerva's art at embroidery, continues to weave patterns in spider-web form). Seldom is the change a positive one, though happy endings do occur: the change of Pygmalion's statue into a living woman who becomes his wife is one case; another is the tale of Ianthe, a girl who has been raised as a boy but fortunately undergoes a sex change on the eve of her marriage to a woman (10.243–97, 9.666–797). More often the change of form is used as a means to defuse a horrific situation and dissipate the tragic pathos which the poet has generated (as when Acis, slain by the jealous Cyclops, is magically restored to life as a river-deity, 13.885ff.). In some stories the metamorphosis is an afterthought, justifying the inclusion of the tale at all (as in the story of Meleager, where it is his sisters, not the youth himself, who are transformed, 8. 533–46). In others a kind of pseudo-metamorphosis occurs, as in the opening book when chaos is shaped into order, or in the tale of Daedalus and Icarus, when the two humans only mimic birds, or *seem* to be gods to an amazed observer (8.220).

How seriously are we meant to take the fantastic events that Ovid narrates? We can be fairly sure that his audience would not have been credulous; elsewhere he himself calls these stories unbelievable.[24] Skilful technique and ingenious modification of literary models matter much more than putting across any kind of message, whether moral or metaphysical. The great qualities of the *Metamorphoses* are wit, pathos and rhetoric, together with abundant gifts for visual description (fortunately Ovid found his ideal illustrator in Rubens). For the duration of a given tale we may suspend our disbelief and respond fully to the force of the character's situation, but the poet's clever editorializing often complicates the effect. Ovid may intervene parenthetically to express shock – or scepticism (1.400 'who would believe it, if ancient tradition did not stand witness?'; 8.721 'this is what the old men told (there was no reason they should wish to lie about it)'). Macabre and horrific episodes are common, though our capacity to empathize may be diminished by the flashes of humour or paradox. The flaying of Marsyas at the command of angry Apollo is potentially a horrendous scene, but Ovid gives him an outrageously clever line: 'why do you tear me from myself?' 6.385). The 'pointed' style (p. 215) is characteristic of his work, and is not confined to the speeches. But although many scenes are played for laughs, there is still beauty and often intense pathos in Ovid's treatment of innocence violated, painful dilemmas, agonies of indecision, fear and desire. In the disturbing story of Myrrha, who lusts for her own father, he skates jauntily over dark waters: the soliloquy of the girl as she struggles with her passion is typically ingenious, but the scenes in which her nurse acts as pander, makes her father drunk and entices him to sleep with a young girl in his wife's absence show a keen insight into human weakness (esp. 10.463–71). Ovid is not simply a wit and a cynic, but in many passages it is clear that a smile is the appropriate response.

Although Ovid undertook to bring the epic down to his own time, the Roman dimension of the poem is less than wholeheartedly patriotic. In the sections which run parallel with his predecessor, his flirtation with the *Aeneid* is deliberately provocative: he fills in gaps left by Virgil, while avoiding the high points. Virgil's detailed narrative of the fall of Troy is among his greatest achievements; Ovid disposes of the city in four words (13. 404, 'Troy fell, Priam too'), and then moves on to the metamorphosis of Hecuba. Dido dominates two books of the *Aeneid*, a mere four lines of Ovid (14.78–81). Aeneas is viewed from a distance, and utters no word in Ovid's version. The wooing of the wood-nymph Pomona by the rural god Vertumnus gets much more attention than the career of Romulus (14.622–771). Throughout, Ovid frustrates the reader's expectations; even in patriotic mode, he does not deny himself sly witticisms and irreverent paradoxes. Julius Caesar and his adoptive son Augustus must both be praised: Ovid does so by declaring that Julius, now divine, observes Augustus' deeds and admits that they are superior to his own: 'he rejoices to be surpassed by him. Yet the son forbids his own deeds to be set above his father's; nevertheless, fame, unfettered and obedient to no man, exalts him in spite of his desire, and in this one thing opposes his commands.' (15.850–4). This is a compliment, but a typically ingenious and perhaps, to Augustus, a faintly annoying one. Hellenistic wit displaces Augustan propriety.

The *Aeneid*, as we have seen, was a work which instantly dominated the literary scene; it could not be ignored. Ovid reacted to it by turning to the romantic, the exotic, the supernatural and the erotic. The response of Lucan in his poem *On the Civil War* (between Pompey and Caesar) was more radical, in both political and generic terms: far more than Ovid he may be said to have composed an 'anti-*Aeneid*'. Left unfinished at his death, his poem is one of the most extraordinary works in ancient literature. In originality of conception and style it surpasses any of the other late epics (his contemporary Statius comes closest). The poem breaks off in the tenth book: presumably it would have run to 12, like the *Aeneid*. It is a historical account of the campaigns leading up to the battle of Pharsalus (book 7), which ended with Caesar victorious and Pompey in flight: in book 8 Pompey is murdered in Egypt. In book 9 much attention is focused on the Republican leader Cato, who figures only rarely earlier but now takes on the role of Caesar's chief opponent. It may be guessed that the poem would have ended with Cato's heroic last stand and Stoic suicide at Utica in Africa, an iconic moment. Lucan's history (drawn mainly from the now-lost books of Livy) is often selective or distorted; he neglects important episodes, exaggerates trivial ones, alters places and personalities to suit his needs (thus Cicero, unhistorically, is present at the field of Pharsalus). Historical precision was never his aim. What he presents is an apocalyptic vision of the dying Republic, as the Roman people first commit themselves to fratricidal civil war and then are plunged into slavery (his repeated term) as subjects of the tyrannical empire inaugurated by Caesar. Whereas Virgil had celebrated Rome's new golden age under Augustus, Lucan laments the loss of liberty and the virtual immolation of the Roman people. He is a powerful reminder that epic, like history, need not be simply the story as told by the victorious side.[25]

Lucan is strongly influenced not only by Ovidian wit and point but by the even sharper theatrical style (and the Stoic outlook) of his uncle Seneca. Like Senecan tragedy, Lucan's epic cultivates the rhetorical and the macabre. Although he deliberately excludes the gods in the sense of not introducing scenes in which deities observe or intervene in the human drama, he relishes episodes involving ecstatic prophecy or consultation of oracular sources: but the insights provided are either ignored or useless. A major set piece is the scene in book 6 where one of Pompey's sons tries to discover the future. In some respects this scene inverts the central underworld episode in the equivalent book of Virgil. Whereas Aeneas had sought the aid of the austere Sibyl, Apollo's prophetess, Sextus Pompeius consults the loathsome witch Erichtho, who, in a scene which Lucan deliberately makes as repulsive as possible, reanimates a corpse on the nearby battlefield and forces it to reveal what the shades of the underworld know of the future. Where Aeneas was consoled and reassured by Anchises' positive vision of future Roman greatness, the dead man demoralizes Pompeius by describing how all the virtuous Roman dead are in despair, while past villains such as Catiline and the Cethegi are exulting at the prospect of Caesar's victory. Sextus is assured that places are being kept in Hades for him and his father: 'be not troubled by the glory of a short life; . . . make haste to die' (6.805–7).

The manic energy of Lucan's verse reflects the dynamism of the anti-hero Caesar: although driven by ambition and malice, he is a better fighter than the older and ineffective Pompey. A superb passage early in the poem characterizes the opponents at length:

> The two rivals were ill-matched. The one was tamed by declining years; for long he had worn the toga and forgotten in peace the leader's part; . . . the mere shadow of a mighty name he stood. Just as an oak-tree, laden with the ancient trophies of a nation, the consecrated gifts of conquerors, towers in a fertile field; but the roots it clings by have lost their toughness and it stands by

its weight alone . . . though it totters doomed to fall at the first gale, while many trees with sound timber rise beside it, yet it alone is revered. But Caesar had more than a mere name and fame as a commander; his energy could never rest, and his one disgrace was to conquer without war. Alert and headstrong, he answered with arms any summons of ambition or resentment; he never shrank from using the sword, followed up every success, and snatched at the favour of fortune, overthrowing everything that blocked his path to supreme power, and rejoicing to clear the way by destruction. Even so the lightning is driven forth by wind through the clouds . . . it flashes out and cracks the daylight sky, striking fear and terror into mankind and dazzling the eye with slanting flame; . . . falling and returning it spreads destruction far and wide, and gathers again its scattered fires. (1.129–57, extracts; Duff's tr., modified)

Even those who are doubtful of the value of biography-based criticism find it hard to deny the relevance of Lucan's career, since he was executed (or rather, forced to commit suicide, in the manner of the day) for treason against Nero, having been implicated in the conspiracy of Piso in 65; in the subsequent purge his father and his uncle Seneca were also forced to kill themselves (Tacitus, *Annals* 15.70). Other traditions, if reliable, are also interesting – that the conspiracy had a Stoic side to it, that the corrupt emperor was to be replaced by the philosopher Seneca, that Lucan and Nero had already fallen out, or that the emperor was jealous of the young man's poetic talent. It is a perennial puzzle that the poem opens with hyperbolic praise of Nero as Lucan's inspirational genius: the high-flown imagery recalls the prologue to Virgil's *Georgics*. Some read the passage as ironic, while others think it pre-dates the quarrel with Nero. Whatever the truth, there are small grounds for seeing the rest of the poem as holding back in any way from indictment of tyranny. Lucan constantly intrudes on the narrative, protesting at the events he is forced to narrate, underlining the significance of the action, denouncing the agents and the consequences. Apostrophe, used sparingly by his predecessors, now figures on every page: the poet thrusts himself into the action. Addressing Caesar, he even refers to Pharsalia as 'our' battle – that is, 'fought by you and recounted by me' (9.985). In this as in other stylistic techniques (metre, vocabulary, profuseness with epigram) he is anti-Virgilian.

In Homer and Virgil it is common for the poet to linger on the death of even a minor figure, reminding us that each individual has dependants, a wife, a home, something they have lost. A Homeric example is the following:

He went after Xanthus and Thoon, sons of Phaenops, both late-born. Their father was worn out by cruel age, and he had no other sons for his possessions after him. Then Diomedes slew them and robbed them of their lives, both of them; to their father he left lamentation and bitter sorrow, for he did not welcome them home returning from battle, and distant kinsmen divided the estate. (5.152ff.)

Precisely this individual attention is rejected by Lucan in a memorable passage which also illustrates his love of the gruesome, his emphatic, demanding rhetoric, and the stark simplemindedness of his historical perspective.

> When the world is dying I feel shame to spend my tears
> on the innumerable deaths and to follow individuals' destinies
> questioning, whose guts did the fatal wound
> pass through? who trampled on his vitals spilling on the ground?
> . . . who strikes his brother's
> breast, cuts off the head, and throws it far away
> so he can plunder the familiar corpse? who mangles
> his father's face and proves to those who watch by his excessive wrath
> that the man he slaughters is not his father? No death deserves
> its own lament; we have no space to grieve for individuals.
> . . . From this battle the people received a mightier wound
> than their own time could bear; more was lost than life
> and safety: for all the world's eternity we are prostrated.
> Every age which will suffer slavery is conquered by these swords.
> How did the next generation and the next deserve
> to be born into tyranny? Did we wield weapons or shield
> our throats in fear and trembling? The punishment of others' fear
> sits heavy on our necks. If, Fortune, you intended to give a master
> to those born after battle, you should also have given us a chance to fight.
> (7.617–46, with omissions; tr. Braund)

Lucan loves digressions, is addicted to curious learning, and constantly indulges the age's devotion to paradox, sometimes to the point of perversity. The reader needs as far as possible to adopt the poet's own extravagant mind-set in order to reap the rewards that the poem has to offer – but they are considerable.

Lucan's was the most iconoclastic of the Latin epics. His younger but longer-lived contemporary Statius paid tribute to him in an admiring commemoration (*Silvae* 2.7), but his own epic the *Thebaid* (probably published about AD 91) took a step or two back towards epic orthodoxy. In particular, Statius reverted to mythical subject matter and fully reinstated the gods as overseers and participants in the poem (Lucan's bold exclusion of the Olympians clearly raised critical eyebrows).[26] In other ways he was certainly much influenced by Lucan (and by Seneca's dark tragedies, some of which covered material related to his own). The influence is discernible in his choice of the theme of civil war culminating in fratricide, his extravagantly rhetorical style, full of pathos and passion, his fondness for scenes involving macabre or spine-chilling effects (ecstatic prophecy, supernatural apparitions, gruesomely described wounds), and his penchant for Stoic-flavoured moralizing. His subject is the conflict between the sons of Oedipus, tyrannical Eteocles and jealous exile Polynices, following Eteocles' seizure of the Theban throne, which leads to war between Argos and Thebes. The conflict is slow to begin: Statius paints the mythological background and brings in other heroes to swell the colourful cast of characters. After many delays and the deaths of most of Polynices' companions (the Seven against Thebes), ultimately the two brothers kill each other in single combat (book 11). The kingship is claimed by Creon, who denies the invading dead burial; this impious act is condemned by Theseus of Athens, and his intervention on the side of right finally brings the tragic events to a dramatic close. The poem is rich in melodramatic climaxes and vicious acts of revenge. High points include the opening of the earth to engulf the prophet Amphiaraus, who is carried down chariot and all, still alive, into Hades, never to return; the noble self-sacrifice of the Theban Menoeceus, whose death ensures that Thebes will be saved (there are echoes here of Roman myths of *devotio* or self-immolation); the blasphemous defiance of the gods by Capaneus, who is struck down from the battlements of Thebes by Jupiter's thunderbolt. Most horrific of all is the mad hatred of Tydeus, whose anger at the man who has mortally wounded him is such that he begins to gnaw the head and brains of his enemy, a cannibalistic act which deprives him of the immortality which Minerva, his patroness, had been about to bestow; when she sees the bestial depths to which he has sunk, she turns away in disgust. One needs a strong stomach to relish Statius, but once read he is unforgettable.

Quite different is the other epic which Statius only began, a poem on the career of Achilles. (The conventional length of the epic form made it an occupational hazard for poets to die without finishing their works: besides Lucan and Virgil himself, Valerius Flaccus and Claudian also left truncated efforts.) The thousand-odd lines which he wrote show a surprisingly light touch; there is humour and a playful imagination in his picture of Achilles as a boy hunting in the hills, then reluctantly being dressed in girl's clothes by his anxious mother, only to find unexpected advantages in the disguise, as it enables him to get close to the beautiful princess of Scyros, with whom his youthful romance swiftly blossoms. When the text breaks off Achilles is en route for Troy and manlier pursuits.

The remaining poets of the first century AD require a brief word. Valerius Flaccus' unfinished *Argonautica* reworks the story of Jason: as in Apollonius, the scenes between the hero and Medea are bound to interest most, though the careful reader can appreciate the ingenuity with which the poet has reworked or altered traditional matter by setting the poem alongside Apollonius, whose work the writer knew intimately. Comparative criticism also has much scope with Silius Italicus, whose *Punica* (17 books!) narrates the Hannibalic war and can therefore be set alongside Livy's account, which survives in full and was evidently Silius' main source. There is much to be gained from seeing how the same events are transformed from historical to epic mode, but the comparison often leaves one questioning Silius' taste and judgement (even Feeney, who rehabilitates everything he touches, cannot bring himself to defend Silius with any real enthusiasm).[27] The constant presence of the gods in his account makes one see Lucan's wisdom in exiling them from historical epic. It is one thing in the world of exotic and primeval myth to accept that a Fury may inspire Turnus to oppose Aeneas, or even that two Furies may be involved in forcing Eteocles and Polynices into madness; it is less easy to take seriously such a being's involvement in the historical misfortunes of the beleaguered town of Saguntum in 219 BC.

From this point onward the pre-eminence of epic is on the wane. There are later works extant, mainly in Greek (some of them seemingly ignorant of their more imaginative Roman predecessors). But although this poetic peak might still be the chief ambition of a poet such as Camoens or Milton, the great days of the genre were numbered. In modern times the rise of the novel as the main narrative form, and more recently the critical hostility towards the public, the patriotic or the rhetorical, have all contributed to the decline of epic in its traditional guise. But any reader with the imagination and enthusiasm to suspend prejudice will be astonished at the richness, the diversity and the sophistication of these masterworks of antiquity.

2

Drama

'Oh misery! Now I'm on the verge of uttering the dreadful truth!'
'And I of hearing it. Yet hear I must.'

Sophocles, *Oedipus the King* 1169–70

I

Drama means something done, and action needs actors. It is likely that Greek (in this case essentially Athenian) drama emerged from a form which consisted solely of choral song, possibly song including narrative or praise of Dionysus, a god closely associated with drama. In that case, the key innovation, ascribed to an almost mythical figure called Thespis, was to introduce an actor separated from the group of singers who made up the chorus – an individual with a name who could engage in dialogue with the chorus, and convey news of events offstage. Thespis, allegedly active at Athens in the 530s, was seen as the founder-figure of tragedy, the most prestigious form of drama (comedy came later); but our first surviving tragedy is Aeschylus' *Persians* of 472, 60 years later. By then there were two actors, and the later works of Aeschylus require three, as do most of the plays of his followers. The history of tragedy can be seen as one of progressive growth in the importance of the actors, while that of the chorus diminishes.

Many features of the Athenian theatre are strange to us.[1] These were open-air productions, forming part of the outdoor celebrations at the annual civic festivals of Dionysus. In the fourth century the theatre was rebuilt to hold 14,000; its scale and structure in the earlier period is controversial, but it would still have held an audience of thousands. The composition of that audience is again hotly disputed: male citizens, adults and youths, would surely have formed the majority, but whether women were admitted is uncertain. Playwrights were authorized and sponsored by the state, and competed for state-funded prizes. At the most significant festival, the City Dionysia, three dramatists each put on four plays, three tragedies and a satyr play (see p. 61). These would take up most of a day, but the plays were shorter than most modern dramas (in our texts, few last more than 1,500 verse lines; comedies were often shorter). The winner was decided not by the audience as a whole but by official judges. In the absence of elaborate visual effects, most of the plays involved simple scenery and depended more on the power of the word than on illusionistic representation. Costumes might be lavish, but props were few and those which were used often carried great significance (the rich fabrics on which Agamemnon treads, or the bow of Philoctetes). Actors and chorus alike were normally Athenian citizens, and were all male. The use of masks made it possible to shift roles: an actor might play three or four parts in the course of a performance, and shift between male and female roles. The apparent restrictiveness of the three-actor limit was further relaxed by the inclusion of silent actors playing supporting roles (slaves, bodyguards and the like).

In general, tragedy dealt with the mythical period, following the lead of epic (Plato called Homer the pathfinder of tragedy, and subjects connected with the Trojan wars remained particularly prominent). Contemporary events were sometimes treated, but only in the early period or at a much later date. The only surviving historical drama is Aeschylus' *Persians*, which dramatizes the scenes at the Persian court when the queen and council of elders receive the bad news of the Greek victory over the Persian fleet at the battle of Salamis. The play culminates with the return of Xerxes, the defeated king, humiliated and dressed symbolically in rags. Even here history is mythicized. The events on stage are distant in place though not in time, and all the characters are Persian: no Greek leader is praised or even named, though some passages allude to particular cities, including Athens. The events are seen from a Persian perspective, though the morality is Greek and little attempt is made at historical accuracy. Yet though the play has a dignity and pathos which makes it more than patriotic chest-beating, it does seem that Greek tragedy normally preferred to avoid the historical, and to deal with political issues more indirectly, through the mirror of myth.

It remains the case that many of the tragedies dramatize themes which have obvious resonances for the Athenian audiences.[2] Several plays are set in Athens: institutions and cults familiar to the theatre-goer are referred to. In the *Eumenides*, the third play of Aeschylus' *Oresteia*, the action moves from the vicious and accursed palace of Argos, where we have witnessed murder and tyranny, to the cleaner air of Athens, where a jury of citizens offer refuge and justice to the wretched Orestes. Athens also helps the weak and defenceless (Euripides, *Children of Heracles, Suppliants*; Sophocles, *Oedipus at Colonus*). The Athenians are shown an idealized version of themselves (as in Pericles' funeral speech). But this is to oversimplify. Many other plays, not necessarily set in Athens, include anachronistic references or present themes which the audience might find highly relevant but also disturbing. The *Antigone*, for example, presents a conflict between the individual religious conscience and the decrees of the state. The *Trojan Women*, set in the immediate aftermath of the sack of Troy, demonstrates the devastating effects of war upon its victims: it has often been suggested that the Athenians' recent massacre of the rebellious citizens of Melos was in Euripides' mind. Tragedy is not a comforting or congratulatory genre, and many of the dilemmas facing the characters on stage are hard to solve. Difficult choices and seemingly inevitable suffering face virtuous characters, and divine vengeance can strike down the innocent as well as the guilty. We can see why Creon is punished, but what of Antigone and Haemon? Tragedy frustrates the expectations of the audience; it can even go some way towards challenging their basic ideological assumptions, about politics, gender, religion and much else. The fact that the gods regularly (not invariably) restore order at the end of the play may diminish but can hardly dissipate the effect of this challenge.

When we ask what is at stake in Greek tragedy, it is hard to come up with an answer that covers all of the 32 surviving plays. But in all of these we are confronted with suffering, usually intense and sometimes involving death, often multiple deaths. The play need not end in a bloodbath, as in *Hamlet*, but danger must at least threaten. Second, the action normally includes conflict, personal or political, often intensified by the close relationship between those involved, for tragedy focuses above all on the family and on intra-familial loyalties and antagonisms. Third, since the leading figures are normally royal or of high status, these conflicts may have important implications for the whole state, as Orestes seeks to regain his throne or Oedipus tries to save Thebes from pollution and plague. It is only occasionally, mostly in Euripides, that more personal plots emerge, where the city's affairs are in the background: in the *Alcestis*, for instance, the focus is on the household of Admetus, and the plot has no real implications for society at large. That play is anomalous in other ways, as the catastrophe is reversed, tragedy averted, and Alcestis restored to life. Here tragedy comes close to comedy (compare *The Winter's Tale*).

A further common element in the tragedies is the divine background. As in epic, the gods have a major role to play in the genre. Though in many plays they do not appear, they are frequently invoked, their prophets appear on stage, oracles are reported, and there is above all a sense of their presence behind the action. When an obscure oracle comes true, or a dream becomes reality, the divine hand is at work, for good or ill. Many plays end with a divine epiphany (the so-called *deus ex machina*), a conclusion in which the god appears on high and interprets events or declares the future. The gods enhance the significance of the action, but it is the humans who suffer the consequences. Thus far the technique is that of epic, but tragedy allows us less access to the actual deliberations of the gods (Zeus rarely if ever appeared on stage), and in Sophocles especially, there is a deeper sense of mystery and ambiguity in divine activity.

Many have seen Greek tragedy (and sometimes Greek comedy) as religious drama in a stronger sense, like medieval mystery plays. On this kind of argument, the significance of the plays lies in their links with Greek religion, especially Dionysiac rituals.[3] The leading expert on Greek religion sees the genre as rooted in primeval rites of sacrifice ('do the greatest poets only provide sublime expression for what already existed at the most primitive stages of development? Human existence face-to-face with death: that is the kernel of *tragoidia*'[4]). But although tragedy includes representation of rituals (supplications and prayers to the gods, burial ceremonies, lamentations, songs of blessing and so forth), the individual drama is not a ritual in the same sense; plays are not performed as an act of worship, but take place (along with other contests) amid a larger festival context. Clearly the genre has considerable religious content, and forms part of a religious occasion, but it is not clear that audiences regarded the plays as religious acts: certainly this was not the only aspect to which they responded. When we hear of re-performances they are not for ritual purposes, but because of the special popularity of particular plays.

A final general point concerns the formal aspect of tragedy. Unlike Homer, whose work is entirely in hexameters, or Shakespeare, who writes in blank verse with only occasional variations, the tragedians employ a great diversity of metres which reflect the complex poetic heritage. (All tragedy is in verse, though the comic poets made very occasional use of prose passages – one of many indications of the stylistic gulf between the genres). The key distinction is between spoken verse (including most of the dialogue between actors) and song. Broadly speaking, the chorus sing, whereas actors (and the chorus-leader when conversing with actors) speak. But there are numerous places where actors do break into song, usually at moments of deep emotion or excitement; some such passages are high points in the play and must have called for virtuoso vocalizing (e.g. Creusa's aria in the *Ion*, in which she reveals the truth of how she was raped by a god, gave birth in secret and exposed the child). In translations (especially prose translations, which flatten out the diversity) these distinctions of metre and tone are harder to recapture, but they are fundamental to the pace and power of the drama.

Some other alleged rules governing Greek tragedy are in fact the prescriptive preferences of later criticism. Influential above all is Aristotle's short monograph the *Poetics*, perhaps written in the 330s BC, which focuses on tragedy and its generic progenitor epic (a lost second book dealt with comedy).[5] Aristotle's treatment is often compressed and elliptical, and many of his key terms (such as 'catharsis') have been expanded and developed by later critics in ways he might well have disowned. He is often said to require unity of time, place and action. Actually he says nothing about place, while he only offers a descriptive generalization on time: 'tragedy strives as far as possible to limit itself to a single day'. That the tragedians in general restricted the timescale of the action, and avoided change of scene, is true, but exceptions are common. Unity of action or plot is more complex, and here Aristotle does indeed set guidelines which concern the coherence and probability of the plot: events should unfold as a chain of consequences, and random elements should not be introduced.

It is easy to underrate Aristotle because we have learned so much about criticism since, but he was one of its founding fathers. His clipped comments are often deeply suggestive, not least in the ninth chapter, where he remarks that poetry, dealing more with generalities, tells us what sort of person would probably or necessarily act in a certain way, and so is closer to philosophy; history, by contrast, deals more with the particular ('what Alcibiades, for instance, did or what happened to him'). Or again, later in the same chapter, reflections on formal structure converge with ideas of 'poetic justice' in the tantalizing comment on the otherwise unknown story of Mitys:

> emotions are more likely to be stirred when things happen unexpectedly but because of each other; this arouses more surprise than mere chance events, since even chance events seem more marvellous when they look as if they were meant to happen. Take the case of the statue of Mitys in Argos falling on Mitys' murderer and killing him; for we do not think that things like this are mere accidents.

So too in tragedy, chance events and apparent coincidences in the end reveal a deeper meaning: *Oedipus the King* is a paradigm case.

II

Our 32 plays span three-quarters of a century. Not all are dateable, but the earliest, as already mentioned, is Aeschylus' *Persians* (472), while the latest certain date is that of Sophocles' *Oedipus at Colonus* (posthumously produced in 401). One play may be later still: it is possible that the *Rhesus*, ascribed to Euripides, is by a later hand, from the fourth century. Each of the three major tragedians composed over 80 plays, and we know the names of about 45 other tragic poets from the period. The fifth-century audience would have had the opportunity to see hundreds of plays, whereas we have only the tip of the iceberg. But what we have is not a random selection: the seven plays by Aeschylus and seven by Sophocles look like a selection made in late antiquity for closer study, including a number of 'classic' dramas: *Oedipus the King* was evidently already recognized as a classic by ancient critics such as Aristotle and Longinus.[6] We have much more by Euripides, who was more readable, highly quotable, and controversial. Many more plays are known in part from later quotations or fragments, but in a survey of this kind only a few that survive complete can be considered.

Already in the fifth century we can see that Aeschylus, Sophocles and Euripides are emerging as the three 'great' tragedians. In Aristophanes' *Frogs*, produced in 405, Dionysus, discontented with the quality of poetry, goes down to the underworld to bring back a great poet to revitalize Athens. The second half of the play is dominated by a contest between Aeschylus and Euripides for the privilege of returning to life; at the end the god chooses Aeschylus, representative of old values and classic verse, and Sophocles assumes the place of honour which the older tragedian is vacating in the underworld. Other lesser figures are mentioned at the start of the play only to be dismissed as inferior. But the work which has done most to establish this triad is again Aristotle's *Poetics*. That essay adopts an evolutionary view of the genre, trying to describe how tragedy attained its true nature, and there are clear indications that he regards more recent tragedy as inferior; the position of Euripides in this process of decline is ambiguous. Modern critics have too often conflated Aristophanes and Aristotle to produce a caricatured account of tragedy's development. According to this conventional schema, Aeschylus was primitive, Sophocles the mature artist, while Euripides brought the genre into decline. Literary history needs to do better than that: in fact Sophocles and Euripides were contemporaries, both producing plays throughout the second half of the fifth century. Although Euripides was younger, he died first, and Sophocles was said to have worn mourning dress in his honour. Both the later dramatists were figures of the first rank; the Aristophanic treatment, which satirizes Euripides as a decadent and corrupting poet, is a masterpiece of mischievous yet admiring misrepresentation.

One marked difference between Aeschylus and his successors is his preference for the 'trilogy' structure: except for the *Persians*, all his surviving works come from a connected series of plays. This makes a total assessment difficult except when we have the whole sequence, as is uniquely the case with his trilogy on the house of Atreus, the *Oresteia* (*Agamemnon*, *Libation-bearers, Eumenides*). With the others scholarship struggles with alternative hypotheses on how to reconstruct the trilogy, and in two cases we are even unsure which place the surviving play occupied. The trilogy structure suited Aeschylus' interest in presenting successive generations of a family, a chain of crime and misfortune: first the death of Agamemnon, then the coming of his son Orestes, grown to manhood, to avenge his father; then the consequences for the avenger after he has committed the terrible crime of matricide. Similarly his Theban trilogy portrayed the doom of Laius, Oedipus and the fratricidal sons of Oedipus – three generations. Still vaster perspectives are exploited in the trilogy on Prometheus, the only surviving tragedy to deal mainly with the gods – in this case, the rise of Zeus to power and his vindictive punishment of the disobedient Prometheus, whose bitter defiance is dramatized in the surviving play, but who must endure centuries of torment before being finally released in the lost *Prometheus Unbound*. (This last case is complicated still further by the possibility that the surviving Prometheus play may not be by Aeschylus but by an imitator.) But trilogies went out of fashion, it seems, as the century wore on. As a result the individual dramas become more intense, yet also more complex in their plots, with more abundant characters and more frequent changes of direction. Euripides' late plays, especially *Phoenissae* and *Orestes*, illustrate the tendency.

To later readers, Aeschylus looked archaic, in his thought, his style and his dramatic technique. In the *Frogs*, he is treated as a spokesman for the good old days when the Greeks won the battle of Marathon (in which he himself fought), but also as a composer of overblown and incomprehensible lyrics. Inherited guilt, ancestral curses, persecuting Furies, vendetta and religious pollution – concepts such as these pervade the world of Aeschylean tragedy, a world of dark powers in which mortals must pray for justice or retribution that may be slow in coming. Austere in characterization, eloquent yet exotic in its polysyllabic style, dominated by long and complex choral odes, his drama does seem to belong to an older world. But this is only one side: Aeschylus, born in the sixth century, is also the poet of democratic Athens, deeply involved with its ideals of reasoned discussion and decision-making, which he dramatizes in mythic terms in the last play of the *Oresteia*, set in a king-free Athens. In his presentation of the doom-laden world of the heroic age, he not only shows us horrific events and catastrophes, but also allows his characters to work towards a difficult resolution. In Aeschylean tragedy there is a strong emphasis on the gods' power, and especially the will of Zeus, who oversees human lives and may bring blessings as well as destruction. Aeschylus is famous for presenting mortals confronted with seemingly insoluble dilemmas, but in the end something positive does seem to emerge after suffering. On the most plausible reconstruction of the *Prometheus* trilogy, after an impasse of generations,

Prometheus is eventually reconciled with a Zeus who may have learned wisdom as he grew older. In the *Seven against Thebes*, the city of Thebes is saved from invasion, though it requires the death of their King Eteocles. Above all in the *Oresteia*, the poet dramatizes the contrast between a darker world of vendetta and savage conflict, and a society in which the rule of law has an important place, where argument and persuasion may prove superior to hate and violence.[7] The refugee Orestes, pursued by the Furies, finds sanctuary in a mythical Athens where Athena presides over an archetypal law court. In this trilogy, although the sufferings and crimes of the past are not forgotten, and the Furies still have their grimmer side as agents of retribution, the emphasis at the close is on the enlightened justice of the court, and the reconciliation of opposed factions among the gods promises prosperity for the future. Some readers have nevertheless felt that the optimism of the last play lacks the poetic power of the earlier parts of the trilogy; to judge by Euripides' reworkings of the myth in the *Electra* and the *Orestes*, he too may have found Aeschylus' idealistic conclusion unsatisfying or anti-tragic.

Above all Aeschylus must be read for his style, which is rich and sumptuous, in contrast with the sparer vocabulary and more orderly sentences of the later dramatists. Vivid imagery and daring word-combinations and compounds create an effect which transcends the many parodies:

> And when he had slipped his neck through the strap of compulsion's yoke, and the wind of his purpose had veered about and blew impious, impure, unholy, from that moment he reversed his mind and turned to utter recklessness. For men are emboldened by base-counselling, wretched infatuation, the beginning of woe. However, he brought himself to become the sacrificer of his daughter, in aid of a war woman-avenging, as a rite to bless the fleet. (*Agamemnon* 218–27, tr. Fraenkel [adapted])

Sophocles is no easier to summarize than his great predecessor. One tendency in his plays, which it is all too easy to use as a formula, is for each to portray a heroic individual, isolated or alienated from those he/she belongs with, whether community or family, angry and intransigent, resistant to persuasion, often defying even the gods. Hence influential readings have grouped Antigone, Ajax, Philoctetes, the aged Oedipus and others under the label 'the Sophoclean hero'.[8] (Qualifications abound: one of our seven plays, the *Women of Trachis*, does not fit this pattern; many different plot-structures may have been detectable in the lost plays; and this heroic stance is not solely Sophoclean, since Aeschylus' Prometheus and Euripides' Medea share some of these attributes.) The pattern is evident, though we must be as sensitive to its variations as its regularities. Through these individuals Sophocles explores the gulf between the ordinary figures of the civilized community and the extraordinary or unusual figure (whether exceptional in his gifts, like Oedipus, or in his wilful violence, like Ajax). To the Athenian audience Antigone's resolution would seem extraordinary in a woman. Her courage in defying a tyrannical male kinsman is set in relief by the more prudent advice of her timid sister Ismene; in the *Electra* there is a similar opposition between the two sisters Electra and Chrysothemis.

Isolation is one side, contact and interaction another. The importance of human communication and trust is strongly brought out in one of the last plays, *Philoctetes*. The hero Philoctetes was abandoned by his comrades on deserted Lemnos, because they could not endure his loathsome wound and his screams. Now that they have need of him, Odysseus plots to deceive him and get what they want; but Neoptolemus, the noble son of Achilles, has qualms. Initially he follows Odysseus' plan, but as he comes to know and pity the wounded Philoctetes, his nature rebels. In scenes all the more astonishing for their brevity, we watch the young man recognize his affinity with the older hero, a role model and father figure, and in this process he chooses his own path in life, rejecting Odysseus' low morality. Subtle and sensitive, this play is fascinating not least as the only extant tragedy without female characters: its concerns are rather with masculine bonding and education as a citizen-warrior. But its lasting appeal comes more from its intimate dramatizing of the workings of conscience.

Sophocles is also the master of dramatic irony, whereby appearances deceive the unwary character on stage, though the audience perceives the truth or anticipates the outcome. This technique is supremely handled in *Oedipus the King*. Oedipus in that play is living an illusion, certain of his own identity and confident of his intelligence; in a key scene he boasts of his mental powers and scoffs at the blind prophet Tiresias, who foresees his doom. Who solved the riddle of the Sphinx, he asks? Where was Tiresias then? 'It was I who did it, I, know-nothing Oedipus.' By the end of the play he is exposed as the man he himself was seeking, the man who slew the former King Laius, now revealed as Oedipus' father; he has walked willingly into the destiny he initially fled, when the Delphic oracle forewarned that he would kill his father and sleep with his mother. When he had sight, he understood nothing and despised the blind seer; now that he has seen the truth, he blinds himself, cutting himself off from normality (isolation again). Sophocles is especially fond of oracles and prophecies, and in his drama they are more than merely plot devices; they are used to illustrate human blindness in a larger, non-literal sense. In a way Oedipus is everyman, not for Freudian reasons but because no one can foresee the future; we all guess wrong, and grope uncertainly towards an ending that may be disastrous.

Alas, you generations of men, how close to nothingness do I count your
life. Where in the world is the mortal who wins more of happiness than just
the illusion, and after the semblance, the falling away? With your example,
your fate before my eyes, yours, unhappy Oedipus, I count no man happy.
(1186–96)

Piety is a quality traditionally ascribed to Sophocles, but with little justification. The gods are important in his plays as in all tragedy, but they are
markedly less conspicuous than in the other two dramatists. Much more is
said through oracles and prophecies. When gods do appear they are formidable figures: Athena in the *Ajax*, or Apollo and Artemis in some lines from
the lost *Niobe*, are not divinities to worship with ease of mind.[9] Choruses, as
in the *Oedipus the King*, may express their desire that the oracles be upheld,
and religious devotion vindicated, but these passages are part of the drama
and need not represent the beliefs or anxieties of the playwright. But
undoubtedly we meet deep religious feeling in the plays, and nowhere more
memorably and numinously than at the close of the last play, *Oedipus at
Colonus*. The aged Oedipus, exiled and wearied by misfortune, finds refuge
in a district of the poet's native Attica (patriotism is satisfied, but that is
hardly the poet's first priority), and passes from mortal sight in a mysterious
end which suggests, without clearly asserting, that the old man has joined
the select group of mortals who are called 'heroes', in a supernatural sense:
beings who retain power after death and receive cult from those who
survive after them. The speech in which a messenger narrates the passing of
Oedipus is unique in tragedy. Just one of its remarkable aspects is that
messenger speeches normally relate scenes of violence or action which
cannot be enacted on stage (e.g. the battle of Salamis in the *Persians*); yet
here there is no violence or conflict, but an ending which is more than
death. Even the eyewitness role of the conventional messenger is abandoned,
for the speaker admits that he did not himself observe the departure of
Oedipus, and Theseus, who did so, is sworn to silence.

In comparison with the dignity and sobriety of Sophocles Euripides has
often been found brash and ostentatious, but that is to underrate one of the
greatest dramatists of any age. Some of his reputation as a showman derives
from his comic portrayal in *Frogs*, still more from Aristotle's ambiguous
praise (he clearly regarded Sophocles as a far greater craftsman). But even
Aristotle commented that 'whatever other defects of organisation [i.e.
structuring his plays] Euripides may have, he is the most intensely tragic of
all poets,' and he illustrates his own points in the *Poetics* as frequently from
Euripides' *Iphigenia among the Taurians* as from the *Oedipus* of Sophocles.
Yet there is a pervasive tendency in criticism to regard him as second-rate,
and this was intensified by Nietzsche, who branded him as the villain who

brought tragedy down from its Dionysiac heights by introducing an intellectual element.[10] Perhaps part of the problem is that we are lucky enough
to have over twice as many plays by him as by either of the others
(17 tragedies, plus a satyr play): alongside milestones of tragic art such as
Hippolytus and *Bacchae* are others which it is hard to rank so high (the
Children of Heracles and the *Andromache*, or the possibly spurious *Rhesus*).
Yet there is no good reason to suppose that all the lost plays of Aeschylus
and Sophocles were peerless masterpieces.

It is true that there is some reason to think that Euripides was less
successful than the others in his own lifetime. He came third in his first
competition, and apparently came first only four times, whereas Sophocles is
said to have been always first or second, never third, and both Aeschylus
and Sophocles were victorious with over half their plays. In addition
there were traditions that he was bookish, misogynistic, unpopular, even a
recluse, but like all ancient biography of writers this needs to be treated
with great caution.[11] What is clear is that Athenian audiences were fascinated
by Euripides.

Any reader of Euripides will be struck by the rhetorical qualities of his
dramas. 'Rhetoric' is a complex term (as a later chapter will illustrate), and
the characters of the other tragedians are neither inarticulate nor unsophisticated, but the spoken word and the powers of skilled, deceptive speech are
especially prominent in his plays. All sorts of people speak at surprising
length and with great ingenuity ('Euripides' in the *Frogs* preens himself on
this 'democratic' innovation), sometimes pleading paradoxical and implausible
cases or putting arguments at a high level of abstraction. In particular,
Euripides is fond of confrontation-scenes in which two (sometimes more)
opponents argue against each other at length, mixing argument and denunciation.[12] The language of the law courts is sometimes used: in *Hippolytus*,
Theseus accuses his son of raping his wife, and Hippolytus makes a self-
righteous defence; the scene ends with the young man being dismissed into
exile. Other famous clashes of this kind include Jason versus Medea, Hecuba
versus Helen (*Trojan Women*), and a three-cornered debate between Jocasta
and her two sons (*Phoenician Women*). It is typical of Euripides that these
highly elaborate debates never resolve the issue; indeed, normally they merely
heighten the antagonism.

Beside rhetorical skill, the characters often wax philosophical. Tragedy in
general is not shy of anachronism, but this is one area where Euripides goes
beyond his predecessors, introducing startlingly 'modern' thought into the
traditional legends. Hecuba ponders the relative importance of heredity and
environment, Orestes the relation of noble character and noble birth; Phaedra
discourses to the chorus on the power of passion and how it can overwhelm
the mind's former good resolutions. 'Modern thought' of a more social

kind is prominent in Medea's searching analysis of the position of women. It is easy to see why Aristophanes and others branded Euripides an intellectual poet, or associated him with Socrates. Sometimes the ideas to which he alludes can be connected with the theories of specific thinkers of the day, but it is unconvincing to see him as a disciple of any one sophist.[13] More important is the fact that by means of these seemingly intrusive passages he narrows the gulf between the heroic age and the world of the audience. Sometimes the contemporary scene seems to loom surprisingly close: in the *Suppliants*, the Athenian Theseus and the Theban herald argue at length about the merits of democratic and monarchic government, with Theseus taking the side of democracy. Even if we allow that Theseus, the favourite hero of Athens, is no ordinary king, the scene is obviously disconcerting.

The plays of Euripides do not dramatize heroic achievement. His are tragedies of suffering rather than of action (though *Medea* is a partial exception). There is a strong emphasis on the victims of war, above all in the *Trojan Women*, which focuses on the women after the sack of Troy, as they wait in misery to be carried off to slavery in Greece. The play has spoken powerfully to many war-haters. When the characters attempt to seize the initiative, the outcome is rarely positive. Phaedra's efforts to preserve her good name bring death to Hippolytus without achieving her objective. Electra and Orestes in the *Electra* take revenge on their mother, but with psychologically devastating consequences for themselves. In the *Orestes*, the deed of matricide makes the young man an outcast rather than a hero; his efforts to escape death by striking at Menelaus' family are first sinister, then frustrated, and finally neutralized by divine intervention. Everywhere we see Euripides' determination to give his audience the unexpected. Traditional stories are modified, unusual variations welcomed: in the *Helen* he adopts the bizarre version that makes Helen a prisoner in Egypt throughout the war, while the Greeks and Trojans fight over a phantom. 'Stock' characterization can be inverted (good King Eteocles becomes a power-mad tyrant). Characterization may also challenge prevailing ideology: women behave with masculine violence, slaves show nobility and virtue, 'barbarian' foreigners express civilized sentiments.[14]

Euripides' genius has a lighter and a darker side. The lighter is demonstrated by the plays sometimes called 'tragicomedies': *Ion, Iphigenia among the Taurians, Helen*. In all of these we have a happy ending involving the reunion of those who have been parted by misfortune or misunderstanding: mother and son in *Ion*, brother and sister in *IT*, husband and wife in *Helen*. After confusion and ignorance come recognition and rejoicing: the plot of the *Odyssey* lies in the background, the recognition-dramas of Menander and his successors in the future. While these plays are full of subtlety and irony, this does not exclude depth and pathos. In particular the *Helen*, which reunites the lovers but against a background of a futile war for an illusion, has a bitter-sweet quality which prompts reflection, not hilarity.

For the darker side of Euripides – or indeed of tragedy, and of Greek religion – we look above all to the *Bacchae*, a play of his last years, which most think his masterpiece.[15] This daunting drama presents the conflict between Dionysus, arriving for the first time in Thebes and demanding worship, and the hapless Pentheus (whose very name means 'sorrow'), the inexperienced king who tries to defy and deny the god. The chorus of 'bacchants', female devotees of Dionysus, proclaim the beauties and the wild ecstasy of the god's cult, but Pentheus is stubborn and suspicious; surely it is all a cover for lustful drunkenness. Dionysus assumes human form, a grim predecessor of Christ, not to save Pentheus but to tantalize and eventually to entrap him. Mesmerized and mocked, dressed in women's garb, the king is led to the mountains where the maddened women of Thebes, led by his own mother Agave, hunt him down and tear him limb from limb. In a horrific scene Agave appears on stage rejoicing, carrying her son's severed head (the detached mask and wig), in the belief that it is a lion-cub she has slain. The play ends with Dionysus revealing his divinity and sending Agave and her family into exile; all are involved with Pentheus' crime of failing to accept the god.

The plot is a traditional one: a god is scorned and exacts his revenge. In this sense, the play must be a celebration of Dionysus. But the fascination of the play lies partly in the interaction between god and man, above all the dialogues between Dionysus and Pentheus. What is happening – does he drive Pentheus mad, or is he calling forth something that lies deep in the king's own psyche? The violence of the Bacchants is no less disturbing, and some have read this politically, as a warning against mob emotion. No single reading can exhaust this paradigmatic tragedy. From another angle, the play can be seen in metatextual terms: a play about playing parts. Dionysus, Pentheus and others assume disguises; and in one key scene Dionysus asks the question which has preoccupied theorists of tragedy: 'would you really like to see what gives you pain?' (815). Dionysus, ironic questioner and manager of the action, is a double of the poet himself. The difference is that the god lacks the dramatist's compassion.

Besides tragedy, these dramatists regularly wrote satyr-plays, usually as a shorter tailpiece after the tragic trilogy. In the textual tradition this genre is very much the poor relation: we have only one complete play, Euripides' *Cyclops*, an entertaining spoof on the famous episode in Homer's *Odyssey* 9. (There are also substantial fragments of plays by the other tragedians: one, Sophocles' *Trackers*, has been brilliantly augmented and modernized by Tony Harrison.)[16] The plays involved mythological burlesque, always with a chorus of satyrs, those hybrid beings, part human part animal (horse or goat), who were among the entourage of Dionysus. While often coarse and grotesque, the plays were not structurally and morally anarchic like comedy. In Roman times, the poet-critic Horace described Tragedy as a dignified matron who does not descend to trivial verse even though she deigns to associate, though modestly, with the cavorting satyrs. (*Art of Poetry* 231–3). The Greek critic Demetrius put it more crisply: the satyric drama is 'tragedy at play' (*On Style* 169). These comments should not mislead. The plays may be skilfully composed but the choruses are a rumbustious lot: there is not much dignity in the antics of the crude, lustful satyrs, who like many characters in Aristophanes' comedy sported massive phalluses, with frequent talk of putting them to use.[17] There are, however, recognizable affinities with tragic plots: *Cyclops*, like *Helen* or *Iphigenia among the Taurians*, is an escape-drama. Sometimes the satyr-play may even have been regarded as a continuation of the tragic trilogy. In Aeschylus' *Agamemnon*, we are told of the storm which dispersed the Greek fleet on its journey home, and those on stage wonder especially about the fate of Agamemnon's brother Menelaus. After the three plays of the *Oresteia* there followed the satyr-play *Proteus*. It is a reasonable guess that this play dealt with the encounter of Menelaus with the shape-changing sea-god Proteus in or near Egypt, an episode already handled with some humour in the *Odyssey*. Reconstruction and guesswork can help a little in defining the typical themes of satyr-drama: early inventions (fire, the lyre, and so on), cultic features, birth and childhood of gods, imprisonment and escape, seem to have been prominent. But in general this is a big gap in our knowledge of the ancient stage.

III

Comedy was a later arrival, first staged at the Dionysia in 486; subsequently it had a more prominent place at a different festival, the Lenaea, which seems to have been less prestigious. According to Plato's *Symposium*, Athenians generally regarded the two genres as requiring different gifts – the same dramatists did not compose both tragedy and comedy (though Socrates, that seriocomic figure, challenges these assumptions). The genres can be treated as polar opposites in countless ways: Aristotle claimed that tragedy showed men as better than they are in everyday life, comedy as baser. Tragedies tend to finish with funerals, comedies with weddings and celebrations. Nevertheless, tragedy and comedy do interact (Euripidean 'comic' plots and happy reunions have been mentioned), and in particular Aristophanes constantly parodies and subverts tragic themes, plots and language. More fundamentally, in his *Acharnians* he makes one of his heroes, Dicaeopolis, declare that 'comedy too knows about justice' – the word for comedy here is a rare punning form, 'trugodia', which obviously plays on the parallel 'tragodia', tragedy. At the very least, this means that not everything in comedy is merely laughable, though few questions are more heatedly debated than whether Aristophanes is ever entirely serious and on what subjects.[18]

Already the discussion is moving from comedy in general to Aristophanes in particular – inevitably. Whereas with tragedy we have three major figures well represented, only one exponent of 'Old Comedy' survives, making comparison and generalization still more hazardous. Eleven plays by Aristophanes have been preserved, ranging from 425 (*Acharnians*) to 388 (*Wealth*). There is then a major gap in our evidence before the only complete play of Menander, the *Angry Old Man* (316, an early work). Menander is the key figure of 'New Comedy'. The terms 'Old' and 'New' are attested in ancient criticism: definition of the hazy category of 'Middle' comedy, also occasionally used in antiquity, is difficult without a single extant example. These terms express the consensus that the genre of comedy underwent a development, indeed changed its whole character (from the topical to the typical).[19] This judgement is hazardous when so much is lost, but we can agree that Aristophanes and Menander were very different; also, that later Aristophanes is different from the earlier part of his oeuvre. But we must always remember that the discovery of a single additional play might refute many reconstructions.[20]

Like tragedy, Aristophanes' comedy follows certain regular plot-patterns and structures, and some of these are clearly traditional: the *agon* or confrontation between two sides (comparable to the conflict-scenes in tragedy, but somewhat less polished); the *parabasis*, a mid-play interlude in which the chorus address the audience directly; the conclusion with festivity and celebration, usually with a heavy accent on drink and sexual indulgence. There are also certain common elements in the plots. Plays regularly begin with an unsatisfactory situation which an individual (the comic hero or heroine) resolves to change, often by drastic, unlikely or impossible means. He or she meets with resistance, generally overcomes the obstacles, and the remainder of the play explores the consequences, which are not always those the protagonist or the audience expected. In *Acharnians* the hero is determined to end the war with Sparta, but when the Athenian assembly is obdurate, negotiates his own private peace embracing his own farm and family, where he engages in profitable trading with other states and indulges the appetites that war has denied. In *Knights* the object is to end the oppressive predominance of a major politician, in *Clouds* to escape creditors by acquiring extraordinary skill in rhetoric. In *Peace* the countryman Trygaeus, despairing of convincing anyone on earth to make peace, resolves to prevail on the gods to bring it about, and prepares to fly to Olympus astride a gigantic dung-beetle: this parodies the tragic motif of Bellerophon on the winged horse Pegasus. As so often, comedy coarsens and renders absurd the lofty aspirations of tragedy. In *Lysistrata* again the goal is to end the war: in this case the principals are the women of Athens, led by the authoritative figure of Lysistrata. By the combined means of a full-scale sex strike and seizing control of the Acropolis (public and private themes are combined), the women reduce the men on both sides to desperate capitulation. As these examples show, the initial situation may be realistic, but swiftly develops into fantasy and absurdity.

Other plays depart from the Athenian setting: in *Birds*, the hero and his sidekick are weary of endless Athenian litigation, and seek a new utopian life among the birds. They acquire wings themselves, become leaders of the birds, found a city in the sky (its name, Cloud-cuckooland, has become proverbial), and in the end overthrow the gods and become kings of the world. In this extravaganza of wish-fulfilment, the normal festive ending to comedy is enlarged to cosmic scale, as the hero Peisetaeros ends up claiming at least some of the power of Zeus and celebrating his marriage to Basileia, who represents royal authority. Comedy is here borrowing and transforming mythic motifs, including the early battles among gods and giants, the succession myth in Hesiod, and the stories of Zeus' potential overthrow by a further successor. Mythical comedy is also represented by *Frogs*, as already described: the descent to the underworld is a recurrent heroic exploit, and Dionysus in this play dresses up as Heracles in a vain effort to profit from that hero's formidable reputation (instead he finds himself hounded for the great hero's unpaid bills and flogged for stealing Hades' pet dog Cerberus!).

These comedies are two-sided. On the one hand there is a strongly anarchic tendency, in that the small man, the man-in-the-street, gets what he wants despite authority, and the inhibitions of law, ethics and etiquette do not apply – the women take control of the state in more than one play, whereas in classical Athens they could not vote or play a political role. Even divine law is overthrown by the megalomaniac triumph of Peisetaeros in *Birds*. On the other hand there is a sense in which comedy is highly conservative, since it regularly proclaims the merits of the good old days: it is the new politicians, the current poets, the new intellectuals, who are satirized as debasing the old ways, and the aim of Dicaeopolis, Lysistrata and others is to get back to the time of 'normal' values and restore peace and prosperity (and, in *Frogs*, good poetry).

The tension between these two aspects is particularly marked in *Clouds*, which is a very atypical comedy (and was not a success when first performed, to the poet's chagrin). This play presents the teaching of Socrates, here portrayed as a charlatan and a corrupting influence. The hero here is less bright and able than most. Although he wants to win rhetorical skill, he is too slow-witted to benefit from Socratic training, and finally sends his son in his place. The results are disastrous, for the lad is transformed into a glib, unscrupulous and immoral sophist. In rage and dismay, the hero burns down the 'Reflectory', Socrates' school for scoundrels; it is unclear whether the philosophers are burned alive or merely run off ignominiously (probably the latter). The new education is treated here with much less sympathy than the poetry of Euripides in *Frogs*. We see dramatized not only the supposed enticements of sophistic teaching but also something of the older Athenians' antagonism to these thinkers. Plato's *Meno*, in which the boorish conservative Anytus gives Socrates a stern warning, shows the serious side of these conflicts: Anytus was later one of Socrates' prosecutors, and Plato in the *Apology* made Socrates allude to *Clouds* as one contributing factor to the hostility toward himself.

The comedy of Aristophanes is highly political, in the sense that it is frequently set in and constantly alludes to the Athens of the poet's day. Living politicians are satirically represented, often obscenely abused. In particular the demagogue Cleon is repeatedly accused of corruption, avarice and boorishness. The virulence of Old Comedy astonishes moderns, but the licence of the festival helps to explain the poets' outspokenness: this is a time at which the common citizen can laugh at and feel superior to authority-figures.[21] The same explanation will cover the equally striking vigour with which the gods are abused or comically represented (the cowardly, inept Dionysus in *Frogs* is not unique: he was earlier cast in the role of a raw recruit in General Phormio's army by the comedian Eupolis).[22] Despite the conventionality of comic abuse, there are some signs that it could go too far. Certain subjects were virtually taboo: comedy could make fun of Heracles or Dionysus, but probably not Athena, the city's own patroness, or Demeter, who presided over the mysteries of Eleusis, part of the Athenian state. Laws were in force for part of the late fifth century restricting the freedom of comedy, and Cleon appears to have prosecuted Aristophanes for maligning Athens in the presence of foreign visitors. Nevertheless, the level of political freedom in comedy may seem one of the strongest arguments for Athens as an 'open society'.

But although Old Comedy is political, it is also fantasy: reality and imaginative absurdity are closely intertwined, making it hard to say of any play or scene that it is (for example) commenting seriously on current events. Although real-life personalities are allowed to appear on stage, they are often distorted or caricatured: the general Lamachus is a pompous windbag, Socrates in *Clouds* and elsewhere is a stock intellectual. In *Knights*, Cleon becomes 'the Paphlagonian', a crooked foreign slave; Aristophanes later complains that Eupolis stole this idea and presented the politician Hyperbolus under the guise of Marikas, another foreign slave. In Cratinus' lost *Dionysalexandros*, mythical allegory seems to have been used: Dionysus disguised as Paris (Alexandros) and starting the Trojan war was somehow representative of Pericles starting the war with Sparta, though we do not know how explicitly this was signalled. These poets show extraordinary abundance of imagination; it may be misguided to tie their plays down to dreary party politics.

Talking too much about plot and themes risks omitting any reference to Aristophanes' comic style. This is gloriously rich, whether we look to the innumerable newly coined words, the puns and plays on stock phrases, the combination of concrete, earthy images with loftier abstractions ('Observe the pleasing combination of lyricism and filth' is one donnish comment),[23] or the constant presence of parody, above all of tragedy but also of other sources, from older lyric poetry through Herodotus to the set formulae and oratory of the assembly. A favoured technique is the final twist of a sentence, destabilizing solemnity into bathos.[24]

> 'I'm in a bad way, such is the passion that is ravaging me . . . I cannot describe it, but nevertheless I shall make it plain by analogy. Tell me, have you ever felt a sudden desire for . . . pea-soup?' (*Frogs* 57ff.)

Or, on a more extended parodic scale, we may cite the following exchange, as Lysistrata detects an obstacle to her master plan:

Chorus leader:	Queen of our great design and enterprise,
	Tell me, why hast thou come so frowning forth?
Lysistrata:	The female heart and deeds of evil women
	Cause me to walk despondent up and down.
Chorus leader:	What say'st thou?
Lys.:	Truth! Truth!
Chorus leader:	What is amiss? Tell it to us who love thee.
Lys.:	'Tis shame to speak and grievous to be silent.
Chorus leader:	Do not, we beg, conceal the ill we suffer.
Lys.:	We need a fuck. Such is my tale in brief.

(*Lys.* 706–15, tr. K. J. Dover)

Literary historians often describe the transition from Aristophanes to Menander as a shift from political comedy to domestic, and account for this by the changed political circumstances of Athens (after 338 subject to Macedonian rule, and at times forced to abandon the democratic system). Detailed scrutiny of the evidence for lost plays may cast doubt on this model, but there is certainly a change of emphasis. Domestic themes, however, were not new: they are important in *Clouds*, *Women at the Assembly* and elsewhere. A famous passage in *Wasps* interestingly prefigures the plots of New Comedy. The anti-hero Philocleon, having been cured of his addiction to jury-service, has taken with equal enthusiasm to the life of party-going and drinking. In one scene the old man has wrecked the party and carried off a flute-girl, to whom he murmurs maudlin endearments:

> If you're nice to me, I'll set you free and have you as my concubine when my son dies, little pussy. Just at the moment I'm not in charge of my own money, for I'm still under age. And I'm kept under very close guard: my son watches me and he's a spoil-sport and extraordinarily tight with money. He's afraid I'll be corrupted, and I'm the only father he's got. (*Wasps* 1351–9, tr. R. Hunter)

The old man is enjoying a temporary rejuvenation, and so behaves like the conventional comic youth, infatuated but unable to indulge his love because he is not financially independent. The inversion of the normal situation here suggests that the more obvious plot is already a well-known one.

Menander is one of the beneficiaries of the twentieth century's rescue operation on the body of papyri found in Egypt. Before this we had only a considerable number of fragments, extracts of one line or several; in 1907 the 'Cairo text' was published, including large parts of three plays and some lesser portions, and in 1959 the only complete play we have was published, the *Duskolos* or *Angry Old Man*. There have been significant further finds, and Menander is far better known and understood now than he could have been a century ago. This is valuable also for our understanding of later writers: Plautus and Terence in their plays were translating and adapting Menander and his peers, and their influence on European comedy, above all on major figures such as Goldoni and Shakespeare, Molière and Wilde, would be impossible to exaggerate.

Whereas Old Comedy was earthy and erotic, New Comedy is more idealistic and romantic: the plot often hinges on a young man desperate to win the girl of his heart, and the play usually ends with marriage. Frequently the girl will be unsuitable at first (a slave or a courtesan), but will turn out to be of respectable birth after all. New Comedy, above all that of Menander, concerns itself with personal relationships, family life and social mishaps. Politics and public life are marginalized. Similarly the rampant freedom of speech, the vicious personal abuse and obscenity, which we associate with Old Comedy are banished from Menander's supremely civilized stage, on which even a slave self-consciously apologizes for using a word like 'shit'. It is unsurprising that the cultivated Plutarch, in a summary comparison, prefers the decorum of Menander to the vulgarity and vivacity of Aristophanes. In Aristophanes, he sighs, 'the tendency to jests and buffoonery is altogether excessive', but he notes with approval that in all of Menander's plays 'there is no homosexuality, and the seductions of virgins end decently in marriage' (*Moralia* 712c). Ancient critics acclaimed Menander for 'holding up a mirror to life', but the praise is exaggerated: he portrays only a part of life, and in a discreetly stylized manner. His plots are not realistic, but they are of this world (no mock-heroic exploits, no fantastic animal choruses). With his generation the ordinary decent man steps into the limelight.

One of the plays which survives in part, the *Shield*, dramatizes the problems facing the family of a young soldier who is presumed dead. An avaricious uncle prepares to marry the young man's sister for her money (in the belief that her brother's property has passed to her), but the clever slave Daos devises a scheme to frustrate and embarrass him, and the soldier, not dead after all, returns to the household, bringing general delight; the play no doubt ended with the wedding of the girl to her previous fiancé. There are various 'stock' elements here, most notably the crafty and resourceful slave, who becomes still more prominent in Plautus. Daos, Latinized as Davus, is the ancestor of Wodehouse's indefatigable Jeeves. The summary does not reveal all of Menander's skill in structuring his plays: the *Shield* begins with a dialogue between Daos and the wicked uncle (who does not at first reveal his motives); thereafter, when the stage is clear, the goddess Tuche (Chance) appears and tells the audience the true situation, making it possible for them to enjoy the ironic developments. This technique of informing the audience but keeping some or all of the characters in ignorance is a standard device, but is here saved from banality by the deferred position of the prologue: the audience at first are in the same state as Daos and the others, and feel for them accordingly.

The *Angry Old Man*, which survives intact, gives us a richer picture of Menander's art. The main plot concerns Sostratus, a young man who has fallen in love with a country girl who lives with her father Cnemon, the bad-tempered misanthrope of the title. His bungling efforts to win the old man's approval are futile until the latter has to be rescued after falling down a well. He emerges still grumbling but willing to compromise with life if people will just let him alone. Interspersed with the main plot are numerous entertaining incidents, twists in the plot, and minor characters, most of whom also find Cnemon insufferably rude and objectionable. Among these is a cook (a stock figure in the comedy of the period), whose glee at Cnemon's discomfiture is amusingly expressed in terms reminiscent of grander genres.

> By Dionysus, the gods *do* exist! So you wouldn't lend a stewing-pot, you crook, to sacrificers? No – you're greedy! Fall in and drain the well dry – then you won't have a dribble of water left to share with anyone! Today the Nymphs have given me revenge on him – and rightly! No-one hurts a *cook* and gets away scot-free. Our art's a sacred one, I think. With *waiters*, though, do what you like! (639–47)

Menander's characterization is light but subtle; even recurrent 'types' are given individuality and delicate touches. The plays are compassionate presentations of human folly and absurdity: his unsympathetic types are not mere stage-villains (except perhaps the uncle in the *Shield*). Cnemon is no monster, despite the cook's indignation, nor is his conversion treated as a complete reversal of character; rather, we gain a more sympathetic perspective on his outlook even as he compromises and accepts that other views are possible. And the end of his longest speech strikes a dour note which is comic but also realistic, as Cnemon defends his conduct as follows:

> If everyone behaved like me, we'd have no law-courts, we wouldn't send each other to prison, and there'd be no wars! Each man would have enough to live on, and he'd be satisfied. Perhaps, though, modern life is more to your taste. Choose it, then. This grumpy, peevish old man won't get in your way. (743–7)

This can hardly be taken as the moral of the play, and earlier remarks in his speech may seem more persuasive (when he proclaims that his earlier isolation policy was misguided); but in a quirky way it does put a telling point.

Menander is said to have taken special care with his plots: an anecdote tells how a friend asked him shortly before the Dionysia if he had finished his play, to which he replied 'Yes, I've composed it; the plot is finished, I just need to add the lines.'[25] Although the situations are conventional and the coincidences convenient rather than plausible, the scenes progress smoothly and effectively, with none of the casual inconcinnity of Plautus. One structural principle which had a long history seems to have come in with Menander: the five-act structure, which is canonical in Shakespeare and many others.[26] But in his plays we have dialogue without song; there are references to the arrival of the chorus, but no choral interludes in our texts, although they do include indications of the breaks where choral songs could be added. In both tragedy and comedy we can see a decline in the chorus's importance in the late fifth century; in Aristophanes' fourth-century plays their role is much reduced, and by Menander's time it seems that the task of composing these *entre-acte* lyrics was too trivial to be the concern of the dramatist. Plautus and Terence, following Menander and his coevals, abandon even the occasional references to the chorus's arrival, although the break-points in the action are often still visible.

IV

Even after the papyrological windfall, Menander offers relatively little of sustenance to those who prefer their plays whole, and his contemporaries have fared much worse. For the remaining body of work embraced under 'New Comedy' we turn to the numerous dramas by the Roman imitators. Our picture of Roman drama is lopsided in several ways. We have no complete tragedies before Seneca in the first century AD, no comedies later than 160 BC, and nothing from the period in between: major works such as Ovid's *Medea* and Varius' *Thyestes* are entirely lost. Moreover, the comedies we have are *fabulae palliatae* ('plays in Greek dress'), whereas we have no representatives of the *comoediae togatae* ('plays in Roman togas'), which apparently grew out of the Greek imitations and may have displaced them. (We do have numerous fragments of early tragedy and Roman-dress comedy, but as usual these are of limited help: imagine reconstructing a Shakespearian play from the extracts in a dictionary of quotations!) Finally, we are less informed than we would like on the native Italian influences which may have partly shaped the work of Plautus and (to a lesser degree) Terence. We know other forms of drama existed: the mime, for example, and other forms of lowbrow farce; but in all probability Greek New Comedy was the virtually exclusive model for their plays, and often the specific source-text is acknowledged.

The recent discoveries have given us some help here: we can set a section of Plautus' *Bacchides* alongside the Menandrian model, some 50 lines from the *Twice-deceiver*.[27] The results are illuminating. Plautus is not just trans- lating but adapting and embroidering, sometimes heightening the farcical element: he changes metre, alters names, adjusts stage business. His proced- ure is not as creative as Virgil's emulation of Homer in the *Aeneid*; but to compare it with Virgil's adaptation of Theocritus in some of the *Eclogues* or with Catullus' rendering into Latin of Sappho and Callimachus is less absurd. Terence is innovative in a different way, as he advertises in more than one of his prologues: rather than simply basing a Roman play on a single Greek model, he deliberately combined scenes from more than one Greek play, even plays by different hands – a practice which seems to have been controversial. There is no certain case of Plautus doing this, though some have suspected him of doing so.

Plautus is said to have died in 184 BC, and two of his plays were definitely produced in 200 and 191. Terence was a somewhat later figure, producing in the 160s, and in some ways seems to belong to a more cultivated period, though this may be more a matter of dramatic temperament than of the advance of Roman culture. Although they draw on the same models and are recognizably working in the same genre, in many ways Plautus and Terence are polar opposites. Symptomatic is the sheer number of the plays: 21 by Plautus survive, and we know of more, while Terence's extant six appear to be all he wrote (it is of course possible that Plautus simply lived longer). Plautus is comically abundant but slapdash, Terence more careful and restrained. Plautus delights in coarseness and vulgarity, Terence avoids the obscene. Even Plautus' villains have their attractive features (Ballio the ultimate pimp in *Pseudolus*). Plautus' favourite characters tend to be outrageous and subversive (crafty slaves, charming courtesans), or exaggerated caricatures (the pompously named Pyrgopolinices ['Towering-city-conqueror'] in *Miles Gloriosus*), while Terence follows the Menandrian lead in crafting less extreme and more subtly characterized personalities. Plautus, like Aristophanes, is extravagant in language, freely coining new words, importing Greek words and phrases into Latin; Terence's language is purer and more correct (one of the reasons he remained so important in the educational curriculum). Plautus includes a wide range of styles, and one of the most remarkable features is the frequency of songs in a variety of metres ('cantica'), sometimes monodies, occasionally duets, perhaps modelled on those in Greek and Roman tragedy but not straightforwardly parodic. There are over 60 such songs in Plautus' extant work, whereas Terence displays much less metrical variety.

Plautus is anarchic, at times even amoral; Terence is less cynical, more didactic, inclined to emphasize the need for understanding and moral improvement. Plautus often spoofs and parodies elements that Terence takes seriously (romantic love, or the sage advice of elders). The poet-critic Horace finds fault with Plautus, complaining that he did not care whether the play was well made provided he made money out of it. Terence (whom Horace quotes in several places) was no doubt more his kind of author, more cerebral and less prone to absurdity and slapstick. Terence, like Horace, was a self-conscious artist. One novelty in Terence is the detached prologue in which the playwright defends or explains his practice. We hear in the prologue to the *Hecyra* that the poet has suffered at successive performances from rival attractions, such as boxing, tightrope-walkers, gladiatorial contests. Horace's satirical sketch of the uncritical play-going public echoes Terence's complaints.[28] Terence's greater restraint and sobriety mean that he is easy to underrate: Julius Caesar wrote that he lacked the *vis* (forcefulness) of Menander.

There is plenty of diversity in the surviving comedies, and the dramatists were evidently always ready with a fresh variation on familiar themes. In the prologue to the *Eunuch*, rejecting the charge of plagiarism, Terence remarks on the conventionality of the comic plots:

> If the playwright is not allowed to make use of the same characters as other writers, how can he still bring on a running slave, virtuous wives and dishonest courtesans, greedy spongers and braggart soldiers? How can he show substitution of a child, deception of an old man by his slave, love, hatred, and suspicion? Nothing in fact is ever said which has not been said before. [tr. B. Radice]

The characters themselves can play on the 'stock' nature of their roles, as when the slave Chrysalus in Plautus' *Bacchides* remarks 'I don't like those Parmenos and Syruses who steal small sums of money from their masters' (649–50). These are standard slave-names, but the joke is that Chrysalus himself was called Syrus in the Menandrian original on which *Bacchides* is based! Characters can be cast against type, audience expectations frustrated: for instance, in the *Hecyra* the stereotyped view of wives and mothers-in-law turns out to be unjustified.

One play which is recognizably different in kind from the rest is Plautus' *Amphitryo*, which uses a plot from classical myth: the story that Jupiter disguised himself as Amphitryo in order to sleep with his wife Alcmena, and the child born of their union was Hercules. In Plautus' play the plot is expanded, with a host of confusions resulting from the presence not only of two Amphitryos but of two slaves called Sosia, one being Mercury in disguise, who has accompanied Jupiter on his sexual adventure. This is a mythical scenario, but there is a clear similarity to the plot involving identical twin brothers, the *Menaechmi* (Shakespeare's model for *The Comedy of Errors*). Interestingly, Plautus calls the *Amphitryo* a 'tragicomedy', probably because of the mythological characters, but modern readers will also be struck by the touching seriousness with which the innocent wife Alcmena, accused of adultery by her mortal husband, is treated.

Of the rest, brief comments on a handful of plays must suffice. Plautus' *Pseudolus* is perhaps the supreme 'clever slave' play, as well as including the monstrous pimp Ballio (the clash between them early in the play is a classic scene: Pseudolus hurls the fiercest insults at Ballio, who smirks and takes pleasure in these as words of praise). The opening scene of *Curculio* includes a marvellous contrast between the adoring lover, the cynical slave who has seen it all before, and the old madame (who sings a brief lyric passage about the love of *her* life – wine!). The *Aulularia* includes the archetypal miser (hence Molière's *L'avare*); Terence's *Phormio* has the best example of a parasite or hanger-on; his *Self-Tormenter* portrays the perennial nosey-parker, in Chremes. It is he who voices the high-minded line 'I am a human being, and count nothing human alien to me', but although this has often been quoted as a philosophic profundity, it serves him merely as a justification for being a busy-body. The *Captivi* is a more sober and serious Plautine drama, with a virtuous slave who switches places with his master in order to help him escape; ingenious ironies of identity ensue. In both prologue and epilogue Plautus draws attention to the unusual qualities of this 'chaste' play: no obscenity, no harlots or brothel-keepers – no women, indeed. 'Poets find few such plays where good men get better' (1033). But in another play a character expresses scepticism as to whether anyone ever benefits morally from watching a play.[29]

Terence's work shows a writer much more concerned with moral dilemmas, especially conflicts within the family, where loyalty is due to both sides. Most of his plots depend on misunderstanding and are resolved by generous and humane behaviour. His *Adelphi* ('Brothers') dramatizes the differing educational practice of the soft-hearted, indulgent Micio and the bossy, bullying Demea. Their conflict over how best to raise their sons is entertaining, but the issues are real and permanent. Terence makes it hard to judge which is in the right: Micio's kindness is more attractive, but his indulgence has not kept his son from excess and deception. There is a moving moment when Micio confronts his son and deceives *him* in turn, making out that the girl he loves is going to be sent away; he does this to teach the boy a lesson, but eventually relents and comforts the despairing lover. Their relationship is much more intimate and affectionate than that between the proud, blustering Demea and his frightened offspring. Hardest to assess is the end of the play, where Terence seems to have modified the Menandrean original. Demea undergoes a transformation (like Cnemon in *Angry Old Man*), becoming or pretending to become generous and extravagant like Micio ('Two can play at that game,' he soliloquises: 'I too could do with a bit of love and appreciation'). By granting favours galore, Demea wins popularity but alarms and astonishes his brother with his new extravagance, and this leaves us with no clear 'winner' or 'right answer'. Terence lacks the fast-moving slapstick, the extravagant farce of Plautus, but he is the more thoughtful and subtle of the two comedians, and the worthy heir of Menander.

V

Tragedy at Rome was composed by major figures such as Ennius; other early figures such as Pacuvius and Accius were much-quoted and admired by Cicero and others, and their work may have had considerable impact on the subsequent development of other genres (such as Virgilian epic); the dramas of Asinius Pollio, composed in the late first century BC, were acclaimed by Virgil and Horace, and are still praised by Quintilian.[30] But only Seneca's plays survive intact – with the proviso that one of these, the *Phoenician Women*, is incomplete and was probably never finished, while two of the plays transmitted under Seneca's name are almost certainly by other hands: these are the *Hercules on Oeta* and the *Octavia*. The last is of special interest as the only surviving example of a historical Roman drama, for it dramatizes a grim episode of Nero's reign, the displacement of his first wife, the noble Octavia, and her supersession by the vicious Poppaea. Seneca actually appears as a character in the play, vainly endeavouring to alter the cruel designs of the tyrant Nero. Since the play appears to predict events later than Seneca's death, he cannot be the author.

The plays authentically ascribed to Seneca are all mythological, concerned with central figures of the Greek legends: the Trojan and Theban sagas, Medea, Phaedra, Thyestes. Each play presents destruction inflicted upon others or self; in five of the eight revenge is central. Phaedra destroys Hippolytus, then commits suicide herself. Medea murders her children, Clytemnestra her husband. Atreus, Seneca's vilest villain, chops up Thyestes' sons and feeds them to the unsuspecting father in a stew, then takes pleasure in revealing the truth about the menu. Greek tragedy often allows some longer perspective or some compensation in time to come, but Seneca's presentation of the human condition is far blacker. It is true that the chorus often, and individual characters sometimes, voice high-minded Stoic precepts, declaring that the wise man can defy the tyrant, that the independent soul may rise above the delusions of wealth and power. But these are doctrines which none of the principals in the tragedies succeeds in upholding (Hercules in the *Heracles on Oeta* does triumphantly transcend human weakness and wins apotheosis, but this can plausibly be seen as one decisive argument *against* Senecan authorship!). Unlike *Macbeth* and *Lear*, these plays do not end with normality restored or with the arrival of a purifying agent. The Senecan plays have often been labelled 'Stoic drama', but it is a naive response to suppose that they merely set up examples of undisciplined immorality to show the audience what to avoid. The Stoic framework seems to serve rather to show the sheer ineffectuality of virtue in the face of supreme evil and corruption. The cosmos responds to the evil deeds of its inhabitants: the stars darken, the sun turns tail and flees, at the atrocities of man. 'We have brought guilt to heaven,' cries Oedipus (*Oed.* 36). These lessons were not lost on the impressionable Lucan.

At about 1,200 lines each, Seneca's dramas are shorter than the average Greek play, and although at first they seem to follow Greek conventions (limited number of actors, a chorus, use of messengers, and so forth), they in fact are plays of a very different kind, more restricted in emotional range and tone, less varied in metre and use of song, and concerned to evoke horror rather than pity. Above all they are declamatory dramas. Eliot remarked that his characters 'all seem to speak with the same voice, and at the top of it'.[31] Gentler emotions are rarely admitted to the Senecan steambath. In Greek tragedy persuasion is sometimes effective, and appeals to compassion do not always fall on deaf ears (one thinks of the moving scene at the end of *Oedipus the King* in which blind Oedipus begs Creon to let him say farewell to his children, and the wish is granted); not so in Seneca. Denunciation and vituperation are the appropriate modes; the winner prevails through brute strength, greater vindictiveness, and the sharper epigrams.

On, my heart, and perform a deed which posterity can never approve, but will never cease to speak of! Some savage, bloodthirsty sin must be ventured, one which my brother might prefer to be his own! You cannot avenge his crimes, unless you surpass them. (*Thy.* 192–6)

The dates and circumstances of composition are mysterious. Seneca was forced to commit suicide in AD 65, when he was over 60, and these works could be the product of almost any period after he reached manhood. They may well come from the period before the accession of Nero, but there is no firm evidence, except that several of them evidently influenced the work of his nephew Lucan, writing in 60–65. But Seneca was in danger under Caligula, exiled under Claudius, recalled after changes in the politics of the court to become first the tutor, then the minister and finally the victim of Nero. Any part of his career might seem an appropriate context for the haunting mood of fear and guilt which prevails in his dramas.

Another difference between Seneca's plays and those discussed earlier in this chapter is that those were unquestionably performed in the theatre, whereas it is highly probable that Seneca's dramas were not composed for actual stage performance but as 'recitation-drama'. Those who argue for the latter position point to the serious problems of staging, with inconsistencies in the text regarding location or movement on stage. Some of these vanish if one ceases to apply criteria derived either from the Greek stage or from modern realistic productions, but by no means all. There can be no doubt, however, that they were written to be read aloud, probably by more than one reader, and even short experiments in this procedure will show them to possess 'dramatic' qualities.

Even the characters in the dramas themselves seem aware of their status as literary figures, as characters with background in a literary tradition. Some have overstated Seneca's novelty here; intertextual allusiveness was also present in the Greek tradition, where Euripides unmistakably imitates and some-times pokes fun at Aeschylean incidents, and both tragedy and comedy allude to previous enactments of the same or comparable plots. Seneca's self-conscious drama queen Medea had her predecessor in Ovid. Ovid made Hypsipyle, Jason's former paramour, passionately pray 'May I be a Medea to Medea!' (*Heroides* 6.151). The role of Medea is set, the character can presuppose it and another character can emulate it. Seneca surpasses this pointed device in the dialogue between Medea and her nurse, where the nurse protests against and Medea aspires to her true and traditional villainy:

Nurse: The Colchians are gone, your husband is unfaithful, and nothing is left to you from all your resources.

M: *Medea* is left!

And, a few lines later:

> *Nurse:*   Medea –
> *Medea:*   Fiam! [i.e. Let me *be* Medea; let me assume the role I was born for]
> (*Medea* 164–6, 171)

These powerful moments of self-recognition and self-assertion point the way to 'I am Duchess of Malfi still.'

The dynamic force of Seneca's monstrous personalities bequeathed something permanent to western theatre: the revenge-tragedy of the Elizabethans, the megalomaniac conquerors of Marlowe, would not have existed without him, though the diabolic mythology of the Christian tradition also makes its contribution. Hamlet's visiting troupe of players, for whom 'Seneca cannot be too heavy, or Plautus too light', give as a sample of their art a grandiloquent passage which seems to parody Marlowe in his most Senecan vein. Shakespeare's own early work *Titus Andronicus* blends the grim narrative of Tereus and Procne from Ovid with the Thyestean feast from Seneca in a heady brew of horror. Titus plays the chef to his enemies with gruesome gusto.[32] The Roman dramatist's other great legacy is his incomparably epigrammatic and pointed style: like his characters, it attracts even as it repels the listener. In contrast with the Greek masters, Seneca has sometimes been dismissed as a creator of crude melodramas; but in the absence of knowledge of the Greeks, it was he who was crucial in transmitting the classical tragic mode to dramatists up to the seventeenth century.

3

Rhetoric

I have often heard Gorgias maintain that the art of persuasion surpasses all others; for this, he said, makes all things subject to itself, not by force, but by their free will, and is by far the best of the arts.

Plato, *Philebus* 58a

[Rhetoric is] in truth the greatest good, and the source of freedom to men for themselves, and at the same time of power for each man over other men in the state.

Plato, *Gorgias* 452d

I

These bold claims may surprise moderns, to whom 'rhetoric' probably suggests either a rather inflated and artificial style or a highly formalized codification of arguments. But rhetoric is important not only as the chief medium of politics in an articulate and argumentative state, not only as the foundation of education throughout the ancient world, but as a formative force in virtually all ancient literature. Literary theorists have recently come to recognize its omnipresence in the modern world as well (though they may prefer to label what they are doing as discourse analysis). This chapter will focus on the ancient orators, above all on the central figure of Cicero, whose importance for the European tradition can hardly be exaggerated; but we will frequently note parallels and connections in other genres, and many of these points will recur elsewhere.

The term rhetoric needs some further definition. At its most specific, it refers to formalized speeches, in law courts or assembly or senate, as delivered by Demosthenes or Cicero and subsequently published; by extension, it can embrace speeches in very different literary genres such as tragedy and history. It can embrace the whole theory and practice of oratory. But it need not be restricted to oratory: if oratory itself is defined as the art of persuasion, that art is not only practised by political orators and advocates. In another type of work, Cicero uses all his rhetorical skills to convince his readers of the worthlessness of Epicurean philosophy. Rhetoric, then, can encompass any form of persuasive communication. According to Cicero, eloquence is the same whatever the theme and size of the audience, even if one is addressing a few intimates or indeed oneself (*On the Orator* 3.23). In the broadest sense of all, any form of communication that seeks to have an effect (intellectual or emotional) on an audience can be considered as a rhetorical utterance. These broader perspectives are largely visible in the major works of rhetorical theory (e.g. that of Aristotle); they help explain the interest of the field to modern theorists, although the latter concentrate on the soundbite rather than the *sententia* (see p. 216). In an era of multi-media communication and round-the-clock access to 'rhetorical' projects such as hard-sell advertising and nationalist propaganda, these themes have not lost their relevance. 'We are freed from rhetoric only by studying its history.'[1]

Speechmaking was of interest to the Greeks from the beginning. We have seen that speeches are important in Homer, and they were much admired by later readers, even used as illustrative examples by critics. Antenor assesses the oratory of Menelaus (laconic, plain style) and of Odysseus (powerful, grand style) with the enthusiasm of a connoisseur. Lawsuits and deceptive pleaders are mentioned in a simile and portrayed on Achilles' shield. Above all, Odysseus in the *Odyssey* is famed for his eloquence, though also prone to lies, flattery and fabrications. Since this hero is also more than once compared with a poet, the close links between oratory and poetic performance are already evident.[2] Further generic affinities developed with the emergence of drama: the orator resembles an actor, not only for his skills in memory, delivery and stamina, but also as one who is playing a part.

Rhetoric proper, in the sense of the art of composing formal speeches in prose, seems to have emerged in Greek-dominated Sicily, following the fall of the Syracusan tyranny (467–6 BC), after which a more open form of government was in power. Aristotle believed that the need for speechmaking skills arose from the legal battles to regain property that had been misappropriated under the tyrants' rule. This association of eloquence and freedom was deep-rooted in ancient thinking about oratory: our expressions 'free speech' and 'freedom of speech' evoke the same ideas. It was in liberated Syracuse and democratic Athens that oratory had a place, not in monarchic Macedonia, still less imperial Persia (fear to speak one's mind is a potent factor in Herodotus' portrayal of Xerxes' court; and to do so is even more perilous under mad Cambyses).[3] The Romans took over the same model: Cicero alludes to these ideas in his *Brutus*, a work which surveys the history of Greek and Roman oratory under the shadow of Caesar's dictatorship. Still more suggestive is Tacitus' *Dialogue on Oratory*, in which he examines the reasons for the decline of eloquence under the empire, contrasting the dull productions of the present with the splendour of the Republican past. Although other speakers dwell on changes in taste and educational practice, the last word goes to Maternus, who gives a political explanation: Republican competitiveness and conflict came close to anarchy, and the constant mood of crisis fostered rhetoric; but the way we live now, with peace and order guaranteed by a benign overlord, leaves little room for more than routine speeches on trivial issues. Nostalgia and disillusionment cloud the speaker's expression of dutiful gratitude for a time when the emperor's rule has 'pacified eloquence itself, like everything else' (38).

This analysis is no doubt over-schematic. The spoken word had its role even in non-democratic states, as it must have in any society where government involves discussion and negotiation rather than a single man's *fiat*. But it is undeniable that the great age of oratory in Greek history was the age of democratic Athens.[4] It was also the age of the sophists, a type of expert who taught young men for high fees: rhetorical skills were particularly in demand. Few speeches survive, however, from the heyday of the democracy, the fifth century. In our evidence demonstration models precede actual oratory. Tradition maintained that a transforming moment was in 427, when the sophist Gorgias arrived in Athens and stunned the audience with his ornate poetic prose. He cultivated rhythmical and rhyming speech, with balanced clauses and verbal music which recalled the style of high poetry. But in fact the textbooks must have preceded the man, as we can see the impact of this style before that date, even in Euripides' early plays. Gorgias, a lover of paradox and ingenious play with witty ideas, clearly contributed to the perception of rhetoric as a frivolous or dangerous game. We have his *Helen*, a remarkable exercise in arguing a seemingly implausible case.[5] In this he defends the notorious adulteress, declaring that she is innocent whether she was induced to follow Paris to Troy by love, by force, by persuasion or by the gods. There is little focus on the mythical scenario: with appropriate changes, this speech could defend any adulteress or indeed any criminal. Particular interest attaches to the section on persuasion, which is out of scale with the rest: Gorgias takes this opportunity to extol his own art with subtle and highly influential formulations.

> Speech is a powerful prince. Its substance is minute and invisible, but its achievements are superhuman; for it can stop fear and remove sorrow, create joy and augment pity . . .
> How many men have been persuaded and do persuade how many on how many subjects by fabricating false speech! For if everyone on every subject

possessed memory of the past and understanding of the present and foreknowledge of the future, speech would not be as powerful as it is; but as things are, neither remembering a past event nor investigating a present one nor prophesying a future one is easy, so that on most subjects most men make belief the mind's adviser. But belief, being slippery and unreliable, brings slippery and unreliable success to those who employ it . . .

The power of speech bears the same relation to the ordering of the mind as the ordering of drugs bears to the constitution of bodies. Just as different drugs expel different humours from the body, and some stop it from being ill but others stop it from living, so too some speeches cause sorrow, some cause pleasure, some cause fear, some give the hearers confidence, some drug and bewitch the mind with an evil persuasion. (*Helen* 8–13, extracts)

In the *Helen* Gorgias speaks in his own person. Another work ascribed to him is the *Defence of Palamedes*, which purports to be a speech by that mythical figure, a clever Greek of the heroic age, who was framed and accused of treason by Odysseus out of envy of his inventions (this story was popular in tragedy). The speech itself is ingenious enough, but it is more important as an early example of 'declamation' – the construction of a speech by a fictional or historical character in order to set oneself a particular rhetorical challenge. In later times the student might be set the task of advising Agamemnon whether to sacrifice his daughter, or urging Sulla to give up his dictatorship and withdraw to private life.[6] The technique is most fully documented from the Roman period: it became a stock feature of rhetorical training, and clearly influenced literature. (An obvious instance is the rhetorical contest between Ulysses and Ajax in Ovid's *Metamorphoses* 13: each argues that he is the proper recipient of the dead Achilles' armour.)

Another much-quoted authority who evidently aroused conservative Athenian suspicion was the sophist Protagoras, who maintained that the skilful speaker can find opposing arguments on every question. This was construed as meaning that the orator could make the worse cause appear the better. Not all Athenians welcomed this news: we can see angry antagonism to the sophists reflected in Aristophanes, and Protagoras in Plato is made to refer to the unpopularity of his profession. Even when oratory was well-established, it was common for one speaker to adopt a 'plain man' attitude and accuse another of being too clever; and professional speech-writers were viewed with suspicion.

By the time of Gorgias' visit, formal textbooks in oratory were clearly current, many of them by practitioners. Prominent in the early theoretical discussions was the argument from probability, illustrated from accusations of assault. If a weak man is accused of attacking a strong man, the weak man should be acquitted – why would he take on an obviously superior opponent? But the strong man should also be acquitted of attacking the weak man: obviously, he would know that others would think him the likely assailant, and would have held back accordingly (Plato, *Phaedrus* 273a–c). Plato also makes fun of the swiftly developing technical jargon ('must we not acknowledge that most admirable Parian, Euenos, for being the first to discover "covert allusion" and "indirect praise"?' (*Phaedrus* 267a)). The fully developed structural and stylistic vocabulary has no place in a book like this, but a few points are central.[7] Oratory could be subdivided (as by Aristotle) into three categories: law-court speeches, deliberative speeches (i.e. those which advocated a particular course of action in the political arena), and 'showpiece' or epideictic speeches. The first two types seek to achieve a concrete goal: to win a case, or carry a resolution. The third does not have an immediate practical end, but aims rather at inspiration or edification: eulogies and funeral orations are among the most obvious examples. Other subdivisions included the different parts of a speech. Division varied, but most law-court speeches include a proem, a narrative section, argument for your own case and against your opponent, and a peroration (often highly emotional). Styles were differentiated, with experts differing on how many styles there were, but a triple division was perhaps the most popular. In this, the three styles were defined as grand, middle and plain (the best orator was master of all, and could modulate between them in a given speech). The skills needed by the orator were also enumerated: *invention*, the ability to find appropriate arguments for a case; *disposition*, the skill to arrange them in the most tactically effective way; *diction* and stylistic ornamentation; *action*, effectiveness in delivery; and finally power of *memory*. A great deal more terminology was devised by successive author-ities; for our purposes it is important to look beyond the technicalities to the larger principles. Major authors such as Aristotle and Quintilian are of particular importance, as they paid careful attention to both the larger debates and the technical detail.

   Although there is massive continuity between Greek and Roman rhetoric, some key contrasts should be mentioned. One arises from our evidence: on the Greek side we have speeches by many hands, and most of all from the figure who later had the highest reputation, Demosthenes. But in Latin the towering figure of Cicero eclipsed all his predecessors, and the representa-tion from later generations is capricious. This contrast is heightened by the degree of detailed knowledge we have of Cicero. Besides his orations we have many other publications and private letters from his hand, making him the only figure of classical antiquity whose biography can be written from detailed first-hand evidence. By contrast we generally know the Athenian orators purely from their own work or from later scholars commenting on their work. Other contrasts are institutional: in Athenian law courts citizens had to speak in their own defence or prosecute in person. Hence the prominence of professional speechwriters like Lysias, who would prepare a version for the litigant to deliver. (Political speeches are another matter.) By contrast Cicero often speaks for others: 'in defence of' Caelius, of Sulla, of Flaccus, and so forth. Finally, status and rank perhaps carried more weight in Rome than in democratic Athens, and we often find Cicero assuming that his very eminence is a point in favour of his client (although having said that, we should admit that these factors did not inhibit speakers: the scurrility and invective in Roman oratory seems if anything to have been more extreme than anything in the Greek speeches).

II

Among the Greeks, some are minor figures of interest chiefly to specialists. Antiphon is notable as the earliest surviving orator (d.411). His extant speeches all deal with homicide; he had the distinction of impressing the historian Thucydides, who thought his self-defence on a charge of attempting to install an oligarchic government the best ever made on a capital charge (8.68). Andocides gained notoriety in one political-religious crisis and was not allowed to forget it; Isaeus specialized in inheritance disputes. Not all the speeches which have come down to us as 'Lysias' or 'Demosthenes' are authentic, for great names attract forgeries. Sometimes this is a gain: we would be the poorer without the speech by a religious maniac impossibly ascribed to Lysias (Lys. 6). There is also a broad contrast between the orators who are simply concerned with the law courts and those who speak on political themes. The former category includes Lysias (who as a non-Athenian was not entitled to take part actively in politics), the latter Aeschines, the inferior antagonist of Demosthenes. Demosthenes straddled both spheres. It is traditional in ancient and modern times to rate public above judicial oratory, but much more of the latter survives in both Greek and Latin, and theory dealt in far more detail with the rhetoric of the courts: many might have to defend themselves on charges of fraud or misconduct, and although in the radical democracy participation in politics was encouraged, the proper moves to make in changing political conditions were much harder to codify. In modern times, with the revaluation of social and cultural history over war and politics, the so-called 'private speeches' (those delivered in the courts) have gained new readers. Not only are they rich quarries for facts about law and behaviour, but also key sources for attitudes and ideology.

The range of these speeches is wide. At one end they may amuse with their very triviality, as when a speaker argues over the proper ownership of a disputed watercourse (Dem. 55). An attractive short piece delivered by a cripple insists that his disability is genuine and entitles him to a state pension (Lys. 24). Others deal with major Athenian institutions, such as the sponsoring or equipping of ships for the fleet (Dem. 51) or the running of the silver mines (Dem. 37). Defences of men who are at risk of losing citizenship rights because of associations with anti-democratic elements shed light on the political antagonisms and in-fighting after Athens' defeat in the war against Sparta (e.g. Lys. 16, 31). Accusations of violence and assault are common (Lys. 3 and 4, Dem. 21 and 54). Some of these speeches are brief and allusive, but there are others that open up a whole unfamiliar world. Aeschines' long indictment of Timarchus argues that because the latter has (allegedly) prostituted himself to a whole series of men, he is legally disqualified from holding public office. This speech is the single most informative document on Athenian laws and expectations about homosexual behaviour. Another speech which has always aroused interest is Lysias' *Defence of Eratosthenes* (1), in which the client defends himself for killing his wife's lover, after finding him in bed with her. The law permitted this if the man was caught in the act and the violence was unpremeditated; the speaker is being accused of having planned the whole thing and set the victim up. For most of the speech he adopts the manner of an injured innocent, who has been naive in trusting his wife too readily, but (or 'therefore') is guiltless of any kind of plot. But in the narrative of his act he strikes a more elevated note:

> He confessed his crime but begged and entreated me not to kill him but to accept money. But I said 'It is not I that will kill you, but the law of the city, which you transgressed, thinking it less important than your pleasures, and you chose to commit an offence like this against my wife and my children, rather than being obedient to the laws and observing restraint.' Thus it was, gentlemen, that he obtained the treatment that the laws decree for men who commit deeds like these – he was not dragged in off the road, nor did he run and take refuge at the hearth, as these men [the prosecutors] claim. (Lys. 1.26–7)

The high-minded declaration and the vivid use of direct speech do not wholly eliminate our unease at the concluding hints of another story. Although we rarely have speeches on both sides of a case, hints of this kind can allow us to reconstruct some at least of the opposing side's position.

By far the most important figure on the public stage is the orator Demosthenes, who from about 355 was active in politics as well as in the courts, and who from about 350 onwards began to press persistently for Athens to oppose the power of Philip of Macedon by every possible means.[8] His surviving speeches urging immediate action, the *Olynthiacs* and the

Philippics, play repeated variations on this theme. Most famous of all is the speech *On the Crown*, delivered in 330 BC. The title refers to a proposal by one of his supporters, Ctesiphon, that Demosthenes should be awarded a crown (i.e. an honorific wreath) for his services to Athens. This proposal was attacked by his long-term enemy Aeschines, who indicted Ctesiphon for unconstitutional action on a number of formal points, but more fundamentally because, Aeschines maintained, Demosthenes' entire career had been a total disaster for Athens. (Aeschines' prosecution speech survives in full, so that this is one rare instance where we can measure two major orators against one another; another case is an earlier clash between these two, 13 years earlier.) In defending Ctesiphon (in which he was successful), Demosthenes was also presenting a defence of himself and his past policy; and on the basis that the best form of defence is attack, he devoted extensive parts of the speech to a vitriolic indictment of Aeschines, whose policy of support for Philip Demosthenes regarded as treason.

By 330, when the case came to trial, Demosthenes' past policy might well seem disastrous. Philip had crushed Athens and the other resisting Greek forces at the battle of Chaeronea (338) and in 336, when the Greeks tried to shake off Macedonian rule after Philip's death, the military genius of his heir Alexander had made short work of the revolt. Although the Macedonian yoke was not as severe as those which later conquerors of Greece were to impose, the loss of independence was a bitter blow, especially to Athens, once mistress of an empire of her own. Demosthenes makes much of the Greek ideals of freedom in his speech, and one reason that it has been highly valued is because in retrospect it seems to have something of the quality of an epitaph on that freedom. The orator's eloquence has often dazzled even sceptical historians, though hard-headed readers will recognize that Demosthenes' pan-Hellenism was pursued in Athens' interests, and may even suspect that there was more to be said on Philip's side than our sources allow us to see.

Demosthenes deals lightly and swiftly with the formal charges of irregularity, where Aeschines' case was strong. Instead he concentrates on his own record as a statesman, repeatedly contrasting it with Aeschines'. He surveys his career in phases, culminating in the role he himself played in marshalling Greek resistance prior to Chaeronea (in particular by securing an alliance between Athens and Thebes). Throughout, Demosthenes presents himself as embodying the highest and noblest ideals of Athens, whereas Aeschines stands for everything that is self-serving, inconsistent and base. One of the least attractive aspects of the speech to modern eyes is the persistent invective concerning Aeschines' upbringing and background: according to Demosthenes, he was of low birth and sordid profession (he was originally an actor), unable to live up to the statesman's role.

Examine therefore, side by side, the episodes of your life and mine, Aeschines, calmly, not cruelly; and then ask our hearers whose fortune each of them would choose. You taught the alphabet, I was a student. You conducted initiation rites, I was initiated. You were a clerk, I was a member of the assembly. You were a third-role actor, I was in the audience. You broke down in your lines, I was there hissing. (265)

It is illuminating, though depressing, to see how much weight such arguments were expected to carry even in a supposedly democratic society.

More positive is the heroic image that Demosthenes paints of Athens' past, and the lesson he draws from that past to vindicate the policy which, under his leadership, she has pursued against the invader from Macedon. In one crucial passage (192–210), he even insists that despite the defeat, they made no mistake. Even if they had marched to Chaeronea *knowing* that they would be defeated, they would have been right to do so. Only thus could they sustain their record as champions of liberty in the fifth-century wars against Persia.

It cannot be, it cannot be, men of Athens, that you erred when you took it upon yourselves to fight the battle for the liberty and security of all. Yes, I swear this, by your ancestors who bore the brunt of the danger at Marathon, by those who held the line at Plataea, by those who fought in the ships at Salamis, and at Artemisium, and those many other brave men who lie in the public tombs – *all* of whom, Aeschines, the city judged worthy of that same honour, not merely the successful and victorious. (208)

Much admired by ancient critics, and memorably discussed by Longinus in *On the Sublime* (16), this passage shows Demosthenes at his best: these are the tones which were imitated by Cicero in his *Philippics* and by Churchill in his war speeches.

III

Besides the mainstream of oratory proper, many other Greek texts provide versions of speeches or insights into the rhetorical genres. Some works were couched in speech form even though they were never delivered, whether as didactic exercises or as pamphlets to publicize the author's views (many of the 'speeches' by the educational theorist Isocrates belong to this category). There are also speeches embedded in other works. Rhetoric strongly influenced Euripides and later tragedians, and some scenes in drama evoke the atmosphere of the courts.[9] One example is the confrontation of Hippolytus and Theseus in Euripides' *Hippolytus*: there the normal process of justice is perverted, as Hippolytus' oath prevents him from revealing the key evidence that would prove his innocence; moreover, Theseus has already sentenced him before he comes back on stage. Similarly, in the *Trojan Women*, although Helen argues that Menelaus should spare her and Hecuba that she should die, the real power in play is not rational argument or prudential considerations but Helen's beauty and Menelaus' renewed desire. Tragedy, like other literary genres, is at least as concerned with ways in which persuasion *fails* as with its successes.[10]

Speeches are also prominent in historiography, above all in Thucydides. His deep knowledge and sophisticated adaptation of rhetorical teaching is obvious. Most of the speeches in his work are of the deliberative type (e.g. the Mytilene debate). In one case, the episode at Plataea, we again see a distorted version of the law-court situation, with the Spartans as judges, Thebans as prosecutors and Plataeans pleading a hopeless defence (3.53–68). One speech stands out as different, the funeral speech ascribed to Pericles, spoken at the burial of the Athenian dead after the first year of the war. This falls into the category known as epideictic, 'show-piece' oratory: it does not aim at a specific goal but celebrates or commemorates. The funeral speech was an important civic occasion, at which the Athenians not only honoured the dead but recalled their history (or an idealized version of it) and enjoyed the glow of patriotic pride. Other funeral speeches survive, but the difference is great: not only is the historian's version more complex and thought-provoking, but it stands in a context. The ideal is memorably stated, but the rest of the history shows us how flawed is the reality.[11] Some would go further, and even see the speech as implicitly pointing to weaknesses or at least contradictions in the Athenian way of life. However, the passage on the spirit of self-sacrifice shown by the dead certainly states an ideal of a kind in unforgettable language, and it may be wrong to deny value to these sentiments because we live in a world where war means something far more terrifying. This extract gives something of the speech's quality: detailed comparison has established that Lincoln drew on this passage in the immortal Gettysburg Address.[12]

> . . . you must yourselves realise the power of the city, and feed your eyes upon her from day to day, till love of her fills your hearts; and then when all her greatness shall break upon you, you must reflect that it was by courage, sense of duty, and a keen feeling of honour in action that men were enabled to win all this, and that no personal failure in an enterprise could make them consent to deprive their country of their valour, but they laid it at her feet as the most glorious contribution they could offer. For this offering of their lives made in common by them all they each of them individually received that renown which never grows old, and for a sepulchre, not so much that in which their

bones have been laid, but that noblest of shrines wherein their glory is laid up
to be eternally remembered upon every occasion on which deed or story shall
call for its commemoration. For heroes have the whole earth for their tomb;
and in lands far from their own, where the column with its epitaph declares
it, there is enshrined in every breast a record unwritten, with no tablet to
preserve it except in the heart. Take these men as your example . . . (2.43)

This inspirational ceremony did not impress every Athenian alike. The
sceptical and disturbing figure of Socrates, self-appointed gadfly of the community, was always prepared to criticize or question the basis for established
institutions, democratic ones not least. In a short work called *Menexenus*,
Plato shows Socrates waxing ironic about the funeral speech: 'How fine a
thing in all sorts of ways death in battle is! You get a handsome and
splendiferous funeral, even if you die poor, and you win high praise even if
you're not good for much.' Nevertheless, he affects to admire the whole
occasion and reminisces about how, listening to the speakers, he feels himself grow prouder and taller and start looking down on any foreigners present.
Sometimes it takes him several days to come down to earth! This mischievous
commentary has a serious point: rhetoric weakens self-awareness and darkens
counsel if it only tells the audience what they want to hear.

We have seen that Athenian literature shows us much evidence for
suspicion of rhetoric and fear of its powers, while also indicating that those
powers do have limits. Plato takes up both strands of thinking and develops
powerful and far-reaching criticisms which embrace both rhetoric and
poetry. One source of his concern is doubtless the condemnation of his
mentor Socrates by an Athenian court persuaded by misguided or malicious
orators (Plato's *Apology* or Defence speech gives us his version of Socrates'
polemically anti-rhetorical response to his accusers). But the issue goes
far beyond this personal loyalty. The power of speech and the basis of
persuasion in argument are of intense concern to him as a philosopher who
inevitably uses words himself and who dramatizes his arguments and ideas
in highly sophisticated literary form. The paradox that Plato himself exploits
rhetorical forms and seeks to move and inspire his readers, not just to
present arguments, was not lost on the ancients: a speaker in Cicero refers
to the *Gorgias* as a work in which 'in the course of mocking the orators
Plato shows himself the supreme orator' (*On the Orator* 1.47).

There are several aspects to Plato's criticisms. First, he disapproved of the
determination of orators to win their case by whatever means, irrespective
of the truth (similarly with the funeral speeches: orators praise Athens and
the dead for virtues they possess and those they do not possess, indiscriminately). In the public sphere, he believed that politicians were too ready to
pander to the desires of the people rather than guiding or instructing them

on the basis of rational morality. This was related to his condemnation of rhetoric as a spurious art, with no serious intellectual foundation and certainly no moral basis: essentially it was a collection of clever verbal tricks. Sophistic teachers aimed at helping their students get on in society; Plato thought that they should be teaching them how to live better and improve their minds and morals. Another criticism concerned the appeal of oratory to the passions (anger, fear, pity) rather than the intellect (this was still more evident in poetry). In the *Gorgias*, Socrates confronts several spokes-men for rhetoric, Gorgias, Polus and Callicles, each more ruthless and less moral than the last. The third opponent, Callicles, is a young man eager to participate in politics. Despite his initial politeness, as the discussion advances he is revealed as an ambitious careerist, driven by his own desires and aspirations to the exclusion of morality: though prepared to compromise with the democratic environment, his real ideal would be to rule as a tyrant (a recurring figure of symbolic horror in Plato). Though the dialogue begins with the civilized Gorgias, the acceptable face of rhetoric, the portrait of Callicles shows what it means to pursue success through a purely instrumental art like rhetoric, without rooting one's ambitions in reason and morality.[13]

The *Phaedrus*, in which the atmosphere is friendlier and more light-hearted, also shows a character confronted with a choice in life: Socrates' friend Phaedrus is said to be wavering between the pursuit of rhetoric and philosophy. Socrates first teasingly mocks, then imitates, then surpasses and transcends, the sample speech by Lysias which Phaedrus reads at the start and misguidedly admires. Socrates can beat the professionals at their own game and also transform the game itself, shifting the form and style into his own ethical-religious mode. In the second half of the work, amid further criticisms of the rhetoricians, Socrates half-whimsically sketches what a true art of rhetoric might look like: above all, it calls for expert knowledge of the human psyche and a quasi-medical understanding of what kinds of argument will appeal to what kinds of mind. Knowledge of the soul and its nature is what Socrates himself seeks; it also formed part of the subject of his speech, though cast in fantastic mythical guise.[14] Plato does not make clear whether he really believed this true art to be achievable, nor how one could ensure that this kind of rhetoric was not abused by amoral practi-tioners. There is a utopian flavour to these proposals, which suits the play-ful and holiday atmosphere of the dialogue. Nevertheless, Plato's general critique of the rhetoric of his time, and of all times, has an irrefutable core.

It is not hard to see Aristotle's *Rhetoric*, a key work of ancient theory, as building on Plato's suggestions in the *Phaedrus*. Aristotle however makes clear from the start that moral supervision of rhetoric, as opposed to the utilizing of moral arguments within speeches, is not his concern. Rhetoric can be abused, but so can all things, except virtue itself. What he does is take the hints of earlier teachers and handbooks and systematize them, at a high intellectual level. But his approach is practical, not critical: 'the proofs furnished by the speech itself are of three kinds. The first depends on the moral character of the speaker [as perceived by the audience], the second on putting the hearer into a certain frame of mind, the third upon the speech itself, in so far as it proves or seems to prove' (i.2). The first two books of this work examine argumentative method and the handling of character and emotion, but the third is especially interesting to moderns as laying the basis for a formal study of style.[15]

IV

Despite Plato's opposition, of which echoes are detectable in later periods, rhetoric was there to stay, and became basic to the educational system (only a minority even among the literate would go on, like Cicero and Horace, to study philosophy at 'university' level). The suspicion which the fifth-century Athenians felt was echoed when the art gained a foothold in Rome: teachers of rhetoric were expelled early in the second and again in the first century BC, though political motives as well as moral may have been relevant.[16] The Elder Cato growled 'rem tene; verba sequentur' (stick to the point, and the words will follow). But although Romans typically looked back to a primitive simplicity, effective speakers must always have been needed (diplomacy follows in the wake of the conqueror), and although Cicero's predecessors have not survived, he tells us enough to show that he was the culmination of a long-standing tradition. He was modest enough not to say outright that in him Roman oratory reached the pinnacle of perfection, but he often implied it, and made others do so in his dialogues (e.g. *On the Orator* 1.95, 3.80; *Brutus* 322). His undoubted vanity need not blind us to his extraordinary achievements, and not in oratory alone.

Cicero, indeed, is remarkable in all sorts of ways. Of all the countless individuals who play a part in the historical and literary creation of ancient times, he is the one we know best (Augustine is perhaps his closest rival). This is because of the bulk of material we have from his pen, but still more because of its range. We possess not only speeches (58 in all, though some are incomplete; 29 from the law courts, the rest political in one way or other); there are works on the theory of oratory, on philosophy and religion, on practical ethics (especially the short and readable essays on friendship and on old age, and the longer work *On Duties*); he was a poet, though little has survived and his efforts here were widely ridiculed; above all, we have over 900 letters from his correspondence with others (this number includes about 100 replies from some of his contemporaries, including men as eminent as Julius Caesar, the younger Cato, Caesar's assassin Brutus, and Antonius (Mark Antony)). Most revealing is the posthumously published collection of letters to his closest friend Atticus, from whom Cicero had no secrets; more variety and greater discretion are found in the equally substantial body of letters to and from a variety of friends. Although some of the letters are formal in manner and were clearly meant to be read by others, the majority are intimate and private. What survives is only a portion of his enormous output, public and personal, and the coverage is irregular, but for the periods from which both speeches and letters survive they constitute detailed source-material such as survives for few periods from the ancient world.[17]

This is all the more fortunate because Cicero was an unusually articulate and intelligent observer, and at some stages a key participant, in the eventful years of the late Roman Republic. Born in 106 BC, he was of middle-class stock from the town of Arpinum, south-east of Rome. Lacking aristocratic background and distinguished ancestors, he had to make his own way, and throughout his career felt keenly the need to establish himself with the noble families who had produced consuls for generations – the upper class of the senate, many of whom patronized or looked down on him. His industry, ambition and above all his great gifts as a speaker made the early part of his career a huge success: he made a great name for himself through his advocacy in the courts, a process which he like others regarded as a means of winning friends and supporters (*On Duties* 2.51, 66). The first speech we have dates from 81, when he was only 25, but his first major coup, in 70, was one of his rare prosecutions, when he successfully indicted the notorious Verres for misconduct and embezzlement as governor of Sicily (Cicero had earlier served there, and his former friends in Sicily had entreated his aid in order to gain recompense for Verres' extortion). His first speech in this trial was so successful that Verres capitulated forthwith (Cicero was not going to let his carefully prepared case go to waste on that account, but published his whole set of speeches anyway). This triumph was all the more impressive as Cicero was opposed by Hortensius, currently regarded as the supreme Roman orator: that case marked the beginning of the older man's decline.

But Cicero sought public office, not just victories in the law courts. He competed successfully for the series of magistracies which culminated in election as one of the two consuls of 63 (the consuls being the supreme magistrates and executive agents of the Roman state, in charge of civic and military affairs alike). Cicero was justly proud of achieving this goal, not only the first of his family to reach such a high rank, but doing so in the earliest possible year permitted by the various age-restrictions on office. In his consular year he took a decisive line in repressing the conspiracy of the disaffected aristocrat Catiline, who after failing twice to be elected as consul on a radical programme resorted instead to armed violence. From this period come his four speeches against Catiline, which are among his most famous (they were published some years later, and include some fairly obvious editing intended to emphasize Cicero's foresight and defend his actions). The crisis culminated in the declaration of a kind of martial law, and Cicero took responsibility for executing a number of Catiline's supporters without trial, following a heated debate on their fate in the senate. This action, which some thought shockingly unconstitutional, was one which he felt obliged to defend for the rest of his life: at one point his enemies used it to drive him briefly into exile. Contemporaries already grew weary of his constant harping on his achievements in that year: Brutus complains of this in a letter to Atticus, and later readers joined the chorus ('his consulship, praised not groundlessly but ceaselessly', sighed Seneca).[18]

Although Cicero assumed that he was now part of the establishment and could look forward to many years as a respected senior figure, events disappointed him. The crushing of Catiline's conspiracy did little to alter the alarming condition of Roman politics. Normal government was increasingly disrupted. Among the reasons for instability were socio-economic unrest in Italy, growing levels of extravagance and misconduct among the governing class, and the excessive power given to the most successful generals, whose armies came to owe their loyalty more to them as individuals than to the state. Cicero is our prime source for the next 20 years, during which the uneasy alliance between Pompey, Julius Caesar and Crassus overshadowed Roman politics, with each man seeking to dominate the other two. The eventual split between Pompey and Caesar after Crassus' death led to civil war in Italy and beyond. Cicero had ties with both men, but sided with Pompey for reasons of personal loyalty, while deploring the bloodthirsty ambitions of both sides. Caesar won this war and established himself as dictator, outraging Cicero's Republican sentiments. The period of Caesar's rule was one of the episodes of enforced political inactivity during which he wrote extensively, producing many of the philosophic works based on Greek teaching which were so important for later European thought (see p. 243). He was not party to the murder of Caesar in 44, but emphatically approved it, and saw that the hour had come for him to take a lead in politics again (he was now, aged 63, one of the most senior figures of the senate: many of his former seniors and rivals had died in the civil wars). He naturally took the side of the assassins, self-styled 'liberators' (Brutus, Cassius and others), against the Caesarian party led by Antony. The antagonism between Antony and Cicero escalated into a war of words alongside the military opposition between these two sides: a series of 14 speeches preserve this conflict and give us a picture of the developing crisis. (Cicero himself called them his 'Philippics', accepting a jocular suggestion from Brutus and aligning himself with Demosthenes.) For a time Caesar's heir Octavian, who flattered Cicero and whom Cicero promoted, seemed to offer a powerful ally who could command the loyalty of Caesar's forces. The unexpected ruthlessness with which Octavian changed sides and made common cause with Antony was fatal to the liberators' cause and to Cicero, for whom Antony had no mercy. He was executed in December 43, and his head and hands barbarically cut off and pinned to the Rostra, the speaker's platform in the Roman Forum.

Even this crude summary will show some of the fascination of a life spent at the centre of so extraordinary an age. But 'at the centre' is itself a questionable formulation. Cicero is central to our evidence, both on politics and on much else ranging from senatorial procedure to the publication and distribution of books at Rome (Atticus, who had a large team of scribes, acted as his 'publisher'). But many have thought him a man of words not of deeds: in this he has traditionally been contrasted with the far more dynamic and radical figure of Caesar.[19] Arguably he was a key player only in his consular year and in the final clash with Antony, whereas in the intervening decades, while always trying to play an important role, he was marginalized, kept at arm's length, even exiled, while the more powerful generals and 'dynasts', as moderns like to call them, dominated the political arena. There is truth in this but not the whole truth. Even Caesar not only had a high personal regard for Cicero but respected his power and influence as a speaker, and indeed feared its potential to shape opinion. In an age which is repelled rather than seduced by power-politics, the versatile, sensitive and warm-hearted personality of Cicero seems much more attractive than the relentless march of Caesar to glory and power, let alone the frigid and calculating ambition of Octavian.[20]

Our chief concern here is with Cicero in his speeches. But part of his fascination is that other parts of his work enable us to get a different perspective on the speeches. It is not only that the theoretical works, above all his dialogue *On the Orator*, show us some of the principles that underlie the practice. Sometimes he alludes to or explains his practice, with pride or self-mocking humour. In 63 he had to defend Murena, his appointed successor as consul, against charges of electoral bribery which might invalidate his election. In a later speech he remarked that none of the jurors in that case had supposed that this was a mere matter of electoral corruption: the key issue, with Catiline still in the field with an army, was to ensure that there were two (reliable) consuls in place on 1 January (*Defence of Flaccus* 98). The same case had obliged him to make fun of the rigid Stoic morality of Cato, one of the prosecutors. Much later he dramatized a dialogue on philosophy between himself and Cato about Stoic ethics. 'You say all sins are equal', comments Cicero in his own work. 'I'm not going to have fun with you now as I did on the same topic when we were on opposite sides in the Lucius Murena case. What I said then was before the ignorant – and I admit I was playing to the gallery a little as well! But our discussion now must be on a subtler plane.' (*On Ends* 4.74) At the time of the trial, he had praised the jurors' perspicacity; now he admits that their philosophic inexpertise was exploited. Or again, the modern reader is baffled by the intricate detail of Cicero's arguments in defence of Cluentius: we may be relieved, though slightly shocked, to find that Cicero boasted of his success in obscuring the issue (he said he had engulfed the jurors in darkness, reports Quintilian (2.17.21)).

The gulf between the highly wrought, theatrical style of oratory and the more idiomatic usage of conversation or an informal letter is considerable. In one letter to Atticus we see Cicero making a joke of his own rhetorical flamboyance.

> As for myself – ye gods, how I spread my tail in front of my new audience, Pompey! If ever periods and clausulae and enthymemes and *raisonnements* came to my call, they did on that occasion. In a word, I brought the house down. And why not, on such a theme – the dignity of our order, concord between Senate and Knights, unison of Italy, remnants of the conspiracy in their death-throes, reduced price of grain, internal peace? You should know by now how I can boom away on such topics. I think you must have caught the reverberations in Epirus . . . (*Letters to Atticus* 1.14.4, tr. Shackleton Bailey)

But although the tone here is light, it would be a mistake to suppose that Cicero did not care deeply about the topics he mentioned. In some ways he cared too much: innately conservative, he longed for the stability of politics in an earlier age. He loved the language of political concord and a united Italy, but did not often probe beyond the words and think about the institutional weaknesses which underlay the high-sounding slogans. By contrast Caesar could cut through the verbiage, declaring the *res publica* a shadow without substance (Suet. *Julius* 77).

Cicero describes his own education and training in the *Brutus*, a dialogue on the history of Latin oratory, and comments on his own speeches in various places, notably the *Orator*, another essay written late in life. There he laughs at the effervescence of his youthful style, exemplified in a florid passage of the *Defence of Sextus Roscius*, in which he describes the archaic punishment for parricides (they were tied up in sacks and tossed in the sea). 'They die, but their bones never touch the earth. They are tossed by the waves, but they are never washed by them. They are cast ashore at last – but find no rest in death even upon the rocks' (72, quoted *Orator* 107). In those days, he declares, he had not come entirely off the boil! Less notorious but still memorable is another passage of the same speech in which he waxes philosophical, elaborating the theme that guilt itself, the ravagings of conscience, is our punishment for crime: we need not believe the old tales of torture by Furies in the underworld (66–7).

Cicero's speeches are mostly datable within a year, often more exactly, so that we can trace his rhetorical development. We can also compare his handling of the same type of case as prosecutor and defender, or observe the transformations which affect some individuals when the needs of a case demand (Catiline, the arch-villain and public enemy of 63, becomes an enigmatic and fascinating personality, a man of extraordinary gifts, a few years later, when it is necessary to excuse young Caelius for being taken in by him). He matches his speeches to his audience: those to the senate are couched in different terms, and a more elaborate style, than he uses to the Roman people gathered in the forum. Appeals to the dignity of Rome and the glory of her conquests are common; by contrast he can shamelessly denounce the unreliability of Greek witnesses (*Flaccus* 9ff., 64ff.) or sneer at the hedonism of the Epicureans (*Against Piso* 63–72), though we know from other works that his real views were more sophisticated.

Some of the speeches are much longer than a modern court would allow, and his handling of the case is not restrained by strict criteria of relevance. Digressions (for instance on Roman history and precedents) are frequent; so are elaborate set-pieces of reconstruction and imaginative embroidery. In Roman courts, as in Greek, much weight was allowed not only to the examination of the defendant's past life but also to the authority and status of the advocates; the best interest of the state and the current political situation might also be invoked. Cicero often thrusts such matters to the foreground and avoids confronting the detail of the charges. It seems clear that Cicero regularly published his speeches, probably soon after the case in question. As with the Verres trial, some speeches were never delivered but appeared first in written form, like open letters or pamphlets. (The Second Philippic is another instance.) While his political orations were no doubt published partly to vindicate his policy or mould opinion, this is less likely to be true with the law-court speeches: here he was probably advertising his own skills and showing off his cleverness. In one letter he speaks of these speeches as giving instruction to younger orators (*To Atticus* 2.1.3, cf. *Philippics* 2.20).

Any reader of Cicero will be struck by the emotional tempo of the speeches. He himself regarded this as crucial to the art of the orator, who must be able to manipulate his audience's sympathy and antagonism. Pity needed to be aroused in the interests of the defence, indignation and

contempt directed towards one's opponent. Cicero was proud of his emotional finales, in which the appeal to pity is usually to the fore (e.g. *Defence
of Milo* 92–105, *Defence of Sulla* 88–91). When several advocates spoke, he
usually brought up the rear in order to put across this appeal with max-
imum impact (*Orator* 130). But equally vigorous, and uninhibited by trivia
like fact or justice, are his character-assassinations. Invective was common in
Roman oratory, and widespread in the culture as a whole (pp. 217f.). Such
outspokenness went much further than Greek courts would have permitted,
but although he insinuates, he does not descend to the level of obscenity.
Rhetoric has its own laws of propriety: 'let us speak no more of shame and
debauchery. There are some things which I cannot decently mention. Your
tongue is the freer because you have committed offences which you could
not hear from the lips of a *modest* enemy.' (*Philippics* 2.47). This decorum
does not restrain Cicero from describing how Antony was once sick in a
public meeting, or making risqué allusions to his extra-marital relations with
the actress Cytheris or the manly Curio. These accusations were common
coin, and it is clear that Cicero and his clients had to repudiate slurs of
the same sort.

Quintilian thought that Cicero surpassed Demosthenes not only in his
power to arouse pity, but in his wit (10.1.107). Humour is one of the joys
of Ciceronian oratory, a constant surprise to those who expect him to be
permanently pompous.[21] Most cynically playful is the *Defence of Caelius*
(56 BC), in which he represents a younger protegé, a well-to-do and intelligent politician whose career is threatened by a prosecution for violence
and murder. (Caelius a few years later is one of the wittiest and most entertaining of Cicero's correspondents while the latter is abroad, reluctantly
serving a year as governor of Cilicia.) Cicero turns the case into a comedy,
persistently making out that the charges are fabricated by a jealous woman
bent on revenge. The woman in question, the aristocratic Clodia, was the
sister of one of Cicero's worst enemies; she may also have been the mistress
of Catullus, but was clearly involved with Caelius. If Cicero allowed us to
examine the charges at leisure and in all seriousness, the case against Caelius
might look alarmingly plausible; but instead he virtually puts Clodia in the
dock, delighting jury and populace with his mocking distortion of the
prosecution's case. Clodia may well have been getting her own back for
being dropped by Caelius. Cicero chooses to highlight this, and pillories
her for her lifestyle, insinuating that she lives the life of a prostitute and
maintaining that as men of the world we can all understand Caelius being
temporarily ensnared by such a woman: we were all young once. In a *tour
de force* of impersonation he calls up the memory of Clodia's ancestor, a
figure of the sternest moral authority, Appius Claudius the blind, consul
of 143, and speaks with his voice (*prosopopoiia*, a recognized rhetorical

technique which here makes for comic melodrama). Through Cicero, the indignant statesman denounces his degenerate descendant.

> Did I dissolve the peace with Pyrrhus so that you might daily establish treaties with lovers of the basest sort? Did I convey water to Rome by aqueduct merely so that you could indulge in nude bathing? Did I construct the road that bears my name so that you could go gallivanting along it, escorted by other women's husbands?

At which point Cicero breaks off in mock dismay, remarking 'But gentlemen, why have I adopted so magisterial a role that I'm afraid the same Appius may suddenly turn round and start attacking my client with that censorial majesty of his?' (34–5) A moment later he adopts a more modern, sophisticated persona, that of Clodia's own brother, who can't understand what his sister is making such a fuss about. If she's lost one lover, there are plenty more to choose from. Appius' archaic moralizing is set against Clodius' shameless loose-living: both are hilarious, both serve to deflect attention from Caelius' own dodgy morals and dubious activities. One scholar writing in the fifth century said that Cicero got his guiltiest clients off the hook with his jokes (Macrobius 2.1.13).

With another major speech, the *Defence of Milo*, we have valuable guidance from an excellent external source, the scholar Asconius (writing in the next century). He composed a detailed historical introduction and commentary, of such quality that we would welcome his aid for all Cicero's works. His sources may have been partly senatorial proceedings, partly the speeches of Cicero's opponents. Milo was on trial for murdering Clodius when they met on the road near Bovillae, south of Rome (the two men were both leaders of unruly gangs); Cicero was determined to show that Clodius had planned to murder Milo, that he lay in ambush for him, and that Milo's slaves heroically defended their master against assault; much of his skill is directed to making this plausible. Throughout, Clodius is painted as a hot-headed thug who will stop at nothing; by contrast the narration of how Milo set out on his trip is given with deceptive simplicity:

> Meanwhile Clodius knew (it was not hard to find out) that Milo was required by both ritual and law to travel to Lanuvium on 18 January to nominate a priest. So he suddenly set out from Rome the day before to set a trap for Milo in a spot opposite his own estate. His departure from Rome meant that he had to abandon a rowdy public meeting at which his usual violence was sadly missed – a meeting he would never have abandoned had he not particularly wished to be present at the scene of the crime at the crucial moment.
>
> Milo, on the other hand, attended the senate that day and stayed until the meeting was concluded. He then went home, changed his clothes and shoes,

waited for a bit while his wife (as they do!) got herself ready, then finally set off at an hour by which Clodius could easily have returned to Rome, had he really wished to that day . . . (27–8, tr. Berry)

Asconius makes clear that Milo was in fact accompanied by numerous slaves including gladiators; that Cicero is misleading his audience as to Milo's time of departure; that Clodius did in fact have a perfectly legitimate reason for being out of Rome on that day. Asconius' own view was that the encounter happened by accident, but his circumstantial account makes clear that Milo was no innocent party, that Clodius was wounded several times and hurried by his entourage to a nearby inn, and that Milo and his men then attacked the inn and finished him off. The more we read Asconius, the more we appreciate Cicero's rhetorical skill in handling a virtually hopeless case. In fact the condemnation of Milo was certain from the start: Rome at this point was under martial law, Pompey and his soldiers were supervising the trial, and Cicero, while courageous to speak at all, did so with much less than his usual eloquence (the speech preserved is an improved and edited version, presumably an effort to redeem himself or restore his self-respect). Milo was condemned and exiled, but his choice of residence, Marseilles, had its compensations. Reading the version of the speech which Cicero eventually published and with remarkable tactlessness sent to him in exile, Milo replied that it was lucky this version had not been delivered, or he would not have had the chance to get acquainted with the excellent mullets that Marseilles had to offer (Dio 40.54).

  Cicero's writings about rhetoric, its theory and practice, have already been mentioned. The most important, the dialogue *On the (Ideal) Orator* in three books, is an attempt to enlarge the conception of the orator beyond the mechanical systems of the handbooks (though Cicero does communicate much technical and practical material in a readable form). The dialogue is set in the past (91 BC), in Cicero's youth, and the participants are major statesmen of the day from whom Cicero learned as a boy: one in particular, L. Licinius Crassus, was close to being his ideal. Cicero's most ambitious goal in this work is to reunite philosophy and oratory. He sees the orator not only as a skilled wordsmith, nor even just a 'good man skilled at speaking' (the Elder Cato's formulation), but as a wise and virtuous statesman, expert in all spheres that are relevant to the art of speech, above all in the law and in philosophy (ethics, he maintains, give the insight into audience psychology that the orator needs; political theory has obvious relevance to practice; physics and logic expand one's imaginative scope and techniques of argumentation). The dialogue is rich in subtle and suggestive discussions of many parts of the orator's task. Besides standard material such as the division of the speech into parts or the four virtues of oratory (linguistic correctness, clarity, ornament, appropriateness), there are many more unusual themes developed with wit and acumen. One fascinating passage which exploits the dramatic date and cast of characters is Antonius' account of how he succeeded in a particularly unpromising case, the trial of Norbanus in 95 BC: among the factors he mentions are his own personal interest in the case, admitted and claimed as a right; the introduction of his own personality and his previous record as persuasive factors; the use of the argument from expediency, supported by historical examples; the arousal of hatred by the prosecutor against the defendant; and the appeal to sentiment and to pity. The emphases here illuminate much that is central to the Roman courts and alien to our own (2.197–204). The vivid dramatic setting, and the combination of smooth and agreeable exposition and wealth of examples, makes *On the Orator* one of Cicero's finest achievements. By comparison the shorter *Brutus* and *Orator*, later and more polemical essays, are less successful, although the former is an important source of historical information and of Cicero's assessments of his predecessors and contemporaries.

V

The dramatic end to Cicero's life, and the establishment of the principate of Augustus a decade later, made it natural to see here a turning point in the history of oratory. This was already the view of Seneca the Elder, writing under Tiberius.[22] We have seen that Tacitus in the *Dialogue on Oratory* sees the subsequent period as one of decline, though one of the speakers, Aper, vigorously asserts the case for optimism and declares Cicero's style long-winded and out-dated ('who nowadays could have the patience for five books against Verres?' 20.1). Seneca and Tacitus are not alone, but some of the assertions of decline come in politically charged contexts; others are implicated in the educational polemic against training in increasingly artificial declamation. In any case, oratory was not stifled by the empire, though it is true that speakers had less chance of influencing policy at the highest levels.[23] No politician could neglect training as a speaker, and major court cases were frequent enough (Pliny mentions many of these, notably the prosecution of Priscus for provincial misgovernment, *Ep.* 2.11: he and Tacitus appeared for the prosecution). Some oratory was tainted by the power-politics of the time. Tacitus is harsh on the so-called *delatores* (informers), men who made almost a profession of denouncing individuals for offences against the regime or for in some way infringing on the dignity of the imperial family.

Although political debate even under good emperors was subject to restraint, another form, epideictic oratory, the rhetoric of praise (and blame) came into its own, especially in honorific speeches addressed to the ruler or other dignitaries. This practice had Ciceronian precedent, in the speeches he delivered under Caesar's dictatorship, of which the best known is the *For Marcellus* (September 46 BC). In that speech he broke silence in order to express appreciation to Caesar for his magnanimity in recalling the Pompeian Marcellus from exile. This speech is an uneasy mixture of tones and themes: fulsome praise of Caesar, whose achievements are said to be beyond adequate expression, measured regret for the recent conflicts, some low-key notes of implicit criticism; and exhortation, though generalized, to undertake much-needed reforms and lay strong foundations for the future beyond Caesar's own lifetime. Hypocrisy is too easy and crude a diagnosis: we see from a letter that Cicero was genuinely moved by Caesar's concession (*Letters to Friends* 4.4). But the difficulty of finding a suitable style in which to address the dictator is palpable; Cicero faces in prose some of the problems which the Augustan poets would partially surmount in verse.

This speech had strong influence on Pliny's much longer *Panegyric* over a century later (AD 100) – an influential work which inaugurates a whole genre (11 later instances survive).[24] This speech is a formal expression of gratitude to the Emperor Trajan for Pliny's election to the consulship: that such a speech would have been an impossibility under the Republic is self-evident but telling. At extravagant length Pliny enumerates Trajan's virtues and achievements, contrasting him throughout with Domitian, the most recent model of the Bad Emperor. Here too the praise is in part exhortation, the enumeration of virtues a programme for the monarch to follow. But there is no means by which that programme can be imposed: all the power lies with Trajan. In the same reign Tacitus wrote that he lived in one of those rare times 'in which you may think what you feel and say what you think' (*Histories* 1.1). Pliny's speech does not refute that claim, but does make clear that it needs sharp qualification. One passage in particular makes the changed condition clear through paradox: 'In your case we have no fears, and are all eagerness to follow your lead. You command us to be free; we will be so! You tell us to express ourselves openly; we shall do so!' (66.4). Polished though it is, much of the speech suffers from this excessive protestation of gratitude. We can understand Pliny sincerely wishing to celebrate Trajan's suppression of informers (34–5) or his generosity from his private purse (50); but the rhapsodic passage in which he thanks the emperor for graciously consenting to the senate's wishes by holding a third consulship seems disproportionately extended (56–62). We know from Pliny's letters that the speech was much expanded for publication. Had Trajan been subjected to the full 80-page version, he might well have had second thoughts about senatorial freedom of speech.

Although no political oratory survives between Cicero and Pliny, the *Panegyric* does not exhaust our knowledge of the rhetoric of the first century

AD. Apart from Tacitus' *Dialogue* already mentioned, many other sources supply evidence for the continuing impact of rhetoric on Roman society. Under Tiberius, the Elder Seneca (father of the philosopher) compiled a book of reminiscences of the best speakers he had heard in his lifetime, in response to the enthusiastic interest of his sons. In this work we find extracts from many unfamiliar figures and some famous ones (including the poet Ovid). Seneca's work provides essential evidence for the training and the taste of orators, and above all for the exercises in so-called declamation, a kind of practice oratory using fictional, historical or even mythical situations. Typical is the invention of a law which is then transgressed for good or defensible reasons: the aspiring orator must then argue one side or the other, and the more ingenious or novel his argument, the more he wins applause. The malign influence of this art has been exaggerated. It certainly pre-dated Cicero (who himself practised it), and indeed arguably goes back to the origins of rhetoric (p. 80 on Gorgias).

The other major figure, at the turn of the century, is the professional teacher Quintilian, an eminent professor of rhetoric and tutor to members of the imperial family. In advanced years he set out in 12 books the 'Institutio Oratoria', what the young orator should know: his massive work ranges from the minutiae of word-formation through the vast range of figures of speech to the moral ideals that should underlie the orator's art (he revived the formulation of Cato, who declared that the orator must be a good man skilled at speaking). He illuminates countless aspects of ancient education and reading practices. More systematic than Cicero's *On the Orator*, more humane than the Greek and Latin technical texts on rhetoric from later periods, his work has been called the Ariadne's thread through the labyrinth of ancient theory on the subject. Quintilian is not overtly political: writing as a successful dignitary under Domitian, he could not afford to be. As a result he makes a very effective contrast with Tacitus in the closely con-temporary *Dialogue*. Quintilian's expansive and donnish complacency seems less immediately persuasive than Tacitus' darker and sharper picture; but his contribution to Western literary culture is the more permanent one.[25]

VI

To follow the subsequent high points of ancient oratory we must move away from Rome to the provinces. Two new trends deserve mention. In the second century the Greek world, long dominated by Rome, seems to have enjoyed something of a literary revival. Massive civic expenditure, ostenta-tious erudition, extravagant oratory and large egos are all in evidence during the period often called the Second Sophistic, in which many orators and writers made themselves impossible to ignore. Major figures included Dio Chrysostom, Herodes Atticus, and Aelius Aristides: their careers were chronicled by Philostratus and their kind were cut down to size by Lucian.[26] The novelist Apuleius, writing in Latin though born and resident in North Africa, had been trained in this tradition and belongs in the same world. One of the oddest speeches of antiquity, and one of the funniest, is his self-defence on a charge of seducing a wealthy widow by use of magic.[27] The case was brought to trial in late 158 or early 159, and the speaker was almost certainly acquitted (otherwise he would hardly have published the speech). In good Ciceronian fashion, he evades the more serious aspects of the case and emphasizes the more trivial. He was accused of writing erotic and other poetry (no doubt this was meant to illustrate his louche character), and repudiates this with ease by citing innumerable precedents and delighting the audience with quotations from his harmless compositions (one of these is a snatch of verse accompanying a gift of toothpaste!). He uses the charges as springboards for satiric displays of his own learning and good taste, while deriding the boorish ignorance of his provincial antagonists. From another angle, he takes the opportunity to build up his status as a philosopher, with extensive quotation from Greek sources with which his accusers cannot cope but with which he and the proconsul presiding are familiar (Apuleius flatters the judge shamelessly throughout). In style, the work is unlike anything that precedes it – florid, full of exotic or invented words, lists and catalogues, allusive and poetic touches – but is itself surpassed by the peerless *Metamorphoses* of his later years (pp. 142–5).

A very different tone dominates the last group of works with which we are concerned. These works also derive from the second century, and are the product of Christian orators, writing in both Greek and Latin – the so-called 'apologists' or defenders of the new religion.[28] Christianity itself will figure more in a later chapter. Its relation to 'pagan' learning and so to oratory was complex. The unselfconscious simplicity of the first three Gospels contrasts with the philosophic depth of John and the rhetorical adroitness of Paul. On the one hand, Christians might repudiate the devious wiles of rhetoric and claim that the truth spoke for itself. On the other, they might, like the apologists, adopt the tools of classical artistry in order to make their cause more widely known and more acceptable.[29] The latter course was inevitable if they sought to influence imperial government. Several of these speeches are addressed to the emperor of the day (Justin to Antoninus Pius, Athenagoras to Marcus Aurelius and his colleague Verus), but this is probably a literary fiction. At most they are pamphlets, which it was hoped that eminent statesmen might read. There are arguments common to the various speeches, no doubt intended to refute widely held prejudices. In particular they reject the accusations of immorality, cannibalism (a wilful misrepresentation of the Eucharist?) and orgies, and assure the emperor that their reluctance to sacrifice on his behalf betokens no disloyalty. There is also much criticism of pagan religion. Here they redeploy many arguments against the gods of myth which earlier philosophers had devised (some of them figure already in Cicero's *On the Nature of the Gods*). Other arguments may have been more important to the insiders, to raise the spirits and strengthen the belief of new recruits: such are the arguments about the relation of Christianity to Judaism, or on the fulfilment of Old Testament prophecies by Christ, and the frequent anticipations of the Second Coming.

The Greek speeches are less memorable than the incomparable oration by the first Latin apologist, the theologian Tertullian (*c*.197), which is more learned, more aggressive and more dynamic in style than those of his predecessors. This speech contains many memorable formulations (e.g. that the blood of the martyrs is the seed of Christianity, 50), and sets forth important arguments which would have lasting influence (e.g. that the Roman Empire has a special purpose in God's design: 32). It is defiant rather than diplomatic: a Roman magistrate who read it would most probably have concluded that the sect its author was defending consisted of dangerous fanatics. Here is a typically vigorous passage, in which he begins by explaining his refusal to pray to any but the true God.

> All this I cannot ask of any other, but only of Him, from whom I know I shall receive it, since he it is alone who gives and I am one to whom the gift is due – I his servant, who alone worships him, who for his teaching am slain, who offer to him that rich and better sacrifice which he himself commanded: I mean prayer, proceeding from flesh pure, soul innocent, spirit holy. Not grains of incense worth a penny, not tears of an Arabian tree, not a couple of drops of wine, not the blood of a decrepit ox that longs for death, and on top of all that filth a vile conscience – indeed I wonder, when the most depraved of priests are examining the victims at your sacrifices, why the hearts of the victims, not the sacrificers, are the ones being inspected! While thus, then, we spread ourselves before God, let the hooks pierce us, the swords gash our throats, the beasts leap on us. The very posture of a Christian at prayer is readiness for any torture. Go to it, excellent magistrates, rack out the soul that prays to God for the Emperor. Here you will find the 'crime' – where the truth of God and devotion to God dwell. (30, Loeb tr. adapted)

A new and powerful theme, with a long and often grim future, has joined the rhetorical repertoire.

We have surveyed the mainstream history of oratory, and given some attention to the ways in which it influenced other genres. Other instances will figure elsewhere, for rhetoric was the basis of education throughout antiquity, and both the practice and the critical vocabulary of other genres were shaped on the model of rhetorical analysis. Rhetorical style might even provide a means to interpret character. Seneca diagnosed Maecenas' personality as dissolute and effeminate on the basis of his self-indulgent poetic technique: the style is the man (*Letters* 114). Rhetoric was often criticized in the ancient world: as inflated bombast, as ignorance feigning expertise, as hypocrisy, or as a means of creating artificial situations and expressions, remote from life's practicalities. From at least the Romantic era onwards it has been seen as inimical to values such as spontaneity and sincerity in art, or as promoting stock responses which inhibit truer understanding of art or life. The positive side should also be allowed some voice. The schooling orators received in delivery, the degree to which they trained their memory, are techniques more relevant in an oral culture, but the achievements of the most successful are still enviable today. More important, rhetorical training promoted fluency and articulacy in debate, skill at organizing and presenting a complex argument, together with an ability, if not to see, at least to argue, more than one side of a question; it sharpened the capacity to detect falsehoods or suspect motives; it encouraged an alertness to precise wording and to the distinctions between related terms; it fuelled the mind with a rich store of apt examples and historic (or semi-historic) precedents. The greater minds were aware that words must not be divorced from thought, and that their own case must be examined as rigorously as their opponent's. The greatest temptation for the skilled orator is to end up deceiving himself.

4

History, Biography and Fiction

To be ignorant of what happened before you were born is to remain forever a child.

Cicero, *Orator* 120

I

A characteristically colourful story from Herodotus alerts us to some of the most striking features and problems in ancient historical writing. A propos of a reference he has made (itself digressive) to the Corinthian ruler Periander, he goes on to tell of an event which took place in his time: how Arion of Lesbos, a rich, successful musician and singer, was sailing from Tarentum to Corinth when the sailors carrying him decided to kill him for his money and dump his body. He pleaded for his life but was getting nowhere, until he asked for the opportunity to give them a song, dressed in his full singing outfit, and promised he would then jump overboard. The crew, pleased at the thought of enjoying a special performance by the Pavarotti of the day, agreed to this; Arion gave them his star turn, leaped into the sea, and was lucky enough to be picked up by a dolphin which conveyed him safely to Corinth ahead of the sailors. He told the whole story to Periander, who after initial scepticism made sure to question the crew on their return, and swiftly exposed their guilt. 'That is the story as the Corinthians and Lesbians tell it,' concludes Herodotus. 'There is moreover at Taenarum today an offering by Arion in the temple, a small bronze figure of a man on a dolphin.'[1]

Herodotus is traditionally the father of history, but already in ancient times he was also branded a liar, or in kinder terms a 'teller of stories' (*fabulae*, Cic. *On the Laws* 1.5). But the story of Arion highlights a number of issues that recur in other writers besides Herodotus. First, it is a marvel, an event which is perhaps not impossible but certainly not something that happens every day. Second, it happens not just to any old traveller but to a figure famous in his own right, a distinguished singer, and one who is in some way attached to the court of another famous man, Periander: in ancient historical writing, major figures tend to attract one another. Elsewhere Herodotus brings together the wise Solon and King Croesus, although chronologically this encounter is hard to accept. Third, it is not just an incident but makes a story, and one with a moral: the crew resolve to commit a crime, that crime is miraculously averted, and their guilt is exposed, leading to punishment. Retribution and revenge are major narrative forces in Herodotus and elsewhere; often, as here, they involve a satisfying didactic element: crime does not pay. Fourth, the story is entertaining in its own right rather than historically significant. It has no consequences, but is told simply because it is enjoyable and makes a moral point. Fifth, the event is commemorated by a monument, the offering allegedly dedicated by Arion. It is plausible enough that this object existed, though it may not have been inscribed or definitely connected with Arion; it may indeed be the origin of the tale itself, invented to explain what was represented. This is 'aetiology', seeking to answer the questions: 'Where did this come from? How did this dedication (or this building, or ritual, or custom) come about?' The surviving relics of the past are the stuff of historical enquiry. Herodotus often says that such and such an object is still there 'visible in my time', as a kind of testimony to the validity of his account. Croesus' dedications at Delphi prompt questions such as: 'Who was Croesus? In what circumstances did he send such lavish gifts?' The same process is visible in much Roman historical writing, especially treating the early period.

Ancient historians were not equipped with modern archaeological methods: they did not excavate or carbon-date, nor could they normally translate older languages such as Linear B or Etruscan, or deal easily with living languages not their own. Herodotus probably spoke neither Egyptian nor any of the languages spoken by Persians, although he wrote at great length about these cultures. The historians were dependent either on oral tradition, which might pass on accounts second-hand or at many removes, or on written works, usually those of earlier historians (they also tried to use other sources, notably poetic texts, but were aware that this was difficult material to use). Books were rarer, harder to obtain, and slower work to read than in modern literate cultures. 'Research' for Herodotus meant firstly going to places and seeing for himself; second-best was to obtain hearsay accounts, if possible from eyewitnesses. Thucydides endorsed this and stressed the need to cross-check accounts. Historians were aware that their informants might be biased. The ideal of historical impartiality was formulated early, seldom sustained in practice. They applied their knowledge of human nature, tested accounts by the criterion of plausibility and probability: certainty was rare. But the fundamental problem for the ancient historian dealing with events he had not witnessed, particularly events of long ago, was the near-impossibility of confirming or refuting the inherited tradition. Herodotus might be sceptical about the story of Arion, but how could he prove it did not happen? In any case it was worth preserving. Sometimes conflicting accounts were told, and the historian adjudicated between them. In all of this there are the seeds of research as we know it, but these pioneers faced formidable obstacles.

There were also different assumptions as to what history should be. Homer's *Iliad*, read as a confrontation between East and West, is a key model for Herodotus, and Thucydides emulates both. The epic influence cast a long shadow. Most important, it imposed a conception of leaders, warfare and political struggles as the central matter of history. Second, it encouraged a sense of history as a dignified genre which should commemorate and celebrate great deeds, a genre with serious, even tragic resonances and a didactic tendency which was often explicit (especially at Rome). Third, it made it inevitable that history should be a *narrative*: other forms of exploration of the past were not unknown, but looked down on. 'I am not disposed,' wrote Cato haughtily, 'to report what appears on the tablet of the pontifex maximus, such as how often the price of food goes up, how often a cloud or something else eclipses the moon or the sun' (*Origins*, F77 P.). History had to be more than a catalogue of magistrates or dates. The result was artistically more impressive but often deprived modern scholars of factual data which the ancient historians thought unsuitable or unreadable. Finally, the awareness of epic poetry as part of the background meant that the relation of historical writing to myth remained an uneasy one. Myths were traditions, and therefore important; the historians believed that the myths in epic and elsewhere preserved some form of historical facts, but they knew that poets exaggerated and recognized that the supernatural elements must be reduced or explained away if history was to emerge. Herodotus retold many mythical tales, Thucydides was much warier; later writers reinstated them in order to make 'universal histories' more complete. Poetry and prose might treat the same material: Ennius' epic poem bore the title *Annales*, meaning 'year-by-year' – that is, a chronological account of history. It is doubtful that any of the Roman historians recognized how much of their history was in fact a glorious myth.

A final general point concerns the status of the writers. It is an important feature of Greek historical writing that most of the major figures were not state employees or court historians; they wrote as independent agents, and whatever axes they ground were their own, not the result of a patron's preferences. Many of them wrote, like Thucydides, while in exile from their own homeland. At Rome the situation was different: apart from Livy, all the major historians were of senatorial rank and wrote their works after reaching mature years in service to the state, whether as statesmen or generals or both. Even Livy, though seemingly not a figure of distinction except for his writing, was clearly a member of the ruling class, on friendly terms with the Emperor Augustus (Tacitus, *Annals* 4.34). Roman politics and Rome's interests or ambitions are central to these men's works; in general, Greek historians adopted a more independent voice and a wider perspective.

II

Some of these general issues will recur, but we must now focus on a few of the key figures of the historical tradition. Time has dealt unevenly with them: Herodotus, Thucydides and Xenophon survive complete (though Thucydides' work was never finished), but Polybius' massive history is truncated; of 142 books of Livy only 35 survive, and we have lost over half of Tacitus' *Histories* and perhaps a third of his *Annals*. The names of many other major and minor historians are known, but some are barely more than names: short extracts ('fragments') and summaries or critical references are often all we have to represent influential writers (for Greek, most of these were assembled and discussed by Felix Jacoby in one of the greatest works of classical scholarship[2]). 'Fragmentary' historians are relevant from the beginning, for Herodotus certainly had predecessors, though they almost certainly tackled less ambitious topics and on a smaller scale than he. One whom he names is Hecataeus, whose works on genealogy and on the geography of the Mediterranean lands represent an effort to order material, temporally and spatially. Herodotus certainly used his works, but the new and crucial ingredient was a large theme: the wars between Persia and the West. Henceforth the great subject (often treated at great length) became mandatory for the historian.

Although Herodotus' *History*[3] chronicles the rise of Persia, its gradual expansion under a series of kings, the revolt of Ionia, the first invasion by Darius, and finally the failure of Xerxes' invasion of Greece (480–79), the sequence of his work is not straightforwardly chronological or geographical, although it involves elements of both. The author in fact includes, and even seems to relish (4.30.1), extended digressions on all manner of subjects, particularly geographical, ethnographical and mythological excursus, incidental stories about characters whose names have come up, and accounts of traditions. Often these passages seem to have no more than a tangential relation to their context or to Herodotus' main subject. But certain motifs recur, such as Greek freedom and Persian despotism, the instability of prosperity, the

perils which attend arrogance or violent action, or the affinities and mis-
understandings between different cultures. From the ethnographic passages in
particular it emerges that the history is from one point of view an examination
of human *nomoi* – not only laws but values, codes of practice, rituals and
beliefs – of a remarkably open-minded kind (later he was branded a lover of
barbarians). Whether or not the author has seen all that he describes (he
himself admits that there is much he has not), he is fascinated by other ways
and other places. He has his preferences (not always Greek), but is moderate and selective in explicit value judgements. A key passage in which he
reflects on the relativity of values also shows that this conclusion is far from
leading him to underrate their importance.

> In view of all this, I have no doubt whatever that Cambyses was completely
> out of his mind; it is the only possible explanation of his assault upon, and
> mockery of, everything which ancient law and custom have made sacred in
> Egypt. For if anyone, no matter who, were given the opportunity of choosing
> from amongst all the nations in the world the beliefs which he thought best,
> he would inevitably, after careful consideration of the relative merits, choose
> those of his own country. Everyone without exception believes his own native
> customs, and the religion he was brought up in, to be the best, and that being
> so it is unlikely that anyone but a madman would mock at such things. There
> is abundant evidence that this is the universal feeling about the ancient
> customs of one's country. One might recall, in particular, an account told of
> Darius. When he was king of Persia, he summoned the Greeks who happened
> to be present at his court and asked them what they would take to eat the
> dead bodies of their fathers. They replied that they would not do it for any
> money in the world. Later, in the presence of the Greeks, and through an
> interpreter, so that they could understand what was said, he asked some
> Indians, of the tribe called Callatiae, who do in fact eat their parents' dead
> bodies, what they would take to burn them. They uttered a cry of horror and
> forbade him to mention such a dreadful thing. One can see by this what
> custom can do, and Pindar, in my opinion, was right when he called it 'King
> of all'. (3.38, tr. J. Marincola)

Interest in *nomoi* overlaps with his central political interests: how men
behave under different types of government, how different societies organize
themselves in peace and in war, are questions of obvious importance for
his main theme – what qualities of mind, body, constitution or climate go
to explain the Greeks' unexpected achievement in repulsing the massive
Persian invasion force?

The range and diversity of Herodotus' work are incomparable, and it is
inexhaustibly entertaining. We are shown strange animals, weird climatic
conditions; we hear of the circumnavigation of Africa and the contribution of the Nile to the Egyptian coastline. He tells many stories for their

own sake (often they are memorable for their humorous aspect, even their punch-lines, as with the anecdote of Hippocleides, who 'danced away his marriage', 6.129), and several times notes that he does not necessarily endorse all that he reports: these accounts are 'what people say'. His horizons are wider than those of most other historians in antiquity. He will tell of small cities as well as great, minor figures as well as kings and tyrants; he gives ample space to women and even children (Thucydides bears much of the responsibility for the narrowing of history's scope). His is cultural history, not just political and military: Arion is not the only artist he mentions.

There is a bleakness in Herodotus' outlook, with his recognition that states which were great in time past are now small, and that good fortune does not remain in the same place (1.5). This sombre attitude (which is not unmixed with a love of life and a fascination with new discoveries) gives depth to his traveller-tales and romantic episodes. His outlook seems close to that of Sophocles, who is said to have known the historian. Most memorable is the scene in which Xerxes surveys his mighty army and admires it, then bursts into tears. When his uncle Artabanus asks what is the matter, he replies that 'it came into my mind how pitifully short human life is – for of all these thousands of men, not one will be alive in a hundred years' time.' Artabanus replies:

> Yet we suffer sadder things in life even than that. Short as it is, there is not a man in the world, either here or elsewhere, who is happy enough not to wish – not once in his life but repeatedly – to be dead rather than alive. Troubles come, diseases afflict us; and this makes life, despite its brevity, seem all too long. So heavy is the burden of it that death is a refuge which we all desire, and it is common proof that God, who gave us a taste of this world's sweetness, has been jealous in the giving. (7.46)

This passage illustrates two other features of his work. One is the use of dramatic speeches and dialogue. Herodotus' narrative includes an enormous cast of characters, and many of them speak or engage in dialogue of various kinds. In some places he presents extended speeches (Solon and Croesus; the debate among the Persian nobles on the virtues of different constitutions; Xerxes and his counsellors debating the advisability of invading Greece). Elsewhere rapid dialogue serves to accelerate a vivid narrative, as at the critical moment in a palace conspiracy in Persia:

> It was dark in the room, and Darius, standing over the two men locked together on the floor, hesitated to intervene For he was afraid that, if he struck, he might kill the wrong man. But Gobryas, aware of his hesitation, cried out: 'What's your hand for – if you don't use it?'
> 'I dare not strike', said Darius, for fear of killing you.'

'Fear nothing,' answered Gobryas, 'spit both of us at once if need be.'
Darius then drove his dagger home – by luck into the body of the Magus.
(3.78)

The inclusion of speeches became a standard narrative device used by historians even when there can have been no evidence for them (in one scene Herodotus even reconstructs the pillow-talk between Darius of Persia and his chief wife (3.134)). Again this is part of the Homeric inheritance. Thucydides was to adopt stricter criteria for including speeches, but in both writers we can see that they are used to emphasize significant moments, to expose underlying motives, and to point to contradictions, delusions and hypocrisy in the speakers' attitudes.

The other point illustrated by Artabanus' speech is the underlying religious feeling that runs through Herodotus' work. Yet the gods are not presented as openly intervening in the world of human events; rather, dreams, omens and particularly oracles convey (however opaquely) signs and warnings to human agents. There are other strands, however, in Herodotus' thinking, which have a more 'modern' feel to them and which complicate his theological picture. He recognizes a qualitative difference between mythological and historical narrative (3.122); he applies the notion of probability or plausibility to stories about religious matters (3.33, etc.), and plays with rationalizations of folk-tale and myth (1.122, 2.57.1–2); he does not generally name gods in the narrative proper, nor does he view them in anthropomorphic terms. His identification of gods across cultures, and his general statement that he believes all mankind has an equal share in knowledge of the divine (2.3.2), show him to be no simple believer. Piety and scientific caution are pleasantly blended in the following comment.

> The natives of Thessaly have a tradition that the gorge which forms the outlet for the river was made by Poseidon, and the story is a reasonable one; for if one believes that it is Poseidon who shakes the earth and that chasms caused by earthquakes are attributable to him, then the mere sight of this place would be enough to make one say that it is Poseidon's handiwork. It certainly appeared to me that the cleft in the mountain had been caused by an earthquake. (7.129)

It does look as though Herodotus moved easily between an older, more poetic and numinous set of concepts and a range of ideas of the kind which we associate with Ionian philosophy. Just as geographically a man born in Halicarnassus was well-placed to understand both mainland Greeks and Lydians or Persians, so Herodotus, born probably in the 490s, was on the cusp between the archaic period and the new intellectual world of the sophists and Socrates. More than any of his successors, however, he is a true original, as well as being a narrator of genius.

Thucydides the Athenian, who wrote a history of the great war between Athens and Sparta (the 'Peloponnesian War' 431–404), died leaving the story incomplete, for he brought the narrative down only to 411; a few passages make clear he lived to see the defeat of Athens.[4] He is in important ways the heir of Herodotus, but at first sight the differences may seem more evident than the resemblances. Herodotus' narrative took him far afield in time and place, embracing Scythia, Babylonia, India, Egypt and Italy, and covering in a selective and unsystematic way over a hundred years of tradition, as well as legendary material going back much further. Thucydides restricted himself to contemporary Greece and presented a tightly controlled war-narrative in annalistic form (each year narrated in sequence), preceded by a book which presented essential background, particularly the causes of the war. Herodotus' theme took him far beyond the limited perspectives of the Greek world; Thucydides was concerned with the conflict between Athens and Sparta and their allies. Whereas Herodotus relished the personal and anecdotal, Thucydides has a much more restricted frame of reference. He deals in detail only with the key players, the leaders and politicians of the two sides, and even the more colourful political figures (such as the notoriously dissipated Alcibiades) are seen only in their public roles. Some of these features may be explained by reaction against Herodotus, whom Thucydides probably thought undisciplined and over-credulous: in a famous passage he remarks that the absence of the storytelling element may put off readers, but that he will be content if others find his account *useful* (1.22). That hope is connected with his belief that the events he recorded were in some way typical, that they would recur in comparable forms 'for as long as human nature remains the same'. The *History* of Thucydides will give not practical advice so much as access to understanding of human nature at a general level, and insight into the processes of history. Later practitioners such as Polybius took him to mean something more trite and far-fetched, and supposed that history could be a manual for the aspiring politician.

Personal evaluations and judgements are frequent in Herodotus ('There is one custom among the Babylonians which is altogether shameful . . .' (i.e. temple-prostitution), 1.199); by contrast Thucydides veils his own opinions and employs in much of his work a coldly analytical (though far from passionless) manner which has deceived many readers into thinking of him as the most objective of historians. Thucydides is an austere writer, exact and detailed in his record of contemporary events, and unusually lucid in his accounts of military campaigns (he himself was a general), but the impression which he gives of god-like impartiality is largely the result of a highly controlled self-presentation. In particular, his methodological chapters have impressed moderns with their emphasis on accuracy and confirmation through witnesses, combined with his dismissal of popular opinion. His efforts to distinguish immediate causes (the spark-points of the war) from the deeper underlying causes represent a powerful analytic tool. He writes with great authority, only rarely admitting uncertainty; when he fails to find out what he wants we sense his frustration: 'I was unable to record the numbers of the Spartan forces because of the secretiveness of their society' (5.68). Unlike Herodotus, he imposes an authorial view rather than repeating and attributing variant versions so that the reader can judge. A striking indicator of his drive towards apparent objectivity is the fact that in the one episode of the war in which he himself appears as a participant, he describes his activities in the third person (an influential technique, used by Caesar and others). But he himself was exiled because of a military failure, and subsequently lived among Athens' enemies. He cannot have been either detached from or indifferent to Athenian fortunes, but his attitude is not a simple one.

Although the *History* includes a great deal of narration of specific campaigns, its larger theme is imperial Athens at its full power and how that power declined under pressure of war and because of inadequate leadership. Thucydides clearly admired the great statesman Pericles, who led Athens into war but died soon after its inception; his successors are systematically exposed as inferior. The power and greatness of Athens are described in many speeches – critically by the Corinthians (as a nation which never rests or allows any others to do so), idealistically by Pericles in the famous 'funeral speech' in which he praises the Athenian way of life. Much of the work is concerned to show the gap between the ideal image of Athens and the brutal reality of imperialism made still harsher by war ('war is a violent teacher' is one of his most famous sayings: 3.82.2). Episodes of unforgettable intensity present the weakening of Athenian morale and power. One of the most memorable is the description of the plague which ravaged Athens early in the war, from which he suffered himself but survived, and which he analyses with a clinical detail that owes something to the emerging medical literature ('all the kinds of extrusions of bile that have been given names by the physicians' 2.49.3); another is the examination of the psychology of civil war, using the particularly bloodthirsty example of Corcyra as a paradigm (3.80–2). In both cases he examines the consequences for morale and morality. The careful self-discipline of his style does not exclude dramatic and suspenseful narrative, with a capacity to communicate the effect of despair and suffering. His narrative gifts as much as his accuracy of detail ensured that later writers took his work as definitive (within its own carefully defined limits). 'He sometimes makes the sufferings appear so cruel, so terrible, so piteous as to leave no room for historians or poets to surpass him' (Dionysius, *On Thucydides* 15). Nowhere is this more brilliantly achieved than in books 6 and 7, his account of the rash and disastrous Athenian expedition in Sicily, which ended in complete defeat ('few out of many returned home'). Here is a particularly vivid and appalling moment from the Athenians' humiliating retreat:

> The Athenians pushed on for the River Asinarus, impelled by the attacks made upon them from every side by a numerous cavalry and the swarm of other arms, supposing that they should breathe more freely if once across the river, and driven on also by their exhaustion and craving for water. Once there they rushed in, and all order was at an end, each man wanting to cross first, and the attacks of the enemy making it difficult to cross at all; forced to huddle together, they fell against and trampled one another, some dying immediately upon the javelins, others getting entangled together and stumbling over the articles of baggage, without being able to rise again. Meanwhile the opposite bank, which was steep, was lined by the Syracusans, who showered missiles down upon the Athenians, most of them drinking greedily and heaped together in disorder in the hollow bed of the river. The Peloponnesians also came down and butchered them, especially those in the water, which was thus immediately spoiled, but which they went on drinking just the same, mud and all, bloody as it was, most even fighting to have it.
>
>   At last, when many dead now lay piled one upon another in the stream, and part of the army had been destroyed at the river, and the few that escaped from there had been cut off by the cavalry, Nicias surrendered himself to Gylippus, whom he trusted more than he did the Syracusans, and told him and the Spartans to do what they liked with him, but to stop the slaughter of the soldiers. (Thuc. 7.84–5, tr. Crawley)

Thucydides' narrative of this campaign is perhaps the high point of ancient military history, and the damning yet sympathetic characterization of Nicias, the virtuous but weak and vacillating general, is a brilliant portrait.

Thucydides' other great innovation is in his use of speeches. Whereas Herodotus included many short exchanges and incidental direct speech, Thucydides' with few exceptions are formalized, complex rhetorical set pieces in a rich, dense style, designed to explore the abstract issues involved in political and military conflict and to shed light on the narrative. Often they are antithetical, with one speaker responding to another: Cleon and Diodotus, Nicias and Alcibiades (but no one counters Pericles' speeches). We see the influence of contemporary formal rhetoric, but Thucydides' argumentation is subtler and more involved. It is also (despite his claim that the speeches are based on what was actually said) startlingly ruthless. Speakers vary, but for many figures on the Thucydidean stage politics is not a matter of lofty aims and loyalties but about the possession and use of power. No writer dramatizes so shockingly the naked thinking of *Realpolitik* ('you now possess an empire that is like a tyranny, one that it may have been wrong to take but it is unsafe to surrender' 2. 63). Perhaps the Athenians and others of his day did not actually say these things, but he clearly saw himself as presenting the realities behind the slogans. The historian as critic, digging beneath superficialities and exposing ugly truths, is a Thucydidean legacy of first importance (such analyses deeply influenced Sallust and Tacitus). The bleakness of this approach may rest on both disenchantment and a changed religious world. Thucydides is aware of religious motivations but tends to underplay them. Sophist-trained intellectualism is to the fore when he makes the Athenians speak as follows to the citizens of Melos, prior to their mass execution:

> Of the gods we believe, and of men we know, that by a necessary law of their nature they rule wherever they can. It is not as though we were the first to make this law . . . all we do is make use of it, knowing that you and everyone else, having the same power as we have, would act in the same way. (5.105)

Thucydides can be criticized for his emphases and omissions, and sometimes modern discoveries (inscriptions, etc.) enable us to amend and supplement him in important ways. But he is supreme among ancient writers on war and imperialism, and his style because of its very restraint has astonishing intensity.

III

The importance of Thucydides is swiftly demonstrated by the fact that several fourth-century historians began their narratives where he left off – even though this terminal point was clearly accidental. Some are hardly more than names (in the case of the Oxyrhynchus historian we lack even the name, though what portions we have show a writer of quality). The only continuator to survive intact is Xenophon, a well-off and cultivated Athenian and another military man. His *Hellenica* or *History of Greek Affairs* covers the end of the Peloponnesian war and the next 40 years, but patchily and with odd biases or misapprehensions.[5] It is a confusing period and Xenophon does not give us the help we really need; he can tell a good story but not give us a sense of the larger developments. The work was not nearly as influential as his other writings, especially the *Anabasis* (*Journey Up-country*), a vivid and intriguing narrative of his journey into and back from Asia Minor on an abortive mercenary expedition which failed to install the younger Cyrus on the throne of Persia and had then to find its way home, partly under Xenophon's command. Ethnography and diplomacy mingle with perennial problems of military discipline in a story from which Xenophon emerges with nearly as much credit as he thought he deserved. His other major work is the *Cyropaedia*, a largely fictitious work on the early life and upbringing of another Cyrus, the founder of the Persian empire, now a near-legend who could be used as a moral exemplar. This long and rather tediously moralizing work had great influence on the novel (p. 135) and also on what is sometimes called the 'mirror for princes' tradition (works in which writers tried to present in attractive ways not-so-subtle teachings for the monarchs of their day). Much shorter is his *Agesilaus*, a rhetorical eulogy of the Spartan king who had taken up Xenophon and who also figures in the *Hellenica*. Eulogy of this kind is the root of biography.[6]

Other forms of historical writing developed in the fourth century, partly in response to the changing times. The omnivorous mind of Aristotle turned its attention to compiling a 'database' of Greek states' constitutions as readily as to assembling anomalies of zoology and botany. The *Constitution of Athens* is the one surviving example, and tells us much we are glad to know, but it is clearly a work of imperfect synthesis, and the absence of historical acumen leads many to attribute it to a research pupil rather than Aristotle himself. Local histories, of Athens and elsewhere, were abundant. But the new tendency was for history to turn more to great men. There was no single 'hero' to Herodotus, and in Thucydides Pericles only figures in the first two books, subsequently present in the work as a neglected ghost; but Theopompus, an acerbic figure of the mid-fourth century, turned from writing *Hellenica* to *Philippica*, a work focused at least partly on the Macedonian King Philip II, who in the mid-century was expanding his influence throughout Greece; in 338 he conquered the mainland at the battle of Chaeronea. But Theopompus, a writer of whom we would gladly know much more, was no sycophant: the racy fragments that survive show him to have portrayed the Macedonian court in caustic and satirical terms ('for though by nature they slayed men, by their habits they got laid by men' 115F225).[7] The historian Callisthenes, who accompanied Philip's son Alexander on his conquests, lost both his historical integrity and his life. He was notorious for inventing portentous fictions to adorn his master's expeditions: the Pamphylian sea drew back its waves, making way for Alexander (124F31), and birds guided the chosen one on his way to consult the oracle of Ammon (F14). But in the end he rebelled against Alexander's Orientalizing megalomania, and was put to death.

Alexander's conquests were important for history in other ways. Not only was he himself a charismatic figure of fiery personality and amazing achievements, but he opened up a vast new field for historical and geographical study, spreading Greek cities across the Middle East and beyond. He created the 'Hellenistic world', that is a world in which some people, some of the time, wanted to *Hellenize* or 'go Greek' and learn about Greek culture. The age is past when this could be seen as a wholly civilizing process: Alexander and his successors sought glory and loot. But many writers gained new opportunities. Greeks wrote about the new lands they could explore (Megasthenes on India); some found it easier to describe imaginary countries than real ones. Native writers also composed works in Greek, in an effort to explain their cultures to the Graeco-Macedonian rulers (Manetho in Ptolemaic Egypt, Berossus in Babylon). The need for new ethnographic writing fuelled a Herodotean revival.[8] Geography becomes an instrument of empire: to map a nation is one step towards conquering it. As for Alexander himself, his career was narrated by many, with differing perspectives, but all earlier accounts are lost; our main narrative, the much later Arrian (second century AD), is a work of industry not of insight, though it can be supplemented by many other late sources, notably one of the longest of all Plutarch's biographies. But the personality of Alexander is beyond recovery, not that that will inhibit more attempts.[9]

There is a tradition that the Romans sent an embassy to Alexander in 323, shortly before his death (Arrian 7.15.4–6). Certainly by that date the Greeks knew of the rising power in Italy. Even Hesiod in the *Theogony* mentions Agrius and Latinus as sons of Odysseus by Circe, 'and they ruled over the famous Tyrsenians' (Etruscans). There were Greek colonists in Sicily and southern. Italy (Magna Graecia) from the eighth century. Callimachus in the third century tells a Roman story in his *Aetia*. The Sicilian historian Timaeus, writing a history of the West while in exile at Athens, was the first Greek historian to give a summary account of Roman history, down to 264 BC, and he wrote a separate monograph on Rome's wars with Pyrrhus of Epirus. By 275, when Pyrrhus withdrew from his attempt to invade Italy because of the cost in manpower (hence the term 'Pyrrhic victory', meaning one so costly that it is almost as bad as a defeat), Rome was becoming a major player in the Mediterranean; over the next century she won victories over Carthage, and finally destroyed her arch-enemy in 146. During the same period her influence over the Greek world was hugely extended. The culminating war with Perseus of Macedon ended with the battle of Pydna in 168, after which Roman control of Greece was swiftly consolidated. 'Liberated' from Macedon, Greece fell under the Roman yoke. Among the many hostages taken to Rome by Aemilius Paulus, the victor of Pydna, was the soldier-diplomat Polybius, who spent many years in Rome and came to admire the power that had defeated his people.

Polybius' *History* took up the tale of Rome's rise from where Timaeus had stopped, covering the period 264–146 BC.[10] Like Plutarch later, he had a dual purpose, to explain Rome to the Greeks and Greece to the Romans; but the former dominates. In 40 books he recounted the rise of Rome to empire, including the wars with Carthage and the subjugation of Greece. The opening of his work (books 1–5 and much of book 6) survives, together with extensive extracts from the remainder. Polybius never became as famous a writer as Herodotus and Thucydides; for one thing, his style is too lumpy and long-winded. He is a powerful polemicist and loses no opportunity to denounce his predecessors (especially Timaeus, whose prestige he despised and feared). But the tale he tells is one of immense drama and scope, full of exciting episodes and guided by two powerful ideas – the Roman appetite for power, which drove them on to extend their empire, and the achievement to which that had led – the unification of the 'inhabited world' (by which he meant the Mediterranean and Asia Minor). Polybius saw that because of the scale of Roman conquest all history within that sphere was now interlinked and must be treated together; his massive narrative advances in stages, following events in one area then turning to explain how matters were developing in another. This results in some dramatic cliff-hangers, as at the end of book 3 where he suspends the account of the Rome–Carthage conflict at a terrifying moment, after the disaster of Cannae (216 BC), when the Romans are expecting Hannibal to march triumphantly on Rome itself.

Polybius was concerned to analyse the sources of Roman power. We see something of his thinking in book 6, which was one of several non-narrative books (a historiographical innovation). There he considers the Roman constitution (which he saw as a kind of hybrid, a 'mixed constitution', combining democratic, oligarchic and monarchic elements) and the military structures of the army. This kind of social-structural analysis is unusual in ancient history, and although the results may be questionable he deserves credit for making the attempt. Many of his points about Roman morale and discipline, and how these are reinforced by legal provisions and custom, go deeper than the conventional self-praise we find in some of the Roman moralists; but he also recognized that the high standards of Roman morality were decaying and that ruling an empire brought danger of both corruption and ambition (e.g. 31.25, cf. 18.35). It is a mistake to dismiss such analysis as trite moralizing; Polybius documents what he says from his own experience and observation, and by the end of his career he was mixing with the highest level of Roman aristocracy. The loss of his later narrative, where his own knowledge would have played a fuller part, is one of the most regrettable in the historical record. Although he over-praises his friends the Scipios (and himself), his work remains a sober and impressive narrative of a key period. In a work dominated by war, his evident expertise in the tactics and techniques of his time inspires confidence in his military narrative. His analysis of the superiority of the Roman legion to the Macedonian phalanx reminds us that wars are won with more than moral superiority (18.28–31), and it does not surprise us that he can describe a detailed system of fire-signalling that he himself had invented (10.43–7)![11]

IV

Rome's prominence in the Mediterannean came at a late stage after a long climb from obscurity; the traditional date of foundation was 753, whereas Polybius was writing in the mid-second century BC, as a privileged outsider. What did the Romans themselves know and say about their past?

Over 500 years elapsed between the foundation and the first known Roman historian, Fabius Pictor (fl. 216), who composed a work in Greek that Polybius knew and used. Like so many works, it is now lost; so is the first history in Latin, by Cato the Censor, entitled *Origins*; so are all the overall histories of Rome by Romans prior to Livy, who began his work in the 20s BC. Livy's enormous work eclipsed them: ancient critics were in no doubt about his superiority as a stylist.[12] Livy managed to chronicle the entire history 'from the founding of the city', drawing on many earlier writers, but he needed 142 books and may have taken as much as 40 years to do it. Notable in his work is the uneven coverage: the first book covers the time when Rome was ruled by kings, a period which the Romans estimated as nearly 250 years; book 5 takes us down to the sack of Rome by the Gauls in 390; by book 21 we have already reached the war with Hannibal (218). Clearly Livy had far more material and wrote more extensively on the later period. (Dionysius of Halicarnassus, a Greek contemporary who wrote voluminously on early Rome, makes Livy look concise, but the length of his treatment is due to rhetorical expansion, rather than added information.)

Livy himself comments on the difficulties he faced. He allowed that the early years were open to neither confirmation nor refutation: 'more pleasing poetic fictions than reliable records of historical events' (preface); he acknowledged that events before the Gallic sack were more obscure because so much was lost when the city was destroyed by fire (6.1). But had full records survived, Livy was not the man to seek them out or master them. Writing on so great a scale, he was inevitably dependent on his predecessors, and often we can see the process of adaptation at work (especially in the books where he is using surviving portions of Polybius).

A framework for history seems to have been provided by the so-called *annales maximi* or yearly chronicles, kept by the priestly authorities. Later writers disparaged these as bare and arid, recording only corn-shortages and eclipses or other prodigies; even if they did no more, they might still form a foundation for history if they did indeed preserve the names of the consuls of each year. But it is not clear whether they went back before the Gallic sack, and even afterwards they might be defective or misleading. However, on this basis Roman history-writing normally adopted a year-by-year chronicle style, and the manner of the *annales maximi* was often imitated through a kind of sophisticated plainness. But if a year-by-year account was being given, many years might be bare of events. Sometimes the historians admitted this: one instance comes early in Livy's second book (2.19): 'The next consuls were Servius Sulpicius and Manius Tullius. Nothing noteworthy occurred. Then came Titus Aebutius and Gaius Vetusius. In their consulship Fidenae was besieged . . .' But normally Roman historians abhorred a vacuum, and Livy's forerunners had energetically filled the gaps in the records. As Rome grew in scale and power there was a natural desire to map out the process of growth, and Roman writers were readier to draw a moral-didactic conclusion in their works – hence the added desire that Rome's rise should be glorious, her wars honourable and just. Partisan loyalties in the present might also affect the representation of the past. Conflicts over agrarian laws, for instance, were retrojected into the early Republic (Livy 2.41 'a form of legislation that has invariably been the source of agitation and upheaval down to present times'). History was often the work of political leaders in their retirement or leisure time (e.g. Cato, Sulla, Sallust); they are unlikely to have discovered the virtues of impartiality when they left the forum. Even less distinguished figures might be prone to self-glorification: the family of the Valerii were unduly prominent in the work of Valerius Antias, that of the Licinii in the history of Licinius Macer; those were not their only fabrications. There were other potential sources for distortion: Cicero complained that funeral eulogies publicized fictional achievements, and feuds were perpetuated in personal memoirs which could mislead the historian who accepted the author's verdict on his enemies.[13] Some episodes were written up on the model of famous passages in Greek historiography, and that way of thinking might also afflict chronology: it is suspicious that the expulsion of the kings of Rome should fall in the same year as the downfall of the tyrants at Athens. Livy was aware of some of the defects of his sources but did not detect them all; more important, he had no means of substituting something better.[14]

In his preface to the whole work Livy set out his aim: to show his reader 'how men lived, what their moral principles were, under what leaders and by what measures at home and abroad our empire was won and extended; then let him consider how, as discipline broke down bit by bit, morality at first foundered; how it next subsided in ever greater collapse and then began to topple headlong in ruin – until the advent of our own age, in which we can endure neither our vices nor the remedies needed to cure them.' Livy is often seen as a complacent and naive writer, but these are not the words of a mere eulogist of the Augustan peace. Had the narrative of his own times survived, we would doubtless find a darker picture than in the initial books or the epic narrative of the Hannibalic wars. Even the earlier books do not deny the presence of arrogance, sedition and cruelty in earlier times, but they do portray Romans as succeeding, time and again, in overcoming obstacles and showing themselves worthy of their city and their destiny. The drama of these developments fired his vivid imagination. In embarking on the bloody rein of Tarquin the Proud, he himself invokes the comparison with Greek tragedy: 'the Roman royal house produced a tragic spectacle to rival those of Greece, in order that disgust with kings might all the sooner usher in an era of liberty' (1.46). Most of the famous tales of Roman heroism and self-sacrifice are in Livy: Horatius keeping the bridge, Gaius Mucius thrusting his hand into the fire; the death of Verginia, slain by her father to preserve her chastity; Cincinnatus called back from the plough to serve his country, Camillus the second founder, compelling the Romans to begin again after the Gallic invasion. Here is his description of the Gauls' entry into Rome, the lower part of which has been evacuated except by the elders of the nobility.

> They assigned a small number of men to guard-duty, for fear that an attack from the citadel or the Capitol might find them unprepared. Dividing into separate looting parties, some of them marched in haste toward some nearby buildings, moving through the empty streets without meeting a soul; others made for the furthest districts, thinking those would be still intact and rich in booty. But frightened by the very silence, they made their way back, in case some trap set by their foes might ensnare them as they roamed the streets. In a large group, they found their way back to the forum and the adjacent districts; there the homes of the populace were shut and secured, the halls of the leading citizens stood open wide. But they felt more inhibitions at intruding on the open houses than the closed; they gazed with wonder not far from adoration at the men seated in the entrance halls of their great houses. Even in their garments and finery they seemed elevated above the merely human; but when one saw the air of majesty that clothed their faces, the stern dignity of their expression, they could be compared only with gods. (5.41.5–8)

Always he emphasizes virtuous conduct, noble deeds and high-minded words: his leaders have dignity enhanced by all the richness of the Augustan prose style (he cuts out some of the jokes of Flamininus that Polybius recorded, Plb. 18.6–7). The glory of Rome, its martial prowess, and the divine destiny of the city are always before his eyes. But unlike the other major Roman historians he was no soldier (his battle-scenes are dramatic but imaginative embroiderings), had no direct experience of politics, and although he often speaks of military losses he is blind to the real human cost of a society committed to almost continuous war. Moreover, when his sources did record Roman atrocities he was inclined to edit or ameliorate them (L.33.10.5, watering down Plb.18.26). He wanted his nation's history to be more honourable and glorious than it in fact was. Other historians have fallen victim to the same temptations.

Livy produced the classic *History* of Rome, but his achievement was self-defeating. The sheer bulk of his work ensured first its abridgement (Martial 14.190), then its gradual disappearance. Under the empire brevity and cynicism replaced amplitude and idealization of the past. Already in his lifetime the senator Asinius Pollio patronizingly referred to Livy's *Patavinitas* (provinciality – Livy came from Patavium, Padua, in north Italy). Readers of Robert Graves' *I, Claudius* will remember Pollio crossing swords with Livy on the proper practice of history; while unhistorical, it is a scene with some insights (ch. 8).

Not all historians in the late Republic were determined to write massive histories going back to the foundation. Monographs on more limited themes were in vogue. Cicero in a famous letter tried to induce L. Lucceius to undertake one on his consulship, suggesting he bend the rules of history a little and praise him even more than he feels justified![15] That work never got written, and the only short account of the consular year which does survive, Sallust's *Catiline*, would not have pleased Cicero at all (though he did not live to see it). Sallust was a somewhat unsuccessful and unscrupulous politician whose career was ended by the death of Caesar, whom he had supported; he turned to history in his retirement. His major work, a history of the civil wars, is lost; the *Catiline* and the *Jugurthine War* are earlier and short, which helped make them popular schoolbooks: the heavy-handed moralizing on the vices of ambition and avarice also attracted the lugubrious reading public of the early empire, who seem to have enjoyed being told that 'you've never had it so bad'. In the *Catiline,* the focus is not on Cicero but on the anti-hero of the title, presented as a figure of brilliant potential but debased by the immorality of his times.

His insatiable spirit constantly sought the excessive, the inconceivable, the over-ambitious goals. After the dictatorship of Lucius Sulla, he had been overwhelmed by a monstrous desire to enslave the state, and did not care a straw what means he used, provided he achieved monarchic power for himself. His savage spirit was forced onward more with each passing day; driving him were his impoverished means and his guilty consciousness of crimes, and both of these motives he had enhanced by the means I have already described. The corrupt state of society also gave added impetus, corruption that was worsened by the presence of the two most damaging though contradictory evils, love of luxury and love of riches. (*Catiline* 5.5–8)

The development of the conspiracy is analysed vividly but without chronological precision or sociological detail; Sallust is far more interested in dramatic scenes and cynical comment on human weakness. The climax of the work is the senatorial debate (in Thucydidean manner, a pair of speeches) after most of the conspirators are imprisoned; Caesar advocates clemency, but Cato's view, that they should be executed, prevails. This conflict foreshadows the later political and military opposition of these two figures, and the scope of the monograph is thus broadened beyond its ostensible subject. The final execution, supervised by Cicero as consul, is introduced by a description of the sinister setting within the prison house.

> With armed guards in position, he personally escorted Lentulus to the prison; the praetors did likewise with the rest. There is a place in the prison which is known as the Tullianum; when one has climbed slightly on the left, it is underground, sunk in a pit about twelve feet deep. Defensive walls surround it on all sides, and the roof above is supported by stone arches; the ugliness of the spot, the darkness and the stench make it loathsome and horrible to look upon. When Lentulus had been cast down into this place, the officers who punish capital offences, who had received their orders, broke his neck with a noose. So it was that this patrician, a descendent of the most illustrious house of the Cornelii, a man who had held the office of consul at Rome, met an end appropriate to his character and his deeds. Cethegus, Statilius, Gabinius and Caeparius were subjected to the same penalty. (55.2–6)

In Sallust's other monograph, the *Jugurtha*, a war of relatively small military importance is made into a paradigm of wartime politics in a corrupt society. Sallust is a moralist first, a Thucydidean stylist second (his tense sentences and archaisms would have offended Cicero as much as the negative approach to Roman values); he was a researcher third or not at all. Given the loss of his most ambitious work, he cannot be a central figure on the Roman historiographical stage: there, his chief claim to greatness is as a formative literary model for the greatest of Roman historians, Tacitus.[16]

The other key figure in historical writing of the late Republic is Julius Caesar himself. The crisp lucidity of his Latin has condemned him to be a beginners' school text for centuries; but only a more informed reader can fully appreciate the skill and deviousness with which he publicizes his own military achievements in Gaul, masking failures or misjudgements, and defends his role in the civil wars against Pompey and the Republican cause.[17] The *Gallic Wars* is not solely a military record; there is room for ethnography as well, describing the Gauls, the Germans and even the benighted Britons.

Caesar called his works *Commentarii*, which was a semi-technical term meaning that they were only unpretentious notebooks, the raw materials for a real history. This was disingenuous: Cicero was enthusiastic about the purity and correctness of the style, and declared that only the inept would attempt to improve on Caesar's own words (*Brutus* 262). That stylistic judgement did not affect Cicero's deep antagonism to Caesar's political aims.

V

Our picture of historical writing under the Republic is much fuller than for the early empire. Despite the initial efforts of Augustus to mask his near-monarchic role, it is clear that the emperor became a crucial focus for historical writing at an early stage, not only as a patron of letters or as the subject of works biographical or panegyrical, but through imperial reigns becoming a structuring principle for historical works (thus Tacitus subtitles his *Annals* 'from the death of the divine Augustus', and emperors' deaths in that work coincide with the ends of books).

The presence of the emperor at the heart of the Roman world had significant negative consequences. Since most of the historians were senators or otherwise prominent in politics, the relations between emperor and senate bulked disproportionately large in their works; it is easy for a reader to forget that millions of citizens of the empire never saw the emperor or even had much idea who was currently on the throne. Also, the posthumous reaction against 'bad' emperors could be so violent that the tradition about them became distorted. Tacitus shrewdly remarks that 'the histories of Tiberius, Gaius [Caligula], Claudius and Nero, while they were in power, were falsified through terror, and after their deaths were written under the stimulus of recent hatred' (*Annals* 1.1); and that 'while we shrink from a writer's adulation, we lend a ready ear to detraction and spite, because flattery involves the shameful imputation of servility, whereas malignity wears the false appearance of honesty' (*Hist.* 1.1). Elsewhere he alludes more specifically to the flattering fabrications of the Flavian historians (*Hist.* 2.101). The praise which the Jewish historian Josephus lavishes on Vespasian and Titus may give something of the flavour of these works, but Josephus' own agenda in his *Jewish Wars* also embraced self-praise and self-exoneration: by declaring that he had foreseen that the Jews' revolt against Rome was hopeless, he sought to defend his own swift conversion to the victorious side.[18] The clearest instance of a Roman historian playing the flatterer is Velleius Paterculus, who served in the army under Tiberius and wrote a short work culminating in an enthusiastic narrative of his reign. This is often condemned or ignored for the very reasons Tacitus gives, and because

Tacitus' own far darker portrait of Tiberius has dominated the perception of the emperor. Velleius does however merit attention on his own terms, as a writer trying to find new ways of expressing loyalty to a changed regime (the Augustan poets had already faced some of the same problems).[19] We may not admire him, but his work is illuminating. There were other difficulties. Autocracy generates secrecy: even highly placed contemporaries might be unsure of the reasons behind new policies (Dio 53.19). Finally, there was the danger of imperial censorship. Book-burning began in the late years of Augustus. Cremutius Cordus was brought to trial under Tiberius, and at least part of the reason was said to be his praise of Brutus and Cassius in his historical works; Tacitus for obvious reasons gave the episode prominence (*Ann.* 4.34–5: Appendix 1.4). Other cases are known (p. 195).

But it is Tacitus who rightly dominates the historiography of the early empire. We have three smaller works complete (though there is a short gap in the *Dialogus*), then substantial parts of his longer and more ambitious historical works. The *Agricola* is a posthumous tribute to his father-in-law, a distinguished soldier; it combines biography with a quite detailed narrative of his campaigns in Britain, including ethnography; there are speeches before a great battle, and then a bleaker account of Agricola's last years, when he was recalled and under suspicion. The work concludes with a powerful passage that owes something to the tradition of funeral eulogy. Besides commemorating his kinsman, Tacitus also makes Agricola an exemplar of the proper conduct of a man of honour in difficult times: 'let it be known . . . that there may be great men even under bad emperors, and that obedience and submission, when joined to activity and vigour, may attain a glory which most men reach only by a perilous career, utterly useless to the state, and closed by an ostentatious death' (42). Tacitus has in mind the showy deaths of the Stoic martyrs, Thrasea Paetus and others, whom he treats with more sympathy in the later *Annals*. The *Agricola* is a rich and complex text; devotees of the history of Roman Britain often neglect its most interesting aspects.

The *Dialogue on Oratory* has been described elsewhere (p. 79); here too the preoccupation with the pressure of power on talent is prominent, and the state of oratory is a barometer for the health of the community. The other early work is the *Germania*, which gives a geographic and ethnographic essay on the various peoples making up the land which caused Rome so many years of war or uneasy peace. Tacitus had no first-hand knowledge and no special qualifications for the task. The facts of tribal affiliations and customs are doubtless often derivative, out-dated or fabulous; what matters is the guiding idea, the use of Germany as a model against which to set the civilization and the decadence of Rome. He plays many variations on this theme, one which continues in his later work. The

Germans are the ultimate 'other', the mirror in which Rome may glimpse its own primitive past (simplicity, chastity, and above all a lost freedom – which among the Germans has become almost anarchic) and also a savagery which is in tension with their primitive virtues. The continued effort to subjugate Germany had lasted 210 years: 'tam diu Germania vincitur' writes Tacitus (37, 'so long is the process of conquering Germany'!). They were still seen as an ever-present threat.

The *Histories* narrate events after the death of Nero, the civil wars which dominated the 'year of four emperors' (AD 69) and from which the Flavian dynasty emerged triumphant. The surviving books are a heady mix of political intrigue, disappointed hopes, powerful battle scenes and fighting within Rome itself. But despite the power of the narrative, this work takes second place to the *Annals*, which take the reader still further back in time, to events after Augustus' death: the surviving books cover the fortunes of the Julio-Claudian dynasty (Tiberius, Claudius and Nero; the books on Caligula and the end of Nero's reign are lost). The structure remains annalistic, as the title suggests; foreign affairs alternate with events at Rome, though often the two are linked or set in deliberate contrast (as when the frontier campaigns of Germanicus or Corbulo are contrasted with the claustrophobic fear and faction-fighting at the centre of power).

In the preface to the *Agricola* Tacitus declared that in his own time Nerva and Trajan had succeeded in combining two things once thought incompatible, the principate (i.e. government by the emperor) and liberty. That rosy view may have been no more than a momentary euphoria or a graceful compliment; in any case, the conflict between these two lies at the heart of his work, as does the corrupting force of absolute power (in one passage he declares that Vespasian was the first emperor who ever changed for the better; that is a damning judgement on the whole of the Julio-Claudian line which forms the subject of the *Annals*). The rulers whom we witness in the surviving books of the *Annals* form stages on a declining curve: Tiberius, monstrous but awesome; Claudius, a pedant, dupe and cuckold; Nero, a matricide and an aesthete (15.67). The behaviour of those who surround the emperor is conditioned by the power of the centre: 'at Rome consuls, senators, equestrians hurled themselves into slavery' (1.7, after the accession of Tiberius). Tacitus never fails to highlight cases of hypocrisy, adulation and paranoia. Pretence and dissimulation are constant motifs: the subject pretends to absolute loyalty, the monarch masks his real opinions and defers his final judgement. Tiberius is the key figure in this pattern, and the six books on his reign represent the height of Tacitus' art, while also dramatizing the sheer impenetrability of imperial history. Tacitus presents Tiberius not as a mere villain but as a disturbing enigma, capable of generosity and efficient action, but also of bitter resentment and cruelty. Again and again

Tacitus has to offer multiple interpretations, or narrates a superficially positive action while also seeking to unmask the real and sinister motive behind
it (the Thucydidean inheritance is strong here: the historian's task is to tear
away pretences in word and act, and to go beyond the superficial meaning).
The tradition about Tiberius was overwhelmingly negative, and Tacitus
faced real difficulties in interpreting the character of the aged recluse. The
summary he gives at the end of book 6, after the emperor's death, has
puzzled many readers and does not do justice to the complex figure portrayed in the earlier narrative. If in the end he failed to resolve the problem,
it is one of the most fascinating failures in ancient historiography. It is made
still more so by Tacitus' unforgettable style, compressed and suggestive,
epigrammatic and involved.

Part of what horrified Tacitus and others about the empire was that under
a bad ruler (and he seems to have assumed that there would be more bad
than good), the subjects are compelled to accede to or even play a role in
crimes and misconduct. In a powerful chapter of the *Agricola* we see Tacitus'
own personal *peccavi*, and that of his class, when he refers to the executions
in Domitian's last years with a rhetorical force that enhances the collective
guilt: 'soon ours were the hands that dragged Helvidius into prison; we
gazed on the dying looks of Mauricus and Rusticus; we were the ones
soaked by Senecio's innocent blood' (45). But it is too simple to say
that Tacitus is imposing the Domitianic template on Tiberius. Rather, the
historian sees both resemblances and contrasts between emperors, and is
seeking to uncover the origins and the inherent moral deficiency of the
institution of empire itself. Yet he saw no alternative: the system was there
to stay, and represented the best hope for Rome's survival. 'It was expedient
that all power should be conferred on a single man' (*Histories* 1.1). 'Tacitus
teaches the tyrants how to be tyrants and their subjects how to behave
under tyrants': the judgement of Guicciardini is at least two-edged.

Important inscriptional evidence helps the modern historian to confirm
his reliability: the text of a speech by Claudius which Tacitus has recast and
compressed, or the invaluable discovery of a senatorial resolution from one
of the tensest moments of Tiberius' reign.[20] We have not even touched on
the abundant factual information in Tacitus' longer works, where we find a
wealth of detail on legionary movements, senatorial resolutions, equestrian
officials, provincial government and municipal policies. But what fascinates
Tacitus most and remains most in the reader's mind are the struggles,
intense and sometimes grotesque, at the heart of the imperial court and
family.

Tiberius indeed wore an angry frown or a treacherous smile. Whether the
young prince spoke or held his tongue, silence and speech were alike criminal.

Every night had its anxieties, for his sleepless hours, his dreams and sighs, were all made known by his wife to her mother Livia and by Livia to Sejanus. Sejanus even drew Nero's brother Drusus into his scheme by holding out to him the prospect of becoming emperor through the removal of an elder brother, already all but fallen. The savage temper of Drusus, to say nothing of lust for power and the usual feuds between brothers, was inflamed with envy by the partiality of their mother Agrippina towards Nero. And yet Sejanus, while he favoured Drusus, was not without thoughts of sowing the seeds of his future ruin, well knowing how very impetuous he was and therefore the more exposed to treachery. (*Annals* 4.60)

In these parts of his work we see a potential novelist – a Dickens or a Balzac.[21]

Already Pliny the Younger admired his friend Tacitus enormously: he was delighted when a provincial visitor at the games, on learning that he was a literary man, asked him 'So are you Tacitus or Pliny?' (Pliny, *Letters* 9.23). In response to an enquiry from Tacitus while the latter was writing the *Histories*, he supplied him with information on the circumstances of his uncle's death in the great eruption of Vesuvius in AD 79 (*Letters* 6.16 and 20). Elsewhere in his letters he gives a vivid picture of his uncle's energy and scholarly curiosity (3.5); his determination to get closer to the volcano and investigate what was happening was the fitting conclusion to a life of indefatigable enquiry. Pliny declares that Tacitus by recounting these events will immortalize his uncle's memory. It is a piquant irony that Tacitus' narrative of the eruption is lost, while Pliny's two letters survive to commemorate his relative in a more personal and informal style, but probably in more detail, than the historian would have permitted himself.

We saw that in the Greek historical tradition authors sometimes took up the challenge of continuing their most distinguished predecessors' work: Xenophon continues the narrative of Thucydides, Polybius that of Timaeus. Similarly Ammianus Marcellinus, writing in the 380s AD, took up the torch of history in the grand manner where Tacitus had ended, and in a work of 31 books described the fortunes of the empire from the death of Nerva (AD 98) to his own lifetime, a narrative of almost 300 years.[22] The first 13 books are lost: this lost section was evidently more summary than the later parts, in which the author was writing partly as an eyewitness; what survives, more than half of the *History*, covers only 25 years, the period from 353 to 378. Ammianus was raised in Syria, probably in Antioch, a Greek speaker writing in Latin; a man of some wealth and status, a soldier and a traveller, he does not see himself as a Roman, but he is a product of the wider multinational empire created by the universal extension of Roman citizenship. Of all the Latin historians, he is the first not to make Rome central to his work. He came there late in life and writes with disapproval of the decadence of its inhabitants (14.6, 28.4). Yet the concepts of Rome as the eternal city, and of the imperial destiny, remain important as overarching ideals.

Emperors are central to his work, as is military narrative. In the extant part he describes the reign of Constantius, the rise, reign and downfall of Julian, and the fortunes of his successors down to Valentinian II. The cast of characters is large, including many would-be usurpers, generals and bishops, informers, defectors and careerists. Lawyers, eunuchs and elephants earn his intense antagonism. He has a satirical tone, and a shrewd eye for failures and defects of character. Justice and stable government are high priorities; morality in high office is desirable, although he recognizes that it is often lacking. He frequently puts forward his opinions and judgements, but on the central figures of his work it is hard to feel complete confidence in his views. For each emperor he presents an obituary, weighing merits against defects; but the comments in the narrative, and still more the narration itself, make the overall evaluation of both Constantius and Julian more complicated than at first appears.[23] He plainly overestimates the worth of his former commander Ursicinus, and although his admiration for Julian is not unqualified, it leads him to some extravagant claims: despite Ammianus, Julian's successes in Gaul were *not* deserving of comparison with Rome's victories over Carthage and the Teutones.[24] Ammianus is fond of these learned invocations of earlier precedent, normally used to show the superior virtue or the greater challenges facing the leaders of his day.[25] They also place his own work against the historical tradition, just as Thucydides had implicitly asserted the superiority of his subject to those of Homer and Herodotus.

Ammianus writes from his own experiences in two major sections of his work. The first concerns campaigns in Parthia under Ursicinus, in which the highlight is his vivid account of the siege of the city of Nisibis (esp. 18.6–9) and of Antiba (19.1–9). The second covers part of the ill-fated Persian campaign of Julian, which ended in the emperor's death and a grim withdrawal after a humiliating treaty (books 23–5). The recurring use of 'we' clearly indicates the account of an eyewitness (which is not to deny that the historian no doubt supplemented his account from other sources). Both make compelling reading and include unforgettable scenes of dramatic reversal or chilling horror. On occasion his pictorial imagination, enriched by wide reading, may run away with him: 'so crowded together were we that the bodies of the slain, held upright by the crowd, had no room to fall to the earth, and in front of me a soldier with his head cut in two, split into two equal halves by a powerful sword stroke, was so pressed in on all sides that he stood upright like a tree-stump' (18.8.12).

Indeed, important though he is as a source, Ammianus deserves to be read as much for the imaginative vigour of his writing. He has often been seen as more Greek than Roman – his curious learning makes itself evident in many a digression, not only ethnography in the Herodotean vein, but on everything from eclipses to obelisks; his metaphors and bold locutions seem to stretch the boundaries of Latin. Even in translation we can relish his acid judgements: on Lampadius, for instance, a man of such self-esteem that he was indignant if even his style of spitting did not attract admiration (27.3.5), or on Sabinianus, that man of low stature and 'small, narrow mind', who was barely able to endure the gentle sound of a party, let alone the din of battle, without showing his apprehension (18.6.7), or on Julian's view of Christian sectarianism ('he knew from experience that no wild beasts are such enemies to mankind as are most of the Christians in their hatred of each other', 22.5.4). Tacitus on Claudius' freedmen finds his match in Ammianus on Constantius' court eunuchs: as bad news came in from the Persian front, 'the forge of the courtiers, hammering day and night at the bidding of the eunuchs upon the same anvil, held up Ursicinus to the suspicious and fearful emperor as a grim-faced Gorgon' (18.4.2). He continues:

> Eusebius then, like a viper swelling with abundant poison and arousing his multitudinous brood to mischief when they were still hardly able to crawl, sent out his chamberlains, already mature, with orders that amid their other duties they should use the soft utterances of their voices, ever childish and persuasive, to batter the reputation of that brave man in the all-too-ready ears of the emperor. (18.4.4)[26]

This Eusebius is a sinister figure, painted by Ammianus as the evil genius of Constantius. The historian sardonically reverses their apparent power-relations, commenting 'if the truth be told, Constantius had considerable influence with Eusebius' (18.4.3). These quotations should give some idea of the mordant vitality of the last great historical work of the Western empire.

VI

Tacitus the historian is often supplemented by or paired with Suetonius the biographer, whose chief surviving work is his collection of short lives of the Caesars from Julius to Domitian. A later author claimed that Tacitus wrote eloquently, Suetonius truthfully! (*SHA Probus* 2.7) More broadly, there was a generally perceived distinction between history and biography. History was the more ambitious, more prestigious form, usually much longer and preserving a loftier style and generic rank. Biography, which began in eulogy, might go deeper into a man's private life, his tastes and habits.

Plutarch, a near-contemporary of Tacitus, emphasized that such details might be more illuminating of a personality than far greater deeds: a jest or a chance remark could tell you more than the fact that a man won a war or sacked a city.[27] Suetonius similarly did not disdain telling details, though his are often more scurrilous and scandalous than the high-minded Plutarch would have tolerated.[28]

Suetonius was writing under Hadrian, probably some time after Tacitus' works had been published. It is debated how much he owes to them and whether his works are in any way a response to Tacitus (probably not much), but the comparison is certainly valuable. A fine example is the flight of Vitellius during the year of the four emperors. Tacitus creates a haunting night-time scene in which the doomed man tries to escape:

> . . . with characteristic weakness, and following the instincts of fear, which, dreading everything, shrinks most from what is immediately before it, he retraced his steps to the desolate and forsaken palace, whence even the meanest slaves had fled. The solitude and silence of the place scared him; he tried the closed doors, he shuddered in the empty chambers, till wearied by his miserable wanderings, he concealed himself in a degrading hiding place, from which he was dragged out by the tribune Julius Placidus. (*Hist.* 3.84)

Suetonius in his version remarks that Vitellius (who was a notorious glutton) originally set out with two companions, a baker and a cook! He also makes the hiding-place explicit: 'he took refuge in the door-keeper's lodge, tying a dog before the door and putting a couch and a mattress against it'. When he is made captive, Tacitus again preserves distance: 'he was led along with tattered robes, . . . amid the invectives of many, the tears of none. The degradation of his end had extinguished all pity.' Suetonius says that 'some pelted him with dung and filth, others called him incendiary and glutton, and some of the mob even taunted him with his bodily defects' (*Vitell.* 16–17).

The first six lives, up to Nero, are much fuller; this no doubt reflects the general perception of the sin-soaked Julio-Claudians as more fascinating (Nero's matricide draws more readers than Vespasian's meanness). Unlike Plutarch, Suetonius does not stick to a chronological scheme: after accession he treats various aspects of the ruler's conduct synoptically (his personal qualities, his moral conduct, his tastes, etc.). Especially fascinating are the sometimes extensive quotations from personal correspondence, mainly of Augustus (a collection of his letters may have been in circulation). Such insights are rare after Cicero. Often the treatment is crude and cynical (sexual habits, warts and body odour are mentioned, whereas Tacitus would have disdained such detail), but it is not nihilistic. Suetonius has an idea of how an emperor should behave, and gives good marks when they are deserved. The scope is wider than in history proper: we learn that Augustus was afraid of thunder, and that he always carried a seal-skin around with him as a form of protection (*Aug.* 90). Cultural interests may be used to prove depravity of character: thus Tiberius is said to have hung in his bedroom a painting of Atalanta fellating Meleager (*Tib.* 44). Racy, fast-moving, full of good stories, the work will never lack readers; unfortunately it is also careless, credulous and prone to unjustified generalization. As the first imperial biography in Latin, it set a pattern followed by the so-called *Historia Augusta* (a concoction of low-level scandal on the rulers from Hadrian on) and others. In formal contexts emperors might be gods, but biography could still drag them down to earth.

The biographical work of Plutarch has already been mentioned.[29] A peaceful, supremely civilized and amazingly well-read Greek, he lived at Chaeronea near Delphi in the late first and early second centuries AD. He is a scholar of much greater talent than Suetonius and a writer of extraordinary range (dialogue, philosophic essay, rhetorical polemic; elsewhere he writes on subjects as different as Isis and Osiris, the intelligence of animals and the reason why the Delphic oracle no longer pronounces its oracles in verse). But the *Parallel Lives of the Greeks and Romans* are his greatest achievement; their influence on Western Europe has been profound, as this is where many people learned their ancient history. Shakespeare's *Antony and Cleopatra, Julius Caesar* and *Coriolanus* derive their plots and much detail from Plutarch through North's translation (1579). The *Lives* were a big project: 22 paired biographies survive, and some unpaired. (The pairs are nowadays normally separated and read independently, although this involves losing some insights.) The rhetorical schools had often tackled comparisons between Greek and Roman figures, literary or historical: Demosthenes and Cicero, paired by Plutarch, are also compared by Quintilian, Juvenal and Longinus. Alexander and Julius Caesar made another natural duo (and Caesar himself, not uniquely, probably aspired to rival Alexander). But the elaborate series of Greek and Roman notables, and the scale and nature of the biographical enterprise, is quite unparalleled. Although many scholars have tried to find Hellenistic precedents, the probability is that the project is Plutarch's own, and the lives, while uneven in length, detail and judgement, are a stunning achievement. They are more readable and captivating than almost any other ancient history (and less bedevilled by military detail than most). Although the aim of the lives is to teach morality through example, the characters are not oversimplified: Brutus and Coriolanus, Antony and Alcibiades, are hardly role-models, but neither can we simply note behaviour patterns to avoid. Plutarch's delight in the story he is telling and his genuine sense of drama normally prevent the didactic undercurrent from becoming too patent.

To the historian they are valuable because Plutarch often includes material which would otherwise be lost. The *Life* of Pericles, for instance, does a huge amount to flesh out the Thucydidean portrait, which focused on his last years and dealt only with his public face. Sometimes the Life enables us to amend Thucydides' picture: Plutarch quotes a comic fragment which makes clear that Cleon was already a prominent opponent of Pericles' defensive strategy, whereas Thucydides, who evidently disliked him, introduced Cleon only after Pericles' death. Much had changed in Graeco-Roman power-structures and politics by the time of Plutarch, however, and his grasp of earlier political issues is not always firm. Where he scores brilliantly is in his characterization.

Very predictably (since the focus is on the active world of public life), his subjects are all male. But *Antony* surprises and delights with its dual star roles, and the closing episodes of the *Life*, as of Shakespeare's play, are Cleopatra's. She is a dazzling creation, a world away from the decadent and intoxicated queen of Augustan propaganda: in Plutarch's account Octavian is vexed at Cleopatra's death, yet cannot but admire her nobility (86). Plutarch describes her neither as an Eastern temptress nor as an elegiac mistress, but as a gifted and clever woman: 'Her own beauty, we are told, was not of that incomparable kind which instantly captivates the beholder. But the charm of her presence was irresistible, and there was an attraction in her person and her talk, together with a peculiar force of character which pervaded her every word and action, and laid all who associated with her under its spell. It was a delight merely to hear the sound of her voice, with which, like an instrument of many strings, she could pass from one language to another' (27). Antony's weakness is sympathetically though still unsparingly demonstrated, culminating in his failure to hold position at Actium when he sees Cleopatra's ship withdrawing (moderns deny that this was a tactical blunder, but the myth is too strong to be altered now).

> Now it was that Antony revealed to all the world that he was no longer guided by the motives of a commander nor of a brave man nor indeed by his own judgement at all; instead he proved the truth of the saying which was once uttered as a jest, namely that a lover's soul dwells in the body of another, and he allowed himself to be dragged along after the woman, as if he had become a part of her flesh and must go wherever she led him. . . . He got into a five-banked galley, and taking with him only Alexas the Syrian and Scellius, he hurried after the woman who had already ruined him and would soon complete his destruction. (66)

But Antony's stature grows again in his death (vindication through a brave end was a frequent motif in ancient literature); he is no ordinary love-sick dupe, any more than Plutarch is a commonplace moralist.

VII

Although Cicero proclaimed history the light of truth and a moral guide to life (*On the Orator* 2.36), doubts had been expressed from the beginning, and it was always clear that some historical works, or parts thereof, were composed to delight, amaze and entertain the reader.[30] Herodotus had already commented that Egypt deserved his special attention because it contained the greatest number of wonders. Marvels and paradoxes continued to be prominent in later writers, especially when describing remoter lands.[31] Such writing was popular, but also suspect. Ctesias, who lived at the Persian court around 400 BC and allegedly drew on Persian records, was generally regarded as a sensational scandal-monger: his aspirations to 'correct' Herodotus do not arouse much confidence. We find many references to the fabulous and unbelievable tales told by writers such as the Alexander historians (and Alexander's achievements, already staggering in reality, passed into the realm of fantasy in the tradition that moderns call the Alexander Romance). Even better attested events could be treated with derision: Juvenal refers to the achievements of Xerxes, who bridged the Hellespont with boats and built a channel through Mount Athos, but adds 'and whatever the lying Greeks have the face to put in their histories' (10.174–5). History could involve exaggeration, imaginative elaboration, or sheer fantasy. In the absence of photographs or other forms of records, readers could not easily assess the veracity of the historian. How would they know whether Megasthenes had given an accurate description of a banyam tree?

For these and other reasons historians were not always believed. Herodotus' credibility was impugned from a very early date. To say nothing of the oblique comments in Thucydides, Cicero commented that the father of history included innumerable fables (*On the Laws* 1.5), and Plutarch, resenting the negative presentation of his native Boeotia, wrote a work on Herodotus' malice. Historians, like modern scholars, did not scruple to attack their rivals: Polybius spends a whole book denouncing the errors and iniquities of Timaeus, and the geographer Strabo criticizes Herodotus, Hellanicus, Ctesias and most of his other predecessors. Modern criticism has sometimes gone further. A recent monograph argued that Herodotus made up most of his source citations, and questioned whether he was even writing history rather than a kind of imaginative narrative set in a historical context.[32] This position is too extreme, but it is true that moderns have often exaggerated the similarity between ancient historical writing and our own (though modern work in this field is far from homogeneous). We have already seen that historians were capable of filling gaps and elaborating on limited data. Rhetorical training encouraged authors not only to include speeches (only Thucydides ever seems to have had qualms about this), but to adopt a subtly rhetorical attitude to their subject matter.[33] The facts, even when known, were not necessarily left to speak for themselves. Vividness and powerful contrasts were valued; so were memorable sayings and stories with a good moral or ironical twist. Cicero's friend Atticus jestingly remarks that orators are permitted a certain freedom in using historical examples, and may adjust them in order to make a point more sharply (*Brutus* 42–4). Historians undoubtedly allowed themselves some such latitude on occasion. But discrimination is needed: different authors will have had different ideas about the legitimacy of adjusting or adding to the information they inherited or acquired, and different criteria would have been applied in different contexts (for instance, more freedom might be necessary or permissible in dealing with very early times or very far off places). We should not doubt, however, that a boundary line existed between truth and falsehood, even though authors might disagree strongly about where the boundary lay. Polybius recognized a difference between history and eulogy, even when dealing with the same man. Lucian condemns inferior historians not only for their style but for their disregard of truth.[34] None of this is to deny the possibility, even the likelihood, of distortion through unconscious biases, undue modernization, or schematic assumptions – all factors which can be discerned also in modern historical writing.

It is noteworthy that writers from an early stage felt it desirable to authenticate their work by claiming it was derived from some obscure or previously unexploited source. Ctesias' citation of Persian records has just been mentioned; he was preceded by Acusilaus of Argos, who claimed to have used an account on bronze tablets which his father had discovered while digging his garden![35] Plato's narrative of Atlantis is quoted as deriving via the sage Solon from an Egyptian priestly tradition. Euhemerus claimed to have travelled to an island in the Indian ocean and discovered there a monument of gold with an inscription recounting the deeds of long-dead kings, Uranus, Cronos and Zeus: on this basis he composed his *Sacred Account*, arguing that the mythical gods were in fact mortals.[36] Philostratus' strange biography of the Pythagorean Apollonius is allegedly based on a text by the latter's disciple Damis (a figure of whom suspiciously little is known). It is clear that many, if not all, of these claims are bogus, and the motif was carried over into fiction proper. Antonius Diogenes evidently carried it to extremes, including not one but two incompatible accounts of his source-material. On the one hand, it is based on studious work in libraries; on the other, it derives from a discovery by Alexander's soldiers at the sack of Tyre of a chest of cypress wood containing tablets on which the narrative was set out in full – so what need for library research? The reader is surely meant to spot the amusing discrepancy. In our own time Umberto Eco mischievously opens his most famous novel by alluding to this tradition

('Naturally, a manuscript'). Perhaps Thucydides was wise never to refer to his sources.

History is the parent of historical romance. The emergence of fiction in the ancient world is hard to track given the gaps in our evidence, but there is no doubt that a tradition of adventurous and often exotic narrative developed during the Hellenistic period. The works classified as novels by modern scholars probably date from no earlier than the first century BC, but it is clear that their roots lie much further back. A key work which shows the writer using a historical figure in fictional ways is Xenophon's narrative of the upbringing and career of Cyrus the Great, founder of the Persian empire (cf. p. 115). This remarkable work radically diverges from the account given by Herodotus in his first book (though admittedly Herodotus commented on the diversity of tradition about Cyrus). Recounting in prose the experiences of an idealized hero in a foreign setting, Xenophon anticipates some of the chief features of the romantic novel. Although the emphasis in his work is on Cyrus as king and commander, there is an important sub-plot involving Pantheia and Abradatas,[37] a pair of ill-starred lovers whose mutual devotion ends in tragedy. Xenophon's priorities are the political and military skills of his hero: the erotic sub-plot is a diversion from his main concerns. His successors reversed the emphasis: instead of fictionalizing a historical character, they placed fictional characters in a quasi-historical setting, as we can see in a number of fragmentary extracts. The earliest clear example of the type, *Ninus*, seems to have put the principal characters' love affair at the centre, while still choosing a distinguished figure of Eastern history as its hero, and giving prominence to his military achievements as well as his emotional ambitions. The handling of the leading character is very different from Xenophon: the youthful king of Babylon becomes a tongue-tied young lover. The sentimental aspects of the genre are still more apparent in the next early example known to us, *Metiochus and Parthenope*. Herodotus in his account of Polycrates of Samos had mentioned a daughter without naming her (3.124), and the novelist makes this bit player the heroine of a romantic narrative: teenage protagonists, love at first sight, parental opposition, travels and troubles, wanderings through foreign lands, and probably eventual reunion. Reconstruction is hazardous, but some fragments give the flavour. 'Parthenope,' rhapsodizes the hero, 'are you forgetful of your Metiochus? From the day you left, as if my eyes were glued open, I have had no sleep . . .'[38] Emotional outpourings are part of the stock-in-trade of the novelists: to some extent their credit can be saved by assuming that they view their characters with a detached irony.

Five Greek novels survive complete, all probably from the first or second centuries AD:[39] the *Ephesian Tales* (or *Anthia and Habrocomes*) of one Xenophon (who may adopt this name as a tribute to the earlier Xenophon),

Chariton's *Chaereas and Callirhoe*, Longus' *Daphnis and Chloe*, Achilles
Tatius' *Leucippe and Clitophon* and Heliodorus' *Ethiopian Tale*. The order
is uncertain, but it is usually thought that Xenophon and Chariton are
earlier than the other three and that Heliodorus, whether second, third
or fourth century, is last of all. This is not unconnected with the more
evaluative consensus that Longus, Achilles and Heliodorus are more sophisticated than the other two: it is better to separate questions of evaluation
from chronology.

The novel of the younger Xenophon is the weakest by common consent, although critics often try to palliate its weaknesses by maintaining
that it is an abridgement of a better version. However that may be, this
passage from the conclusion gives some idea of the characteristic themes of
the genre.

> And when all the rest had fallen asleep and there was complete stillness,
> Anthia put her arms around Habrocomes and wept. 'Husband and lord,' she
> said, 'I have found you again after all my wanderings over land and sea,
> escaping robbers' threats and pirates' plots and pimps' insults, chains, trenches,
> fetters, poisons, and tombs. But I have reached you, lord of my heart, the
> same as when I first left you in Tyre for Syria. No one persuaded me to go
> astray . . . I remain chaste, after practising every device of virtue. But did you,
> Habrocomes, remain chaste, or has some other beauty eclipsed me? Has no
> one forced you to forget your oath and me?' With this she kept kissing him,
> but Habrocomes replied, 'I swear to you by this day that we have longed for
> and reached with such difficulty, that I have never considered any other girl
> attractive, nor did the sight of any other woman please me; but you have
> found Habrocomes as pure as you left him in the prison in Tyre.'
> They made these protestations of innocence all night and easily persuaded
> each other since that was what they wanted. (5.16)

The adventures that she describes are typical: the longer and more ambitious novels play ingenious variations on these basic ingredients. In four of
the five novels mentioned, the principals are young lovers, either betrothed
or recently married, who are separated by events and forced to wander
through foreign lands undergoing all manner of misfortunes. Frequently
they attract unwanted attention, and sometimes are obliged to submit to
captors or oppressors. Misunderstanding, deception and coincidence reach a
near-Dickensian complexity: sometimes one believes the other is dead, sometimes both labour under this kind of misapprehension. Sham deaths through
drugs, as in *Romeo and Juliet*, play a regular part in encouraging such error.
But in the end, thanks to good luck and divine providence, they are
reunited, more experienced though not much wiser (character development
is limited, and subordinated for the most part to the constraints of plot).

It is not always easy for the reader to keep track of events, particularly in the longest and most complex of the novels, that of Heliodorus (10 books). What is lacking by way of plausibility and depth of characterization is compensated for by a fluent and attractive narrative style, involving regular set-piece speeches, descriptive passages, and curious learning. Quotation and allusion pay homage to many classical models, from the *Odyssey* through Plato to Hellenistic pastoral. This highly literary texture, combined with the sophisticated handling of conventional motifs and situations, make it likely that the novel was aimed at the educated reader. The notorious pronouncement by Perry, that the genre was read by 'children and the poor in spirit', is now only quoted in order to dismiss it.[40]

The odd one out among the surviving five works is Longus' *Daphnis and Chloe*. Here the main characters are hardly more than children, growing up and learning, very gradually, about sexuality and each other. The normal routine of an abduction and separation through travel is avoided, events being confined to an idyllic rural setting on Lesbos, where the two are being brought up in innocence by shepherds. The dangers and misfortunes here are on a much reduced scale; the happy ending is never seriously in doubt. Many will be content to enjoy the descriptive charm of the work, and the comically naive presentation of the soon-to-be lovers. More sophisticated interpreters have spun many a complicated web around the work, exploring themes such as nature and culture, or seeking allegory of religious initiation. This last approach has been attempted with several of the novels, and gains some support from the undoubted importance of Isis in the *Metamorphoses* of Apuleius (see pp. 143–4). It is true that Egypt, which exercised a fascination on the Greeks not confined to the religious, figures frequently as a destination in the novels, and that Heliodorus in particular seems to give a special significance to the cult of the Sun God; and divine Providence often seems to guide the wandering lovers or protect them in adversity (as when a miraculous shower of rain puts out the fire which is about to consume one of our heroes (Xen. *Eph.* 4.2)). Gods do not appear in the novel, but there is a sense of their presence offstage. This does not, however, entitle us to read the works as mystical allegories in any strict sense. It remains a tantalizing fact that the heyday of the Greek novel, the first two or three centuries AD, sees the development of a range of Christian fictions, the 'apocryphal' narratives of the Apostles and other religious heroes: the best known are the so-called Acts of Paul and Thecla (second century). Many of the motifs are similar: hardship, wandering, torture survived and virginity preserved. But in this variation the happy ending is not marriage but martyrdom or life in service to Christ. Whether pagan or Christian texts influenced one another remains an open question, but they recognizably cater for some of the same tastes.

The similarity of the surviving novels is deceptive and may be the consequence of some kind of moral censorship of the tradition (idealized lovers, virtue rewarded). Some of the lost works about which we know something were clearly more varied and racier. Papyri give us glimpses of several works, reinforced by summaries and brief references. Antonius Diogenes' 24-book opus on 'The Incredible Things beyond Thule'[41] was a long narrative of unbelievable events, parodying earlier travel fantasies or tall tales (even the title may suggest this, if it also claims to 'go beyond' the accounts given of the remote island of Thule by earlier writers). Evidently it was also a tour de force in narratological terms, involving an elaborate system of multiple internal narrators. Different again (cruder and focusing more on the erotic) was a work known as *Iolaus*, in which a character disguised himself as a eunuch in order to gain access to a girl, probably during some religious rite from which males were barred.[42] Other works went in more for the macabre and grotesque: cannibalism and orgies (Lollianus) – 'my piece is raw!' complains one diner on human flesh – or nightmarish pursuit by eunuchs with their ears and noses chopped off (Iamblichus).[43] The improbabilities of the genre reach mind-boggling levels in Iamblichus' *Babylonian Tale*, which included twin brothers who were both identical in appearance to the hero, thus doubling or trebling the potential for mistaken identity.[44]

The comic fiction of Lucian, which does survive intact, provides further evidence for the fertility and entertainment value of the genre. His outrageous *True History* is an extended spoof on fantastic travel stories. Having sagely criticized his predecessors and correctly identified Homer's Odysseus as 'the founder of this school of literary horseplay' ('he spun many such fanciful stories to the Phaeacians, who knew no better'), he goes on to declare that he has no true story to relate, since nothing worth mentioning has ever happened to him. 'My subject, then, is things I have never seen or experienced or heard tell of from anybody else: things that do not in fact exist and could not ever exist at all. So my readers must not believe a word I say.' This mischievous honesty recalls and subverts the more positive claims of historians to be using eyewitness accounts.

The ensuing narrative includes a river of wine, giants, a city built on a giant cork, a trip to the Moon, an encounter with the dead in Elysium, and an episode in which our hero sails inside a whale and makes landfall in its belly. 'There was land, with hills, formed, I suppose, by the settling of the mud the creatures swallowed.' His comic imagination is inexhaustible: a high point is the wild absurdity of his description of the Moon-dwellers.

> To be beautiful on the moon is to be bald and hairless . . . on comets, the
> opposite holds true . . . They grow beards just above the knee . . . when they
> blow their noses, a bitter honey emerges. . . . Their eyes are removable . . . they

often lose their own and have to borrow other people's. Some of them, the rich, have a large stock in reserve. (1.23–5)

When his ship makes the return journey from Moon to Earth, they pass the floating city of Cloud-cuckooland, familiar from Aristophanes' *Birds*: 'I thought of the dramatist Aristophanes, a wise and truthful man, whose writings arouse undeserved disbelief.' (29) The fun of the work is obvious to any reader, and most could also cope with the clever allusions and additions to stories from the *Odyssey* and Herodotus. It is refreshing to encounter an ancient text which was evidently composed to amuse the reader, and which continues to do so without fail.

VIII

The death of a certain Petronius during Nero's purge of suspected conspirators in AD 65 makes entertaining reading. This man was a courtier, high in Nero's favour on account of his self-indulgent lifestyle and sophisticated taste. Having lost the emperor's goodwill and being obliged to commit suicide, he ostentatiously avoided the heroic or Stoic manner cultivated by his contemporary Seneca, and spent his final hours listening to light songs and frivolous verses (Tacitus, *Annals* 16.18–20). In his will he did not flatter Nero or list gifts to the emperor, but sent him a detailed catalogue of his recent debaucheries, listing names and sexual positions which Nero had supposed entirely secret. His death was parodic and outrageous: if this man was not the Petronius to whom the *Satyricon* is ascribed, they were certainly soul-mates.

Petronius' surviving work is only part of a considerably larger whole. What we have are substantial portions of books 14, 15 and 16. The total number of books is unknown: one guess is 24, the number of books in Homer's poems, which would suit the intermittent epic parody. But we cannot even be sure that the novel was completed before the author's death. What is clear is that it was an extended narrative of episodes in which the characters drifted from place to place, getting involved in shady activities (theft, fraud, perhaps even murder) and often undergoing humiliating experiences. The parts we have are set in south Italy (probably Puteoli and certainly Croton). The main character, Encolpius, is also the narrator (but an unreliable one): he is infatuated with a pretty boy who accompanies but more than once deserts him, and he falls in frequently with other no-gooders who exploit or get the better of him. The plot line is evidently a parodic or low-life version of the Greek romantic novel. Instead of noble heterosexual lovers devoted to one another, we have here a homosexual pair with little in common, and infidelity is frequent on both sides. Many of the stock motifs of the novel are redeployed (e.g. storms and shipwreck): the high-flown sentiments of the genre are exaggerated to the point of burlesque, especially in the hero's bouts of self-pity, which lead him to contemplate suicide (94). The tone constantly fluctuates: ecstatic reunion gives way to despair or embarrassment, temporary success is swiftly followed by exposure or fresh disaster. Whereas in the Greek novel we saw that the actions of the principal characters are overseen by divine Providence, and that Helios or Aphrodite may be looking after the interests of the faithful lovers, in Petronius' book the hero is cursed by the anger of Priapus, a phallic and normally comical deity (139), and is therefore stricken by impotence at the most inconvenient moments (129–30, 132; cf. p. 172). As this suggests, eroticism and sexual comedy are prominent in this novel, and the title no doubt alludes to these themes: *libri Satyricon* ('books of satyric doings') suggests the lustful and grossly physical nature of satyrs, those goat-like followers of Dionysus.

Only one major episode of the work survives completely intact, the famous dinner party hosted by the wealthy freedman Trimalchio. Other scenes are scrappier: some involve the sexual antics of the main characters, others rowdy quarrelling and tempestuous travels. An entertaining sequence involves a get-rich plan by the ingenious poet Eumolpus, who proposes that they fool the greedy citizens of Croton into thinking that he is a rich man close to death, so that they can live off the fat of the land because the citizens will do anything for them, even prostitute their children, in the hope of being mentioned in his will. This plan is still in progress when the text breaks off: as an added refinement, Eumolpus is in the course of stating the terms on which the legacy hunters will inherit – they will have to eat his body after his demise!

The structure of the work is loose and picaresque. Unconnected inset stories are introduced as entertainment for the characters (ghost-stories at Trimalchio's feast, a tale of a widow's infidelity to defuse hot tempers on board ship (61–3, 111–12)). Digressions are frequent, some of them involving declamatory speeches (88), even a declamation against declamation (1–2); there are comments on works of art, and particularly poems. The text is scattered with short verse passages, often banal but deliberately so. Eumolpus himself is allowed several long renditions, but he receives little respect from others. 'Some of those walking in the colonnades interrupted his recitation with a shower of stones. Being familiar with this sort of appreciation of his genius, he covered his head and fled . . . I was nervous myself in case they thought I was a poet too' (90; cf. 92.6, 8). But the text is multi-faceted. Eumolpus is a clown, but his comments on epic may embody semi-serious criticism of Petronius' contemporary Lucan (118).

The account of the dinner held by Trimalchio has always been the most popular part of the novel. Flamboyantly wealthy, the host takes a naive delight in his own possessions and in the abundance of his hospitality. Cheerful and self-important at first, he becomes increasingly morbid as the evening grows on, even reading his will and designing his funereal monument over dinner. Constantly parading his supposed learning, he exposes his hopeless ignorance. Rich foods and wine, and an endless succession of courses and entertainment, do not compensate for the grossness of his company and the tastelessness of his boastful conversation. It is not surprising that our layabout heroes are constantly laughing at him behind his back while guzzling his lavish fare.

Trimalchio clapped his hands and exclaimed: 'so wine, sad to say, enjoys longer life than poor humans! So let us drink and be merry. Wine is life-enhancing. This is genuine Opimian that I'm serving. Yesterday the wine I provided was not so good, though the company at dinner was much more respectable.' So we got started on the wine, taking the greatest pains to express our wonder at all the elegance. (34, tr. P. G. Walsh)

Gossip of this sort was being bandied about when Trimalchio came in. He mopped his brow and washed his hands with perfume. He waited a second or two before remarking: 'Excuse me, my friends, but for some days now my stomach has not responded to nature's call. The doctors are at a loss. But in my case pomegranate-rind and pinewood dipped in vinegar have done the trick. I now have hopes that my stomach will be regular as before. Anyhow, my inside is rumbling like a roaring bull, so if any of you want to relieve yourself, there is no need to be ashamed. None of us was born rock-solid. I can't imagine any torture worse than having to hold it in. This is the one thing that even Jupiter can't forbid. I see you're grinning, Fortunata, but that's how you keep me awake at night. But even in the dining room I don't forbid anyone to ease himself, and the doctors forbid us to keep the wind inside. If anything heavier is imminent, everything's ready outside – water, chamber-pots, the other bits and pieces. Believe me, the vapours attack the brain, and flood through your whole body. I know quite a few died that way through refusing to face the facts.' We thanked him for his generosity and consideration, and hastened to choke our laughter by taking frequent swigs of the wine. (47)

Trimalchio is a grotesque but brilliant creation. Despite the lead given by the educated narrator, it is hard merely to sneer at him: he is a sympathetic and good-humoured host, generous but absurd.

The conversation at the dinner table is just as fascinating. Petronius has taken great pains to characterize the different participants, especially through their style. Trimalchio's fellow freedmen speak in a highly colloquial, idiomatic style quite unlike the main narrative of the novel. It may not reproduce but is certainly a great deal closer to popular Latin: short snappy sentences, proverbial sayings, swift changes of subject, slangy insults. The vividness and vigour of these passages make them quite exceptional in classical prose, with its bias toward the elevated and the rhetorical.[45] The opposition is made explicit when one of the speakers challenges Encolpius' companion, the rhetorician Agamemnon:

> Agamemnon, am I right that you are saying 'why is this boring man prattling on?'? I'm doing it because though you're the expert with words, you're saying nothing. You don't belong to our patch, so you sniff at the way we poor buggers talk. We know you're off your head with all that education. I tell you what: can I persuade you to come out to our country place one day, and take a look at our little house? We'll get a bite to eat there – some chicken and eggs. It'll be a pleasant outing even if the weather this year has turned everything upside-down. We'll certainly get enough to fill our bellies. My little feller is growing fast, ready to sit at your feet; he can divide by four already. He's a smart lad, made of the right stuff, though he's crazy about birds; I've already killed three goldfinches of his and told him that the weasel ate them. But now he's found another hobby; he's very fond of painting. . . .
>
> I've bought the lad some law books; I want him to get a smattering of the law to cope with our property. Law is where the bread is; he's had enough literature to mark him for life. If he shies at law, I've decided that he must learn a trade as a barber, or auctioneer, or if the worst comes to the worst an advocate – some career that only death can rob him of. So every day I rail at him: 'Believe me, education's for your own benefit. Take a look at Philero the advocate. If he hadn't applied himself, today he wouldn't be able to keep the wolf from the door . . . Education's a real treasure; a profession's something for life.' (46, extracts)

Of course this is not a transparent window on to real life: these men and their preoccupations are distorted through the perception of Encolpius the narrator and Petronius the author. But the light-hearted mimicry of low-brow conversation and its vitality is extraordinarily successful, and has few parallels in ancient literature.

We have already met Apuleius as a distinguished advocate, philosopher and sophist, brought on trial for seducing a woman by magical arts (p. 101). By far his greatest work is the so-called *Golden Ass* (the original title may have been *Metamorphoses*), the one complete Latin novel to survive (in 11 books), and a masterpiece of stylistic virtuosity. It can still be read with delight by moderns who know nothing of Apuleius' background or period. The prologue declares that it will include interwoven 'Milesian tales', an allusion to a Greek tradition of storytelling, usually crude and erotic. The promise, like much else in the work, is deceptive, for although the novel includes sexual misadventures, it is composed in a far more sophisticated style and appeals to a more intellectual and erudite readership. Written in the first person, it tells the story of a certain Lucius, a likeable young man travelling in northern Greece, who is foolishly excited by the idea of magic. Discovering that the mistress of the house where he is staying is a witch, he ignores the explicit and implicit warnings he receives, and is determined to learn more. Soon he is making love to her maidservant, eager to get access to the magic potion which can transform him into a bird. Unfortunately, the maid mixes up the jars and by the end of book 3 Lucius finds himself not a bird but an ass! The rest of the work recounts his misfortunes: carried off by brigands, rescued but consigned to hard work in a mill, maltreated by a malicious boy, bought and sold and stolen by a variety of owners, repeatedly beaten and abused, but occasionally given better treatment. Even his occasional good fortune is comical, as when his good taste in food and wine delights his owners, or when he is obliged to sleep with an infatuated woman, a scene both tender and burlesque. Although he retains his human wits, he cannot speak or communicate with other humans: only the reader has access to his thoughts and can enjoy his commentary – often knowing, sometimes naive. The traditional association of the ass with stupidity is exploited, as Lucius makes remarks such as 'clues that were ambiguous but not obscure to an intelligent ass like me' or 'my readers are probably saying by now: "Oh god, do we have to put up with an ass philosophising?"' (7.12, 10.33).

Apuleius' plot is not original. His novel is clearly a cousin of the short novella (an abridgement of a longer work) preserved in the manuscripts of Lucian and entitled 'Lucius, or the Ass'.[46] This follows the story-line of books 1 to 10 very closely: until we near the climax there is hardly a sentence which is not paralleled in the Latin writer. Apuleius' far greater length is attained partly by greater scene-setting and characterization, partly by the addition of subsidiary tales or inset narratives (most notably the famous tale of Cupid and Psyche which straddles books 4–6). But the Greek 'Ass' ends with risqué farce: when Lucius has been restored to human shape, he hurries round to the woman who had been besotted with him as an ass, only to find that when she inspects his much-diminished equipment, she finds him so inferior as a lover that he is swiftly out in the street, and ruefully sets sail for home! This version of the story is highly entertaining but has no moral and no deeper meanings.

Apuleius' final book takes a very different turn. Lucius in ass form escapes and finds his way to the sea, where he prays inwardly to the goddess Isis and is granted a vision of her in all her glory. In a speech of unsurpassed splendour, she promises him that he will be restored to human form at a given moment in her followers' procession next day, and also guarantees him salvation if he devotes himself to her for the rest of his days. All this comes to pass. Lucius is rebuked by Isis and her priest for his fatal curiosity, his obsession with magic, and his previous sinful ways; we begin to see that the picaresque novel has been a disguised pilgrim's progress, with Lucius finally shedding his lustful past and discovering religious truth. Previously Lucius' curiosity has been his undoing (as is also the case with Psyche in the mythical inset narrative of books 4–6): in the last book this is neatly reversed, as the new devotee of Isis rebukes his readers and warns them not to seek to learn more of the initiation-rituals than is permitted (11.23). The ass-shape itself gains new significance, for Isis describes it as 'this vile beast that has always been hateful to me' (11.6). This alludes to the cult and myths surrounding Isis: Seth or Typhon, the deity who murdered her husband Osiris, was identified with the ass. Further complexities emerge when, almost on the last page of the novel, Lucius is described as 'a man of Madauros' – that is, from Apuleius' own town in Numidia, north Africa (11.27). This contradicts the earlier statement that he comes from Corinth (2.12), and it seems inevitable that we are meant to see Lucius as somehow resembling or at least momentarily associated with the author. Needless to say, this does not turn the novel, or even the final book, into autobiography: but it is attested that Apuleius had been initiated into many mystery-religions, and the elaborate account of Lucius' process of induction, through several stages, into the cult of Isis could not have been written by one who was not both well-informed about and keenly interested in this religion.

Modern criticism of this novel broadly divides into two schools. On the one hand there are those who take the conversion narrative as the authentic climax of the work, and see the 'progress' of Lucius from folly to salvation as in some way exemplary: if not advocacy of the cult of Isis, at any rate of some form of philosophic (Platonic?) teaching. On the other are those who see the work as a showpiece of cultured, sophistic entertainment, in which the initiation of the gullible Lucius is the final grotesque adventure and even the visions of Isis can be read as self-deception or hallucinations. The highly original work by the late J. J. Winkler (*Auctor & Actor*, 1985) reached new heights of scholarly ingenuity in presenting the book as an immensely intelligent and complex confidence trick, a predecessor of Escher or Borges, in which the reader is constantly baffled and forced to choose an interpretation without having the means to do so. The final book, on this reading, is a conundrum focusing on the nature of religious choice, a dramatization of the leap of faith which the reader, like Lucius, is forced to make. In a post-Winkler world, it is no longer possible to read the novel 'straight', as a heartfelt personal testimony (it was never easy to do so without setting aside much of the farce and fun of the earlier books). Whatever variation one opts for, the work must be seen as a seriocomic hybrid, a contradiction in terms, as the title 'Golden Ass' suggests, with its double implication of ass enhanced by human intelligence and of man lowered to the level of beast. So too we find Platonist philosophy and spirituality in a grotesque and crude setting, a world of fantastic transformations and generic fluidity. The author's inimitable style mirrors this ambiguity, with simple syntax but complex phraseology, high-flown circumlocutions and exotic archaisms combined with extravagant invented terms and colloquial forms: Greek idioms infect Latin speech-patterns and vocabulary. Flaubert's description is memorably pungent: 'One smells there the odour of incense and of urine; bestiality is linked with mysticism.' The admirers of Evelyn Waugh and of Martin Amis will find equal gratification in Apuleius' finest work.

Novel writing did not enjoy much prestige in antiquity, perhaps because (unless we include the earlier Xenophon) the form developed after the classic period on which most critics focused. Those who do mention the genre tend to be negative. The killjoy Julian the Apostate approves history as useful, but continues by saying that we must reject 'all the fictions composed by writers of the past in this form of history, narratives of love and all that sort of stuff'. The Latin authors fared no better. Quintilian nowhere mentions Petronius, and a later critic dismisses literature which aims only at entertainment through fiction: 'realistic narratives full of the imaginary adventures of lovers, with which Petronius engaged himself and Apuleius too, amazingly, sometimes trifled'; such things must be rejected by a philosopher and relegated to 'nurses' cradles'.[47] Ancient judgements are interesting, but we are not obliged to follow them, especially when the disparaging verdict clearly arises from a high-minded philosophical agenda. Whatever our verdict on the Greek novels, the Roman instances are undoubtedly masterpieces. This seems an uncontroversial case in which the Roman imitators surpassed their models; it is also striking that in this genre the parody is more successful than the original (the readers of Richardson and Fielding may well reach the same verdict on the early English novel).

5

Erotic Literature

... take this short message to my girl,
unfriendly words.

May she live and flourish with her lovers,
whom she holds in one embrace, three-hundred strong,
loving none of them truly, but with each and all alike
bursting their groins.

And let her not look back at my love, as of old;
for it is dead and gone, through her fault, fallen
like the flower on the edge of a meadow, once struck
by the passing plough

Catullus 11.15–24

I

In earlier chapters we have been looking at particular genres, virtually all of them recognized in antiquity and amenable to survey as inherited literary forms. In this chapter and the next two the discussion will be broader and more thematic. This chapter deals with literature involving desire and its fulfilment or frustration. Needless to say, this embraces a very wide range of genres, and I shall be largely ignoring some which have already been discussed. The main focus will be on smaller-scale and more 'personal' types of literature – lyric poetry, epigram, some pastoral poetry, and amatory elegy.[1] Prose will not be ignored, but these themes are more prominent in poetry: the chief exception is Platonic dialogue, of which more below.

There are many ways in which classical scholarship can make fresh advances, but the most dramatic is by the discovery of new evidence. The publication in 1974 of a papyrus (detached from a mummy-wrapping) containing the longest piece so far known by the early poet Archilochus of

Paros was one striking example. (One of the original editors presented it to an Oxford audience at a meeting which gathered to hear a paper mysteriously entitled 'Last Tango on Paros'.)[2] We have perhaps the second half of a poem presenting a man and a woman engaged first in dialogue, then in some form of lovemaking. Here is a translation of what survives.

> * ... '... holding off altogether ... endure.
>
> But if you are eager and your passion drives you,
> inside our house there is one
> who feels great desire even now,
>
> a lovely maiden, tender. I believe
> that she is perfect in form.
> She is the one you should make [your own].'
>
> Such were her words. But I answered,
> 'Daughter of Amphimedo,
> a fine and [virtuous?] woman,
>
> whom now the damp earth covers,
> many are the delights the goddess gives
> to young men,
>
> besides the holy deed. One of those will suffice.
> At our leisure, when the ...
> grows dark,
>
> you and I shall determine together, with god's goodwill.
> I will do as you ask me.
> Great is [the desire in me.]
>
> Do not bar me, dear, from ...
> inside the precinct and the gates.
> I shall hold back towards the grassy
>
> meadows. Be sure of this now. As for Neobule –
> someone else can take her.
> Ugh, she's over-ripe, twice your age.
>
> The maidenly flower has lost its bloom
> and the charm she once had is gone.
> She is insatiable.
>
> A madwoman, overstepping the limits.
> To hell with her.
> Let nobody press me
>
> to take on a wife like that;
> I would be a laughing stock to my neighbours.
> It's you I want, and badly.

*   Dots indicate gaps in the text. Bracketed words are possible but not certain ways of filling a gap. We do know that the end of the passage marked the end of the whole poem.

For you are one I can trust, and not treacherous;
she is ferocious,
and has a plethora of lovers.

I'm afraid that if I pressed on there too eagerly,
I'd be fathering blind and stillborn pups
like the bitch in the fable.'

These were my words. Then taking the maid
I laid her down among the blooming flowers.
In a soft cloak I wrapped her,

cradling her neck in my arms,
. . . she stopped . . .
[quivering?] like a fawn

and gently I touched her breasts with my hands
. . . her young flesh was revealed
her prime of youth was approaching

and as I caressed her lovely body all over,
I let go my white strength
while I touched her golden [hair?].   (fr 196aw.)

The narrator is seeking sexual gratification with a young girl. When the passage begins she is trying to fend off his advances, recommending another girl in the house, Neobule. The man's reply, while courteous to her, vigorously rejects Neobule as lover or bride; he then makes a limited concession to her protestations, by suggesting something less than full-scale lovemaking; without waiting for an answer, he then moves swiftly into action. The description which concludes the poem is vividly sensuous, making clear that the man gets his way, yet it does not lack tenderness. How far do they go? This is much disputed, but it seems unlikely that he actually enters her: we would need to be told as much, after his proposal of an alternative. (Others, however, opt for deliberate ambiguity at the end.)

Four central points about this new fragment are relevant to many other texts. First, although the poem is told in the first person, we cannot assume that it is autobiographical. This point may seem self-evident, but is often ignored. The characters in a poem, including the narrator, are characters manipulated by the poet: in principle Archilochus (or, in later poetry, Catullus, or Propertius . . .) could have made up the whole scene. First-person narrative produces vividness, it does not guarantee direct access to experience. Second, it seems clear that the situation in this poem involves non-marital sex. This reflects a general tendency in ancient literature (and indeed much modern): marriages are not as interesting as affairs. When husbands and wives are the subject, it is normally because they are separated or unhappy, whether because of infidelity or some other source of distress. When Odysseus returns to Penelope, the story is over. Marriage resolves the earlier difficulties at the end of Menander's plays, as in Shakespeare's comedies. Love poetry focuses on the lover (usually but not always from the male perspective). Third, we observe the difference between the narrator's flattering and reassuring style as he addresses the girl and the savagery with which he dismisses the alternative of Neobule. Ancient erotic poetry often involves a hate-poetry element. Either the abandoned lover hurls invective at the former beloved, or the lover who has been rejected angrily warns the beloved that beauty will not last: one day there will be retribution. Poets are powerful: they can immortalize their darlings either for good or for ill. Later tradition claimed that Archilochus had directed such vicious poetic abuse at Lycambes and his daughters (Neobule was one of them) that some or all of the family hung themselves in shame. Propertius said that Catullus' poetry had made Lesbia more famous than Helen herself (2.34.88), but neither figure was famous only for her virtue.

The fourth point concerns genre and audience expectations. The poem is in an iambic metre, and iambs were (at least later, and visibly in some of Archilochus' own work) associated with aggression and violent, forthright language (these are the implications, for example, of Catullus 40).[3] Genres handle the same themes in different ways: explicit description of sex would be out of place in epic, and even in oratory the speaker must frame his references with apologetic comments (Aeschines 1. 37f., 76, etc.). Iambic readily admits obscenities, but these are avoided here, metaphor being preferred, and even this degree of anatomical precision is rare in love poetry of the middle range, such as Latin elegy. We do not know enough of Archilochus' practice or his audience's assumptions to be sure what they would have made of this, but we do know that Neobule was prominent elsewhere in his poetry, and not always in a negative light. Whether she was real or fictive, we seem to be dealing with a developing situation. Again the parallel of Catullus comes to mind.

Before we move on to other specific cases, some further general comments on sexual roles and situations are necessary. No amount of special pleading can conceal the fact that both the Greek and the Roman world were male-dominated (as, of course, was every society before the late twentieth century). Women were subordinated, did not have voting rights, often were barely allowed a role in society outside marriage. Pericles in Thucydides declares that the highest praise for a woman is to have nothing said about her, good or ill. This general situation had its consequences for literature (as a female chorus complains in Euripides' *Medea*). Almost every major and minor writer surviving from the ancient world is male. Women do, however, bulk large in myth, literature and art. One obvious tendency is for literature to magnify male fears of women getting out of control (the adulteries and child- or husband-killings in tragedy are extreme examples). Misogyny was not rare. Hesiod develops at length in both his poems the tale of Pandora, the first woman, who brought so much evil into the world. Semonides in a satirical poem lists ten different types of woman, comparing them with animals ('another is from a monkey . . .') and listing their faults. Only one (the bee-type) represents a doubtless rare ideal.[4] In general it was assumed that men married not for companionship but to have children. The concern for legitimacy of heirs and continuity of property placed severe restraints on the freedom of citizen wives.[5] Men, by contrast, could and often did enjoy themselves elsewhere. Class distinctions also mattered: slaves were available for sexual gratification, as were prostitutes of various levels of sophistication. But because love poetry thrives on portraying the unattainable, we often see men in despair at being unable to win a woman's favour, although she may be of low birth, even a courtesan (poor men in love with haughty rich courtesans are common in comedy).

A survey of the various genres reveals certain 'standard' situations: the lover in pursuit of the beloved, whether in desperate devotion or more whimsically and flirtatiously; the lover jealous at the success of a rival; the lover parted from the beloved, and either confident (for a time) in the other's fidelity, or miserably anxious and suspicious. We have already mentioned the aftermath of the affair, generating hatred and abuse (though sometimes the lover still continues to express longing and desire while knowing it is hopeless, as in Catullus). An alternative approach involves greater detachment, with the poet amusedly observing the human comedy endemic in the lover's condition: this attitude is especially cultivated by Horace. Or again, the text itself may betray the speaker: in Theocritus we can see that the Cyclops has no chance of winning the sea-nymph Galatea, and similarly Virgil's Corydon is whistling in the dark, as the reader sees before Corydon finally admits it to himself. Occasionally we find poems that celebrate success and ecstatic joy, though it seldom lasts (for one notable case, see appendix 1.3).

Homoerotic poetry is also common, and follows many of the same patterns. Male relationships are far better known than female, though we turn in a moment to the most famous instance of female homosexuality, Sappho. In ancient times bisexuality was fairly common, and exclusive preference for one sex or the other may have been relatively rare. The idea that some people are intrinsically or by nature homosexual was probably not common, though Aristophanes in Plato's *Symposium* develops it in a fantastic context.[6] However, long-term same-sex relationships do seem to be familiar: Agathon and Pausanias in the same work of Plato are recognized as a 'couple'. Much emphasis in modern discussion has been placed on the active–passive distinction, treated as crucial in the classic discussion of Greek homosexuality by Dover:[7] to be the active partner in a homoerotic act was manly and respectable, to be the passive, or at least to admit to occupying the passive role, was potentially a source of shame or a subject of abuse. Derisive treatment of 'pathics' is common in Aristophanes, Catullus and Martial, not to mention the scurrilously comic *Priapean verses*. Foucault and others have argued that whichever the gender, what matters is the power-relations between partners, and that in male–male relations, power belongs to the penetrator. But there is some risk of excessive rigidity here: 'romantic' relationships clearly existed, and lovers' devotion could be admired without attending to their relative status and power. Aeschylus could dramatize Achilles' affection for Patroclus in explicitly erotic terms; the lovers Harmodius and Aristogiton were commemorated for 'liberating' Athens because they assassinated Hipparchus after a personal insult.[8]

Chastity was demanded of women before marriage and marriage was generally arranged early. On the male side there seems to have been no special value placed on sexual self-restraint: the chaste Hippolytus in Euripides is seen as peculiar and self-righteous by his more lustful father. Certain religious and philosophic sects may have prescribed abstinence, and the Orphic notion that the body was in some way base has influenced Plato. But virginity as a virtue in itself (as opposed to a requirement for the priestess of certain cults, to avoid religious pollution) seems to be a phe-nomenon of the Christian era. Some thinkers in antiquity might maintain that the body is a prison, none that it is a temple.[9]

II

It is a painful loss that we have so little poetry by Sappho, the greatest female poet of antiquity: what we have is enough to help us understand her ancient admirers' praise of her as 'the tenth Muse', or even 'the female Homer' (T27, 57, 60 Campbell).[10] One complete poem survives, and significant portions of some others, but of slightly over 200 fragments many are only a line or two, or merely a word. Not that those lines are devoid of force: their very separation from context gives them a special quality of limpid mystery.

I loved you, Atthis, once. You seemed to me a little child. (49)

Love shook my heart like a wind falling upon oaks on a mountain. (47)

Towards your lovely selves [female] my thoughts are unchangeable. (41)

You came, and I was longing for you. You cooled my heart which was burning with desire. (48)

Who was Sappho and what was her position, her social context? Unfortunately we have little that is reliable. More than with most poets, the ancient
evidence is fragile and conflicting. She thinks of herself as a poetess ('it is
not right that there should be lamentation in the house of those who serve
the Muses. That would not be fitting for us' (150)). Her own words imply
she expected her poetry to last (esp. 55). Some of her verses are clearly
composed for special occasions. This applies particularly to the wedding-
songs, in which she touchingly dwells on the passing of virginity (114), or
more light-heartedly acclaims the size and strength of the bridegroom: 'lift
high the roofbeam, carpenters! . . . The groom is coming, a rival to Ares,
much larger than a large man' (111). In other places she speaks affectionately
of many women (the names include Abanthis, Anactoria, Atthis, Gongyla,
Irana), though also dismissing or attacking others (rivals?). Aphrodite is
frequently invoked or described as present. Several poems refer to painful
partings, or to memories of those who have gone away. Older scholars tried
to avoid the natural conclusion, and imagined Sappho as running some kind
of girls' finishing school: this is a notion readily caricatured, but a circle of
friends, probably companions prior to marriage, still seems the most plausible solution, whether we suppose they met for practice of song or of ritual
or both (training in sexual techique has also been suggested!). Whatever the
circumstances, it is hard to deny the eroticism of many of these poems: in
particular poem 94, though in a damaged context, seems to allude to the
fulfilment of desire, whether Sappho's or another's:

> 'and honestly I wish I were dead.'[11]
> She was leaving me with many tears and said this. 'Oh what bad luck has
> been ours, Sappho. Truly I leave you against my will.' I replied to her thus:
> 'Go and farewell and remember me, for you know how we cared for you.
> If not, then I want to remind you . . . and of the good luck we had. You
> put on many wreaths of violets and roses and crocuses together by my
> side, and round your tender neck you put many woven garlands made from
> flowers, and . . . with much flowery perfume, fit for a queen, you anointed
> yourself . . . and on soft beds . . . tender . . . you would satisfy desire . . .'

More revealing, and more clearly springing from artistic technique as well
as emotion, is the one complete poem we have, which uses the conventions
of invocation and prayer (perhaps modelled on the prayers of heroes in
Homer) to produce a complex effect: on one level an appeal to Aphrodite
for aid, on another an admission that this aid has been sought before and
perhaps will be again. The poem is neither self-pity nor self-mockery,
neither simple worship nor parody thereof. By dramatizing her emotions
and commenting on them through the goddess's mouth, Sappho shows her
own ability to step back from them.

Dapple-throned immortal Aphrodite,
daughter of Zeus, weaver of guile, I entreat you,
do not afflict my heart, lady,
with pain and agitation;
But come to me yourself, if ever on another time
you heard my call from far away,
and heeded me, if leaving the golden house
of your father you came
harnessing your chariot. Lovely swift sparrows
brought you, over and around the black earth,
their wings whirring as they bore you from the heaven
through the midair;
and speedily they arrived. Then you, blessed one,
a smile on your immortal face,
asked me what was the matter with me this time,
and why this time I was invoking you,
and what I wanted most to happen to me,
in my lunatic heart. 'Whom am I to persuade this time
to call you back into her affection? Who,
Sappho, is treating you badly?
For if she runs away, soon she will pursue you.
If she refuses gifts, well, soon she will give them.
If she does not love, soon she will love indeed
even against her will.'
Come to me now also, and liberate me from
cruel cares, and accomplish what my heart longs
to accomplish; and you yourself
join me as my comrade-in-arms.   (poem 1)

Some grounds may also be found for seeing in her poems a deliberate adoption of a stance that contrasts with male values. In 16 she begins by saying firmly that 'some say a host of cavalry, others of infantry and others of ships, is the most beautiful thing on the black earth; but I say it is what one loves'. She goes on to illustrate this by means of the myth of Helen, often condemned by post-Homeric poets but here viewed with sympathy. Then come thoughts of Anactoria far away (has she left Sappho as Helen left Menelaus?), whom she would rather see than Lydian chariots and infantry. In another poem, 44, she treats not the martial exploits of Hector, but his glorious wedding to Andromache. More subjectively, there is perhaps a sensuous delicacy of language in Sappho's verses when dealing with love, which contrasts with the frivolity, even the cruelty, of many of her masculine peers.

We are better informed about the context of some other early love poetry. Much of it was evidently composed, like some related types, for performance at the symposium (drinking-party).[12] In its best-known form, immortalized by Plato, this was a semi-formalized gathering of a group of intimates, a setting in which men could relax, converse, listen to music or singing, and often sing or perform themselves. It sometimes had a political aspect: private parties were a suitable meeting-place for conspirators. The poems of Archilochus, Alcaeus and others show us the sort of resentments and recollections which might be aired, and often there might also be cause for celebration ('now is the time to drink and get drunk, now that Myrsilus is dead' (Alcaeus 332, where Myrsilus is one of the poet's political antagonists)). But erotic themes were common, sometimes combined with references to the sympotic setting itself. Theognis in a splendid poem addresses his beloved Cyrnus, assuring him of his future renown (237ff 'I have given you wings . . .'): thanks to Theognis, his name will live forever. 'At feasts and banquets you will be present on all occasions, in the mouths of many, and to the clear-toned sound of pipes young men, with seemly grace and loveliness, their voices fair and clear, will sing of you' [tr. Miller]. But after a dozen lines or so of these assurances there is a sting in the tail, and the final couplet is one of reproach: 'but you do not even pay me slight respect. You cheat me with words, as if I were a mere child.' This behaviour too Theognis immortalizes.

Recurrent in this poetry is the motif of 'falling in love again', which we have already seen in Sappho. Ibycus compares himself with an aging race-horse reluctantly returning to the track (287). Anacreon uses more violent imagery (413): 'Once again Love has beaten me like a blacksmith with a great hammer, and plunged me into a winter torrent.' But in general his manner is lighter and more good-humoured: he calls for water, wine and garlands so that he may box with love (396)(these are suitable weapons for the challenge); he ruefully admits that his white hairs are not attractive (358); he offers a 'Thracian filly' expert instruction, but his promises of expertise seem unlikely to convince the girl to accept him as a 'rider' (417). More melancholy is the elegist Mimnermus, whose lines on love swiftly pass to thoughts of age and death (1 West). The symposium celebrates the joys of the present, intensified by the awareness that soon it will pass away: 'then he will lie in the deep-wooded ground, sharing no more in the drinking-parties and the lyres and the lovely call of the flutes' (anon. *PMG* 1009).

III

The most vivid dramatization of the flirtatious erotic interchange of young, well-born Greek males is to be found in the earlier dialogues of Plato, especially the *Lysis, Charmides* and *Symposium*.[13] Greek educational practice and Athenian social constraints meant that women were normally denied the opportunity to engage in intelligent conversation with men. The world of Plato's dialogues is a masculine one: no woman participates in the discussions (although later Plato's school, the Academy, does appear to have admitted some). Furthermore, the main figure of Plato's work, his mentor Socrates, is represented as strongly attracted to young men. At the opening of the *Protagoras* a friend asks him 'where have you just turned up from, Socrates? No doubt fresh from hot pursuit of the delightful Alcibiades?' From one point of view this makes him a comic figure, all the more so as he is a man of advanced years and somewhat grotesque appearance (in the *Symposium* Alcibiades compares his looks with those of a bestial satyr). But Plato uses the erotic theme to make important points about Socrates' priorities. In the *Charmides* the setting is the wrestling school, and the centre of attention is the beautiful youth after whom the dialogue is named. Although Socrates often talks as though he is entranced by such youths' good looks, he is actually much more interested in testing the calibre of their minds. Critias suggests that Charmides will be a gorgeous sight when he has stripped off to exercise, but Socrates responds: 'before we see his body, should we not undress him as regards his soul?' (154d–e). Plato treats these topics with decorum and charm: Charmides himself is a modest and self-conscious lad, and it is fitting that the subject of their enquiry should turn out to be moderation or self-restraint. In the *Lysis* Socrates stage-manages a conversation which includes two young lovers. The eagerness of the one and the coyness of the other make delightful theatre in themselves but are also used to make moral points about both love and the proper conduct of argument (205e, 210e). Again, in the *Gorgias*, Socrates says that his love is directed at two recipients, Alcibiades and philosophy, and that the former is changeable and fickle, but the latter always remains consistent and says the same thing (481d). There is no doubt which Socrates will side with if the two conflict, and this is part of what the *Symposium* shows.

The *Symposium* and the *Phaedrus* are closely related, but the first is probably the earlier and is certainly the more accessible. This dialogue is set in the house of the tragedian Agathon, who has won his first victory in the Dionysiac contest and is holding a celebratory party for close friends. Others present include Socrates, Phaedrus, a self-important doctor called Eryximachus, and the comic poet Aristophanes. Having indulged themselves to excess the previous night, the company decide to enjoy the evening in a more moderate and cultivated manner, and it is agreed that each will make a speech in praise of Love (throughout, the concern is with love between men). This device allows Plato to give full rein to his powers of characterization and stylistic parody: speeches by Phaedrus, Pausanias, Eryximachus, Aristophanes and Agathon all differ in approach and offer partial (in some cases superficial) insights. The longest and most philosophically challenging speech is that of Socrates himself. Whereas earlier speakers had dealt with love as a phenomenon of this world, and as a source of pleasure for its own sake, Socrates sees love of beauty in an individual as a lower rung on a ladder which will lead the philosopher eventually, through self-discipline and contemplation, to a higher beauty, the essence of beauty itself, more or less identifiable with goodness and wisdom. Such insight will bring man as close to god as is humanly possible. From mythology (Phaedrus) and social commentary (Pausanias) we have moved to a form of religious mysticism, which Socrates ascribes to the teaching of a prophetess, Diotima. It follows that merely physical enjoyment is a trivial and even a distracting goal: Platonic love, though widely misunderstood nowadays, really means not only abstinence but transcendence of the physical. (These ideas are explored from a different angle in the *Phaedrus*, where more attention is paid to the relations between physical lovers, though it is still better if they abstain as far as possible.) The speech sets a high ideal and transports the dialogue to a more otherworldly plane: 'how would it be if it were possible for any of you to look upon Beauty itself, in its uncontaminated, untainted, undiluted form, not stuffed full of human flesh and colouring and lots more mortal rubbish – but what if any one of you could look upon that divine and unitary essence of Beauty?' (211e). Socrates does not claim to have achieved this himself, but it is made clear that this is his aspiration, and the earlier part of the work shows that he has more chance of doing so than his agreeable but worldly companions.

The last part of the *Symposium* is a delightful surprise, as the party is gate-crashed by the drunken Alcibiades, glamorous playboy and politician, a colourful and controversial figure. Plato has an ulterior motive here, as many Athenians evidently blamed Socrates for Alcibiades' political misdeeds, which brought great harm to Athens in her war with Sparta.[14] Plato is concerned to show that Socrates was not Alcibiades' corruptor but his good angel. When he learns what they have all been doing, Alcibiades insists on making a speech of his own, in praise not of Love but of Socrates. His speech is as eloquent as Socrates' but completely different – disorderly and risqué, full of lively images and reminiscences of campaigns: where Socrates aspired to the absolute, Alcibiades is bogged down in physicality and particulars. The core of the speech is both richly comic and thought-provoking. Alcibiades describes his own fascination with Socrates and desire to benefit from his wisdom, which led him to follow him around, invite him to a private supper, insist on his staying the night – 'for all the world as though *I* were a lover laying a trap for my beloved!' (217c). The point is that to all appearances it is the wealthy, successful, handsome Alcibiades who is the 'catch', whereas he finds himself driven to pursue the old and ugly Socrates. In the end he abandons all shame, gets into bed with him and tries to seduce him into revealing his treasures of wisdom, but Socrates banteringly resists even these overtures, mischievously reminding him of the proverbial 'gold in exchange for bronze': what Alcibiades offers is not sufficient to persuade Socrates to give up *his* treasures. With chagrin the young man admits that he slept as innocently that night as if he had been in bed with his father or brother (219).

The dramatic technique needs spelling out here. Alcibiades arrives only late in the symposium, disrupting the moderate and decorous party that had been in progress before: he has missed Socrates' speech, which might indeed have had some wisdom to communicate to him. After his own speech deep drinking becomes the rule. Alcibiades, despite his enormous talents and opportunities, has effectively made his choice: a life of physical and moral self-indulgence, which will lead him on in the near future to further riotousness and eventually to betray his country. The *Symposium* is partly designed to show him as Socrates' most tragic failure.

The *Phaedrus* can be contrasted with the *Symposium* in several ways: whereas the latter is set indoors at night in a company of a dozen or so fellow-diners, the former takes place on a hot summer's day in a country setting, by the banks of the river Ilissus outside Athens, and involves only two participants, Socrates and Phaedrus. The tone of the *Symposium* alters with each speaker: there is immense variation between the intensity of Socrates' account of mystical ascent and the fun and farce of Aristophanes and Alcibiades. The atmosphere of the *Phaedrus* is calmer, the tone more consistently good-humoured, without the *Symposium*'s variety of style and mood: only in the central speech of Socrates does a more intense and poetic style become prominent. But both works share a preoccupation with two themes, love and rhetoric. Phaedrus is shown as a young man at the crossroads in life, with a soul divided in loyalty between philosophy and rhetoric, Socrates and Lysias. The themes intertwine in a variety of ways, but by the end of the work we can see that Socrates' affection for Phaedrus is not only deeper than that of the absent Lysias, but also such as to lead him on to a better life. For Plato, philosophic speech is a purer rhetoric, and reaches depths in the soul that the more superficial oratory of the rhetoricians cannot reach (cf. p. 88).

IV

There are several poetic genres which seem to emerge, or gain full momentum, in the Hellenistic age. The most abundant is the short epigram, usually composed in elegiac couplets.[15] The epigram originates as a practical form, inscribed on stone and particularly used for epitaphs on the dead, sometimes those who have died in war, sometimes beloved relatives: premature death prompts pathos or sentimentality. The epigram, becoming 'literary', turned predominantly to fictional situations. Funereal themes continue, but the genre developed a much larger sphere: it embraces reflections on mortality, descriptions of works of art, riddles, anecdotes about famous men, and not least erotic themes. Many of the major Hellenistic poets practised this form, among them Callimachus, Theocritus, Leonidas and Asclepiades: the last seems to have been a key figure, who either originated or set the pattern for the erotic epigram. The contribution of Posidippus now needs radical reassessment, after a papyrus find which multiplies our knowledge of his work fivefold.[16] A later figure, Meleager, compiled an anthology of the best in the field around 100 BC, and this forms one of the roots of the much later 'Greek Anthology', which assembles thousands of epigrams from across a millennium, arranging them by topic, not by author.[17] Thus book 5 contains love epigrams concerned with women and book 12 poems about love of boys, in both cases from a wide variety of periods. The treatment is equally varied, though certain recurring patterns are evident. There is a greater degree of artificiality and graceful use of convention than in the earlier lyric age, as when the poet addresses the lamp that witnesses his union with the beloved, or the unhappy lover lies prostrate outside his boyfriend's/mistress's closed door, or represents himself in pursuit of Eros, who is playing the role of a truant boy.[18] But often we find a freshness in the clever use of standard motifs or variations on a theme. One example is the epigram ascribed falsely to Plato, where a neat idea is expressed with simplicity:

> You watch the stars, star of mine. If only I were the sky,
> so as to gaze upon you with many eyes. (AP 7.669)

More elaborate is the hedonistic self-pity of Asclepiades, which combines a number of recurring motifs in the genre:

> Drink, Asclepiades. Why these tears? What's wrong with you?
> You're not the only one cruel Cypris has taken captive,
> Nor has bitter Eros sharpened his arrows for you alone.
> When you're still alive, why lie in the dust?
> Let's drink Bacchus' drink, unmixed. Day is a finger's breadth.
> Shall we wait to see the lamp once more, summoning us to sleep?
> Come, drink, unlucky lover. Not so far off now, you poor fool,
> Is the time when we shall have rest for a long night.   (16 Gow-Page
>   = *AP* 12.50)

Poems like this lie behind famous verses of Catullus (5 and 8), and although Asclepiades addresses himself, similar sentiments addressed to the beloved echo down the centuries to inspire Marvell and Herrick.

Female poets are also found in Hellenistic literature, though they are scarcely more numerous than in earlier times. In the Greek Anthology are several female epigrammatists: Anyte, Hedyle, Moero. More interesting is the enigmatic figure of Erinna, whose ancient readers compared her not only with Sappho but with Homer. She died, it was said, at 19 years of age, but before this composed a hexameter poem of 300 lines, entitled *Distaff*, of which scrappy fragments survive.[19] This poem commemorated and lamented her youthful friend Baucis, who also died young (it is possible that Baucis' early death has been transferred to Erinna herself). Little is certain, but we seem to hear the survivor recalling their childhood together – the 'tortoise' game, a form of tag; playing with their dolls and toys; fear of a bogeyman (Mormo the monster). A cryptic transition speaks of forgetfulness and climbing into bed – were the two girls cowering under the sheets together, or does the poem move on in time to marriage? Words for death, grief and lamentation appear, and also the names Aphrodite and Hymenaeus (god of marriage). Any attempt to base a narrative on these frustrating indications must be hazardous, but we glimpse a childhood closeness parted first by adulthood and expectation of marriage, then by premature death. The intimate hints of childhood strike a note seldom heard in masculine voices.

Moderns will think of pastoral poetry as another separate genre invented in the Hellenistic age, although it is not clear that contemporaries of Theocritus, its chief exponent in Greek, perhaps its inventor, would have recognized it as such.[20] The poems which he composed about the loves and singing-contests of herdsmen in a remote and delicious rural setting are transmitted along with a great many other poems which are either set in the city or in mythological times: almost all are in hexameters, the metre of epic, but with differing dialect; some might be classed as 'epyllion' (p. 33), for example the tale of the infant Heracles slaying snakes which attacked him in his cradle (Th. 24). It is not certain that Theocritus would have thought it proper to set his 'pastorals' apart from the rest of his 'idylls' (the title, which is probably not authorial, seems to mean 'little pictures', vignettes – miniature genre scenes?). Even within the pastoral poems there are distinctions: poem 3 is romantic (a lover serenades his beloved, regaling her with mythological examples of lovers in distress), while poem 4 is faux-naif realism, concluding with country crudity.

Besides definitely rural and definitely mythic, there are some borderline cases, notably poem 1, in which the semi-mythological figure of Daphnis is a rustic herdsman but is being persecuted (like Hippolytus) by a vengeful Aphrodite, whom he has scorned or insulted. Love is a central theme in

Theocritus' poetry, but it can be presented in many different forms. Poem 1 contains an intensely pathetic narrative of Daphnis' death. Poem 15 includes a lament for Aphrodite's beloved Adonis. Elsewhere low humour meets lofty myth, as the Spartans are presented as singing a boisterous wedding-song for the nuptials of Menelaus and Helen (18). This bold, adventurous poet is no mere painter of pretty country scenes. He is a master of both the tragic and the comic mode of love. Poem 2 richly exemplifies the former, poem 11 the latter.

In poem 2 Theocritus does something quite unusual for a classical male poet: he assumes a female voice throughout (dramas or other forms in which *part* of the work involves quoting the speeches of a woman are quite different). The voice is that of Simaetha, a woman who has fallen in love with a seducer called Delphis, and now finds to her deep distress that he is in pursuit of another. In desperation she resorts to magical spells in an effort to draw him back.[21] The whole poem is set at night: first Simaetha is alone with her maid, to whom she gives impatient orders ('Throw them on the fire, Thestylis. Poor fool, where have your wits gone? Am I now a laughing stock even to you?'). Then she despatches the maid to her lover's house to conduct further rites: 'take these magic herbs, and knead them over his threshold while it is dark, and whispering say "I knead the bones of Delphis"' (59ff.). Once alone, she begins to recapitulate her experiences, narrating them to the Moon (identified with the witch-goddess Hecate). 'Where shall I begin? Who brought this curse on me?' We hear of her first encounter with the man at the roadside ('And when I saw him, madness seized me'), of her feverish longing, waiting and hoping for 10 days, of how she confided in her maid and sent a message: of the young man's arrival, his smooth-talking flattery (quoted in direct speech), and of how they came together as she had hoped.

> And to tell you no lengthy tale, dear Moon, all was accomplished, and the two of us reached our desire. And no fault had he to find with me till yesterday, or I with him. But today . . . there came to me the mother of Philista, and she told me many other things, and that Delphis was in love . . .

The poem reaches its climax as she renews her spells with a more threatening tone: 'Now with my love magic shall I bind him, but if he hurts me still, then so help me Fates, he shall beat upon the gates of Hades: such are the evil drugs I keep for him in my box, learned from a foreigner from Assyria.' But we are given no suggestion that these charms are likely to be effective, and the portrait of Simaetha is first and foremost that of an unhappy, abandoned woman: the eerie magical processes, her invocations, her references to the precedents of mythic sorceresses like Circe and Medea, complicate but do not diminish our sympathy. By contrast Delphis is painted in merciless colours, as a selfish womanizer. The poem strongly influenced Virgil, who imitated it not only on a small scale in his own pastorals, but also in his narrative of Dido's despair.

In poem 11, by contrast, seriousness and sympathy are hard to sustain for long: the humour of the situation is too evident. Here Theocritus gives us the charming picture of Polyphemus, the monster from the *Odyssey* (see p. 26), as a boy Cyclops, suffering from puppy-love for the beautiful sea-nymph Galatea. He is still young, under his mother's care (line 67); he is not dangerous, merely grotesque. His protestations of wealth, his attempt to palliate his ugliness, are touching but comical.

> I know, fair maid, why you run away. It's because I have one shaggy brow all across my forehead, one long and single brow from ear to ear, and single is the eye beneath, and broad the nostril above my lip. But even so, I tend a thousand herd of cattle, and draw and drink from them the finest milk. I am not short of cheese either, in summer or autumn or in the depths of winter; my racks are ever heavy. (30–37)

The alert reader recognizes the allusions to the contents of the grown-up Cyclops' cave in Homer. Similarly there are witty anticipations of the unfortunate Polyphemus' future fate: '[in my cave] I have logs of oak, and fire undying beneath the ash, and you may burn my soul, and my one eye too, than which nothing is dearer to me.' When a few lines later he wishes a stranger might arrive in a ship and teach him how to swim, we know that the hoped-for visitor will be less benevolent. At the end of the poem he comes to his senses, but only to a degree:

> O Cyclops, Cyclops, where have your wits wandered? You would show more sense if you went and plaited cheese-crates, or gathered fodder for the lambs. Milk the ewe that's nearby; why pursue one that flees? You will find, perhaps, another and a fairer Galatea. Many a maiden urges me to spend the night playing with her, and when I listen to them, they all giggle in delight. It's plain that on land I too am somebody. (72–9)

The reader can only smile at Polyphemus' face-saving self-deception. In this poem several factors reduce our empathy: the mythical setting, the monstrousness of the Cyclops as we remember him from the *Odyssey*, the fact that these two non-lovers are of different species from us and one another; and not least, the jocular framing device by which the Cyclops' speech is enclosed within a poetic letter from Theocritus to his friend Nicias, offering the tale as an example of how singing can bring a cure for love. The poem is perfect in its own terms, but its detached and mocking approach to the lover did not attract Virgil so much as other Theocritean treatments: in his own imitation, while not eliminating the humorous element, he removes the grotesquerie of the situation, heightens the emotion, makes the lover a human countryman and the love itself homosexual, and shortens the framing introduction, using it only to make clear that song did *not* bring release. By contrast Ovid was obviously delighted by the Theocritean treatment, and expands it into a substantial episode of the *Metamorphoses*: there the Cyclops is both comic and monstrous, and there is a third party, Galatea's handsome lover Acis, whom the Cyclops jealously hates.[22]

V

In some ways it would make sense to move directly to the Virgilian development of pastoral and of love as a central theme in that genre; but first should come some comments on the Roman context and especially on that key figure of the generation before Virgil, Catullus (fl. 50s BC).[23]

Although Latin literature is poured into Greek moulds, Greek attitudes were not theirs. By the first century BC Rome was capital of an empire larger than any lasting Greek dominion, and the luxuries of empire – precious metals, jewels, scents, fine wines, statues and works of art – were imported or looted from the conquered nations.[24] The Romans were more moralistic and therefore more hypocritical than the classical Greeks. Marriage was idealized even more (the mother of the Gracchi comes to mind), though adultery was common and divorce and remarriage tolerated. Women had greater freedom and more influence behind the scenes, even in politics: although no woman could have spoken in the senate, the mother of Brutus was a formidable figure at a family council.[25] Homosexuality was proscribed by law, though accepted in private life as long as it did not involve seduction of Roman citizens.[26] Young men's escapades were frowned upon, with the reprobates of Roman comedy being expected to mend their ways after marriage, and Cicero's indulgent comments, in his defence of Caelius, on the inevitability of young men sowing wild oats, represent a bold and uncharacteristic tactic to get his client off the hook. The youth of Rome were expected to serve the nation, in the military or political sphere, and 'leisure', a Greek ideal, meant 'idleness' to the likes of Cato. The well-educated would also be aware of philosophical objections to passion: Stoics counselled suppression of emotions, while Epicureans suggested indulgence in no-strings affairs which would not disturb one's peace of mind. Lucretius denounces the folly of erotic passion at great length at the end of book 4. It is all the more remarkable that the love-poets of Rome around the turn of the millennium developed what may almost be called an alternative lifestyle, an erotic career-pattern, a 'life of love'. Although this is most explicit in Propertius (1.6) and Ovid (*Am.* 1.15), it was Catullus who laid the foundations. Catullus tells his Lesbia that they should 'live and love', and place the smallest possible value on 'the mutterings of stricter old men' (poem 5).

Catullus is most famous as the poet of Lesbia, but his work is much more varied than that of his successors, the love-elegists. He writes affectionate poems to his friends, insults and abuse to his enemies, sometimes light-hearted insults even to his friends; his concerns embrace literature good and bad ('Volusius' *Annals*, shit-smeared sheets'), friends loyal and disloyal (on the latter he has no mercy), gossip, travel and mythology. Politics interest him very little: a few impertinent squibs against Julius Caesar ruffled the great man's pride, but when Catullus' father brought about a rapprochement, there were no hard feelings. The longer and more ambitious poems such as his 400-line epyllion on Peleus and Thetis parade their learning and technique: it has taken longer for readers to accept that the short poems too are carefully crafted artefacts, and that Catullus, though apparently writing of his own experience, is not giving us a versified diary or unprocessed autobiography. He is a poet steeped in Greek literature, one who translates Sappho and Callimachus. Many of his poems take up a hint or topic from Greek epigram and develop it in a new way. The famous poem on the death of Lesbia's sparrow is a good example: poems on dead dogs, chaffinches and other pets are abundant in the Greek Anthology, but Catullus adds a touch of grandiloquent humour.[27]

> O Venus and you Cupids, shed
> A tear, and all in man that's moved
> By beauty, mourn. Her sparrow's dead,
> My darling's darling, whom she loved
> More than she loves her own sweet eyes,
> Her honey of a bird. It knew
> Its mistress as babes recognise
> Their mothers, and it never flew
> Out of her lap, but all day long,
> Hopping and flitting to and fro,
> Piped to her private ear its song.
> Nevertheless, now it must go
> Down the dark road from which they say
> No one returns. Curse you, you spiteful
> Swooping hawks of death who prey
> On all things that make life delightful! –
> That was a pretty bird you took.
> Bad deed! Poor little bird – by dying
> See what you've done! Her sweet eyes look
> All puffed and rosy-red with crying.   (poem 3, tr. J. Michie)

A particularly clear instance of artful rewriting comes when Catullus adapts an epigram by Callimachus:

> *Callignotus swore* to Ionis that he would never hold any boy or girl dearer than her. *He swore*, but they speak truly who say that oaths sworn in love do not reach the ears of the immortals. And now he is burned by a masculine fire, but of Ionis there is, as they say of the Megarians, 'no word and no account'.

Catullus' adaptation runs as follows:

> *My woman says* that she does not wish to marry any man other than me, not if Jupiter himself were her suitor. So *she says*, but what a woman says to an eager lover should be written on the wind or in rushing water.

The imitation seems certain because of the repetition of the key verb in lines 1 and 3: *omose* (swore/he swore) in Callimachus, *dicit* (says/she says) in Catullus. There is a general difference of tone and situation, however. First, Callimachus' poem is about two other people: he is merely a detached and rather amused observer. It is Ionis who is suffering, not himself. By contrast, Catullus puts himself at the heart of the poem, shifting the narrative from third to first person, although in line 3 he is still capable of generalizing, referring to himself and his like as 'an eager lover'. Second, following on from that, in Callimachus it is the male who is the deceiver, the one who swears falsely, whereas the female is deceived. Catullus switches the sex roles, putting himself in the girl's place. (He does this in other poems too.) Third, the relationship is more serious: marriage is explicitly mentioned, whereas there is nothing to suggest that in the Greek epigram. Fourth, in Callimachus the protestations are in the past, the disillusionment in the present. In Catullus we have something more complicated, with the assurances of Lesbia being given now: 'she says'. But Catullus is only half-convinced: there are misgivings and uncertainty even at the heights of the relationship.[28]

Some 25 poems out of 116, mostly short, deal with Lesbia. It is natural for readers to try to put them in a sequence, to see what the 'history' of the affair was; but either Catullus or his later editors have made it hard to do so. Enthusiasm and infatuation are prominent in the early kiss-poems, 5 and 7. Disillusionment comes in 8, where he is saying 'farewell, girl'. It seems that 11 is the termination, but in 13 he is referring to her again as 'my girl', and the affair is on again, though after some dispute, in 36, which is immediately followed by despair and outrage in 37. Similar strange sequences figure elsewhere. Either Catullus' book is not in the order he would have chosen, or he was not trying to provide a chronological sequence but rather a more elusive and fragmentary account, a series of snapshots which focus on the themes of passion and betrayal.

Even the most biographical interpreters must accept that these poems contain some fiction and exaggeration: nobody would suppose on the basis of poem 11 that Lesbia literally burst the groins of 300 adulterers (see p. 146 above). Even the more moderate list of named rivals deducible from Catullus' own verses might cause scepticism. In 77 he accuses Rufus of betraying him, in 82 he denounces Quinctius, in 91 Gellius, in 40 he threatens retaliation against Ravidus; in 37 Lesbia has set up shop as a prostitute in a sleazy tavern and is taking on all comers, including Egnatius. In 58 she is a whorish figure in back alleyways, sucking off the 'descendants of great-hearted Remus'. Or one might take the only long poem devoted to Lesbia, poem 68b. In that rich and complex poem we are told that a friend called Allius lent Catullus his house so that he could meet secretly with Lesbia there, for which Catullus expresses his undying gratitude; he recalls her appearance there, like a goddess's epiphany, a poetic amplification and enhancement of the relationship, of a piece with the elaborate comparison which follows between their love and the short-lived union of Protesilaus and Laodamia, figures from the myths of the Trojan war.

In any case, Lesbia is clearly a pseudonym, used as a tribute to Sappho of Lesbos; Ovid already commented that it was a false name; not until two centuries later does Apuleius give the woman's alleged identity, asserting that Lesbia was in fact one of the Clodia sisters. He does not say, though modern scholars have often assumed, that it was the sister who also had an affair with Cicero's friend Caelius. Whether Apuleius or his modern followers are right or wrong matters less than what Catullus achieved in literary terms. First, he presents the affair as something all-important and sublime, a love that dominates his life, and one which, though not a marriage, partakes of something of its seriousness and demands the same kind of commitment as a marital partnership (see especially the language of 87 and 109). Within his own poetry he makes clear that his mistress was in fact married to someone else, which makes his expectations still more paradoxical. Second, he dramatizes it in a developing narrative that takes us through different aspects of the relationship, from ecstatic delight through discontent and tension to outright antagonism, rejection and revulsion. Third, he relates it to other aspects of his life – his friendships, his brother's death and his own literary ambitions (for Lesbia is conceived as a sophisticated woman who appreciates fine poetry). There *may* have been comparable things in the early Greek lyric poets or in the erotic poetry of the Hellenistic period. But the evidence we have certainly makes it look as though Catullus is the key figure, the inventor of romantic love as a positive ideal.[29]

Between Catullus and the elegists of the Augustan age flits the ghost of Cornelius Gallus, whose works are largely lost. Here too the papyri have been kind, though less so than with the more widely read Greek poets: in 1979 the earliest known Latin papyrus was published, containing about 10 lines of Gallus' poetry.[30] Otherwise we know of him from the tributes of his followers and from his appearance in the *Eclogues* of Virgil, who was a close friend. On the best guess, he took over some of the Catullan motifs, applying them to his mistress Lycoris. This was another pseudonym, and this time we have better evidence for the real model, an actress Cytheris, whose presence at an otherwise respectable dinner party shocked Cicero. As a statesman of importance, Gallus probably brought politics and campaigning more into his poetry, perhaps dramatizing the conflict between love and duty. The new fragments show that he called Lycoris his 'domina', implying his own devotion to her was slavish: this motif was developed by his successors. In this period elegiac couplets, a metre used for a wide range of themes in Greek poetry, come to be closely associated with the theme of love: where other themes are introduced, they are often seen as in conflict or tension with love.

The book of 10 bucolic (pastoral) poems by Virgil, known inaccurately as the *Eclogues* ('Selections'), is bound to suffer from being treated under the single heading of love poetry, for it contains much else, and part of the perfection of the work is that each poem sheds light on the others, themes recurring and interweaving in fascinating patterns. Inheriting motifs and situations from Theocritus, Virgil intensified them, creating a beautiful but fragile rural world, a place of tranquillity and entrancing song, threatened and sometimes overwhelmed by outside forces such as warfare, death and the city. (Whereas Theocritus had placed Simaetha in the town, Virgil makes the jilted woman a countrywoman whose husband has deserted her and gone to the wicked city.) Love in the *Eclogues* can sometimes be idyllic: charming shepherdesses pluck apples and keep house for their lovers. It can be tragic and disastrous, as in the cameo of Pasiphae and the bull, one of many grim love-tales recounted by Silenus in poem 6 (see p. 215). In other poems normal human love can be frustrated and disappointed, as in poem 2, Virgil's adaptation of Theocritus' Cyclops-poem (11), in which the simple countryman Corydon suffers from the sophisticated disdain of the urban Alexis, his master's favourite. At the end of the book Virgil brings Gallus into his poetry, an elegist wandering unhappily within a rugged yet tantalizingly lovely landscape in Arcadia (not the normal Virgilian setting, despite his imitators). Gallus is still grieving, as in his own elegies, over the loss of Lycoris, who has gone off with another man. Virgil takes over phrases and motifs from Gallus' elegies, both complimenting and perhaps teasing his friend, whom he represents as literally 'dying' of love, as the mythical

Daphnis perished from Aphrodite's curse in Theocritus 1. These are learned literary games, which Gallus himself would have relished; they are also generic games, as Virgil blends pastoral with elegy and shows both what they have in common and how he himself is determined first to transform then to transcend his genre. The poem ends with Gallus wasting away (wasting his talents, perhaps, as a poet?), while Virgil prepares to 'rise up' and go on to pastures new (Milton in his imitation, *Lycidas*, saw clearly the symbolic implications). Yet he does not dismiss or despise Gallus, but expresses his own affection for him, a creative love that counters Gallus' self-destructive and self-torturing love. Readers who have tried to apply crude literalism to the *Eclogues* (suggesting that Gallus was on furlough in Arcadia!) are as far astray as those who have attempted to decode rigid allegories. Subtler critical tools and tactful interpretation of symbolic meanings are necessary, but on one level at least the poem is doing literary criticism, illuminating the beauty and weaknesses of Gallus' art and testing Virgil's own capacity to go further.

VI

Tibullus and Propertius, poets of very different tastes and talent, were composing alongside one another in the first decade of Augustus' reign (probably Propertius published first, around 29). Tibullus died in 19 but Propertius went on developing. Ovid is a much younger figure, born in 43 BC and reaching manhood when Augustus was already established and major poets had already celebrated the new order in important works (which explains much about Ovid's self-consciously subversive stance).[31] The variety of their work defies summary, but Tibullus is the smoother and more agreeable of the earlier pair, Propertius more daring in language and ambitious in scope. Tibullus favours a country setting and paints attractive fantasy-pictures of life with his mistress; Propertius prefers the town, with all its temptations for Cynthia and himself. In the eyes of later readers, ancient and modern, Catullus is above all associated with Lesbia (though other, lesser amours are mentioned), and Gallus with Lycoris. Tibullus is less committed to a single mistress: not only Delia but a second girl Nemesis and a boy Marathus figure in his poetry. He is also less strongly wedded to the life of love in opposition to other pursuits: he can turn his pen to celebrate the birthday of his patron Messalla, or the origins of Rome in a poem which may show early knowledge of the *Aeneid*.

The transmitted text of Tibullus also includes some elegiac poems by others, among them the poetess Sulpicia, who appears to have been related to his patron. As the only female writer in Latin from the classical period she has commanded a good deal of interest: it is intriguing to see some of the standard elegiac language used in the opposite direction, addressed to a pseudonymous young man.[32] There are also poems praising or referring to Sulpicia, whether in the voice of her lover or of a third party: the two groups must be related, and may even be by the same poet. In any case the splendid hauteur with which she dismisses her lover when he has been dallying with a prostitute, and the frank though euphemistic delight when she declares her desire fulfilled ('worthy woman has been with worthy man'), strike notes hard to parallel elsewhere in elegy. Yet the total length of both groups of poems is little more than a hundred lines.

Propertius develops and intensifies several Catullan ideas and themes: among them the 'life of love', a life of enslavement to a cruel and capricious mistress, and the developmental narrative, more clearly structured in his work (his first book begins with a reference to the start of his affair with Cynthia, and the third book builds up to the end of their relationship, coinciding with the end of the book). Self-pity, reproach, jealous accusation, passionate concern and melancholy disillusionment, are all notes struck in his poetry: what is absent is the vicious frankness and crudity which Catullus uses to shock his readers and invigorate his verse. One technique which Catullus used in the long poem 68b but not much elsewhere is particularly favoured by Propertius: the mythological analogy. The poet's love for Cynthia is compared with the passions of mythical heroes and heroines, often drawn from Hellenistic models. These allusions may exalt the present-day affair to mythic status, foreshadow a sorrowful end to Propertius' hopes, or show by implication how far the modern reality falls short of the glorious past. Mythical names are abundant, sometimes obscure, always exotic, creating verbal music.

> As the girl from Cnossos, while Theseus' keel receded,
> lay limp on a deserted beach;
> as Cephean Andromeda in first sleep rested,
> from hard rocks released at last;
> And as a maenad, no less tired by the ceaseless dance,
> swoons on grassy Apidanus;
> so Cynthia seemed to me to breathe soft peace,
> leaning her head on relaxed hands . . .   (1.3.1–8, tr. G. Lee)

Propertius' work is not monolithic. The first book is dominated by Cynthia, but ends with three poems on quite different topics, pointing towards other poetic options, on the one hand lush mythological eroticism, on the other sterner contemporary themes of civil war and a kinsman's death. The second book, influenced by Tibullus' longer elegies, is experimental, dramatizing developing situations and also introducing some engagement with Augustan politics. The poet is unsympathetic towards the ruler's moral and military goals: 'no son of mine will be a soldier' (2.7; for another example, see appendix 1.3). Books 3 and 4 bring the Roman context ever more into the foreground, as the theme of the affair becomes one among several which interplay in complex ways. Book 3 shows the poet constantly expressing a (clearly contrived) longing to break free from Cynthia's yoke and from the poetic path in which his passion confines him. He aspires to higher things, pushing at the limits of elegy as Virgil pressed hard the boundaries of pastoral: he will don the mantle of the Roman Callimachus, or sing Bacchus' praises in lofty dithyramb, or journey to Greece and gain inspiration from the ancient fountainhead of poetry. The choice of poetic role itself becomes a subject for poetry.

Book 4 marks a new start. Here Propertius declares himself a patriotic poet; Roman myths displace Greek. This book is less easily classified under the heading 'love poetry': the poet undertakes a Roman *Aetia* (cf. pp. 207–10), anticipated as a future project in 3.9. But already in the first poem, there is a conflict between his aspirations and his former calling: love will be present in the book, sometimes the love of other characters, past and present; but eventually the poet's former mistress reappears, in two of his finest poems. In 4.7, Cynthia is dead: her ghost haunts Propertius' dreams as she complains of his infidelity and defends her own behaviour. In 4.8, as a deliberate contrast, we have an episode from her life, where she returns from a trip with a rival to discover Propertius glumly attempting to revel with two prostitutes ('they sang to a deaf man, they bared their breasts to a blind man . . .'). Her anger is terrifying: the tarts are driven off, Propertius is forced to grovel at her feet. Neither poem is a realistic portrait of a real woman, and editors' unease about their un-chronological ordering is misguided: nowhere is Cynthia's status as a literary construct more evident. The contrast of the two poems is heightened when we recognize that they embody epic parody. The first recalls the scene in the *Iliad* in which the ghost of Patroclus rebukes Achilles for sleeping and neglecting his funeral rites; the second is a richly ingenious reversal of the *Odyssey*: here the wanderer who returns and wreaks vengeance on intruding 'suitors' is the woman, and, unlike Penelope, Propertius is unable to take pride in his fidelity. In every book, almost every poem, Propertius shows his ability to redeploy the motifs of elegy in new and witty forms.

Horace, who was composing lyric poetry alongside the elegists in the 20s, never mentions Propertius, though he cannot be unmindful of him in a passage where he comments sardonically on the pretensions of a Roman Callimachus (*Epistles* 2.2.100). He addresses teasing poems to Tibullus and another poet in the same field, Valgius, advising moderation in their expression of self-pity (*Odes* 1.33, 2.9). He evidently thought elegy too long-winded and monotonous: this is unfair but understandable given his own penchant for variety and compression. Love is only one of his many themes, and he prefers to comment wryly on the deluded passions of others: he himself rarely addresses the same girlfriend twice, and in general affects either an Epicurean detachment or the expertise of a Don Juan. Venus' cruel game is one which wise heads will avoid; a seasoned warrior, he will hang up his arms (though not without a final plea to Venus: 'touch that arrogant Chloe just once with your lash'); watching his juniors, he exclaims in pity and distress on learning who has them in her toils (*Odes* 1.33, 3.26, 1.5 and 1.27). He eyes his friends' conquests with a connoisseur's perception, but disclaims any interest on his own account: 'those arms, that face, those smooth calves, I praise with complete detachment: you can't suspect one whose lifespan has now hurried past . . . the year 40' (2.4). Visualizing the poets in the underworld, he imagines that a larger crowd will surround the manly Alcaeus, whom he takes as his prime model, than the plaintive Sappho (2.13). He was probably closer to Augustus' circle than Propertius, and politics is treated with some seriousness in his work (see pp. 191–4); as for personal relationships, friendship matters more in his poetry than *eros*. Here too he follows Epicurean principle.

When we turn to Ovid, it is hardly possible to confine ourselves to his first work, the *Amores*, though it is here that he most obviously follows the lead of the other elegists. All his earlier work is dominated by the love theme, which he treats with endless inventiveness. The tone is light-hearted, even cynical: Ovid takes delight in representing himself as being in love, but we never believe him. Whereas with the other poets there is room for debate about the reality of their mistresses, Ovid tells us that Corinna is a fiction, and takes pleasure in the fact that girls are going round town claiming to be Corinna.[33] It is too simple to say that Propertius or Tibullus takes the genre seriously, whereas Ovid sends it up: there is plenty of humour, though often less overt, in Propertius, and even Catullus parodies some erotic motifs. Nor can we safely say, as some have said, that Ovid exhausted the genre, or made it impossible to write: Statius' friend Pomponius Stella still writes amatory elegy. But in Ovid the artificiality of the conventions are foregrounded, exaggerated or literalized.[34] The elegiac lover is traditionally pale and thin: Ovid urges his mistress's doorkeeper to open up – or just open the door a few inches, which will be enough for his wasted form! Propertius deplores Cynthia's use of cosmetics; Ovid makes fun of his girl's misfortune in having used a dye which has made her hair fall out. (Prop. 1.2, Ov. *Am.* 1.14). Even potentially painful topics avoided by the others are turned to ingeniously witty account by Ovid (impotence, 3.7; abortion, 2. 13 and 14). Clever comic scenes are numerous: the lover at the same party as his mistress and her man, the problems of having fallen for two people (1.4, 2.10). In one delightful sequence we find Ovid first protesting his innocence to Corinna: how could she possibly think he would ever touch her maid? The next poem is a frantic message to the maid: 'how did she find out?' (2.7–8)! The reader need not seek depth of emotion, far less political correctness, but there is much harmless enjoyment to be had. What he does take very seriously, for all the humorous treatment of the topic, is the future direction and ultimate fame of his own poetry (1.15, 2.1, 3.1, 3.15). This theme outlasts even love in his oeuvre, remaining his consolation in exile on the Black Sea.

Ovid's other most successful work of this period is the *Ars Amatoria*. This is no Kama Sutra, but closer to light social satire, presented through parody of the didactic manner. It should really be rendered 'Art of Seduction': the first book tells the eager reader how to pick up girls (the theatre or the games are good hunting-grounds), the second how to keep them. In book 3 (a later addition), he begins by declaring his intent to arm the Amazons to retaliate, and gives advice to women on how to fight back. Not content with this, Ovid also composed *Cures for Love*, illustrated with his usual abundant mythical precedents (the remedies suggested include travel, hunting, focusing on the girl's uglier features – or starting another affair). Those who complain that all this is deplorable, let alone immoral, merely show that they are as humourless as the elderly Augustus, who used the *Ars Amatoria* as pretext for sending Ovid into lifelong exile.

VII

We have mainly been considering higher genres, those taken seriously by ancient and modern critics alike. There was of course much prose and verse of a more low-grade or at any rate low-life nature: scurrilous anecdotes about politicians and thinkers, alleged memoirs of famous courtesans and sexy novellas – the cruder ass-meets-girl Greek novel paralleling Apuleius' *Metamorphoses* is an interesting example (p. 143). The victorious Parthians were shocked at the risqué reading ('Milesian tales') that they found in the backpacks of Crassus' soldiers after the battle of Carrhae (Plutarch, *Crassus* 32). Innuendo and sexual jibes were common, as we can see in Pompeian graffiti:[35] often they focused on the supposedly degraded role and actions of the passive homosexual. In Tacitus we read of a memorable riposte by a defendant under Claudius. The prosecutor showered him with accusations: corrupting the troops, bribery, adultery, and of playing the pathic, 'unmanly acts'. At this point the accused broke silence: 'Ask your sons, Suillius,' he replied. 'They can testify to my manhood' (i.e. *he* has degraded *them*, not played the passive role himself). The prosecutor's reaction is not recorded (*Ann.* 11.2).

As for verse, not all who imitated Catullus saw him as the tender poet of Lesbia: for Martial he was the exemplar of the witty and often outrageous epigrammatist. Martial's own poetry includes many erotic epigrams of the kind which older translations left in Latin, or, operating on a strange national stereotype, rendered into Italian! In book 11, stimulated by the freedom associated with the Saturnalia, he excels himself in obscene fireworks. The results are often entertaining, sometimes clever, perhaps even arousing; but scatological content does not guarantee quality. More imaginative is Petronius' novelistic narrative of the sleazy antics of his anti-heroes in the red-light districts of Campania. Here a firm though meandering plot gives a framework to their bizarre and often humiliating experiences, recounted in a mixture of prose and verse (cf. pp. 139–52). The narrator Encolpius is suffering from the wrath of Priapus, and critics have detected the influence of epic, in which angry gods bring misfortune on wandering heroes. Priapus has cursed him with impotence, so that in delightful or horrendous circumstances alike he is doomed to failure and derision.

In one scene after a typical let-down he denounces his penis in mock-heroic rage: 'Is this what I have deserved of you, that when I am in heaven you should drag me down to hell?' But he gets no response: the organ merely 'turned away, keeping its eyes fixed upon the earth, nor did its appearance change at my unfinished speech, any more than pliant willows – or poppies with slumbering stems' (Petr.132). Petronius shamelessly appropriates to this grotesque context verses from one of the most memorable scenes in Virgil, the moment when Dido's ghost turns silently away in Hades, ignoring her former lover's grief-stricken appeal. The 'poppies' are imported from another Virgilian context, the pathetic end of the boy Euryalus: 'willows' suggests at least a hint of firmness, 'slumbering stems' renewed inertia. The vulgarity of the topic is redeemed by the ingenuity of the literary imagination.

We have seen something of the variety and complexity with which ancient attitudes to sex and erotic emotions were shaped in literary forms. After these subtleties we may end with something simpler, a short poem by a woman or in a woman's voice from early Greece, of timeless simplicity.[36]

> The moon has gone down,
> the Pleiades have set. Midnight is here,
> the time is going by,
> and here I lie alone.

Perhaps loneliness is more of a cultural universal among emotions than most.

6

Literature and Power

Let there be Maecenases, and Virgils will not be lacking.
Martial 8.55

I

Despite the claims of some high authorities, literature is not a hermetically sealed zone. Behind every text there is an author, and authors must exist in some relation to their society: sometimes that relationship is one of dependence on others, often mediated through some form of patronage. In this chapter we consider the shape these relationships might take in ancient Greece and Rome. An oppositional relationship is of course also possible: some authors (such as Plato) had sufficient wealth, status or self-assurance to be able to write as they pleased, even if it flew in the face of popular opinion or ideology. Others might have to suffer for what they wrote: the outspokenness of Athenian comedy was restricted by law for brief periods, and Roman satire attracted distrust. Exile or even execution might be the fate of an over-bold author under the more oppressive emperors; censorship, even book-burning, were not unknown.[1]

The writer himself was not powerless, although that power might often have to be exercised with caution. In the *Odyssey*, the bard of the Ithacan court, Phemius, evades punishment with the rest from the returning avenger. He does so not just by dissociating himself from the suitors' crimes, but even before that by asserting the power of his art. 'I supplicate you, Odysseus: respect me, pity me. There will be sorrow for you hereafter, if you slay a bard, one who sings for gods and men. I am self-taught, and god breathed all kinds of paths of song into my mind. I am fit to sing at your side as by a god' (*Od.* 22.344–9). Several points of lasting significance appear in this speech – not only the claim both to personal ability and divine inspiration, but the flattering implication of Odysseus' own near-divine status, which Phemius can commemorate, and the unspoken threat of what may happen if he fails to respect him: 'there will be sorrow for you . . .' may imply more than remorse, for it is poetry that preserves men's memory, and Odysseus must guard against his name being remembered not for heroic acts but for shameful deeds. The power of the poet to immortalize is a long-enduring theme, and can be transferred to prose. Tacitus declares it the historian's highest task to commemorate virtuous actions and to ensure that evildoers fear posterity's condemnation.[2]

Phemius, like Demodocus in Alcinous' kingdom, seems to be a resident poet, though the *Odyssey* also mentions bards who travel from place to place (17.382–7). One reason for travel might be to attend major festivals and compete in contests: Hesiod won a prize in a poetic contest at the funeral games of Amphidamas on Euboea (*WD* 656–7). In the *Theogony*, which some have thought might be the song which won on that occasion, he is notably respectful about kings, and his comments there were influential: the eldest of the Muses attend on kings and give them statesmanlike eloquence; 'from Zeus come kings; and blessed is the man whom the Muses love' (96–7). A good king will need and reward good poets. Such indeed seems to be the view of many of the kings or minor rulers of the next centuries.[3] 'Court poetry' is difficult to chart in detail, with the gaps in our knowledge, but Ibycus and Anacreon were certainly resident for a time in Samos, under the wealthy Polycrates (d. 522). Anacreon seems subsequently to have gravitated to Athens during the last years of the 'tyranny' there. We see that wealth and power attract talent, a basic principle of the patronage system. But the readiness with which these poets move from one centre of patronage to another prefigures the situation of Simonides and Pindar in the late sixth/ early fifth centuries, as major artists of recognized status and not hangers-on of a particular individual. With Pindar above all, many patrons would have felt proud to have been able to commission so famous a figure.[4]

One fragmentary lyric by Ibycus is noteworthy for its combination of the mythical and the contemporary. He recounts various aspects of the Trojan war, drawing to a close with references to some of the most handsome young warriors taking part: Hyllis, Troilus and others, and concluding: 'among them, for beauty always you too, Polycrates, will have undying fame, as my song, my fame can bestow' (*PMG* 282). There is more than a hint of the erotic: the poem was probably composed when Polycrates was still a youth (perhaps 540s BC?). More important is the way in which the poet moves easily between mythical examples and the present day: this is a constant feature of praise poetry in antiquity. The poet glorifies his subject by setting it on a level with the great achievements (or, here, the great beauties) of myth. Pindar compares the illness of Hieron with the mythic wound of Philoctetes (*Py.* 1.50ff), or the mutual devotion of Thrasybulus and his father Xenocrates with the affection between Antilochus and his father Nestor (*Py.* 6); more bizarrely, Theocritus finds precedent for the brother–sister marriage of Ptolemy II with Arsinoe in the incestuous union of Zeus and Hera themselves (17.128–34). Horace recounts the conflicts of the Olympian gods and the giants, monstrous forces of unreason, and hints at analogies in the firm rule of Augustus which has pacified irrational opposition (*Odes* 3.4). There are innumerable other examples.[5]

Myth provided the means for the writer to elevate himself as well as his subject. By comparing his theme (sometimes explicitly) with those of Homer or other distinguished poets, he enhanced his own status. A clear example is provided by the newly discovered elegiac poem by Simonides, celebrating the Greek victory at Plataea.[6] Having recounted the death of Achilles at Apollo's hands and recalled the crime of Paris, which began the Trojan war, Simonides continues:

> And so after sacking the town famed in song, they returned to their homes,
> (mightiest of heroes), the Danaans, leaders in combat;
> on whom immortal glory has been shed, thanks to that man who received
> from the Muses, violet-tressed daughters of Pieria,
> all truth, and gave the swift-doomed race of demi-gods a name that lives on
> for later generations.
> But hail and farewell now, son of a glorious goddess, the daughter of
> Nereus the sea-dweller. But I for my part
> call upon you as my supporter, Muse of many names, if indeed you pay
> heed to the prayers of men.
> Arm now also this fluent array of my song, so that others will one day
> remember
> the men who defended Sparta (and Hellas), warding off the day of
> slavery. . . .
> They did not forget their valour, and (the tale of them has reached)
> heaven's height; the glory of those men will last forever.
> Forth they came, leaving behind the Eurotas and the city of Sparta,
> setting out with the horse-taming sons of Zeus, heroes, on their side,
> and Menelaus, mighty ruler. . . .
> The son of godlike Cleombrotus led them, best of men, Pausanias . . .
>   (Simon.11.13–34 W: bracketed phrases indicate supplements where
>   the text is missing)

From Trojan war to Persian war, from heroic Greeks battling Trojans to fifth-century Greeks battling Persians, from Achilles to Pausanias (regent of Sparta and general at the battle of Plataea) – the analogies are firm and clear, with also an unspoken analogy between Homer, the poet who 'received from the Muses all truth' and Simonides himself who calls on the

Muse for aid with 'my song' 'also'. Eternal fame is promised for both subjects. We do not know the context of Simonides' poem, but it is a plausible guess that it was composed for a Spartan-dominated audience, perhaps even to glorify Pausanias himself. (A lot depends on how much was made of the contribution by other Greeks in the lost portions.) What is clear is that Simonides, like Aeschylus in the *Persians*, is giving the Greek victory heroic status, but unlike Aeschylus he singles out living individuals. Broader pan-Hellenic celebration need not exclude more local glorification: as Pindar remarks, at Athens you will win praise for singing of Salamis, at Sparta by celebrating Plataea (*Py.* 1.75–80). But it is clear that this kind of poetry appeals to a wider audience besides a particular family or patron group.

Pindar, the greatest of the Greek lyric poets and the only one to survive in bulk through a manuscript tradition, must now claim more detailed attention.[7] Ancient editors assembled his poems in 17 books: they classified his work as falling into a wide range of genres – hymns, dithyrambs, maiden-songs, songs for banquets, and other forms – but what we have are most of his victory-odes ('epinikia'). This is a genre which seems strange to moderns, although much progress has been made in defining its conventions. These poems celebrate people who have been successful in athletic events at the major festivals (the Olympian, Pythian, Isthmian and Nemean Games), held every two or four years and involving a wide range of contests, including wrestling, boxing, running and racing in chariots. Participants tended to be aristocratic, those who could afford the leisure for training, or in some contests the equipment (as in the chariot races, where the patron would be represented by a professional driver). The winners had immense prestige, and were regarded as winning glory for their cities too. Some made a career of athletics, and might win a string of victories. Besides the thrill of the sports themselves, the games had a religious dimension: not only natural ability and training but divine blessing was needed to achieve success. The effort and training needed to achieve victory were seen as analogous to the struggles of heroes such as Heracles to accomplish their legendary feats. Pindar and other poets in this genre (Bacchylides is his best-known rival) treat the victor as representative of human prowess, and success as a symbolic moment of achieving one's full potential. Curiously, the events themselves are rarely described (contrast the vivid narration of the chariot race in *Iliad* 23): what matters most is their deeper meaning and the way in which success defines the human condition. For Pindar does not only sing the praises of the victors: he also reminds them of their limitations and the subordination of mankind to the gods.

There are 45 odes that survive complete. The chronology is not as certain as is sometimes assumed, but on the conventional dating they range from

498 BC (*Py.*10, composed when Pindar was about 20) to 446 (*Py.* 8). Not all are victory-odes in the strict sense, but the exceptions still show many similarities. They average about 70 lines, but there is some tendency for the odes celebrating Olympic or Pythian victors to be longer (these games had greater prestige). How they were performed is disputed, but most probably a performance by a chorus, back at the victor's home town, was normal: in many cases Pindar would himself have been present as a guest-of-honour, and probably trained the chorus. Some shorter odes may have been performed at the celebrations after the games themselves. The victor's family would no doubt keep the poem as a valued heirloom; even the city might attach special importance to it (we are told that *Olympian* 7 was inscribed in gold letters and dedicated at the temple of Athena at Lindos in Rhodes). For the ode normally praises not only the individual's success but the community to which he belongs, including its gods, its festivals and its mythical traditions. One of the greatest of Pindar's poems, *Pythian* 1, not only honours Hieron of Sicily for winning the chariot-race but also celebrates his foundation of the new city of Aitna (beneath Mount Etna, which is vividly described), and the campaigns through which he has kept at bay the threatening Carthaginians and Etruscans. In particular, Hieron's victory in the battle of Cyme is mentioned, and set on a par with the mainland Greeks' victories against the Persians. Foundation legends of cities and peoples may also be included: Cyrene (*Py.* 9), Rhodes (*Ol.* 7), the colonization of Libya (*Py.* 4). As these examples suggest, Pindar found patrons all over the Greek world: in Thessaly, Cyrene, south Italy, Asia Minor and especially in Sicily (14 odes) and Aigina (11).

From early in his career Pindar's victory-odes follow certain patterns, though none is exactly like another. (Comparison with the practice of Bacchylides shows that some of the pattern is of Pindar's own devising: the genre has considerable flexibilty.) Besides the indispensable praise of the victor, specifying the contest and recounting previous victories by the honorand or his ancestors, we find reflections by Pindar on his own art and the power of poetry (often he makes connections and draws analogies between his own achievement and the victor's); there are also generalizing reflections of a moral or religious cast. Gods or other supernatural powers are invoked, as the poet reminds us of the sacred nature of the festivals or seeks divine endorsement of the victor's triumph, and most odes either begin by calling on some god or do so soon after the beginning.

Most but not all of the odes include at least one extended mythical narrative (only nine odes, all short, omit this). Usually this is introduced after a passage of praise for the victor, and we normally return to the contemporary situation at the end (but there are two striking cases where the myth concludes the ode: *N.* 1 and 10). The myth is often the most

powerful and memorable part of the ode, and usually serves to enlarge the
perspective while also being a further means of praising the victor, either
from the deeds of his ancestors, or through legends associated with his
locality or with the origins and history of the games. *Olympians* 1 and 10
tell of different aspects of the establishment of the Olympic Games.
Similarly the Pythian Games, held at Delphi, were associated with Apollo,
who is mentioned in almost every Pythian ode and plays a prominent role in
the myths of several. Many more local traditions or variants on myths are
preserved in Pindar, who is also prepared to revise or 'correct' tradition in
order to uphold the dignity of the gods. (Thus he rejects the tale that
Demeter inadvertently committed an act of cannibalism: 'not for me to call
any of the blessed gods a glutton: I stand aside' (*Ol.* 1.52).) Often the
relevance of the myth to the victor is obvious – the tale of Heracles wrestling
with the mighty Antaeus serves to glorify the champion fighter Melissus
(*Isthm.* 4); sometimes it is more subtle or many-sided. In a few cases the
connection is obscure, but the colourful narrative and elevated language can
be enjoyed for their own sake. The myths are not always positive: darker
notes are struck in some of them, with tales of wrongdoing or disaster used
to set the virtue and good fortune of the victor in higher relief (*Py.* 11,
Clytemnestra's murder of Agamemnon; *Isth.* 7.40ff, the foolish ambition
of Bellerophon). As often in antiquity the category 'myth' is flexible,
and historical events can be treated as myths, provided that they seem
sufficiently remote and romantic. Both Pindar and Bacchylides allude to the
death of Croesus, a historical Lydian king of the previous century.

Pindar's language is highly poetic, full of compounds, unusual words and
florid metaphors; his tone is normally grave but has a lightening humour;
his narratives are often selective and wayward, highlighting certain details
and leaving the listener to fill in the background; direct speech brings drama
and variety. In one of his most famous poems, the myth concerns the hero
Pelops (after whom the Peloponnese was named). As a boy he is beloved by
Poseidon and for a time dwells among the gods: but the sins of his father
cause him to be returned to the mortal world. Poseidon has not forgotten
him, however, as this extract shows:

Therefore the immortals sent his son back again
to dwell among the short-lived race of men.
And when, toward the time of his youth's flowering,
his chin and jaw were darkening with soft hair,
he set his thoughts upon the ready marriage

that might be his by wresting fair-famed Hippodameia from her father,
the king of Pisa. Drawing near the white-flecked sea, alone in dark of night,
he hailed the loud-resounding god

of the trident, who close by
the young man's feet revealed himself.
To him he said: 'Come, if in any way the Cyprian's
loving gifts impose a claim, Poseidon,
to gratitude, then shackle Oinomaos' brazen spear;
dispatch me on the swiftest of all chariots
to Elis; draw me near to mastery.
For thirteen men, all suitors, he has killed,
and so puts off the marriage

of his daughter. Great risk does not place its hold on cowards.
Since we must die, why sit in darkness
and to no purpose coddle an inglorious old age
without a share of all that's noble? But for me,
this contest is a task that I
must undertake; may you bring to fulfilment that which I desire.'
So he spoke, and the words he handled
were not without effect. Exalting him, the god
gave him a golden chariot and a team
of tireless winged horses.

He took strong Oinomaos down and took the maiden as his bride,
begetting six sons, leaders eager to excel.
But now he has a share
in splendid blood-sacrifices, reclining by the river-course of Alpheos,
in his well-tended tomb beside the altar
that many strangers visit. Fame gleams far and wide from the Olympic races
of Pelops, where the speed of feet contends,
and utmost strength with courage to bear toil.   (*Olympian* 1. 65–96,
      tr. Miller, with slight alterations)

Here many of Pindar's themes are united: ambition for fame in spite of risk, the favour of a god to the man who is worthy, the continuity from the mythical past to a present which still remembers and commemorates the achievements of heroes like Pelops, just as Pindar's poem has preserved the memory of Hieron, victor in the chariot race at Olympia in 476 BC.

Pindar presents himself as the 'guest-friend' and intimate of his patrons, enjoying an easy relationship with the great and able to give them his counsel. It is likely that he himself was an aristocrat (*Py.* 5.75, if this refers to the poet himself), at home in the world of high birth and inherited wealth. This makes it easier for him to treat the addressee as a friend rather than an employer; the poem he produces may be described as a precious gift like rich wine in an ornate drinking-bowl (*Ol.* 7.1ff.), a treasure-house of hymns (*Py.* 6.7), or even a palace-like structure (*Ol.* 6.1ff.). Explicit reference in literal terms to commission and fee are rare.[8] Poets as spokesmen of the Muses were expected to dispense didactic advice (as Hesiod did to his idle brother, or Theognis to his beloved Cyrnus). Pindar gracefully bestows well-phrased wisdom: in extract or translation it may sound commonplace, but his recipients would have known it was appropriate to the genre. Even a powerful monarch like Hieron may be addressed as with authority:

> Guide your people with a rudder of justice; on an anvil of truth forge your tongue. . . . You are the steward of many, and many are the sound witnesses that will see deeds of both sorts. . . . Do not be deceived, my friend, by shameful gains, for the posthumous acclaim of fame alone reveals the quality of men who have passed away to chronicler and bard. The kindly excellence of Croesus does not perish; but universal execration holds down Phalaris. . . . (*Py.* 1.86ff.)

Such passages should not be read as serious warnings: the audience is not meant to suppose that there is danger of Hieron becoming a sadistic tyrant like Phalaris. The king is encouraged to go on doing what he is already doing – sometimes perhaps to do what he is already intending to do (as possibly in *Py.* 4.277–99, where Pindar urges Arcesilas to recall Damophilus from exile). This poetic strategy provided an important model to later poets such as Theocritus and Horace, who needed to find an appropriate tone in which to address a ruler. Even prose authors might use the same technique, as in Seneca's work *On Clemency* (addressed to the young Nero!).

Although formalist criticism, inspired by the important work of Bundy, has tended to evacuate biographical and historical elements from Pindar, giving central place to the generic conventions of praise poetry, this can be overdone.[9] Pindar has his own opinions, though courteously masked. He is naturally loyal to his native Thebes, and devoted to their 'cousins' the Aeginetans, for whose continued well-being he prays in his last poem: in a period when Aegina was threatened by Athenian imperialism, it is hard to exclude an extra-literary dimension (*Py.* 8.1–20, 88–100). In *Py.* 7 he hints at the misfortunes of his addressee Megacles, exiled from Athens: 'I rejoice at your recent success, but this grieves me, that envy requites your noble deeds.'

Pindar was popular, and swiftly became a classic. Herodotus quotes a well-known phrase; Plato's speakers cite him frequently; one of Aristophanes' choruses mocks the Athenians for their gullibility, saying that envoys from allied states can get anything they want from the assembly by citing Pindar's line 'o shining Athens, violet-crowned, celebrated in song, bulwark of Greece, famous Athens, divine citadel'; 'and at that very word "crowned" you sat up on the tip of your tiny buttocks'.[10] We are reminded of Socrates' sarcastic comment on the Athenians' susceptibility to flattery. (p. 87). But although artists and sophists gravitated to Athens, there seems to have been no fully developed system of patronage in the radical democracy, where publicly funded forms of poetry were preferred (as in the dramatic festivals). It was elsewhere, for instance at the court of Macedonia, that rulers still tried to assemble talented poets and thinkers. Euripides emigrated to live there in the last years of the Peloponnesian war, and composed at least one play in honour of King Archelaus. The younger tragedian Agathon was also induced to accept this royal hospitality. Tradition had it that Socrates was invited too, but politely declined, saying that he did not want to be put in the position of being unable to give adequate response to good treatment.[11]

We have seen that Pindar avoids laying too much stress on financial aspects of his art, preferring more metaphorical descriptions. Other authors (especially those writing in 'lower' genres) refer with fewer inhibitions to the mercenary Muse. The poet in Aristophanes' *Birds* (904ff.), who offers encomia on the newly founded Cloud-cuckooland, is clearly out for profit: his sample wares are made up of snatches from Simonides and Pindar. Simonides acquired a reputation, in or after his lifetime, for money-grubbing. Aristotle tells a story about him: 'When the victor in the mule race offered Simonides only a small fee, he refused to compose a poem since he took a poor view of writing in honour of mules; but on being given an adequate fee he wrote: "Hail, daughters of storm-footed horses".' Yet (says Aristotle drily) 'they were the daughters of the asses too.'[12] The question of poetic independence versus financial dependence has exercised many modern critics, and some classical writers were evidently sensitive about the issue: Horace equivocates about the topic in several passages. Juvenal and Martial, adopting the deliberately cynical pose of their genres, repeatedly assume that poets want cash before all else: Juvenal paints Statius as prostituting his poetry for hire (7.82–7).

II

Alexander the Great made a difference, in poetry as in so much else. He had an epic poet called Choerilus, notoriously bad. Later connoisseurs drew the proper conclusion: rulers needed to be more discriminating in whom they patronized. Moreover, gross flattery or distortion of history invited derision, with Callisthenes' encomiastic history of Alexander being a byword for its flattery, and Onesicritus regarded as not much better. A pleasant anecdote tells of Onesicritus reading aloud an account of Alexander's meeting with the Amazon queen, and of one of Alexander's generals, Lysimachus, iron-ically asking 'And where was I when all this was happening?'[13] Horace, writ-ing to Augustus, emphasizes the need for judgement in choice of poets, and Suetonius tells us that Augustus accepted the need for caution. 'He took offence at being made the subject of any composition except in serious earnest and by the most eminent writers, often charging the praetors not to let his name be cheapened in prize declamations.'[14]

Epic, as we saw in an earlier chapter, was the royal genre, and could be adapted to historical events. We know of many examples from the era of Alexander and his successors, when monarchies far greater and more enduring than any since the Persians could offer patronage on a scale undreamt of by Samos or Sicily in the archaic period. Perhaps fortunately, these successors of Choerilus are lost. But epic on the wars and achievements of kings was not the only possible form of praise poetry, and not necessarily the most effective. Poets might prefer to adopt more indirect forms of praise, and often patrons might be delighted by the ingenuity and wit demonstrated by a more devious approach.

The master of indirectness and the apostle of ingenuity is the poet Callimachus, born in Cyrene in Egypt, and active at the court of Alexandria under the early Ptolemies (the line which ruled Egypt in the Hellenistic age, running from Alexander's general Ptolemy to the famous Cleopatra).[15] Callimachus (see also pp. 207–10) was writing mainly in the period 270–245. He is one of the representatives of a learned literary elite patronized by the Ptolemies, making use of the rich resources of the great library and 'museum' they founded at Alexandria. The name means 'shrine of the Muses' – perhaps the first ever externally-sponsored scholarly foundation, for the schools of Plato and Aristotle were funded by the founders and their pupils. A satirical writer, Timon, speaks of 'many bookish inmates maintained in multiracial Egypt, perpetually squabbling in the Muses' birdcage'.[16] Callimachus' poetry constantly seeks unexpectedness of content, subtlety of form. Crude longwindedness is despised; the poetry of Antimachus, a writer of the previous century whom Plato had admired, is dismissed as 'obese and opaque' (F398). A justly famous passage in which Callimachus pronounces on poetry is known as the 'prologue to the *Aitia*', perhaps prefaced to a new edition of this poem or of all his works. Here he proclaims his poetic credo, using language and imagery that pervade the work of his Latin imitators.

> . . . away with you, deadly tribe of Envy. And in future judge wisdom by its art, not by the Persian measure [a unit of several miles]; and do not expect from me the birth of a loud-resounding song. Thundering is not my task, but belongs to Zeus.
>
> For when I first set my writing-tablet on my knees, Lycian Apollo said to me: 'dear poet, be sure to rear your sacrificial victim as fat as can be, but keep your Muse thin, my friend. And this too I advise: do not tread the track where wagons have gone before you, nor drive your chariot in the same path as

others, nor on the broad highway, but follow the untrodden paths, even if
you have to take a narrower route.' I obeyed his words; for I sing among
those who love the clear call of the cicada, not the din of asses. Let others
swell till they resemble that long-eared beast, but may I be the slender one,
the winged one, yes oh yes, that I may sing as I feed on the dew that falls as
sustenance from the heavenly sky, that I may cast off old age anew, age that
now lies as heavy upon me as three-cornered Sicily on the dreadful Enceladus.
    (F 1.17–36)

Not everyone agrees that this is a manifesto against bombastic epic, but
it is at least a manifesto against something, even if that something is a
construct of everything Callimachus dislikes. Ancient commentators tried to
identify Callimachus' targets, and modern speculations have gone further
with less evidence. But what matters is the inspirational insistence on 'thin-
ness', subtlety, and on pursuing untrodden paths. 'Make it new': Callimachus
put it more imaginatively than Pound. His Latin followers not only rework
the scene with Apollo (Virgil translates it almost word for word at the
beginning of *Eclogue* 6); they also develop the opposition between crude,
clichéd, long-winded writing and the subtler, sophisticated art which the
author himself can offer. Frequently this becomes an antithesis between epic
and whatever genre the poet himself favours: pastoral in the case of Virgil,
lyric for Horace, elegy for Propertius and Ovid. The patron, if he has taste
and learning, should also accept the canons of Callimachus, and not insist
on being presented with inflated or inferior stuff. Thus what in Callimachus
was a polemical piece of self-assertion becomes in Augustan poetry an
elaborate strategy to enable poets to define their poetic identity and retain
their independence.

Before turning to Rome, however, we should look further at the praise
poetry created for the rulers of the Hellenistic era. It becomes obvious that
such productions could be lengthy and tedious as well as devious and
original. One of Theocritus' poems (17) is written in praise of Ptolemy
Philadelphus and is obviously composed in the hope of winning the king's
patronage. Like anything this poet writes, it is polished work, but the praise
is unrelieved and the superlatives grow wearisome. Much wittier and written
with a lighter touch is the parallel poem to Hieron II (16), in which the
poet allows his purpose to emerge through self-mocking description of the
difficulties that a poet finds nowadays in securing a patron: everywhere
the wealthy find convenient excuses ('I only wish I had some money
myself'; 'who would listen to another poet? Homer is sufficient for all'),
so that the poet's 'Graces', sent out to knock on promising doors, come
home empty-handed. But in Sicily (it is hoped) he will find a patron who
appreciates his art, a monarch strong in taste as well as in war. Most successful
of all, because most indirect and entertaining, is poem 15, a dramatic piece

set in Alexandria.[17] Most of the poem deals with two women of Syracusan birth, who are now resident with their husbands in the great city. One woman, Gorgo, calls on the other, Praxinoa; there is a lively, humorous passage of chat and gossip, including much complaint about their husbands, and they then decide to go to the royal palace and attend the festival of Adonis. A new scene ensues as they cope with crowds and rudeness in the street. In the palace they marvel naively at the beauty of the tapestries, fend off with coarse abuse a man who criticizes their accents, then listen entranced to the professional singer whom Queen Arsinoe has sponsored to sing the lament for Adonis. This song, some 40 lines long, is included in the poem and carries it on to a quite different plane of religious mourning and plaintive erotic longing. The poem concludes with Gorgo's final words, impressed but unabashed. Reality returns: she must be getting back to cook supper before her husband gets cross. The whole piece is astonishingly vivid. It also indirectly praises the royal house, not only by demonstrating their taste and religious devotion, but through more incidental details: 'I'm told the queen is putting on a lovely show', says Gorgo (23), and in the crowd Praxinoa declares that the king has done the people many a good turn since his father went to heaven, not least stamping out pickpockets and muggers, 'ruffians who come up to you sneakily in the street Egyptian-fashion' (48). The compliments to the royals are humorously distanced; by putting them in the mouths of these women, Theocritus avoids any hint of sycophancy.

A still more ingenious example is Callimachus' poem on the lock of Queen Berenice, which was probably a separate composition subsequently incorporated in the *Aetia*, at the end of book 4 (balancing another poem for Berenice at the opening of book 3 and so framing the second half of the *Aetia*). Although some of the Greek original survives, we have a fuller idea of it from Catullus' translation (poem 66). Berenice had dedicated a lock of her hair to one of her predecessors as Queen, now a divinity. The lock had vanished, but by a flattering conceit it was said that it had been translated to the stars and become a constellation (as figures like Orion and Ariadne had been in older myths). The Callimachean poem is put in the 'mouth' of the lock of hair itself – despite the honour of being placed in the stars, it still laments the separation from the beloved head of its mistress! The whole concept is light-hearted and witty: and the poem included some risqué references to the brother–sister marital relations (see 66. 11ff. – the Greek original is mostly lost here): 'at the time that, blessed with recent marriage, the king went forth to harry the Assyrian borders, bearing the sweet scars of the nocturnal struggle he had waged to win the spoil of her virginity'. The tussles of the bedchamber give way to more outdoor campaigning. Callimachus seems to cultivate this indirect or bizarre style of compliment in all of his laureate passages.

A still more startling case is in Callimachus' hymn to Delos, a poem mainly concerned with the misfortunes of Leto, who is persecuted by Hera and so cannot find a place to give birth to her divine children, Artemis and Apollo. Delos will eventually be her refuge, but before that she comes to Cos – whereupon her own unborn child, Apollo, warns her to move on, because Cos is reserved for the birth centuries later of another god! Addressing his mother from within her womb, Apollo prophesies that this island will become the birthplace of Ptolemy II, Callimachus' present patron, and he goes on to tell of that monarch's triumphs: 'O Ptolemy who is yet to be, these are Apollo's prophecies to you' (*Hymn* 4.188). The device is extravagant but undeniably striking – it allows the poet to avoid the obviousness of straightforward statement, the monotony of a catalogue of victories. These lessons were not lost on the Roman poets, although they generally imposed a greater seriousness of mood. The prophecy by Anchises in the mythic past of events in Virgil's present is not entirely dissimilar.[18]

The frequency with which rulers from this period onwards are given divine status, after death or even in life, amazes the modern, and will be discussed further in a later chapter. Context is all: ceremonial ritual serves to reinforce civic loyalty, and high poetry takes these themes as an opportunity to elevate and give colour to potentially prosaic subjects. The rulers themselves were not for the most part deluded megalomaniacs: we relish the dry wit of the Macedonian Antigonus Gonatas, who when hailed as a god remarked 'the man who empties my chamber-pot has not noticed it'.[19]

III

In Rome there are more complex distinctions to be made, partly because this was a more hierarchical, stratified society, and partly because writings by Greeks would be viewed differently from those by Romans. Greeks, even cultivated men, were perceived by Romans as hirelings, who had a clearly subordinate relation to the ruling class of the dominant power. Poets and literary men might form part of the entourage of a Roman statesman, as the Epicurean poet-philosopher Philodemus attended upon Cicero's contemporary Piso. The relationship of Roman to Roman would be different, but how different depended on the writer's status and rank. Hierarchy mattered, but *politesse* masked its importance. Although Rome, unlike Greece, had a highly developed patron–client system, the actual title 'client' was avoided, at least in cultivated circles: often the term 'amicus', friend, was preferred (we remember Pindar's regular self-presentation in terms of guest and host). The terms are of very varied application, and the fact that one was a 'client' of X did not necessarily mean one was financially dependent on him. Moreover, by the first century BC many of the upper classes were busily writing verse or prose works, which they frequently dedicated to one another, or requested such dedications. This could happen between equals, without any issues of 'patronage' being involved. Cicero composes the *Topica*, a work on logic, in response to a request from the lawyer Trebatius. Caelius, writing to Cicero, hopes for a work dedicated to himself (*Letters to Friends* 8.3). Catullus asks for consolatory verses from Cornificius (poem 38). Hence the precise power-relations and the levels of intimacy between writer and recipient are not easy to diagnose, and we should not be swift in reaching cynical conclusions.

In considering these questions we come naturally to the circle of poets commonly labelled 'Augustan' – the poets who dominate the literary scene during the reign of Augustus, and who celebrate his achievements and (sometimes) his ideals. Virgil and Horace are the most significant figures, while Propertius and (later) Ovid may be seen as offering less wholehearted support. This is a period on which we are unusually well-informed, and despite some uncertainties the works of these poets can for the most part be dated quite precisely. The poets make frequent reference to the events of their time: the defeat of Cleopatra, the ending of the civil wars, Augustus' status as bringer of peace and victor in foreign wars, the dedication of temples, the passing of moral reforms, the celebration of the 'festival of the era' (Ludi Saeculares), and so forth. We see them dealing with the problems of treating the new order appropriately in poetry of different kinds. They do not necessarily address Augustus directly (indeed, there is some tendency to avoid doing so); often their poems are dedicated to other notables, not least the key figure of Maecenas, a friend of Augustus but a poet and bon viveur, wealthy and influential but not himself holding an official role in politics. The importance of Maecenas' role as tactful intermediary can hardly be overestimated.[20]

'Augustan poetry' is a simplification. We are dealing with a developing situation. Virgil and Horace both began writing during the so-called triumviral period, between the murder of Julius Caesar in 44 and the battle of Actium in 31. Neither was at first a supporter of the future Augustus: Horace, indeed, fought on the opposing side at the battle of Philippi in 42. Both poets came round gradually, partly under the influence of Maecenas. Octavian's position was only secure from the time of Antony's death in 30 BC; he assumed the title Augustus in 27. There is a fundamental difference between the poetry of the 30s, a time of instability and political unrest culminating in war, and that of the 20s, when the supremacy of Augustus was increasingly established, and the Roman state began to enjoy unaccustomed peace and prosperity. The decade of the 20s sees the publication of some of the masterpieces of the age: the *Georgics* were probably finished in 29, and the next decade saw the appearance of the elegies of Tibullus, three books of Horace's *Odes*, the first three books of Propertius, and the early books of Livy's *History*; during this period Virgil was composing the *Aeneid*. This was a time when the tact of Maecenas, the spirit of recovery and hope, and the energy of the writers were almost miraculously combined. The later period, from about the death of Virgil in 19, sees the regime more settled, and Maecenas seems for some reason to become less important (Tacitus, *Annals* 3.30): even in the work of Horace, who was probably closest to him, he is mentioned only once after 19 BC. Augustus himself may now have found time to take a closer interest in poetry, and certainly he figures more prominently in it.

It has always been difficult to assess the 'court-poetry' of the Augustans. Cynical readers have seen the poets as sycophantic hacks, composing panegyrics to order; more idealistically, they have been seen as rising to the great opportunities of the age and giving poetry a higher status by boldly adopting national themes. The great work of Sir Ronald Syme, *The Roman Revolution* (significantly published in 1939), saw analogies with the propaganda-machine of fascism and Nazism, and his ominous chapter-headings 'The National Programme' and 'The Organization of Opinion' have set the agenda for much criticism ever since.[21] But propaganda in modern times can exploit mass literacy and a wider range of media; in antiquity monuments and celebratory games reached a far wider audience than sophisticated verse. At most, one would have to see the 'message' of poetry as directed to the senatorial and equestrian class. In any case, Maecenas was no Goebbels, and it is unrealistic to see the poets as mere squeaking puppets. A writer did not have to choose to write about Augustus: Tibullus, writing under the patronage of the aristocrat Messalla, never mentions him. One might be in the circle but not of it: Propertius addresses Maecenas in only two poems, displaying clear reluctance to praise Augustus; when he does turn to patriotic themes it is as the heir of Callimachus, not the client under Maecenas' direction. Moreover, some of the themes which are prominent in Virgil and others, not least an interest in the early history and traditions of Rome, had already preoccupied writers of the previous generation (Cicero in his *On the State*, Atticus in his work on chronology, Varro in his *On Families of Trojan Descent*). The interest of the *Aeneid* in aetiology, the telling of stories to explain the origins of rituals and institutions, did not spring from thin air.[22] Similarly, Cicero had urged on Caesar the need for moral reform and increase of the birth-rate, and some of these measures were in fact enacted by Caesar's heir. Augustus, who sprang from a deeply traditional background, was responding to impulses shared by contemporaries. We may grant that his own preoccupations have to some degree guided the decisions of the poets. Yet the freedom with which they approached these subjects in a variety of styles, and the frequency with which they politely declined to embark on grander or more military themes, suggest that they were not obliged to produce poetry to order.

To illustrate some of these points we must turn to examples. One of the earliest texts of the period is Virgil's *Eclogues*, composed around 40 BC. In this book Maecenas is never mentioned; Virgil seems to be under the protection of the Republican Pollio, an ally of Antony, and in *Eclogue* 4 he honours Pollio as consul of 40 BC. The opening poem of the book is a memorable and courageous piece. Using the framework of a Theocritean idealized landscape to make very un-Theocritean points, Virgil dramatizes the consequences of the recent land confiscations in several regions of Italy (including his native Mantua), a process dictated by the need for Octavian to settle his veteran soldiers as promised. The poem is a dialogue between two herdsmen, Tityrus and Meliboeus: the former is contented, the latter wretched.

> Tityrus, you lie beneath the shelter of a spreading beech-tree, practising sylvan poetry on your slender pipe. We are leaving the territories of our homeland, the fields we love; we are driven from our home; you, Tityrus, at ease in the shade, are teaching the woods to echo the name of lovely Amaryllis. (1.1–4)

It emerges that Meliboeus and others have been driven from their homes so that a 'barbarous soldier' may reap the benefit of all their devoted labour. Tityrus' humble plot is secure, however, for he has boldly journeyed to Rome and sought the aid of a wonderful youth, who is not named but seems to be almost divine in his power and benevolence – at least as viewed through the naive eyes of Tityrus. The poem sustains the contrast, with Tityrus rhapsodizing on the saviour-figure who has rescued him from misfortune, while Meliboeus, though not grudging his friend his good fortune, laments the carefree existence he must leave behind and anticipates a life of exile, in which 'I shall sing no more songs'.

Since antiquity readers have tried to connect this with contemporary events and indeed with Virgil's own life. Servius saw the poem as at least partly allegorical: Tityrus represents Virgil and the young man is Octavian. This reading oversimplifies, not least ignoring the fact that Meliboeus seems to get the best poetry. Tityrus, an ageing slave with a small and marshy property, is not a convincing image of Virgil. But the relevance of the land confiscations can hardly be denied (later in the *Georgics* Virgil mentions in passing 'pasture land such as unhappy Mantua lost'). This is neither eulogy nor an attack on Octavian: it is a dialogue, and both sides need to be given weight. There is no need to question the young man's generosity to Tityrus, but what of Meliboeus and his like? A similar situation, with different characters and still gloomier mood, appears in *Eclogue* 9: there too the peace of the countryside is invaded by armed forces, and the shepherds lament that the songs they love are powerless and are slipping from their memory. Already in his earliest work we see some of the typically Virgilian ideas: the hatred of war and violence, the sense of loss when rural tranquillity is disrupted.[23]

The *Georgics*, a decade later, is dedicated to Maecenas, and Octavian is glorified in several passages.[24] The opening of the poem shows that Virgil is following the path of Callimachus. In an extravagant passage he imagines that the ruler may in due course be deified, and will join the 12 signs of the zodiac ('already blazing Scorpio is contracting his claws and allowing you more than your fair share of heaven', 1.34). The hyperbole and the daring imagery, as in the opening of the third book, may suggest that at this relatively early date the poets were unsure how to address Octavian appropriately (one of Horace's early poems honouring the great man, *Odes* 1.2, shows some of the same extravagance and uncertainty of tone). More memorable is the conclusion of the fourth book, where Virgil contrasts himself and 'Caesar' (Octavian). He describes him as 'thundering by deep Euphrates', the river of Parthia, dealing out laws to willing subjects, and aspiring to Olympus. He then continues 'during that time, delightful Parthenope [Naples] nursed me, Virgil, as I blossomed in the pursuits of inglorious leisure, I who once played at shepherd's songs and (bold in my youth), sang of you, Tityrus, beneath the shelter of a spreading beech-tree' (*Geo.* 4.559–66). The contrast is richly suggestive: foreign wars defending the frontiers, as opposed to luscious peace at home on the Bay of Naples; aspiration to godhead versus 'inglorious leisure'; conquest and lawgiving in contrast with poetic composition – and 'play' at that. The poet's freedom to compose in secure peace depends on the conqueror's success and on the stability that law and Roman order impose; yet the poet, for all his frivolity, has himself been a critic, for the allusion to the opening line of the *Eclogues* recalls the negative treatment of earlier acts by Octavian in that poem. Those youthful works were 'play', yet the poet describes himself as 'bold'. The lines are subtle and flattering, but far from simple: if Virgil now accepts Octavian as a saviour-figure, he reminds the reader of other judgements and other values. From our own distant perspective, we may reflect on which of these two men's achievements have lasted longer.

IV

In turning to Horace we face a far greater abundance of evidence, because so much of his work is in autobiographical form. Although we must beware of taking his poetry, however intimate and realistic, as a window on his life, it is safe to assume that the relationship with Maecenas was of real importance to him (and vice versa: Maecenas in his will urged Augustus to 'remember Horatius Flaccus as you would myself'). Maecenas is addressed in 16 poems and mentioned in others, far more than any other addressee. They are close enough for Horace to tease and even jokingly reproach him: he alludes to his friend's infatuation with an actor, laughs at his hypochondria, utters mock-curses on the excessive dose of garlic in his food. Maecenas' personality was a colourful one – flamboyant in dress, notorious for his luxurious table, his taste in jewels and fine wines, his effeminate style of writing (which Augustus deplored: Suet. *Aug.* 86), and even for his walk (Sen. *Ep.* 114.4).

A common type of poem in Horace is the invitation to dinner. It seems likely that this was a conventional form, perhaps not least from client to patron.[25] Philodemus, whose work Horace knew, wrote an elegant epigram to Calpurnius Piso in this vein:

> Tomorrow your poetry-loving friend is carrying you off,
> after the ninth hour, dearest Piso, to his simple hut,
> for the annual dinner on the twentieth.* If you leave
> your dish of udders and your toasts in the Chian wine of Bromios,
> you will at least see companions wholly true, you will at least
> hear talk honey-sweeter than the land the Phaeacians knew.
> But if you ever turn your eyes, Piso, even upon me,
> we shall hold a rich twentieth instead of a simple one.   (23 Gow-Page
>   = *AP* 11.44)

Here is Horace's version of the same motif:

> My dear Maecenas, noble knight,
> You'll drink cheap Sabine here tonight
> From common cups. Yet I myself
> Sealed it and stored it on the shelf
> In a Greek jar that day the applause
> Broke out in your recovery's cause,
> So that the compliment resounded
> Through the full theatre and rebounded
> From your own Tiber's banks until
> The echo laughed on Vatican hill.
> At your house you enjoy the best –
> Caecuban or the grape that's pressed
> At Cales. But whoever hopes
> My cups will taste of Formian slopes
> Or of the true Falernian
> Must leave a disappointed man.   (*Odes* 1.20, tr. by James Michie)

---

* i.e. a dinner commemorating Epicurus. Both men were Epicureans, and Horace largely shared this philosophy.

Horace too offers a wealthy man simpler fare and friendship, but the dinner will be a private one for the two kindred spirits; the wines are Italian (a typical example of Horace's Romanizing of Greek lyric). The language is more austere, less gushing; he avoids the misplaced eroticism of Philodemus' final couplet. By referring to a public acclamation for Maecenas on recovery from a serious illness, he both flatters his patron and shows his own concern: the two have something more to celebrate than an annual event commemorated by all Epicureans. 'Sabine' wine may remind us of Horace's Sabine estate, which was a gift from Maecenas and strengthens the bond between them. Moreover, the phrase 'noble knight' alludes to Maecenas' membership of the class below the senatorial rank: he is represented as a modest man, unwilling to claim the high office that he might (in Latin the expression is an oxymoron: 'clarus', the adjective, is normally applied to senators). Such self-restraint shows that he will appreciate Horace's inferior wine even though he himself has the wealth to lay down four much more distinguished vintages. So Horace's poem includes more biographical detail and also says more about his friend's character, whereas Philodemus confines himself to superficialities.

Accepting Maecenas' patronage meant an admission that Horace was on the wrong side in his ill-fated career as a soldier. He dwells on this in several passages, and turns it to account in a poem which welcomes back an old friend, now free to return to Italy thanks to the amnesty decreed by the generous victor (*Odes* 2.7). Perhaps because these events were so recent, in the *Satires* he avoids overt engagement with politics but has plenty to say in praise of Maecenas on a more personal level: friendship and the proper conduct of friends become regular subjects of his poetry. In one famous poem (*Sat.* 1.5, the 'Journey to Brindisi') he accompanies Maecenas on an important diplomatic mission, but his narrative is all about the humorous incidents en route (noisy frogs, rustic clowns or a girl who stood him up), and the poem ends just when the serious business is about to begin. Was Horace being discreet, or did he really have no more to tell? In the *Odes*, in which he models himself on Alcaeus and Pindar among others, public events are more prominent. The poem on the downfall of Cleopatra (1.37) can readily stand comparison with Virgil's narrative of Actium: she is painted as an alarming Oriental who poses a terrible threat, but her final suicide is treated as heroic ('no humble woman this'). To enhance her status is a compliment to Octavian, who has not fought and conquered a decadent drunken woman, but a figure who finally commands respect.

Most famous among Horace's public poems is the remarkable series of six odes which begin the third book, the so-called 'Roman odes'. Nowhere else do so many odes in the same metre come together. They are evidently meant to be seen as a group, and the opening of 3.1, in which Horace announces himself as a bard addressing and enlightening the younger generation, must apply to them all. The group is varied, however: praise of moderation, chastity and other good Roman virtues; denunciation of modern vice and depravity; romanticized recollection of Horace's youth and how he was marked out as a poet with a future; extended narrative of mythic events (war in heaven, or the ascension of Romulus) and of one memorable historical episode (the story of heroic Regulus, a figure of the Carthaginian war). Augustus' name figures, and he is praised in emphatic terms (the poet even anticipates his deification); but Horace's references are brief, and he seems more concerned to give the new ruler a context in the traditions of Roman morality and history. These poems are not all to modern taste, and not only because of their Augustanism (Wilfred Owen was not alone in disliking 'the old lie,/ *Dulce et decorum est pro patria mori*' ('It is sweet and fitting to die for one's country')). But they represent a sustained effort to give expression to the ideas of Augustus without descending into mere slogan-writing. Whether they all succeed or not, they include some of Horace's most ambitious poetry (3.4 is the longest ode he ever wrote). For the critic of Augustan poetry they are indispensable documents.

But Horace is more at home with more private scenes and prefers to be on the fringes of great events, an onlooker rather than a participant. His attitude is epitomized in *Odes* 3.14, a poem which blends public and private: Horace's concept was imitated by both Propertius and Ovid.

People of Rome, we were lately told that Caesar had sought the laurel won by death, like Hercules; but now he returns victorious from Spanish shores to the gods of his own household.
Let his wife, rejoicing in her exceptional husband, come forth worshipping the just gods, and the sister of the beloved leader, and with them, adorned as suppliants, the mothers of maidens and of young men newly saved.
And you, boys, and girls who have not yet known husbands, beware of ill-omened words.
This day for me is truly one of celebration; it will remove black cares; no more need I fear unrest or violent death while Caesar guards our lands.
Go on boy, fetch fragrant oil and garlands, and a cask of wine that remembers the Marsian war, if any jar has been able to elude wide-ranging Spartacus.
And tell clear-voiced Neaera to waste no time but put myrrh on her hair and tie it up. If there is delay thanks to her odious door-keeper, then come away.
Greying hair mellows the spirit that once was eager for dispute and heated quarrels. I would not have borne such treatment in my hot youth, in the days when Plancus was consul.

From public ceremonial reception we pass to a private party; from chaste girls and boys to a less-than-chaste companion. The reader needs to recognize the allusions to Roman history: the 'Marsian war' and 'Spartacus' hint at the violence that has plagued Italy for the best part of the century, only recently brought to a close by Augustus; and 'Plancus' consulship' marked the battle of Philippi in 42, at which Horace had fought against the ruler he now welcomes back from foreign wars. 'In my hot youth' is like 'bold in my youth' in Virgil's mouth: Horace acknowledges his past but recognizes that the present is a time with better prospects of safety for all citizens. Yet there is a note of wistful nostalgia in the reference to his advancing years and whitening hair. Age brings better judgement but removes some of youth's passionate enthusiasms.

In the *Epistles* Horace treats patronage from a more ethical standpoint, and uses his own relationship with Maecenas as an illustrative example (1.7); but he also acknowledges that such relations can be conducted on a cruder and more self-interested basis (1.17 and 18). His own behaviour is sometimes seen in these terms by critics, but we can at least say that the evidence suggests Horace enjoyed a closer and more informal relationship with Maecenas than other poets. The exact proportion between affection, shared attitudes and self-interest cannot be divined, but the extreme version of the cynical position, which assumes that personal friendship could not exist in Roman society, that self-interest and personal advantage were all that mattered, defies not only common sense but the abundant evidence of Cicero in his letters and not least his essay *On Friendship*.[26]

The death of Virgil and the eclipse of Maecenas changed the position of the poets and especially of Horace, who now found himself centre-stage. The short biography of the poet by Suetonius tells us that several works were commissioned by Augustus himself. Pre-eminent among these was the poem known as the *carmen saeculare* ('poem for the century'), written for the celebration of a major religious festival in 17 BC. In terms of public recognition this was the peak of Horace's career, but the ceremonial quality of the poem has alienated most modern readers. There is certainly more of a laureate flavour to the late collection, *Odes* 4, although it includes some great poems. Only a minority of the poems of book 4 are untouched by the public world in which the poet has now found an established, and publicly acknowledged, place. The emperor is addressed directly, the victories of his stepsons celebrated. Although the writing is as polished as ever, the poetic handling of themes is perhaps less nuanced. In book 3 we were told, with rhetorical urgency, that immoral behaviour needed to be curbed; in book 4, we hear that it has been. Horace dwells more on the Pindaric theme of poetry's power to give immortality. It is hard not to feel that poetry is being kept on a shorter rein, and that Augustus' sympathies are less broad and generous than those of Maecenas. That would not be inconsistent with evidence in Suetonius.[27]

The 'Life of Horace' just mentioned quotes a letter from Augustus to the poet in which, with heavy-handed humour, he reproaches him for addressing none of his chatty verse epistles to himself ('Are you afraid that it will count against you with posterity if you are known to have been my friend?'). From the Hellenistic age onwards it became common to dedicate works in both prose and verse to monarchs or great patrons of the day. Pindar's odes had provided precedent, but the older epic and drama, public poetry, lacked a single recipient. This remains true of Virgil's *Aeneid*, but Lucan and Statius feel obliged to address their epics to the emperor of the day. The procedure became conventional, and in some cases may be no more than a courtesy. 'Your commands' became a cliché of prefaces. Pliny tells a delightful story of a recitation at which the poet grandiosely began 'Priscus, you bid me . . .', whereupon Priscus, the patron, impatiently interrupted him, declaring 'I don't bid you do anything!' (*Letters* 6.15)[28] Whatever one supposes about the imperial addressees of Vitruvius' treatise on architecture or Pliny's *Natural History*, it is a little difficult to believe Apollonius of Citium's claim that he undertook his commentary on Hippocrates' work *On Dislocated Limbs* at the express request of Ptolemy Auletes.[29] Nevertheless, the convention could not be ignored: that the Stoic Chrysippus addressed none of his philosophical works to kings could be taken as a sign of arrogance (Diogenes Laertius 7.185). So too at Rome: although Quintilian's great work on rhetorical training is dedicated to a friend, a later passage pays suitable compliments to Domitian (4.pr.2–6).

V

Literature had indeed from now on to take full account of the emperor. Elegy, with its rejection of public themes and its commitment to the erotic, was open to question, and there are some daring (or at least mischievous) passages in Propertius. Augustus' intolerance of immorality exploded in the condemnation of Ovid in AD 8, exiled to the Black Sea, never to return. Ovid wrote that he had been brought to disaster by a poem and a blunder: the poem was certainly the *Ars Amatoria*, hardly new at the time of his downfall. The blunder will never be known for certain, and many wild theories have been proposed, from adultery with Augustus' granddaughter to seeing the Empress Livia bathing! What mattered was the disturbing precedent, that writers could be punished for their words as well as their acts. By a sobering irony Ovid's last works mirrored what may well be his first: in his early years he had composed a series of fictional letters supposedly sent by mythical heroines to their lovers, lamenting their desertion or complaining of misfortunes (the *Heroides*). In the period of exile, between AD 8 and his death nine years later, he composes a long series of letters to his wife, his friends and the emperor himself, describing his own misery in far-off Tomi, pleading for clemency or intercession. Long despised as lachrymose and sycophantic, these works are now being reconsidered and seen to be more subtle and more sympathetic, perhaps even slyly subversive. But whatever the reader's verdict on the poems, Augustus' verdict on the poet was unalterable, and Tiberius (whom Ovid never addresses and who may have been his enemy) was as immovable as his predecessor.[30]

Around the same time as Ovid's exile Augustus ordered the destruction of other 'not-approved' works such as the satirical verses of Cassius Severus, who lampooned men and women of the upper classes (Tac. *Ann.* 1.72, 4.21). Writers became much more self-conscious about what they made public: the historian Labienus ended a reading of his history by rolling up the work and saying 'What I pass over now will be read after my death' (Seneca the Elder, *Controversiae* 10 pr.8). Tacitus gives a star role to another historian, Cremutius Cordus, who was condemned under Tiberius, and who makes a ringing speech in defence of literary freedom (*Ann.* 4.34–5; see Appendix 1.4). Tacitus says that Cordus' work survived in secret, and was later republished; but Quintilian comments that it survived only in mutilated form. Emperors could at least try to deny works to posterity. Under Domitian, even the copyists who transcribed another seditious history were crucified (Suet. *Dom.* 10.1).

It is significant that we begin to hear more of critical, satirical or oppositional literature when it is threatened with suppression. Lampoons and abuse had always been congenial to the Romans. Caesar's troops sang obscene verses at his triumphal procession over the Gauls: 'men of Rome, lock up your wives; we're bringing home the bald adulterer'. Cordus in Tacitus reminds his judges of the offensive verses Catullus and Calvus directed at Caesar, of the invective exchanged between Octavian and Antony. But under the empire it became unsafe to treat the eminent until they were disgraced or dead. Horace is uneasy with personal abuse in his satires, unless of stock or fictional figures; Juvenal concludes that the risks are too great, and he will direct his mockery at the dead. Biographers had to be careful: although under the Flavians Nero's memory was execrated, it proved fatal to celebrate Nero's senatorial opponents, the so-called Stoic martyrs (Tac. *Agr.* 2). Even unpolitical genres could be dangerous: the Roman public had long been accustomed to see contemporary reference in lines delivered on stage (Cic. *Defence of Sestius* 118ff). In the late Republic, at a time when Pompey was unpopular, cheers went up when an actor spoke the line 'it is

to our misfortune that thou art *great*', since this was taken as an allusion to
Pompey's favourite title (*Letters to Atticus* 2.19.3). Double meanings and
dangerous choices of subject could now be perilous: to dramatize the tyrant
Atreus or Thyestes could be maliciously represented as treason.[31]

The consequence, diagnosed by Tacitus, was that emperors must be
flattered when alive, denounced when they were dead (*Ann.* 1.1). The same
author might adopt both roles: the exiled Seneca addressed laudatory
appeals to Claudius through his freedman Polybius, and composed the
panegyric for Nero to deliver at the funeral of his predecessor ('when the
speaker passed on to speak of Claudius' foresight and wisdom, few could
refrain from laughter . . .' *Ann.* 13.3); but Seneca was also apparently the
author of the hilarious skit on the death of Claudius, known as the
Apocolocyntosis ('Pumpkinification', an invented word based on 'apotheosis',
deification). A medley of prose and verse, colloquialism and parodied
grandeur, with some affinities to the tradition of 'Menippean satire' to
which Petronius' novel belongs, this short work describes the humiliating
experiences of Claudius' ghost on arrival at Olympus, where he finds the
established gods, including the deified Augustus, none too pleased at the
idea of such a misbegotten misfit joining their ranks. He would have been
consigned to play dice with a defective dice-box in Hades had he not been
rescued by Caligula, who recognized him as his 'slave' (having treated him
like one throughout his life). The piece was no doubt received with much
hilarity in Nero's palace.[32]

The other period in which we can see most clearly the workings of imperial
and court patronage is the end of the first century AD.[33] From the Domitianic
period, seen by the senatorial class as a time of tyranny, we have Statius' elegant
Silvae; from the better times which follow, Pliny's *Letters* tell us much
about literary society; while the poetry of Martial begins with Domitian's
predecessor Titus, then straddles the reigns of Domitian, Nerva and Trajan.
In Martial's earlier work praise of Domitian reaches a peak in books 8 and
9, but he hastily suppressed the first edition of book 10 (which no doubt contained more of the same) when the emperor was murdered in early 96, and
his subsequent work duly honours the new rulers. Tacitus and Juvenal did
not publish until after Domitian's assassination, but much that they write looks
backwards (especially Tacitus' *Agricola* (p. 124) and the viciously parodic
fourth satire of Juvenal, which uses mock-epic motifs to portray the emperor's
council meeting to discuss what to do with an enormous turbot).

Antagonistic and satiric writing has an immediate appeal; it is much harder
to do justice to writers such as Statius, who as a professional poet had no
choice but to work with the regime and pay poetic tribute to the dominant
figure on the throne.[34] In his epics the praise of the emperor is confined to
the dedications. The five books entitled *Silvae* are a different matter. The

collection is strangely named. The title ('Woods' or 'Raw material') may suggest poetry that has not been given its proper finish, as Statius pretends that these are casual, even impromptu pieces. Tone, metre, length and subject matter vary, but there is a consistent Statian style: elevated, flattering, richly adorned with mythical references and elaborate descriptions. The shortest and best-known poem, in which the poet asks Sleep to visit him, is quite untypical (5.4). The poems are almost all concerned with notable occasions in the lives of eminent acquaintances, such as a wedding, the birth of a son, a funeral or a dedication of a statue or small temple. Like Pliny in prose, he celebrates the families, the villas or the careers of his friends.[35]

Most of the poems were evidently commissioned, although a few are more personal (above all the lament for his father, 5.3, and the verse-letter to his wife, 3.5). Some are relatively light-hearted, in the Catullan manner: the verses on the death of Melior's parrot (2.4) are an amusing adaptation of motifs from Catullus and Ovid. But when the emperor himself is honoured, Statius' tone could not be more solemn and extravagant. The great equestrian statue of Domitian is celebrated in tones of awe, and the engineering works on the new Via Domitiana provide a springboard for broader panegyric (1.1, 4.3). Poem 4.2 expresses the poet's gratitude at having been entertained for the first (and only?) time at the imperial dinner table. The comparison between emperor and king of the gods, with which Horace had only flirted, is here taken to its logical limit:

> I feel as though I am reclining with Jupiter amid the stars and receiving the immortal draught proffered by the hand of Ganymede . . . The Thunderer's palace next door gapes at [your house] and the gods rejoice that you are lodged in a like abode (do not hurry to mount high heaven yet!) (4.2.10–12, 20–2)

It is pointless to question Statius' sincerity: at this date no other tone was permissible, and it is more rewarding to admire his dexterity in facing the rhetorical challenge. However, we may still prefer the poems to lesser men, which admit a more relaxed and even playful tone.

Among his techniques of praise and glorification the use of mythology is especially notable – not only adopting the bardic role of Orpheus himself, and not only peopling landscape with Pans, Nereids and other beings, but including mythological narratives relating to the real-life events. Thus Rutilius Gallicus' recovery from illness is ascribed to the medical attention he has had from the physician gods Apollo and Asclepius (1.4), whereas in mourning a dead youth Statius visualizes his journey to the underworld, with reminiscences of the classic scenes in Virgil (2.1). Best of all, a charming fantasy involving Venus and Cupid is offered to 'explain' the success of Pomponius

Stella in softening the heart of Violentilla and winning her as his bride: the treatment skilfully combines motifs of love elegy (which Stella himself wrote) with the more conventional marriage song (1.2). We may recall the extended use of mythical paradigms in Pindar, but there is a significant difference. Pindar, though encouraging his patrons to emulate the mythic heroes, regularly warns of the limits that confine human aspirations: 'seek not to become Zeus' (*Isth.* 5.14). By contrast it is standard practice for Statius to declare that the present instance *surpasses* mythic precedent, human or divine (e.g. 1.1.52–3, 1.4.125–6, 3.1.115–16, 3.4.39ff., 4.3.145–52). Pious prudence is superseded by hyperbolic enthusiasm. Roman grandees may outdo the achievements of mythological heroes, provided they never receive praise that exceeds the emperor's.

The mechanisms of patronage continued beyond the Flavian period: Hadrian's enthusiasm for the arts was notorious, and we catch intermittent glimpses of the literary scene under the Antonines through the sadly fragmentary letters of Fronto; in later centuries much can be done with the correspondence of Symmachus (fourth century), whose letters emulate those of Pliny.[36] The panegyrical poems of Claudian shed much light on the court of the Emperor Honorius at the end of the fourth century, but his poetry, celebrating wars, consulships and marriages (and abusing the emperor's rivals), lacks the personal detail and humorous warmth of more versatile authors such as Horace. But the periods we have considered in more detail, Augustan Rome and Domitianic Rome, offer particularly rich evidence of literary activity and interaction. The two reigns may seem to represent polar opposites. The rule of the first emperor was frequently seen as a golden age, whereas Domitian was assassinated and his memory execrated. Both verdicts are oversimplifications: the reign of Augustus already saw the beginnings of Roman 'court' literature, and modern historians have gone far in rehabilitating Domitian as an administrator, despite the condemnation in the ancient texts. At the very least, the relief that his death caused stimulated some of the most remarkable writings of Latin literature, above all those of Tacitus and Juvenal. The literature of the empire cannot be studied without awareness of its historical dimension. Virgil would not have been the poet he was without Augustus, and Tacitus would not have written as he did without Domitian.

7

Aspects of Wit

I believe that a witty man can discuss any subject more easily than humour itself.

Cicero, *On the Orator* 2.217

I

This chapter is not a collection of classical jokes. Such a chapter could be written, and would indeed have ancient precedent: a Byzantine joke-book containing 265 funny stories does survive, and the tradition is evidently much older.[1] Even in his lifetime Cicero was famous for his wit, and Caesar had his subordinates send him choice examples; collections of the bons mots of Cicero and Augustus, among others, were available to Macrobius in the fourth century AD.[2] Major writers such as Aristotle, Demetrius and Cicero himself pondered the nature of humour.[3] There will be little theoretical discussion in this chapter. Rather, I shall be considering a number of authors and traditions in ancient literature, not all of them obviously comical, but all in one way or other adopting a parodic, oblique, ironic or self-consciously ingenious approach to their material. One major genre, comedy, has already been discussed in chapter 2, and will be only briefly mentioned here. I first consider parody and the distortion or unexpected redirection of established genres. In section III the main subject is the learned artifice of the Hellenistic age, exemplified above all by Callimachus and emulated by his Roman disciples (IV). In section V artifice is seen on a smaller scale, and a more verbal form of wit is discussed, with special attention to the 'pointed' style found throughout 'silver' Latin literature and quintessentially in the epigrams of Martial. The remaining parts of the chapter turn to humour as a weapon, the aggressive mockery of invective and the more ambiguous genre of satire, which shifts between direct criticism and ironic collusion with vice. Inevitably these categories will sometimes overlap: for instance, parody is an important part of the technique of satire, and pointed wit is found in other genres than epigram.

Although the aim, as usual, is to engage mainly with individual authors, some more general points may provide something of a framework. Two important contrasts are frequently in play in this chapter: between the high and the low, and between the sophisticated or urbane and the crude or rustic. The first antithesis is closely bound up with issues of genre (Introduction, part II): high genres such as epic, tragedy and history tend to sustain a serious or sombre tone (as does philosophy insofar as it is concerned with fundamental issues of morality and salvation). By contrast 'lower' genres not only readily admit humour but often employ it as a weapon to attack or at least poke fun at higher genres. Elegy snipes at epic, satire parodically takes up serious philosophical themes, comedy burlesques tragedy. The opposition is of course not so simple: the higher genres contain more variety and self-conscious fluctuations in tone than this description allows; but subtle and complex works are simplistically represented as monolithic and ponderously serious in the polemic of the lesser genres. Moreover, 'high versus low' suggests a bipolar hierarchy, but there are a number of levels in the generic ladder, and places are not rigidly fixed: poets and critics might differ as to whether satire was superior to elegy or the reverse. The other antithesis, urbane versus crude or rustic, reflects the social milieu in which much of the literature discussed here emerged: above all, the rich cultural life and literary society of the great metropolises, Alexandria and Rome. Probably no author from earliest times has ever wanted to be regarded as anything but subtle and sophisticated, but it is in the fifth century, in the time of Aristophanes and Euripides, that this claim becomes a regular boast, and by contrast writers regularly accuse their opponents of crude work, naiveté and vulgarity (e.g. Ar. *Frogs* 1ff.). However, variations in this pattern are found. Sophisticated writers can portray crude or low subject matter in witty style or with knowingly learned humour. Low-life scenes are keenly observed in the *Mimes* of Herodas; the ultra-refined dramatization of rural simplicity is the essence of Theocritean pastoral. The same attractive technique is seen in the many scenes from Callimachus onwards in which gods or heroes are entertained to unaccustomedly simple fare by ignorant but well-meaning country-dwellers. The Greek novel cultivates similar effects, dramatizing the naive responses of young lovers as they tearfully learn the ways of the world (or, in Longus, the ways of love). In many of the epigrams of Catullus and Martial, the coarse language of the Roman streets is introduced to give a spicy shock to the reader: yet the versification and the literary conceits are as skilful as in their less forthright poems. The gross and the subtle or tender may be juxtaposed, or even combined in the same poem (Catullus 11, quoted on p. 156). Urbane writers observe and denounce those whom they find lacking in tact or taste; but they may also deliberately set aside these standards themselves, boldly writing in 'tasteless' or immoderate fashion (invective, curse poems, erotic abuse); often they claim to be driven to these lengths by an enemy's vile behaviour (e.g. Ovid in the *Ibis*), but we should not be too ready to take these protestations at face value. In short, in all these contexts our authors are adopting a deliberate pose, and nowhere is the distinction between author and internal narrator more important. Psychoanalysis of the poet in an effort to explain the violence or irrationality of his outbursts may be quite misconceived. Similarly, we should not necessarily see works such as Juvenal's satires as having, or intended to have, a direct impact on the society in which they are composed. Often the poet may not be struggling to amend morality or avenge an insult, so much as inviting admiration for the author's ingenuity, or the reader's participation in an ironic and cultivated game.

II

Parody may be present in literature from the beginning: the Homeric narrative technique of playing variations on a theme or motif might be thought to encourage it. Some critics argue that the scene in book 14 of the *Iliad*, in which Hera puts on her most alluring outfit in order to seduce Zeus, is a parody of warriors arming themselves for the battle. In the relation between the *Odyssey* and the *Iliad* we can sometimes discern a kind of parodic effect, though particular cases are hotly disputed. One plausible case is the exceptional use of a lion-simile when the shipwrecked Odysseus, naked and hungry, emerges from the undergrowth and frightens the Princess Nausicaa and her maids: 'he advanced like a mountain lion, sure of his strength . . . if flocks are penned in a strong-built fold, his hungry belly [NB!] urges him on to go after them even there. Thus Odysseus prepared to go among the fair-tressed maidens, for need pressed hard upon him.' Normally in the *Iliad* such a simile would be used when a hero entered battle. Odysseus is humble and in need of help, so that the simile is incongruous: this is only how he appears to the terrified girls. (6.130ff., cf. esp. *Iliad* 12.299ff.)

Parody is a rich vein throughout Greek and Latin literature, but we should distinguish between direct mimicry or burlesque of a specific model text and a broader, more generic approach, which is perhaps more common. Pre-eminent among the former is Aristophanic parody of Euripidean tragedy, although even here the imitation often extends beyond a single play. In *Acharnians* and *Women at the Thesmophoria* he sends up a notorious sequence from the tragedian's play about Telephus, but in what is surely his supreme travesty of Euripides' art (the parody of his lyrics in the *Frogs*), multiple sources can be recognized. Here the parody depends not only on verbal detail but on a conception of Euripides already expressed in the play – as a writer who pulls down tragedy from its traditional grandeur to trivial themes expressed in hifalutin diction. In particular Aristophanes is mocking the lyric monodies, redolent of self-pity and full of emotional repetitions and colourful compounds, as recently exemplified in Euripides' *Helen* and *Orestes*. But there are also phrases reminiscent of earlier plays. We are to imagine that the heroine has awakened from an alarming dream which she now describes: but the sinister nightmare turns out to have been foreshadowing a quite un-tragic disaster, the theft of a rooster.

> O darkly-shining murk of Night, what unhappy dream do you send to me, a messenger from invisible Hades, with a soul that is no soul, child of black darkness, terrible shuddering vision, black-corpse-shrouded, with a look that is deadly, deadly, with great big fingernails?
>
> But, handmaidens, kindle a lamp for me and lift the dew-water from the rivers in pitchers, heat the water that I may wash away the divine dream (ah, god!)! So that was it! My household, gaze upon this ominous sight! The rooster that was mine, it was snatched away by departed Dulcie! Nymphs born of the mountain, and Manias, help me!
>
> Unhappy am I! I was attending to my own work, winding the distaff full of its twine in my hands, making a skein, so that in darkling murk I might take it to the marketplace and sell it.
>
> But he is flown, is flown to the upper air, on the light-most tips of his wings; he has left me sorrows, sorrows; tears, tears I cast, I cast from my eyes, wretch that I am!
>
> But Cretans, offspring of Ida, seize your arrows and come to my aid; nimbly plying your limbs encircle the house. And let virgin Dictynna, lady of the hunting net, fair one, come with you through the houses on every way, with her little bitchlets.
>
> And you too, Hecate, Zeus's daughter, come, upholding the fiercest torch-lights twin-fiery in your hands, accompany me with light to the home of Dulcie, so that I may enter and catch the thieving girl in the act! (*Frogs* 1331–63)

The repetitions, the play with dark-light images, and the frequent invocations are all mannerisms of late Euripides; the ominous dream is a commonplace of tragedy; but the triviality of the heroine's misfortune mockingly reflects the way in which Euripides had admitted some everyday or down-to-earth details to a number of his tragedies, notably the *Electra*. This is not, of course, a fair representation of Euripides' style: like most stylistic parodies, it exaggerates and extends particular effects, so alerting the audience to the artificialities of tragic conventions and the extreme nature of tragic emotions. This passage well illustrates the antitheses outlined earlie – generic opposition parallels the class-distinctions implicit in the genres in question, since tragedy normally deals with mythical kings, comedy with contemporary commoners. The domestic crisis, like the name of the thieving girl, is appropriate to comedy.

Many passages of ancient literature depend for their effect on a know-ledge of literary norms, and often also of social convention. Parody regularly works by distorting or reversing these conventions. Catullus offers us a good example in poem 13, an invitation poem to Fabullus. This was evidently a regular literary form (poems by Philodemus and Horace are quoted on p. 190). In ancient society as in our own a guest might be expected to bring a contribution (cf. Hor. *Odes* 4.12), but Catullus, protesting his poverty, asks Fabullus to bring the whole meal, including wine and a girl. His own contribution will be only an expensive perfume (perfumes and oils were common at Roman parties; the ancients did not have soap), which will fill the room with sensuous fragrance. This choice offering of his own suggests his poverty is in fact due to extravagance.

Poem 6 is an entertaining little piece which also inverts a traditional form. Catullus asks Flavius the identity of his secret lover. This seems to be a parody of the type of epigram in which the speaker has spotted a clue that his friend is in love. One example is a poem by Callimachus.[4]

> The guest kept his wound hidden. How painful
>   The breath he took (did you notice?)
> At the third toast, and the petals dropping
>   From the man's garlands littered the floor.
> He is badly burnt, by the gods; I don't guess amiss.
>   A thief myself, I know the tracks of a thief.

Naturally, to emphasize the addressee's discretion and the speaker's insight, the clue is sure to be a small one, easy to miss: a blush, a reluctance to drink, a sigh or a sad silence (Hor. *Odes* 1.27). Contrast this tactful, elegant perceptiveness with Catullus' deliberately rumbustious mockery:

> you're in love with some hot little slut, and ashamed to say so. For that bed of yours may be dumb, but it still cries out that you're not spending solitary nights – it's soaked in Syrian scented oil and garlands; those pillows . . . the creaking tottering shaken frame of the trembling bed – no, it's hopeless, absolutely, to hush it up. You wouldn't be showing such exhausted, shagged-out flanks if you hadn't been engaged in some naughty goings-on . . .

In Catullus, the clues are glaringly obvious, the poet is triumphant rather than tactful, and goes on to promise, or threaten, to immortalize Flavius and his girl in elegant verse – a promise the poem in a sense fulfils, while still not exposing her name.

Horace too is a master of these techniques. By this date another well-established form was the 'sending-off poem', addressed to a friend or beloved who was embarking on a journey, usually a dangerous one overseas. It was customary to pray for favourable winds, particularly the kindly west wind or Zephyrus. Horace himself wrote such a poem, addressing Virgil, a close friend (*Odes* i.3). In one of his iambic poems, attacking a foe called Mevius, he does the opposite: since he wishes Mevius to come to grief, he calls on south, east and north wind all to blow together and wreck the ship; instead of anticipating celebration of a friend's safe return, he promises to sacrifice a goat to the storm winds once he hears that Mevius is 'rich prey for the sea-birds' (*Epodes* 10). Another choice example is his parody of the hymnic form, in *Odes* 3.21. In party mood, he invokes the wine-jar he plans to use as though it were a god (his 'cellar', as was common, is in the loft of his house, so the conventional request to a god to 'descend' is given a clever point).

III

The most important author to be confronted in this section is Callimachus: for a full appreciation of his work, some context is necessary. This, however, is not easy to provide given the state of our evidence. Callimachus was writing in the third century BC at the court of Alexandria, in the so-called Hellenistic age (conventionally regarded as starting in 323 with the death of Alexander). Of his own works, the most famous in ancient times are fragmentary for us, and his predecessors are even less easy to reconstruct. From the preceding century we have very little verse (Menander's comedies are not helpful in approaching the *Aetia*); if we go back to the fifth century our evidence is more abundant, but after Pindar it comes largely from the dramatic genres. Writing Hellenistic literary history is like piecing together an enormous jigsaw where at least 80 per cent of the pieces are missing, and those which survive are often wholly defaced or damaged and obscure. Bold assertions and dogmatism are misplaced here.[5]

It is not hard to find authorities who repudiate such caution. A common approach has been to contrast the direct and creative literature of the classical era with the subtle but imitative and introverted scholar-poetry of the Hellenistic world; often this kind of evaluation is openly linked with the view that Greek literature lost its inspiration at the same time that the Greek world lost its freedom (we see here the bias of our Athenian perspective on the earlier period): literature is obliged to become subject to royal patronage or else to bury itself in erudition. This is a caricature, but something like it underlies most of the older readings. More recently studies have focused more on specific authors rather than attempting global generalizations.

It does seem true that (some) literature becomes more self-conscious and bookish, though we must beware of putting this development too late.[6] Euripides was able to allude to generic conventions and even invented some features of his plots. The younger tragedian Agathon appears to have invented an entire myth, composing a play about the previously unknown Antheus (Arist. *Poetics* 9.1451b21). Some of the ingenuity and intertextual games which older critics associated with the third century can be convincingly found much earlier. But although earlier poets might use older sources and allude to them, they seldom cited them (particularly not prose sources, as Callimachus does in passages that prefigure the learned footnote). Again, it may be true that writers since literature began have bemoaned the fact that so much has already been done, but this concern for novelty seems to take on a new urgency in the Hellenistic age.[7] Various strategies were adopted to deal with this burden of the past: old genres combine, new genres emerge, or old ones are turned to fresh use; motifs which were minor in earlier poetry become major concerns (aetiology, metamorphosis); themes of prose are transferred to verse (philosophy, astronomy); relatively straightforward speech-acts are made more convoluted or enormously extended (curse poems). Furthermore, it is not easy to find a poet before the Hellenistic era who wrote with equal authority in poetry and prose, as did Callimachus and Apollonius; still less, perhaps, to find writers of any sort who wrote so much, on such a range of learned topics. Callimachus is credited with writing more than 800 books; even if that is not believed, the list of his productions is remarkable. His prose works included books on nymphs, on local names of months and of fish, on birds, rivers, 'wonders' and much else. He is said to have 'arranged' (edited?) the poems of Pindar and Bacchylides. Particularly important was his catalogue or bibliography of the library at Alexandria, organized by subject: the ancient description is 'tables of those who have distinguished themselves in every form of culture and of what they wrote'. This seems to be an unprecedented enterprise. Apollonius similarly wrote about problems in Homer and Hesiod, as well as on Archilochus.

The work of Aristotle and his school in the previous century had established the ground-rules of scholarship in a wide variety of fields. The Hellenistic writers followed in their wake, and the scholarship fed back into their poetry.[8] The rich resources of the library fuelled their imagination and deepened their learning. This is most obviously true in their use of obscure local histories and myths, but goes much further, into fields such as ethno-graphy, astronomy, even anatomy (Apollonius' moving account of Medea's physical distress as she suffers from love seems to hint at contemporary medical knowledge of the nervous system (Ap. Rh. 3.763)). Now that Alexander's conquests had opened up the world, Greeks were scattered across the three known continents. Callimachus himself was born in Cyrene in north Africa and moved to the great capital of the Ptolemies, Alexandria, in Egypt; we do not know how often, if at all, he set foot in mainland Greece.[9] It would hardly be surprising if he viewed the classical authors and the old country with intense interest, although whether his attitude was more nostalgic, envious, superior or admiring, or a mixture of these, is hard to determine.

'Bookishness' is difficult to define, but one definition might be satisfied by a poet who makes a poem out of a prose text. As far as we can see, Aratus, a contemporary of Callimachus, was the first to do so. Taking Eudoxus' astronomical treatise, he produced a version in epic hexameters, the *Phaenomena* ('Visible Signs', i.e. the constellations), which itself had phenomenal success. Callimachus wrote an admiring epigram about it, and Latin poets seem to have thought it a necessary part of their apprenticeship to translate it into their own tongue (Cicero, Ovid and Germanicus Caesar, nephew of the Emperor Tiberius, are among those who did so). Aratus was one of a number of poets who set themselves the challenge of treating thoroughly recalcitrant and technical material in attractive poetry. Nicander tried the same trick, writing on poisonous snakes. Cicero remarked that Aratus and Nicander had no expert knowledge of their subject matter. That may have been unfair, but they certainly set a pattern. Lucretius in his poem on Epicureanism, Virgil in his *Georgics*, Manilius' Stoic poem on astronomy, even Horace in his *Art of Poetry*, are similar undertakings. But although modern critics join ancient poets in elevating Aratus to the stars, nobody has succeeded in showing Nicander to be any less poisonous than his subject.

Less ambitious and more absurd experiments were not lacking. Lycophron wrote anagrams, numerous epigrammatists composed mathematical riddles (*AP* book 14, cf. *SH* 201); the papyri have thrown up evidence of letter-games, including palindromes and hexameters containing every letter of the alphabet (*SH* 996). Connoisseurs of pointless exercises must admire the dedication of Timolaus, who introduced an additional line after every line of the *Iliad*, doubling the length without marring the sense (the opening is preserved, *SH* 849). More obviously frivolous was Sotades, who rewrote the *Iliad* in the louche metre named after himself (elsewhere associated with jocular abuse and pornographic subjects). Homer remained the fountainhead of literature, but clearly awed reverence was not the only possible attitude for later writers to adopt. The prize for perverse ingenuity must go to the poet Nestor of Laranda, who, noting that the books of the *Iliad* were regularly designated with the 24 letters of the Greek alphabet, set himself the task of composing a version which abstained from using the letter A in book 1, the letter B in book 2 . . . This monument to Oulipo-like self-denial does not survive.[10]

Callimachus' six hymns and about 50 short epigrams survive intact; the rest of his work must be painfully reconstructed from quotations by other authors and from a welcome flood of papyri. We can now speak with more confidence about his major work, the *Aetia*, than was possible 50 years ago. This poem, composed in elegiac couplets, stood first in editions gathering his collected works, prefaced by the polemical defence of his art and reply to his critics (p. 182), and was evidently regarded as his most significant: when Latin poets allude to him as a model, they generally invoke the *Aetia*. The title means 'Origins' or 'Causes': in this work Callimachus explored the explanations behind a wide range of rituals, festivals or religious objects such as statues, casting his net across the whole Greek world, and in each case telling or dramatizing a myth which 'explained' the reason that a cult is celebrated in a certain way. Cities' foundation-legends also featured. In its final form the work was in four books, but it is likely that books 3 and 4 were later additions. Its length cannot be known for certain, but it was considerable. Books 3 and 4 totalled at least 2,000 lines.[11] (Callimachus' most famous saying, that a big book is a big evil, may well not have been made with reference to poetry [F 465].) We cannot be sure of the number of episodes or in some parts their order: the ancient summary, which sets these out in sequence, offers invaluable help where we have it, but is incomplete. It does seem clear that individual episodes were self-contained, though sometimes similar tales were juxtaposed (F 44–7, two tyrannical figures, Busiris and Phalaris; F100–1, two statues of Hera on Samos).

In the first two books, however, a unifying structure was provided. Callimachus represented himself as encountering the Muses on Helicon, in the same fashion as Hesiod long ago (p. 29), but in a dream. (Probably some interpreters had already read Hesiod in that way.[12]) He questions them about the things which puzzle him in religious practice, and they answer. Many of the questions are bizarre and obscure: 'Why have the Parians preferred to sacrifice to the Graces without flutes and garlands?' (F 3); 'How is it that a man of Anaphe uses shameful words when sacrificing to Apollo, and the city of Lindos honours Heracles with blasphemy?' (F 7.19). Rather than a religious devotee, Callimachus presents himself as a passionate researcher: in one sequence he already has three possible explanations from his own enquiries, and merely asks the Muses to arbitrate (F 79: why do women summon Artemis to aid them in childbirth, though she is a virgin?). In another he seems to have offered the goddesses a poetic lecture on the early colonization of Sicilian cities by Greek settlers: in our scrappy text this goes on for at least 20 lines before he gets to the point with a fresh question (F 43). This novel use of the Muses as both inspiration and re-search assistants delighted the Latin poets, as did the extraordinary mingling of learned detail with whimsical and often colourful narrative.

The Muses were not Callimachus' only source. In one fragment, possibly but not certainly from the start of book 2, the narrator is being entertained at a symposium in Egypt, hosted by a cultivated friend, and starts talking to his neighbour, a visitor from the island of Icos. They swiftly find each other congenial: both prefer good talk to heavy drinking. The poet warms to the theme: 'let us, Theogenes, put talk in the cup to mend the tedious draught; and tell me in answer to my question the thing my heart yearns to know . . .'. We might expect enquiries about politics or personalities or even poetry, but the poet's appetite for cultic detail is insatiable: 'tell me, why is it the tradition in your country to worship Peleus, king of the Myrmidons? What has Thessaly to do with Icos?' (F 178). Much of the response is lost, but it evidently involved a story that Peleus, the mythical father of Achilles, had been killed on Icos, and the inhabitants had established a feast-day in his memory. The charm of the scene-setting is a prelude to a further venture into the mythic past.

New evidence combined with old has made it possible to see more of the overall structure of books 3 and 4.[13] It now seems clear that book 3 began with a poem of Pindaric cast (though in non-Pindaric metre) celebrating a chariot-race victory won on behalf of Queen Berenice in the Nemean Games. This was balanced at the close of book 4 by another poem in her honour, the *Lock of Berenice*, discussed in the previous chapter (p. 184). Thus court poetry provided a frame for the second half of the poem, but seems to have impinged very little on the numerous stories told in between. Nor did this honorific purpose demand ponderous seriousness; Callimachus' ingenuity and wit are as evident here as in his other compositions for royal figures. The first part of book 3, besides celebrating the victory, seems to have included a myth, again in Pindaric fashion, which narrated the origin of the Nemean Games, supposedly founded by Heracles to commemorate his triumph over the Nemean lion (traditionally his first labour). In the typical manner of the Hellenistic period, attention is displaced from the 'natural' high point, the combat with the lion. Instead much is made of Heracles' sojourn with an amiable peasant, Molorchus: the setting is humble, the diction suited to epic (we recognize the story-pattern familiar from Callimachus' *Hecale*, the entertainment of a great hero in simple sur-roundings). Particularly delightful is the description of Molorchus' efforts to trap the mice which pester him by night: one fragment mock-heroically describes his setting of a primitive mousetrap.[14] With mischievous humour Callimachus tells how the old peasant listens closely and catches the sound of the mice, and compares this to a trembling doe hearing the roar of a lion-cub – we are meant to think of the lion which Heracles will shortly fight, and to see Molorchus' exploits as a small-scale analogue to that heroic deed (*SH* 259.10).

Just as not all the tales in Ovid's *Metamorphoses* make much of metamorphosis, so in the *Aetia* aetiology is not always prominent. One of the best-preserved sections is a love-story, the tale of Acontius and Cydippe. Acontius, in love with the girl, sent her a letter which she read aloud, and found herself reading out a vow to marry Acontius. Her parents tried to arrange a more eligible match, but she fell ill each time. In the end, after consulting an oracle, her father yielded and Acontius' dearest hopes were fulfilled (F 67–75, about 150 lines of which about 100 are intact). The narrative does include ritual, but the poet self-consciously refuses to be explicit about its origin ('For they say that once upon a time Hera – dog, dog, refrain, shameless soul of mine! You would sing even of that which it is not lawful to tell!' 75.4–5). The tone shifts with bewildering virtuosity: from narration of the girl's sickness to praise by Apollo of the birth and lineage of Acontius, to an intimate and teasing address by the narrator to Acontius regarding his wedding-night:

> I do not think, Acontius, that in exchange for that night, on which you touched her maidenly girdle, you would have taken either the ankle of Iphicles who could run upon the corn-ears, or all the wealth of Midas of Celaenae. And my verdict would be endorsed by all who are not ignorant of the stern god [of love]. And from that marriage a great name was destined to arise . . .

From the wedding-bed we jump down the years, as the poet refers to the clan that still existed on Ceos in his own time, who claimed descent from Acontius (aetiology reasserts its place in the poem). But the episode concludes with a remarkable passage in which Callimachus pays tribute to his source, naming a local Cean historian so obscure that only five other passages in ancient literature refer to him,[15] and summarizing for 20 lines the content of his work, before reverting at the end of the whole episode to Acontius.

> This love of yours we heard of from Xenomedes of old, who once set down the whole isle in a mythic memorialising, starting with how it was inhabited by the Corycian nymphs, whom a great lion drove away from Parnassus . . . and how Ceos, son of Phoebus and Melia, caused it to take a different name . . . and how of its four cities one, Carthaea, was built by Megacles . . . and blended with these themes, dear Cean, that old man, committed to truth, told of your fierce passion; from there the youth's story raced to my Muse. (F 75.53–77)

In this conclusion the poet again addresses the lover with affectionate direct-
ness, yet simultaneously emphasizes the gulf between his own time and the
tale he tells, while also implicitly contrasting his own style of narrative
(selective, vivid, fast-moving verse) with the conscientious cataloguing of
the local chronicler. 'That old man' stands in contrast with 'the youth', with
the poet himself sharing the enthusiasms of both.

IV

Callimachus can never have been easy: indeed, he was a byword for
obscurity.[16] In the fragmentary state in which we are obliged to read them
the *Aetia* pose formidable difficulties. But there is no question that his
reputation stood very high, and his impact on the classical Latin poets,
especially the elegists, can hardly be exaggerated.[17] Apart from particularly
famous passages such as the prologue to the *Aetia* or the Acontius-story,
the whole concept of aetiology as a means of linking legendary and later
times, while not invented by Callimachus, was given powerful backing by
his example. The other aspects of his work which had lasting influence
include the obvious premium he placed on learning, the allusive and selective
use of obscure sources or little-known variant legends, and the intriguing
ways he found of combining very different types of story or poetry within
a larger structure, whether by digression, inset narrative, or juxtaposing
of episodes with a common theme. Important also is the blending or reshaping of genres, as most clearly seen by the way he incorporates Pindaric
themes in aetiological elegy. Certainly his famous prologue was known at
Rome as early as Ennius, and Catullus translated one long section of the
work (66), but we see his influence most clearly with the major poets of the
Augustan age. Two works in particular stand out, the last book of Propertius'
elegies (in which the poet styles himself a Roman Callimachus), and Ovid's
poem on the Roman calendar, the *Fasti*.

The Romans were naturally much concerned with the origins of Rome,
with all its political and imperial significance: antiquarianism is hard to
separate from patriotic celebration of the past. The *Aeneid* had traced the
mythic origins of Rome's power and customs: both Propertius and Ovid are
strongly influenced by Virgil's recent master-epic. Whereas Callimachus seems
to have abjured epic ambitions, Propertius regularly engages with the higher
genre, and with Ovid the relation between epic and elegy comes close to
an obsession. One particularly inspirational section of the *Aeneid* was the
hero's visit to the future site of Rome, and especially the emphasis Virgil
laid on how small and simple everything was then, but how mighty it would
become. Pastoral or rural innocence is contrasted with urban magnificence.

This motif is taken up and constantly reworked by the elegists. It opens Propertius' book, and occurs at least six times in the *Fasti*, as well as providing a premiss for many episodes. Although Callimachus enjoyed contrasts of a different kind, and is not indifferent to the large spans of time he sometimes covers, the variety of his scenes and the relative absence of moralizing mean that the past–present antithesis is not prominent in his work. But in Propertius and Ovid the contrast between present and past, great and small, modern (decadent?) and primitive (barbarous?), are fundamental: on the one hand Rome's past is an example to the present, on the other it contains dreadful tales of cruelty and vice (Tarpeia, Tarquinius). Above all there is the dark foundation-myth with the killing of Remus, however much some versions might try to exonerate Romulus from guilt. Further, Ovid in the *Ars amatoria* had stated a preference for the modern: 'let others delight in ancient times; I congratulate myself on being born at this late date. The present age suits my personality best' (3.121–2); the preference also makes itself felt in the *Fasti*. This admiration for modern sophisticated living adds further complexities to the view of Roman history provided by these poets.

As for the Callimachean influence, this is perceptible in subject matter, form (more clearly in Ovid's case), and narrative technique or tone. Propertius' fourth book begins with a poem which presents the poet as a split personality, who on the one hand aspires to write of myths and origins ('I shall sing of sacred rites, and days, and the ancient names of places'), but on the other is drawn back to the erotic subjects of his earlier work. The first poem also powerfully sets out the contrast (and conflict?) between past and present, with past embracing both myth and history. The rest of the book pursues these oppositions through Callimachean means. In some poems Propertius is present as character, whether lover or bard, while in others his place is taken by alternative speakers (as Simonides speaks from the grave in an episode of the *Aetia*, F 64). Some poems are aetiological, others erotic; significant juxtapositions are found (4.3 shows a modern wife devoted to her soldier husband; 4.4 the traitorous Tarpeia, infatuated with the soldier who leads the opposing army in an episode of Rome's past). Other literary forms are incorporated into elegy: 4.3 is an epistle and 4.11 a kind of defence speech; 4.6 resembles a Callimachean hymn, while also drawing on the *Aeneid*. Generic blending and misdirection of the reader are frequent. It is hard to draw the interpretation of the book together, but it is clearly significant that the book ends with the values of the past asserted in the present, through the speech of the virtuous matron Cornelia, a recently deceased kinswoman of Augustus, who is represented as defending her stainless career before the judgement of Hades (4.11). Eroticism is forgotten, Propertian liaisons trumped by aristocratic marriage, and Roman morality redeemed. But the book speaks with many voices, and in earlier contexts Roman dignity and heroic achievement are treated in more light-hearted vein. As in Callimachus, the device of a concluding piece of 'court poetry' is a significant feature but cannot decisively shape our reading of the entire book.[18]

Ovid's unfinished work on the Roman calendar covers only the first six months of the year, one book for each month. Exile intervened and he either did not write or did not revise the second half of the poem, which would have included the months recently renamed after Julius and Augustus. The surviving books have undergone some revision in exile, but the project may have been abandoned. Ovid is Propertius' ablest pupil, outstripping his master in scale if not in subtlety. Just as his erotic poetry develops Propertian themes to the point of near-parody, and just as the epistle of Arethusa in Propertius (4.3) provides the germ of Ovid's mythical epistles (the *Heroides*), so the *Fasti* builds on Propertian foundations. Also important, however, is the whole background of antiquarian literature on Rome's past, most importantly the work of Varro. This work has set its mark on many of Ovid's discussions, for instance of the Lupercalia, a major festival in February (2.267–452). The calendar itself had been radically overhauled by Julius Caesar and to a lesser degree by Augustus, lengthening the civil year so as to restore parity with the solar cycle. Moreover, the pre-eminence of Augustus and the imperial family meant that the festival calendar now included many entries commemorating notable dates in the great man's career (birthday, victories in war, the date on which he assumed the name Augustus, etc.): it was no longer simply the calendar of the traditional cultic events.[19] All of this made the calendar a potential subject for patriotic literature: it did not make it an easy one. (A case in point is the Ides of March, the date of Julius Caesar's assassination, the subject of a particularly controversial passage.) But Ovid's imaginative gifts produced a work almost as varied and ingeni-ous as the *Metamorphoses*, and one which is rich in the ambiguities of tone and ideology that have most attracted modern critics.[20]

Ovid's format is closer to that of the *Aetia* than the one used by Propertius. Each book consists of separate episodes for different dates, varying greatly in length and depth of treatment. He uses the device of interviewing a deity or deities prodigally, but without the 'realistic' technique of describing an encounter in a dream: Ovid is able to meet and question Janus, Mars, Venus, the Muses and Flora in broad daylight. Another Callimachean device which delights him is that of multiple explanations (the poet's authority is not final). In one sequence, indeed, three Muses offer three different explana-tions for the name of the month of May, and each is supported by two of her fellow-Muses, there being nine in all: impasse. Ovid refuses to arbitrate, asking that the favour of every Muse alike attend him: 'let me never praise any one of them more or less than the rest' (5.1–110). A similar divine encounter opens book 6: Ovid meets Juno, Hebe and Concordia, each with a different explanation for 'June': the scene is explicitly reminiscent of the Judgement of Paris, but Ovid is canny enough to prefer none of these deities to the others.

As for the explanations themselves, often couched in narrative about mythical figures, divine and human, these vary hugely in style (and plausibility). Some are taken over from older sources, or elaborated; others may well be Ovid's inventions. There are extended dramatic tales told for their own sake: the vivid account of the rape of Lucretia concentrates so much on the lust of Tarquin and the noble agony of his victim that we forget that the story took its start from the date which traditionally marked the Regifugium or flight of the kings from Rome (24 February; 2.685–852). There are also ludicrous episodes of sexual comedy which introduce a note quite alien to Callimachus (Augustan elegists were readier than the Greeks to draw on lower genres such as the farcical mimes).[21] A fine example is the scene where Faunus, a lustful rustic deity, is fired with desire for the lovely Omphale, whom he has seen in the company of Hercules, her enslaved lover. One night he sneaks into the cave where the two reside, and hopes to have his way in the dark. Feeling cautiously around the bed, he detects Hercules' shaggy lionskin and moves hastily to the other side: there he meets silky drapery, and is hopeful of success. Ovid's readers will have foreseen Faunus' disappointment, for a traditional part of the story of Omphale and Hercules was that she forced him to dress up as a woman, while she donned his attire: so when Faunus mounts the bed 'he pulled up the skirts, and . . . there lay bristling thighs rough with thickly massed hair' (2.347–8). A moment later Hercules thrusts him out of the bed, lights are kindled and the would-be rapist is humiliated. And that, Ovid sagely pronounces, is why Faunus requires his worshippers to come naked to his rites – or, if foreign explanations (i.e. Greek mythology) do not satisfy his readers, fear not: he has an alternative Roman version, concerning Romulus and Remus, which observes a higher level of decorum.

V

Ingenuity is also discernible on the more detailed level of words and names. As the pathways of myth became overpopulated, writers sought more obscure figures and referred to them in more recherché fashion. Even Homer had used patronymics ('son of X') to refer to his characters. When Patroclus is first mentioned in the *Iliad* the audience is expected to recognize him in 'the son of Menoetius' – one of the many indications that this is traditional poetry (1.307). By the Hellenistic age this was too easy, and far more elaborate periphrases become common. Ovid delights in testing his readers in this way: thus 'Asopiades' means Aeacus, 'Abantiades' can mean either 'son of Abas' (Acrisius) or his grandson (Perseus).[22] Ovid's curse poem, the *Ibis*, pullulates with examples: for most of the poem, he calls down the fate of hapless victims or wicked villains of myth on the head of his anonymous enemy. Normally each couplet contains a reference, often highly elliptical and mannered, to a specific myth.

> And when you wish to return to years of fresher youth, may you be cheated like the aged father-in-law of Admetus! (441–2)

> May you be as fiercely stung by poisoned snake as the daughter-in-law of aged Oeagrus and Calliope, or as Hypsipyle's child, or the man who first with sharp spear-point struck the hollow timbers of the suspect horse. (481–4)

We are reminded of the malicious dinner-party quizzes of the Emperor Tiberius (who enjoyed the more recondite Hellenistic poets): he liked to set scholars obscure puzzles: 'Who was Hecuba's mother? What name did Achilles take when he hid among the women? What was the subject of the Sirens' song?' (Suet. *Tib.* 70).

Ovid in the *Metamorphoses* also shows us another way in which schoolroom material could be amusingly deployed in poetry, in his handling of mytho-logical time. Since many of the myths had emerged quite independently, it naturally proved difficult to correlate the generations of heroes and work out the exact sequence of the great wars and exploits: poets might differ, for example, as to whether certain heroes were old enough (or too old) to go on the *Argo*'s expedition. Prose mythographers struggled with these problems, but Ovid makes light of them. A favourite technique is to allude to impending events, but incongruously or parenthetically: in narrating the battle to defeat the Calydonian boar he mentions Castor and Pollux, and helpfully adds '(they were not yet stars in the heavens)' (8.372). When Medea is gathering herbs for her magic, among them is a plant 'which had not yet become famous for its transformation of Glaucus' body' – this acts as a 'trailer' for a later episode in the poem (7.233, anticipating 13.904ff.). Not only myth but history is treated freely: Ovid makes the Roman King Numa a disciple of Pythagoras, though learned opinion, as he certainly knew, had concluded that chronology forbade this.[23]

Although we now accept that all literature is deeply intertextual, the Augustan poets have proved a particularly fertile field for those seeking evidence of many-layered allusiveness. Virgil in his early pastorals offers a rich example. The myth of Pasiphae, who was afflicted by a perverse passion for a bull, is being narrated by Silenus:

And he comforted Pasiphae (happy woman, if only herds of cattle had never existed!) in her desire for the snow-white bull. Ah! unhappy maid, what insanity seized you! Yes, Proetus' daughters did make the fields echo with their deluded mooing, but none of them ever sought so shameful a union with the beasts, however much they each feared the plough on their necks and constantly searched for horns on their smooth brows! Ah! unhappy maid, now you wander upon the hillside, while he [the bull] is resting his snowy flank on a bed of soft hyacinths . . . (Vg. *Ecl.* 6.45–53)

This highly allusive style expects a lot from the reader. Inset within Pasiphae's tale is a brief comparison with the more obscure story of Proetus' daughters, who were cursed by a deity with madness which led them to suppose they had been changed into cows (though they were not). Further, ancient commentators tell us that the repeated address to Pasiphae, 'Ah! unhappy maid!', echoes a line of Calvus, a poet of the previous generation (friend of Catullus), which occurred in his poem about Io: 'Ah! unhappy maid, bitter is the grass on which you will feed!' (fr. 9 Courtney). This line was evidently addressed by the poet or a character to the wretched Io, whose myth involved her being transformed into a cow and persecuted by Juno. The echo is not fortuitous, as the bovine theme is present in all three stories: Pasiphae would have liked to be a cow, and will behave as one; the Proetides thought they were cows but were not; and Io did not wish to be a cow, but became one! The arch ingenuity is patent. It may not remove the horror and tragedy of Pasiphae, but it complicates our response and arguably diminishes our degree of involvement.

Although periodization of literature is generally suspect and the designation of the first century AD as a 'silver' age is particularly unpopular nowadays, there is one aspect of the style of that age uniting most of the authors, which earlier criticism classed as 'silver' – namely, the so-called pointed style, evident in the authors' love of witty or paradoxical formulations, compression and epigram. Of course, gnomic generalizations go back at least as far as Hesiod, and sharp one-liners are common for instance in the lives of philosophers. (Alexander the Great to Diogenes the Cynic: 'Is there anything I can do for you?' Diogenes: 'You can stand out of my light.') But the pointed style is something sharper and more paradoxical. In attempting to define it, critics have quoted Pope's definition of wit as 'what oft was thought but ne'er so well expressed'. This is not adequate, as in silver Latin epigrammatic phrasing is often used to express what was *never* thought: a striking or counter-intuitive assertion, twisting convention or defying expectation. Virgil offers some instances: an example is the line from book 2 in which Aeneas advocates entering battle against all odds: 'the only safety for the vanquished lies in not hoping for safety' (*Aen.* 2.354). It is notable that this is the final line of his speech: this was a popular place for a striking epigram, often called a *sententia*. Rhetoricians cultivated the device; unfortunately, as Quintilian dourly remarked, there are not as many good epigrams as there are paragraph-ends (8.5.13–14).

We cannot do more than sample the self-conscious cleverness of these writers. Seneca the Elder anthologized the declamatory orators of his day, and provides an invaluable guide to the emerging taste of the period. His remarks on Ovid's one-sided skill as a speaker are intriguing: the poet found argumentation on points of law dull, and greatly preferred the exercise of composing persuasive speeches, with the opportunities these offered for emotional appeal. In the course of the next century, Lucan, Seneca, Tacitus and Juvenal in particular elevate the technique to dazzling levels of ingenuity. The concision of Latin reinforces the effect; word-play and repetition of a word in a different sense often sharpens the wit. Sometimes the comment is on human nature. Commenting on Domitian's persecution of Agricola, Tacitus writes: 'it is natural in a man to hate the one he has injured' (we would expect 'who has injured him', but La Rochefoucauld would have appreciated the subtler point (*Agr.* 42).) More famous is the historian's final verdict on the Emperor Galba: 'while he remained a citizen he seemed superior to a citizen, and by universal consent he was fit for empire, had he not become emperor.' ('capax imperii nisi imperasset.' *Hist.* 1.49). Or take Seneca: 'they do not want to live, they do not know how to die' (*Letters* 4.5). Here the point is that those who lack the insight of philosophy cannot die well. Similarly Seneca like other Stoics makes much play with the language of freedom and slavery, arguing that enslavement to one's passions is the true slavery: paradoxical doctrines lend themselves to startling expression.

'Epigram' can refer to detachable sentences like those just quoted; but we should not neglect the genre of epigram itself. The earlier Greek epigrammatists tended to compose sentimental reflections, and sometimes dramatized a developing situation, but although they occasionally take the reader by surprise in the final line, it is not the regular pattern. That technique, the 'closural thunderbolt', becomes more prevalent in the first century AD with Greek poets such as Lucillius and Nicarchus, but reaches its peak in Martial (writing mainly between 80 and 105).[24] He is by far the most productive writer of epigrams in antiquity, composing over 1,500 poems. His range is huge: literature, politics, country life, a friend's villa, food and drink, patrons and clients, celebration of birthdays and other occasions, *objets d'art*, love-affairs male and female, amorous and obscene, and much more. The dominant tone is light: he frequently mocks the sober-sided traditionalists emblematized by Cato, and brings a cynical eye to bear on society. Only when dealing with the emperor and his entourage does he lapse, inevitably, into courtly caution. He strongly influenced Juvenal (to whom several poems are addressed), both in subject matter and in his deployment of pointed expression and unexpected conclusions. A few examples out of many:

> Paula wants to marry me, but I don't want to wed Paula.
> She's an old hag. I would though – if she were older. (10.8)
> [The point is that she would then be closer to death, and he would not have long to wait to inherit her money.]

> Why don't I send you my little books of verse, Pontilianus?
> For fear you might send me yours, Pontilianus. (7.3)

> Diaulus used to be a doctor; now he's an undertaker.
> As an undertaker, he performs just the same as he did as a doctor. (1.47)

> Lycoris has buried all her female friends.
> I wish she was a friend of my wife! (4.24)

And finally, one of a sizeable number of epigrams that reflect, humorously or provocatively, on the status of his own genre in contrast with the grandiosity or bombast of higher forms:

> Believe me, Flaccus, the man who calls them trifles and jokes doesn't know what epigrams really are. The real trifler is the one who writes of savage Tereus' feast or your indigestible dinner, Thyestes, or of Daedalus, fitting liquefying wings to his lad, or Polyphemus feeding his flock of Sicilian sheep. Far from my slim volumes are all such inflated themes; my Muse is not bloated with tragedy's crazy robes. 'But these are the subjects that all readers praise, admire, adore.' True enough: that's what they praise, but mine's the work they actually *read*. (4.49)

In such a vast body of work it is inevitable that some poems fall flat or do not hold so much interest for the modern reader. But there is something here for every taste; it comes as a shock to read that Pliny did not expect Martial's poetry to endure (*Letters* 3.21).

VI

A variety of genres involve verbal assault or invective against a named opponent. Oratory in both Greece and Rome permitted personal attacks on a man's family, reputation, tastes and behaviour.[25] Aeschines was derided for his career as an actor, Demosthenes was accused of foreign birth and Timarchus of acting as a male prostitute. Crudity and vicious abuse were endemic in Roman culture. Many of their best-known names had their origins in clumsy insults: Brutus ('Thicko'), 'Crassus' ('Gross'), Cicero ('chickpea').[26] Obscene language was regularly directed at political opponents in epigrams or pamphlets, or chanted by mobs of popular supporters. Physical features were fair game, in an age unfamiliar with political correctness: Cicero mocked Piso's bad teeth and Vatinius made fun of Cicero's varicose veins. Rude songs about Clodius and Clodia were chanted in the Forum in 56 BC; Cicero himself is not above insinuating that their relationship is incestuous.[27] These attacks were designed to damage a rival's status and so had a practical effect on politics. In verse genres such as iambic (traditionally associated with insults and aggression), curse poetry or satire, the relation to reality is less easy to determine. Sometimes external evidence may assist: we know that Julius Caesar took offence at some of Catullus' lampoons. Elsewhere it is lacking, and readers are sceptical: can we really believe that some contemporaries felt that Horace was being more aggressive in his first book of satires than the laws of the genre allowed? (*Sat.* 2.1.1ff.). In other cases we may be unsure whether the abuse is serious or humorous, and in some cases the aggression may be directed at a fictional figure or a stock butt. Latin poets, more conscious of possible misrepresentation than the Greek, regularly insisted on the gap between life and art. Martial echoed Catullus and Ovid, declaring 'my page is wanton, my life respectable'.[28]

Traditionally criticism has seen a contrast between the earlier ages of classical poetry (when, it is argued, poetry sprang from and dealt directly with experience) and later times (when it became more 'literary' and conventional, with traditional topics crowding out real-life reference). More recently this strong opposition has been qualified, though not wholly abandoned: the impossibility of drawing a dividing line between periods, and increasing awareness of the subtlety and self-consciousness even of the early poets, have combined with arguments about the inescapable literariness of texts. We no longer assume that Sappho wrote a love poem because she had just discovered she was in love; why should we assume that Archilochus wrote a hate poem simply because someone had injured him? Fiction and fantasy play a part in literature as far back as we can see, though that is not to say that these works have *no* roots in reality. It remains possible to contrast different authors' handling of the same types of material, even if the contrast is between personae rather than poets.

One contrast which remains impressive even in the changed state of criticism is between the aggressive poetry of archaic Greece, that of Archilochus and Hipponax, and their Hellenistic and Roman successors. The conclusion of a poem which has been ascribed to either Archilochus or Hipponax (more probably the latter) survives on papyrus, conveying a powerful impression of vicious enmity. His foe is to suffer shipwreck, but not to die:

... drifting, struck by the waves. And at Salmydessus, when he lies naked, let the topknotted Thracians seize him – in a kindly way, of course!* There he will have his fill of sufferings, eating the bread of slavery – himself stiff with cold, and from the scum may piles of seaweed heap over him, and may he gnash his teeth like a dog lying face downwards in helplessness right by the edge of the surf, tossed by the waves. This I would desire to see him suffer, the one who wronged me, who trampled our oaths beneath his feet; he who was once my friend.   ('Strasburg epode', Hipponax 115 W)

Callimachus also wrote iambic poems, in the first of which he introduced the ghost of Hipponax rising from Hades to rebuke the wrangling scholars of Alexandria; but this is a Hipponax without his old aggressiveness. By drawing the fangs of the older poet, Callimachus goes a long way to ironize the invective out of iambic, and Horace in his so-called *Epodes* finished the job. In the tenth epode (already mentioned on p. 204) he imitates the Greek poem just quoted, but whereas Hipponax had written in terms of a betrayal of trust, the only crime of which Horace accuses Mevius is that he 'stinks': shipwreck seems excessive. Elsewhere Horace blusters and complains, denouncing anonymous figures or indulging in mock-abuse. His vigorous mockery of ugly old women does not reveal a psychological defect but shows him tackling a safe, well-established subject for aggressive writing.[29] For much of the collection his iambic persona is an ineffectual or inadequate one:[30] this is best captured in a poem in which he plays the thwarted lover determined on revenge, but frustrated by his own nature, even his name: 'O Neaera, due to suffer greatly through my manly wrath! For if there is a spark of manhood in Flaccus, he will not endure it...' (*Epode* 15) 'Flaccus' means Horace himself (Quintus Horatius Flaccus), but its literal sense is 'floppy' – the juxtaposition in the Latin with 'manhood' wittily deflates Horace's 'hard man' pretensions. (A parallel in the *Satires* makes doubly certain that Horace used this form of his name deliberately.)

Horace's relative restraint in handling the iambic genre can partly be explained by his inferior status and the need to tread carefully in the troubled politics of his time (similar points apply in the *Satires*, which he was writing contemporaneously). The leaders of the senate and the armies did not have to be so circumspect. Martial quotes a highly obscene epigram against Antony by Augustus, praising its Roman outspokenness (11.20).

You who read Latin verses with gloomy malice, just cast an eye over these six risqué lines by Caesar Augustus. 'Because Antony is fucking Glaphyra, Fulvia [Antony's wife] has resolved on the proper punishment: that I'm to fuck her. What, me fuck Fulvia? If Manius begs me to bugger him, am I to do that too?

---

* This is sarcastic: the Thracians were a byword for ferocity.

Not if I'm in my right mind, I won't! 'Either do me now, or let's go to war', are her words. But my cock is more precious to me than life itself. Let the trumpets sound, let battle commence!' Augustus, you know how to speak with true Roman frankness; your precedent acquits my light-hearted little books.

Martial's contemporary Pliny, defending his own writing of obscene poems, cites a long list of distinguished Romans who, like him, wrote 'little poems with little severity' (*Letters* 5.3.2): the list includes several contemporaries of Catullus and an impressive array of emperors. Pliny remarks that the well-rounded Roman gentleman has experience of comedy and mime, and that to indulge in this form of composition as a leisure pursuit is no cause for embarrassment. The difference, however, is that Augustus' epigram on Antony and Fulvia was meant to wound, and the wit served political ends, whereas most of those Pliny names are merely indulging in a kind of after-dinner game.

Curses are another sub-type of aggressive speech, and one which the superstitious might suppose capable of having a tangible effect. They were a prominent feature of earlier literature such as tragedy (Oedipus curses his ungrateful sons in Sophocles' *Oedipus at Colonus*), but in the Hellenistic period this kind of verbal attack seems to have developed into an independent genre. Here too the direct link with real antagonisms grew thinner, and in the surviving examples the accent is on ingenuity and learning. Ovid's *Ibis*, our best complete example, has already been mentioned: Greek precedents included Euphorion's *Thracian* (*SH* 413–15), in which the speaker calls down mythological curses on someone responsible for a death: may the victim perish as the successive consorts of Queen Semiramis did! Most bizarre of all is the so-called 'tattoo-elegy' (*SH* 970), in which the poet threatens to tattoo appropriately ominous myths on every portion of his enemy's anatomy: 'on your head (I shall put) a great and ruthless stone (such as) hangs over the head of Tantalus . . .'.[31]

VII

More interesting, and more richly represented, is the genre of satire, which Quintilian rightly claimed as wholly a Roman province (Horace and others said that the genre owed its origins to the public and personal frankness of Old Comedy, but the debt is small). The form and meaning of the term 'satira' or 'satura' are disputed: most popular is an interpretation that takes it to mean some form of mixed and tasty food, like the stuffing of a sausage (as we shall see, food is a major concern, even a controlling metaphor in satire). Juvenal alludes to this when he talks of human life as the 'fodder' of (or in) his book (1.86).[32]

There are four key figures in the satirical tradition: Lucilius, Horace, Persius and Juvenal. Lucilius, who lived in the second century BC and was a friend and protegé of the Scipio family, survives only in fragments – numerous, but often difficult and tantalizing. We know enough to see that he was a varied and voluminous writer, whose work eventually occupied 30 books (Horace thought him far too fluent and slapdash). Politics, contemporary life and manners, anecdotes about individuals, philosophy, sex and literary comment all figured in his work. Some links between him and his successors are clear: although he used other metres, he established the hexameter as the regular verse form for satire, and took up the opportunity this offered for parody and spoof of epic, which normally dominated that metre (a famous episode included parody of Ennius' treatment of the council of the gods). One book appears to have been occupied by an account of a journey he made with friends from Rome to southern Italy and Sicily, recounting amusing incidents and landmarks en route: Horace's extant 'journey to Brindisi' (1.5) is an imitation of this. Later generations saw two chief qualities: outspokenness (both in willingness to use crude terms or obscenities, and in being prepared to attack powerful political figures), and the autobiographical element, the use of his own life and activities, dramatized in his verse (no doubt selectively and sometimes through caricature). He was not averse to self-mockery: in one fragment someone remarks 'we've heard he has invited some friends including that crook Lucilius' (929 Warmington). But he also boldly asserts his individuality: 'but as for becoming a tax-farmer of Asia, a collector of pasture-taxes, instead of Lucilius – *that* I don't want; in exchange for what I am – for this alone of all things, I'm not taking the whole world' (650–1). Lively, nonchalant, versatile and colloquial, and clearly only an occasional moralist, Lucilius even in truncated form is an attractive writer. In the game of wishing for the resurrection of lost literature he would come high on many people's lists.[33]

Horace is a more careful writer in every sense: we have mentioned his irritation at Lucilius' loose style and verbosity, and also his reluctance to criticize contemporaries too freely. A reader who expects satire to be a hard-hitting critique of individuals or of the politics and fashions of the day will find little of this in Horace. Indeed, although he uses the term 'satire', he seems to prefer 'Sermones' as a title for his two books in this genre. This word means 'chats' or conversations, and Horace cultivates an informal, good-humoured style which, although full of well-turned phrases, only occasionally resorts to high style or elaborate similes, mythical references or the like; instead we find homely illustrations from nature or crafts, brief snatches of dialogue with an imagined opponent, and that staple of unpretentious didacticism, the animal fable (above all his delightful version of Aesop's story of the town and country mice (p. 254)). He tones down Lucilius: few obscenities, no Greek, no rare or invented words, more orthodox language. The *Satires* include much humour, but inviting a smile not a guffaw. But thoroughly Lucilian, and one of the most charming aspects of the collection, is the dramatization of his own everyday life in Rome, a delightful montage of realistic detail which nevertheless sustains the literary fiction of a simple man living a moral life and writing poetry which is at worst harmless and perhaps even does some good.

> I step out whenever I fancy, on my own; I enquire the price of vegetables and meal; I often wander through the cheating Circus and the Forum as evening comes on; I stand watching the fortune tellers, then head home for a dish of leek and pea minestrone. My meal is served by three slave boys, and a white marble slab has on it two cups with a ladle; next to them stands a cheap cruet and an oil flask, with its saucer, of Campanian ware [i.e. cheap pottery]. Then off to bed I go, not bothered about having to get up early . . . I lie in bed till ten, and then take a stroll; or after reading or writing for my own quiet enjoyment, I have oil applied (but not the sort that dirty Natta uses after stealing it from the lamps). (1.4.111ff., tr. Brown)

Horace produced two books of satires, probably about five years apart (*c*.35 and *c*.30 BC), containing a total of 18 poems. There is less variety than in the larger oeuvre of his model, but the first book still has considerable range: kindly moralizing, autobiographical anecdote, dramatic dialogue framed by racy narrative; there are even some poems which do not include Horace at all (1.7–8), setting puzzles for critics who try to see the book as a closely coherent entity. Horace in all his works (apart from the *Epodes*) draws on philosophy, which at least in its moral aspect he took seriously (see pp. 254–6). Interweaving Epicurean advocacy of the simple life free of ambition and greed with glimpses of his own humble upbringing from which he has risen to be on friendly terms with Maecenas, he shows himself off to advantage, without undue boasting and with sufficient fooling or self-criticism to avoid setting himself up as a model for others. Politics and the great events of the day are occasionally glimpsed in the background; but in the main Horace preaches an ethic of tolerance and mutual goodwill while strongly recommending quietism: politics is something which should be avoided and left to those who are equipped to undertake such tasks. It would be naive not to perceive that Horace is lending support to Maecenas and Octavian, even though that support is expressed indirectly and by implication.[34] Nevertheless, his satires are more concerned with personal morality (without attacking living personalities), and the aggression of Lucilius is a thing of the past. Persius effectively contrasts his two predecessors:

Lucilius carved up the city, along with you, Lupus, and you, Mucius, and smashed his molars on them. Crafty Flaccus [Horace] touches every fault in his laughing friend, and once admitted, plays around the heartstrings, cleverly thumbing a keen-scented nose at the community. (1.114–18)

The implication is clear: vicious aggression achieves less than intimate and subtle humour. The contrast between Horace and Juvenal in their brands of satire can be explored in similar terms.[35]

Horace is famous for his irony, but this is hard to pin down. One objective fact is that in the second book we find him less ready to pronounce in his own person: some poems are dialogues, in others a series of spokesmen are introduced, vociferously moralizing with or without his endorsement, and often occupying the greater part of the poem. In the enormous poem 2.3 the Stoic Damasippus denounces vice at extraordinarily un-Horatian length (and with little of the poet's sense of humour). More successful is 2.7, in which we find a dialogue between Horace and his slave Davus, who takes advantage of the temporary freedom of speech allowed by the Saturnalia to give his master a talking-to. Various aspects of Horace's character are criticized: his inconsistency, his idealization of the past, his alleged preference for the country and rural food (yet look how fast you move if you get an invitation to one of Maecenas' posh dinners), his lust, his ennui, and so forth. The poem is intriguing: on the one hand it echoes much of what Horace himself criticizes in others (so does he in fact know better than Davus allows?), on the other we do recognize some features which have figured in the *Satires* themselves (e.g. 1.2, on his erotic antics). But Davus is not a truly convincing authority-figure: quite apart from his legal status, his 'philosophy', as he admits, is third-hand platitudes, all picked up from the doorkeeper of Crispinus, a long-winded pundit whom Horace elsewhere despises (line 45). Horace himself, however, is not shown in a good light: at the end of the poem he loses his temper and fights back, but with the threats that a master can wield, not with argument or reasoned self-defence. We are pleased to see that the poet can criticize himself, but he also represents himself as unable to take the criticism. Why should he expect his addressees to respond differently?

Persius is the most difficult and the least important of the satirists. His six poems are all that survive from a short life, of which his adult years were spent under Nero's reign. Whereas Horace was eclectically Epicurean, Persius is dogmatically Stoic. His poetry is much more sternly philosophic in its bias, and although there is sardonic wit at the expense of bad men (and bad poets), we miss the variety of tone and subject in the other satirists. He is also very much a writer's writer: his style is dense with allusions and often obscure without detailed exposition. There are dramatic moments and

vigorous dialogue exchanges; there is an eloquent tribute to his mentor, the
Stoic Cornutus, which bears comparison with Horace's touching tributes to
his father; but the stability of the ethical standpoint diminishes the element
of self-mockery and self-parody which is so important elsewhere in this
genre. Nevertheless, he has many pungent passages, and some may find his
moral firmness a welcome alternative to Horace's elusive ironies and Juvenal's
anarchic violence.

The satires of Juvenal, and particularly his earlier work (books 1–2,
containing poems 1–6), come closest to the modern conception of satire as
an attack on moral or political misdeeds. In his later work we see some
modification of tone and more positive 'teaching', but the keynote of his
most characteristic work is *anger*. 'Facit indignatio versum': 'rage is the
source of my poetry.' (1.79)[36] Juvenal does not remonstrate, he denounces.
Poem 1 opens his first book with a whirlwind tour of modern Rome and its
vices, accumulating examples of greed, vice and folly: informers, adulterers,
gamblers, legacy-hunters, arrogant patrons and envious clients. The style of
his writing is as intense as the emotion he conveys (or fabricates): highly
rhetorical, sometimes grandiose. This should warn us not to take his
account as literal truth; nor indeed does he focus on the Rome of his own
day. Writing under Trajan, he looks back sometimes at the period of
Domitian, sometimes to the crime-soaked era of the Julio-Claudians (con-
veniently remote for a satirist who prefers to attack the dead). He regularly
adopts an epic-tragic tone to emphasize the enormity of his subject: he will
recount crimes that exceed the atrocities of the Sophoclean stage, and satire
must don the tragic buskin (6.634ff., 655–61, 15.29ff.). But the vices are
not all equally serious: to write a tedious epic is to Juvenal as vile a crime as
to murder one's husband, or deflower and defraud one's ward. The moral
fervour is not sustained throughout, nor does the style remain consistently
high.[37] One of Juvenal's most effective weapons is the startling and deflating
anti-climax.

> I would value
> A barren offshore island more than Rome's urban heart:
> Squalor and isolation are minor evils compared
> To this endless nightmare of fires and collapsing houses,
> This cruel city's myriad perils – and poets reciting
> Their work in the heat of *August*!   (3.5–9, tr. Green with slight change)

The early poems share a preoccupation with life at Rome: Juvenal is the
poet of the capital. After the overture of themes in poem 1, we meet
hypocritical philosopher-sodomites in 2. Poem 3, a high point in his work,
consists mainly of the long speech by Juvenal's friend Umbricius, who is

leaving Rome permanently in disillusionment with life there ('What am I to do at Rome? I haven't learned how to lie. If a book is poor, I cannot praise it or demand a copy . . .'). Most of the speech is a vividly particularized catalogue of the miseries of city life: danger from muggers, fires and accidental disaster take second place to the humiliations of life as a hanger-on of some patron, forced into sycophancy by the need to keep up with those able social-climbers, the Greeks. 'I cannot endure a *Greek* Rome, citizens!': satire, like invective, thrives on xenophobia. Poem 4 recalls the grim atmosphere of Domitian's court, while also parodying a panegyric of that emperor by Statius: a grandiose account of the emperor's inner council debating wartime strategy becomes a mock-heroic account of their confusion on discovering that the palace contains no dish large enough to contain the bloated fish which has been presented to the ruler of the world.

Poem 5 reverts to the patron–client relationship, already prominent in 1 and 3. The setting here is a dinner party, employed also by Lucilius and Horace (*Sat.* 2.4 and 8). Such an occasion is ideally suited to present the character of a host through the fare he offers, the way he engages with his guests and the quality of his conversation (Petronius surpasses even the satirists on this theme, in the dinner-party of Trimalchio: see p. 141). Food itself can be seen as a moral symbol: plain and healthy fare is contrasted with gross gluttony. The appetite is the measure of the man.[38] Sometimes the food serves as a literary metaphor: particularly since Callimachus, obesity and over-rich food symbolize inflated overblown style, while tasteful restraint at the table reflects moderation and subtlety in one's writing. But the direction of Juvenal's poem is different, focused on the spirit in which the hospitality is given and received. The seed of the poem, as often, can be found in Martial, who also treats the topic of a patron who entertains his entourage but provides them with a meal grossly inferior to what he himself is consuming. (The civilized Pliny treats such meanness with contempt, *Letters* 2.6.) Martial wrote:

> You sample oysters enriched in the Lucrine lake, but I get a mussel that cuts my mouth as I suck it. You have choice mushrooms, I get pig fungi. You match yourself against a turbot, while I am faced with bream. Golden turtle-dove swells you with its massive rump, while I'm served a magpie that died in its cage. Why do I dine without you, Ponticus, when I'm supposed to be dining with you? (3.60.3–9)

In the same way but at greater length, Juvenal presents the malicious Virro gorging himself on luxury delicacies and vintage wine, while his clients struggle through mouldy bread, eel fed from the sewers and disgusting plonk. Even the tableware and the slaves are contrasted. Although in the bulk of the poem Juvenal has apparently been on the client's side, there is a sting in the tail:

> He's no fool to abuse you like this. If you can swallow
> The whole treatment – why, you deserve no better. Some day
> You'll find yourself meekly bending your shaven pate to be cuffed,
> Like a public buffoon, well inured to the whip, a worthy
> Companion for such a feast – and for such a friend.   (5.170–3, Green)

Neither patronizing arrogance nor dutiful self-abasement deserves the satirist's sympathy.

Space forbids any detailed consideration of all 16 satires. A few stand out. The massive poem 6, itself occupying a whole book, forms a prolonged and unmerciful condemnation of marriage (and for the most part of the female sex). Although structurally weak and offensive to modern sensibility, it is an extravaganza of invective, and many of the malevolent portraits are sharp and amusing even if we go on to condemn them. Juvenal himself is perhaps not wholly serious in his misogynist fervour: it is a witty touch when he declares that even if one could impossibly track down that *rara avis*, a perfect woman ('beautiful, proper, rich, child-bearing, supplied with venerable ancestors, more virtuous than any Sabine bride'), such a paragon would be unendurable. ('Yes, I prefer a regular tart to you, Cornelia, mother of the Gracchi, if along with your mighty virtues you bring majestic disdain . . .' 6.166ff.).

The later satires, moving 'beyond anger',[39] are less urban and more urbane. There is more space given to argument and the hot-blooded declamatory style gives way to more reflective moralizing. Cynicism and sardonic comment on human weakness are not lacking, but there is a somewhat more constructive moralizing attitude. The development has a price: we miss the frenetic energy, the mordant rhetoric of the early work. Most famous and most successful of these later poems is the tenth, which Johnson adapted and reshaped within a Christian moral framework as 'The Vanity of Human Wishes'.[40] Here Juvenal, amplifying a well-worn theme with his dazzling eloquence, enumerates the foolish ambitions of mankind, the things for which they misguidedly pray: power, gifts as an orator, military prowess, long life or good looks. In each case he chooses examples from history and mythology to show the disastrous outcome to which each supposed blessing can lead (thus Cicero's eloquence led to his execution, 10.114–26). His conclusion is that it is better to leave the gods to grant us gifts as they think fit: the positive finale is flat compared with the vigour of the negative arguments, and this is perhaps the only section where Johnson unquestionably surpasses his model. As logic and philosophy Juvenal's argument is insubstantial: by taking extreme and dramatic cases he fails to establish any general rules. That is not the point. What makes the main part of his poem unforgettable is the powerful rhetoric with which he describes each example, imaginatively recreating their hopes and ambitions, only to dash them down. The famous passage on Hannibal, in the section on military glory, is perhaps the finest example.

> Put Hannibal in the scales: how many pounds will that peerless
> General mark up today? This is the man for whom Africa
> Was too small a continent, though it stretched from the surf-beaten
> Ocean shores of Morocco east to the steamy Nile,
> To Ethiopian tribesmen and new elephants' habitats.
> Now Spain swells his empire, now he surmounts
> The Pyrenees. Nature throws in his path
> High Alpine passes, blizzards of snow: but he splits
> The very rocks asunder, moves mountains – with vinegar.
> Now Italy is his, yet he still forces on:
> 'We have accomplished nothing', he cries, 'till we have stormed
> the gates of Rome, till our Carthaginian standard
> rises in Rome's red-light zone.' A fine sight it must have been,
> Fit subject for caricature, the one-eyed commander
> Perched on his monstrous beast! Alas, alas for glory,
> What an end was here: the defeat, the ignominious
> Flight into exile, everyone crowding to see
> The once mighty Hannibal turned humble hanger-on,
> Sitting outside the door of a petty Eastern despot
> Till His Majesty deign to awake. No sword, no spear,
> No battle-flung stone was to snuff the fiery spirit
> That once had wrecked a world: those crushing defeats,
> Those rivers of spilt blood were all wiped out by a
> Ring, a poisoned ring. On on, you madman, drive
> Over your savage Alps, to thrill young schoolboys
> And supply a theme for speech-day recitations!   (10.147–67,
>   tr. Green with one adjustment)

A single passage of this quality is sufficient to vindicate 'silver' Latin poetry against accusations of decadence. Juvenal offers many more.

VIII

One more author demands a place. No account of ancient humour would be complete without the most accessible and agreeable of late prose writers in Greek, the iconoclastic Lucian of Samosata (writing mainly c.160–180).[41]

His versatility means that he also figures elsewhere: as a composer of fantastic travel-tales, as a critic of historiography, as a sceptical commentator on
new religious cults. His works are abundant (over 70 dialogues, essays and
rhetorical set-pieces), but mostly short, light-hearted and highly readable.
At times he will take a typical rhetorical genre and show his mettle with it:
the encomium of a figure from history (Demosthenes); the mock encomium
of a fly; or an argument in praise of some unlikely subject (pantomime
dancing; astrology; the life of a parasite).[42] His favourite theme is human
pretension or fraud: he constantly mocks the pomposity of learned men,
know-alls, philosophers, rhetorical teachers, even the gods themselves (these
are the gods of poetic mythology, and his lively treatment of these should
not be misconstrued as atheism or even as an attack on superstition).

Lucian himself expresses his pride in his innovations of form,[43] for several
of his works combine elements from Platonic dialogue, Old Greek comedy,
and the mixed form of prose and verse known as 'Menippean' satire (named
after a much earlier writer, a Cynic philosopher of the third century BC).
Perhaps his finest pieces are the comic dialogues in which he dramatizes
the adventures of a spokesman, sometimes the Cynic Menippus himself,
sometimes a figure called Lykinos, or 'the Syrian', or Cyniscus, or Parrhesiades
('son-of-free-speech'): for the most part these figures are indistinguishable,
and represent a bold, insolent, mocking version of Lucian himself. Several
works describe Menippus' journeys to Olympus or Hades and his amusement
at what he finds there (the discomfiture of tyrants and other pompous
windbags in Hades is a common theme). In one short piece Zeus is interrogated by Lucian's mouthpiece and finds himself in difficulties dealing with
some tough questions about the relation between fate, his own will, and the
rest of the gods ('Zeus interrogated', no. 20). Although philosophy is never
treated with much depth, Lucian is familiar enough with the schools and
their doctrines to satirize them, often through their main exponents. In the
'Fisherman' the dead philosophers are so indignant at Lucian's treatment of
them that they return to life, threaten and manhandle him, and bring him
to trial before personified Philosophy: but the trial turns out to vindicate
the author's cynical view of Philosophy's unworthy followers.

Scepticism is the guiding principle, best exemplified in the *Menippus*, also
called the *Consultation of the Dead*. This is an entertaining variation on the
traditional journey to Hades to gain wisdom from a prophet or sage.
The idea goes back to the Gilgamesh epic, but Lucian's main sources are
the *Odyssey* and Plato's myths of the afterlife. In frustration with the diverse
views of philosophers here on earth, Menippus determines to seek the Real
Truth from the ghost of the prophet Tiresias. In the course of his journey
he sees many famous figures now brought low, and reflects on the power of
chance; he also brings back report of a new decree that rich men who

commit crimes in their lifetimes are to be reincarnated as donkeys and to continue in that shape 'for 250,000 years, passing from one donkey to another and being employed as beasts of burden, driven to and fro by the poor' (20). Both the concern for justice and the doctrine of reincarnation are a down-to-earth version of Plato's sublime conclusion to the *Republic* (p. 239). As for the wisdom of Tiresias, the old man finally relents and whispers the answer to Menippus: 'The best way to live is to be an ordinary human being. Give up all this metaphysical rubbish. Just live in the present, and go your ways laughing a lot and taking nothing all that seriously.' (21) In some ways Lucian is a distant descendant of the comic hero in Aristophanes, who so often seems like a version of the common man, impatient with pretension and arrogance, keeping his feet firmly on the ground. Lucian would have had a great deal of fun with his more humour-less interpreters, some of whom have tried to label him a spiritual pilgrim or even a proto-Marxist critic of Roman imperial society.

But there were many more serious and searching analyses of philosophy and religion in the ancient world than those of Lucian, and in the next two chapters it is time to look at these in some detail.

8

Thinkers

Vain is the word of a philosopher that does not heal any suffering of man.

Epicurus fr. 221

I

Defining the subject of this chapter is not straightforward; nor can a firm distinction be drawn between this chapter and the one that follows. Thinkers can be and often are also believers; believers are capable of argument and rational justification. While the majority of authors in the present chapter would today be counted as philosophers, some are not so regarded (notably Virgil and Horace), others are nowadays more famous for other things (Cicero). Also, it must be remembered that this is not a history of ancient philosophy, but a survey of ancient literature: otherwise the almost total neglect of the towering figure of Aristotle would be indefensible. It may be helpful to distinguish between professional teachers of philosophy, often associating themselves with a particular school or sect, and those influenced by them, whether as pupils educated by a professional or more freely using ideas derived from philosophic writings. The first group would include Plato (with reservations outlined in the following pages), Aristotle, Epicurus, Epictetus and others; the second would include Virgil, Horace, even Cicero, whose knowledge of philosophy was great and whose influence was greater, but who always regarded himself as a well-informed and enthusiastic amateur. 'Influence', of course, can cover a wide range of effects. There is no doubt that Lucretius was taught by Epicureans (though we cannot name them) and remained a passionately committed adherent of that philosophy; but many who had been trained in philosophy would have heard a variety of teachers and might not be wholeheartedly convinced by any one school's doctrines. Here the idea of 'eclecticism' is valuable: an eclectic picks and chooses, partly accepting the principles of a variety of schools. Horace presents himself in this way in the *Epistles*, though allowing that it lays him open to charges of inconsistency.

Only a privileged few in antiquity got any sort of education beyond basic literacy (the vast majority would not get that far), but those who did would first study poetry, grammar and rhetoric. Philosophy was for advanced students, a kind of tertiary education (Cicero and later Horace studied at Athens somewhat as a modern student might go to university). Only well-off parents would be able to give their sons this opportunity; for many, rhetoric was the essential goal, and competence as a speaker or advocate would open enough doors. In both Greece and Rome philosophy was often unpopular: it could be dismissed as pointless verbal nitpicking or seen as dangerously subversive.[1] The high moral principles preached by philosophers were not always sustained in practice, and this allowed their enemies to scoff at them as hypocrites; Socrates' well-known predilection for beautiful young men led to frequent allegations that later teachers had an ulterior motive in instructing the young.[2] Nevertheless, at least the names and some of the chief doctrines of major philosophers (obviously in a simplified form) were fairly widely known. Athenian comedy could treat Socrates as a stock butt, and later alluded to Plato's Forms or his doctrine of the Good; Cicero in his public speeches parodies Stoic and Epicurean positions which he can explain with more sympathy elsewhere; similarly Lucilius in his satires, and Lucian in his dialogues, assume some familiarity with the major schools. Part of this knowledge may be ascribed to readings and recitations of some of the more attractively written texts; also significant are travelling performers or street-corner moralists, preachers of simplified morality in punchy rhetorical form: these men were authors of what modern critics call 'diatribes', a form of popular moralizing as practised by the Greek Bion, whose work influenced far subtler artists such as Horace and Plutarch. There are analogies here with the travels and edifying oratory of St Paul. But for the most part it is fair to say that the more detailed the philosophic discussion, the more rarefied the audience.

Philosophy can mean many things. The earlier writers whom Plato saw as in some sense his predecessors, those whom we describe as 'Presocratic philosophers', often dealt with material which might be regarded as part of physics, astronomy or cosmological speculation. Later categorizations sometimes divided the field into logic, physics and ethics: that is, philosophers studied the nature of argument, the nature of the universe, and human nature (which included political theory, with man being seen as fundamentally a part of society). These different aspects might be ranked in varying orders of importance, depending on the writer's aims. Thus Horace disparages physical speculation and gives priority to ethics, while Seneca, though clearly knowledgeable about logic, can dismiss it as trivial. Religion also formed part of the subject matter of philosophy: to consider the nature of the universe is partly to consider what laws, or what powers (if any) govern it and what effect the existence of these powers has or should have on man. It is disputable how far theology existed as a subject in the ancient world, but any theological discussion was mostly derived from philosophers; hence the overlap between this chapter and the next.

Even in the modern world, many literary works have a philosophic agenda (Musil, Mann), and some professional philosophers rise above the level of textbook prose; but in the ancient world it was more common for a philosopher to write in a self-consciously literary and rhetorical way. Philosophic ideas were expounded in verse as well as prose (in Greek by Empedocles and others, in Latin above all by Lucretius): yet it is recognized that this may create a conflict of priorities, that (as Plato put it) 'there is an ancient quarrel between poetry and philosophy' (*Republic* 10.607b–c).[3] Some thinkers deliberately wrote in an un-literary, unpretentious way (Epicurus, Sextus Empiricus) or expressed contempt for poets and their fancies. Stoics notoriously despised rhetorical ornament, and Cicero felt that they did their cause no service by adopting a brutally plain style. This reflected his own concern with rhetorical persuasion and its methods (ch. 3), but the point goes deeper. A modern philosopher may hope to convince readers, especially colleagues, of the correctness of a particular argument, or the inaccuracy of a previously held view; he or she does not normally expect to influence a reader's whole way of life (exceptions, such as Nietzsche, tend to be controversial and are often marginalized). But an ancient philosopher was often seeking to achieve just this: to make a pupil see things in a new way, or at least to influence his priorities in life and perhaps through him to have an effect on society more widely. It makes sense in the ancient world to speak of 'conversion' to philosophy.[4] Plato often compared philosophy to medicine; we may see it as having an affinity to psychotherapy. In view of this aim, not simply didactic but inspirational, the use of literary form (especially of emotional appeal) becomes comprehensible. Philosophy distrusts rhetoric but cannot do without it; though valuing reason above all, the philosopher also seeks to appeal to the whole person, to instil enthusiasm and kindle the appetite for knowledge. A memorable passage of Plato's *Phaedo* illustrates the point.

'The two of you seem to have that childish fear that when the soul departs from the body, the wind will disperse it and blow it away – especially if one happens to die not in calm weather but when a powerful wind is blowing.'

Cebes laughed and said: 'Try then to persuade us, Socrates, as if we were afraid; or rather, not as though we were afraid ourselves, but maybe there is a child inside us who entertains fears of this kind. Let us try to persuade him not to be frightened of death as if it were a bogeyman.'

'Well, then,' said Socrates, 'you need to sing a charm over him every day until you charm away his fear.'

'And where will we find a good singer of charms like these, now that you are leaving us?' (77d–8a)

II

The origins of Greek philosophy are obscure to us. In some ways a kind of proto-philosophic thinking exists in the early poets: Hesiod in particular seeks to define the order of the world, through the combined metaphors of cosmology and genealogy, through myths which explain the way things came to be as they are (Pandora, Prometheus), and through description of the good and bad society. But historians normally trace the beginnings of philosophic thought to a number of writers from the sixth and fifth centuries, usually known as the Presocratics, thinkers and theorists who came before Socrates. These include Thales, Heraclitus, Anaximander, Empedocles, Parmenides, Anaxagoras and others; Pythagoras and his followers are also often included in this category. They are not a coherent group: some of them knew each other's works, but their views (and styles of exposition) were diverse. Our understanding of them is hampered by the fact that they do not survive in full: we have only fragments, and the valuable but slanted overview of Aristotle, who surveys the history of philosophy up to his time but is naturally viewing it through fourth-century eyes and with his own priorities in view. We can at least say that many of these men were trying to analyse causes and processes in the world, partly through observation, but partly *a priori*, and to define general principles to explain reality. Some identified a first principle: for Thales it was water; for Heraclitus, fire; for Anaxagoras, mind. Democritus formulated a theory of atoms which was developed centuries later by Epicurus. It is a fascinating study (and has been attempted by many distinguished scholars) to try to reconstruct their ideas from our tantalizing evidence; but despite their obvious importance it is more urgent to turn to less nebulous figures and to works which survive complete.

Later writers often saw Socrates as marking a significant shift in the direction of philosophy. According to Cicero he drew down philosophy from the heavens (the cosmic speculations and physical theories of the earlier thinkers) and brought it into the cities and homes of men (*Tusc.* 5.10): that is, he replaced natural philosophy with ethics. The antithesis is no doubt overdrawn; in any case, it raises the problem we constantly face with Socrates, that he left no writings of his own. Any statement about him has to depend on the work of others, above all Plato: a rival portrait in various works of Xenophon presents a more down-to-earth and less penetrating thinker, perhaps more congenial to conventional Athenian opinion. Other sources introduce still more diversity: the satirical presentation of Socrates as a crank and crook (Aristophanes), or the clipped summary comments in Aristotle (partly but not clearly distinguishing him from Plato). This 'Socratic question' has been much debated. The view adopted here is that we must read and relish Socrates as a character in Plato's dialogues: the real man existed, and may or may not have held various views ascribed to him in Plato, but some of what he says there he may have believed without defending his views in these terms, other things he is most unlikely to have thought, and the dividing line can never be firmly drawn. The problem is confounded by the difficulty of determining *Plato's* views, for Plato himself never appears in the dialogues. It is too simple to say that Socrates is Plato's spokesman or always voices opinions we are meant to find sympathetic.

It is indeed hardly possible to sum up Plato. The scale of his oeuvre is large: five thick volumes in modern editions, containing about 30 certainly genuine works, ranging in length from a mere 10 or 20 pages to the vastly ambitious *Republic* (10 books) and *Laws* (12 – his last and unfinished work). He was active as a writer and teacher for half a century after the death of Socrates, his mentor, in 399 (he probably wrote nothing before this). The detailed chronology of his work is hard to determine, though some progress has been made in dividing his writings into periods, early, middle and late. More controversial is the attempt to chart development in his thought: is it characterized more by continuity or difference? The range of his intellectual interests is matched by the dazzling variety of his style: despite the strong competition (Herodotus, Thucydides, Demosthenes, Plutarch . . .), Plato is universally recognized as the greatest Greek writer of prose.

Irrespective of chronology, some continuing strands in Plato's work can be singled out for special attention (though we shall be ignoring works of the highest interest on theory of knowledge, on language, on pleasure, and much else). The impact of Socrates was evidently a decisive factor in shaping his approach to philosophy. If we may draw on Plato's own text at least for biographical detail (some of it confirmed by other sources), Socrates was an elderly man by the late fifth century, when Plato came to know him; a poor man, son of a stonemason, but on familiar terms with many of the most wealthy and prominent Athenians; eccentric in manner, but vigorous in mind and body; detached from but critical and sceptical of politics; ready to perform his military service and other duties like a loyal citizen, but also prepared to refuse to obey orders from the post-war government which he regarded as immoral. Although Socrates is doubtless idealized, he remains a human, sympathetic, fascinating figure, his intellectual sharpness balanced by his persistent modesty and ironic self-deprecation.

The young found his conversation challenging and exciting, for in his keenness to get at the truth he was ready to question conventional opinion about ethical, political and religious ideas; older Athenians were alarmed by this questioning, and suspicions grew that Socrates was a bad influence. Eventually he was put on trial for corrupting the young and persuading people to believe in new gods and doubt the traditional religion. According to Plato's presentation of his self-defence, Socrates provoked the jury by refusing to give up his way of life or make concessions; as a result he was condemned to death and accepted this verdict, though more diplomatic behaviour might have won him a milder penalty. Several of Plato's best-known works dramatize these events. The *Meno* foreshadows the trial, including the hostile figure of Anytus, one of Socrates' accusers. The *Crito*, a short and thought-provoking piece, shows Socrates in prison, resisting the urgent appeal of his friend Crito to take advantage of a plan for escape and flight. He replies that having accepted the validity of the laws of Athens and the right of the Athenian court to pass judgment on him, he must abide by their decision and stay where he is.

Above all there is the *Phaedo*, again set in the prison-house and commemorating Socrates' last day, even his dying moments, when he takes the poisonous dose of hemlock that the Athenians prescribed as a method of execution. This is one of the greatest of the dialogues. The narrator, Phaedo, vividly describes the scene, with a group of Socrates' intimate friends seizing every last moment of conversation with the condemned man. Even the jailor who reluctantly administers the poison expresses his respect for the good-humoured victim. The discussion concerns the soul's fate after death: Socrates expounds and tries to justify his conviction that his soul is immortal and that it will survive him; that, indeed, life free of the body's demands is a purer and better form of existence, a liberation from the prison of physicality (the analogy with the prison-house setting is evident). Socrates' calmness and confidence, even gaiety, as he approaches his death are contrasted with the doubts and distress of his companions, who question him about his views and anxiously present possible objections. It is made clear that the arguments for the immortal soul are provisional, not final: Socrates declares that the others must go on testing and developing them after he has gone. But his own assurance that death is not the end is inspiring, and his dying words seem to be a further suggestion of the 'better life' theme: 'Crito, we owe [the sacrifice of] a cock to Asclepius. See to it, will you, and don't forget.' As Asclepius was the god of medicine and healing, the implication may be that Socrates is about to be 'cured' of life's afflictions. The closing words of the *Phaedo* underline the author's intention to vindicate and glorify Socrates' memory: 'Such, Echecrates, was the death of our friend, the best man, I would say, that we have ever met, and the wisest and most just as well.' The *Phaedo* shows us the death of a philosophic martyr: there are many later examples of this scene, in which deliberate choice of the moment of death preserves the dignity of a virtuous man, who dies after suitably serious and high-minded conversation with intimate friends. The Stoic Cato, opponent of Julius Caesar, chose this form of death (and reread the *Phaedo* – twice! – before falling on his sword). Seneca and the other Stoic figures of Nero's court followed the examples of Socrates and Cato; the convention was sufficiently well-established to be parodied by Petronius (p. 139).

To preserve the memory of Socrates Plato also has to reconstruct Socrates' milieu, Athens' aristocratic society at one of the most memorable periods in her history. Other major figures of the period are also re-created on the Platonic stage: the comedian Aristophanes, the generals Nicias and Laches (suitably involved in a search for the definition of that very military quality courage), and several of the so-called sophists, the management consultants of the fifth century, whom Plato regularly casts as foils to Socrates; while they are self-satisfied and have all the answers, he is never satisfied and persistently asks more questions. The *Euthydemus* contrasts the superficial gamesmanship and logic-chopping of two particularly vain and vacuous sophists with the more serious ethical and educative aims of Socrates. Perhaps the liveliest and most exhilarating picture of these Athenian salons comes in the *Protagoras*, which highlights one of the greatest of the sophists, for whom Plato had considerable respect, and shows him in action, teaching and debating with an enthusiastic audience, including both amateurs and fellow teachers. Socrates joins the group, listens to a set piece by Protagoras, and then begins, little by little, to unsettle the great man and point out the flaws in his assumptions. The debate includes digressions (one in particular tries to shed light on the issue by examining a poem by Simonides), but is chiefly concerned with the relationship of the virtues: can you have one without the others? A lot of ground is covered in 50 pages: these more accessible works are fast-moving and enjoyable, even exciting to read. Any serious reader will want to look back and try to work out where Protagoras goes wrong and what he should have said at certain points. To attract and stimulate able thinkers to ponder these arguments must surely have been among Plato's aims.

Perhaps no aspect of Plato's Socrates is more famous than his claim that he knows nothing: though allegedly declared the wisest of men by the Delphic oracle itself, he resisted this description, and concluded that he was wiser than other men only in being well aware of his own ignorance (*Ap.* 20–3). In many dialogues he is shown seeking to learn from others, but he is often disappointed. A common pattern is for him to try to learn from those who should be knowledgeable about a particular subject, or their own profession (Ion the poetic performer, or Gorgias the authority on rhetoric). But questioning of self-styled experts often leaves them exposed, irritated and abashed: they tend to equivocate or plead another engagement when Socrates urges that they continue in search of the truth together. Unsurprisingly, some interlocutors were sceptical about Socrates' apparent modesty, and many readers have agreed that he knows more than he is telling. Closely related to Socratic ignorance is his famous irony, expressed in his optimistic expectations of learning from each new encounter. The Greek word for irony sometimes means hypocrisy, and some of Socrates' critics refused to look deeper. But irony, in a number of senses, is central to Plato's portrait of him: he is deeply serious when he seems light-hearted; he masks passionate commitment behind an easy-going exterior; he finds insight where it would not be expected, but thinks nothing of questioning high authorities. Irony is also present in Socrates' style of speech and his frequent apologies for his inexpertise as a speaker. As many passages show, he is capable of rising to heights of eloquence that outclass the rhetoricians, and in pursuit of a nobler cause than theirs. These techniques enrich the text, but they also make its interpretation more difficult. Socrates' teasing manner makes it hard to determine how far an argument is meant to be accepted, and sometimes a long sequence may be dismissed as merely 'play'. Just as Socrates' irony was surely developed and extended by Plato, so too the questing, unceasing nature of Socrates' activity, which does not expect to reach a conclusion, is echoed and enriched in the often paradoxical and bewildering conversations of the dialogues. Irony, the dialogue form, and Socrates are connected: in the non-Socratic *Laws* Plato uses other techniques to modify the tone and maintain some open-endedness, but the magical quality is gone. 'Few of us read the *Laws*', remarks Plutarch (*Mor.* 328e).

'Is Socrates really serious about this, or is he just fooling around?' asks Callicles, a character in the *Gorgias*. Socrates' argument so far has led them to the conclusion that we should ensure that our friends get convicted and punished for any wrongdoing, while our enemies get off scot-free. Callicles goes on to protest that this will lead to turning society upside-down. Paradox and counter-intuitive conclusions are typical of philosophy, not least Plato's.[5] Many of his dialogues question popular assumptions and conventional belief. Thus in the *Protagoras* a challenge is offered to the Athenians' cheerful assumption that anyone is entitled to their own opinion in the assembly. From criticizing existing society it is a natural step to designing an ideal one. Others seem to have done so before Plato (some of them are mentioned by Aristotle in the *Politics*), but the *Republic* is the first surviving example. This dialogue has many aspects, and the political side may not be the most important, but it is surely the most influential. The central books sketch a 'utopia', a redesigned and highly regulated state which can only come into being, as Socrates puts it, when philosophers become kings or kings philosophers. Whether Plato himself believed this could ever really happen or not, and how far he attempted to implement these plans in his own time, are hotly contested questions. Many aspects of his proposed state are antipathetic today, while some were found bizarre even in his own time (e.g. the communistic aspects and the sharing of wives). Aristotle in the *Politics* made some penetrating criticisms, and later authors often referred to it as a fantastic creation, or the impractical dreams of an idealist (thus Cicero, complaining of Cato's refusal to agree to a compromise against his principles, remarks that 'he acts as though he's living in Plato's state rather than this cess-pit of Romulus's' (*Att.* 2.1.8)).

The *Republic* is ill-named in English, since the word suggests to us a democratic state or at least a community with a broadly based government. The Greek title was *On the State*: this was Latinized as *Res publica* and later inappropriately Anglicized. The society Plato describes is a hierarchical one governed by an intellectual elite, the 'Guardians', who have been painstakingly trained in all the necessary arts, above all mathematics and philosophical argument. Education and state control thereof are also important subjects in this wide-ranging work. The philosophic Guardians, through their training, will not only understand how to deal with everyday moral problems, but will be able to apprehend the absolute truths and the truer, higher forms of virtue, justice, beauty and so forth. According to the so-called Theory of Forms, a central theme in Plato, actions and objects in our imperfect physical world are pale reflections or inadequate imitations of their perfect archetypes in a transcendent non-physical world; as we perceive the things of our world with our eyes, so through philosophic discipline we may come to perceive the archetypes, to see the truer reality, with our mind's eye. Here we recall the *Phaedo* (on the superiority of the soul to the body), and the *Symposium* (on the love which is no longer content with particular lovers but aspires to absolute beauty). In different works Plato explores different aspects of this metaphysical vision and uses different images to illuminate it. One memorable instance in the *Republic* is the extended simile of the prisoners in the cave (appendix 1.2). Again we see Plato working with paradoxes: power in the state should be given only to those who are least inclined to accept it, and who do so only as a reluctant duty.

Besides the ethical and the political, a third strand running through Plato's work is a concern with religion. In the *Euthyphro*, probably a very early dialogue, Socrates is shocked to find that Euthyphro is acting as prosecutor of his own father for manslaughter. This prompts a discussion of the nature of piety (Socrates is always ready to seek out definitions of moral terms). Euthyphro is soon entramelled in a neat dilemma which still perplexes students beginning on Plato today: is what is pious approved by the gods because it is pious, or is it pious because it is approved by the gods? The relation between religion and morality is a leitmotif in ancient thinking. Plato evidently respects much of the traditional system of ritual and the moral structures which it provides for human life, while contemptuous of traditional mythology and determined to establish a firmer foundation for belief in the gods, rooted in reason and philosophically defensible. Criticism and revisionist readings of myth were current in his time (see p. 271); Plato goes much further than most in condemning and (in the *Republic*) censoring the blasphemous words of the poets. But poetry is still quoted with admiration and affection by his speakers, and myth remains important in his own work.

Where old myths were inadequate, Plato devised his own. Philosophy does not altogether shed its poetic and imaginative past. Especially at the end of dialogues (*Gorgias, Phaedo, Republic*) and when dealing with subjects like the gods and the soul's fate after death, Plato uses myth where religious truths are not accessible by argument alone; the emotional advantages of ending on an other-worldly and inspirational note will not have been forgotten. Most famous is the myth at the end of the *Republic*, the story of a man called Er, who seemingly died on a battlefield but returned to life on his pyre and described what he had been permitted to see of the afterlife, including punishment for wrongdoers and rewards for the good. The *Republic* so far has argued that justice is its own reward; with that argument formally concluded, we are allowed to see what blessings a virtuous life will bring after death. Er's account is a rich mixture of poetic imagery, astronomical and cosmological science, and theories of Pythagorean origin about transmigration of souls: training and morality remain important, since the choice of another life is dependent not only on past deeds but on an individual's personal character ('the responsibility lies with the chooser; god is not responsible'). This visionary account, narrated in Plato's loftiest style, was hugely influential. Cicero in his *Dream of Scipio* (set at the end of his own dialogue *On the State*) imitated it though characteristically giving it a more political and Roman slant. The detailed comparison of the two sheds much light on the differences between Greek and Roman thought: here we may mention that Plato offers his myth as the tale of an ordinary man, an everyman, whereas Cicero uses a historical authority-figure, the elder Scipio; that the experience of Er is simply narrated, whereas Scipio gives a didactic exposition to his living relative; that in Plato's account of the choice of lives no nationalistic or political agenda is present, whereas 'Scipio' gives assurance of posthumous rewards for those who have given service to the state (there is some tension with the other running theme of the triviality of human life against the background of the cosmos).[6] Also unthinkable without Plato is the reshaping of the themes of temporary death and a vision of judgement and reincarnation in the sixth book of the *Aeneid*.

Plato was the first to establish a philosophic school, the Academy (named after a minor hero (H)ekademus, whose shrine was on the site): the term has come to stand for a place where learning of all kinds, not just philosophical, is pursued for its own sake. After Plato the Academy continued to exist, though its teaching practice varied at different times. One important tendency was to develop the negative, questioning attitude that went back to Socrates: Cicero was attracted by this approach, which avoided firm doctrinal commitment and sought only to criticize false positions and establish what was probable, while suspending final judgement. By contrast a tradition also developed that claimed to preserve Plato's true or secret teachings, his 'unwritten doctrines', which bore little relation to the contents of the dialogues.[7] This tradition flowered eventually in the more mystical and religious neo-Platonism known to us especially from the third century AD, above all in Plotinus.

Perhaps the most important literary legacy of Plato was the dialogue form itself. It made possible the vivid re-creation of personalities and historical occasions, the vigorous expression of opposing points of view, with argument enlivened by humour or polemic; it allowed for short-cuts, adjournments, urbane courtesies; the scene-setting itself could contribute to the work's deeper significance, or simply charm the reader with delightful description (the country setting in the *Phaedrus* performs both functions). Criticism is of course possible. Some readers find the dialogue form unsatisfying because, although the interplay and conflict of views are enjoyably dramatized, the individual speakers are partial or prejudiced, and many arguments are not developed in full detail. Others may feel that this is an admission of the inevitable, and that even the longest and most impersonal treatise merely disguises a particular standpoint and omits many alternative lines of argument. Philosophy is a search, not a solution.

III

Aristotle too used dialogue form, but with a significant difference. Unlike Plato, he included himself as a character, and seems to have led or concluded some of the discussions; at the very least, his voice would have special authorial force.[8] Cicero and Plutarch seem to have followed

Aristotle's lead rather than Plato's, as well as dropping much of the incidental conversation and bantering humour of Plato's earlier style: participants make long speeches rather than engaging in cut-and-thrust exchange. But comparison with Aristotle is impossible because his more 'literary' works, intended for a general audience, do not survive. What we have are the so-called 'esoteric' works, which seem to represent something closer to the author's own texts for teaching and exposition to committed students. In any case, Aristotle must be set aside as a figure of more importance for the history of philosophy than of literature. This may seem cavalier in dealing with the 'master of those that know' (Dante), but to sum up his huge achievement in ethics, political theory, rhetoric, logic, causation, physics, metaphysics, botany, biology, the study of animals and so forth in a few paragraphs would be farcical. One general point can be made, that whereas Plato saw the world we inhabit as imperfect and looked beyond it to a superior realm, Aristotle seems more concerned with the exact scrutiny and understanding of things as they are, although bringing to that study a sharp and sceptical attitude based on experience of life. A more specific point, relating to literature: an important aspect of the *Ethics for Nicomachus*, one of his best-known works, is the examination of human character, its development and potential corruption, including the idea of virtue as a mean between two undesirable extremes (thus courage falls between the extremes of rash boldness and cowardliness). His categorization of moral and emotional attributes and his terminology permeated later thinking about ethics and also the treatment of ethical themes in literature: his pupil Theophrastus developed some of these ideas in witty pen-portraits of defective human types (the *Characters* – e.g. the superstitious man, the chatterbox, the busybody).[9] It is not absurd to suppose that playwrights such as Menander may have learned from these thinkers new ways of creating characters and giving them individuality. The two fathers in Terence's *Adelphi* (based on a Menandrian play) can be seen as representing two extremes, excessive generosity versus meanness, over-indulgence versus over-strictness.

Something must also be said of the schools which emerged after the death of Aristotle, in the Hellenistic age. The most important are Stoicism (named after the Stoa or Porch in Athens where Zeno, their founder, used to teach) and Epicureanism. (The Cynics, founded earlier by Diogenes and notorious for their rough living and bluntness of speech, are less significant and more negative: they tended to mock and reject society but without much of a constructive programme, though intellectuals such as Epictetus and Julian might compose idealized portraits of how the true Cynic could or should behave.) Stoicism and Epicureanism were natural opposites. The former maintained that virtue was its own reward, all other goods being 'indifferent'; that is, it did not matter whether one was rich or healthy, as that did not contribute to one's moral condition: a wise man might be happy while being tortured on the rack. They set a demanding ethical standard: few men were thought ever to have achieved the status of true wisdom. Whereas Plato had made God transcendent, a power above or outside the universe, the Stoics thought God was immanent in the universe itself, permeating it, and that each human individual had a spark of divinity within himself. The world was ordered and governed rationally by God for the good of the whole, though whether this divine order took account of the fortunes of individuals might be questioned.

By contrast, Epicurus maintained that the most important goal for human beings was to achieve 'calm' (*ataraxia*, freedom from disturbance), and further argued that we should aspire to pleasure and the avoidance of pain (already in his lifetime this was misinterpreted as advocacy of mindless hedonism, but in fact he taught that human nature could be content with the satisfaction of very simple needs). Epicurus also argued for a complex atomism, according to which all things come into being by chance combination of these atoms: no divine plan (in contrast with the Stoics' emphasis on God and Fate), and no permanency. The soul is mortal, and death is not to be feared. He did not, however, simply eliminate the gods, but declared that they existed in a region between the worlds, everlastingly at peace, unconcerned with human beings, who might however still worship them and try to emulate their tranquillity. Finally, the two schools were opposed on the relation of man to society. The Stoics considered that individuals had a duty to one another and should work together for the common good, virtue being expressed in action; Epicurus, however, recommended withdrawal from public life, since ambition and political activity can only bring distress and fear. For him the ideal was to 'live unknown', with a few intimates and friends. More than any other ancient thinker he anticipated Voltaire's advice, to 'cultivate one's garden'. (Because Epicurus had bequeathed a piece of property in Athens, including a garden, to his followers after his death, his school was often referred to as 'the Garden'.) Epicureanism may seem like a soft option, but it took courage to deny so many fundamental assumptions, including the perennial human hope that life itself has some meaning; and Epicurus was famous for his own brave endurance of pain during his final illness.

Again we face problems of evidence. No early texts of Stoicism survive, so that the system (an evolving one) has to be reconstructed from scrappy references and later summary accounts. With Epicureanism we are better served: the late work of Diogenes Laertius, *Lives of the Philosophers* (second century AD), quotes extensively from Epicurus' didactic letters and his most famous sayings (Diogenes used a variety of sources in different parts of his work, and his treatment of Stoicism is much less valuable). There is also the long poem of Lucretius, the greatest single text on Epicureanism, of which more shortly. But the fullest and most accessible account of many aspects of Hellenistic philosophy is in the philosophic works of Cicero, whose importance in transmitting knowledge of Greek thought to later times cannot be exaggerated. He was an enthusiastic reader of philosophic books throughout his career, widely read though firm in his own preferences (he generally adhered to the Academic standpoint, though admiring the Stoics: for Epicureanism he had little time, being equally resistant to their atomistic theories and their opposition to a public career). He even claimed, with some exaggeration, that his own speeches were steeped in philosophy: he had in mind the generalizations and high-flown discussions of principle.

His philosophic writings were mainly composed in rapid bursts of activity, when political circumstances barred him from playing the role he wanted to in public life. Between 55 and 52 he composed his works on political philosophy, *On the State* and the *Laws* (alongside the dialogue *On the Orator*, partly concerned with the need for rhetoric and philosophy to be combined). More important was the larger body of work which he completed at astonishing speed between late 46 and the end of 44, during Caesar's dictatorship and the months after his assassination: the *Academic Questions* (on epistemology); the *On Ends* and *Tusculan Disputations* (on ethics); the *On the Nature of the Gods*, *On Divination* and *On Fate* (on theology and questions of predestination); the shorter dialogues *On Old Age* and *On Friendship*, and the enormously influential *On Duties* (*de officiis*), not a dialogue but a volume addressed to his son, dealing with questions of social responsibility, obligation, self-interest and, in short, the duties of a citizen.

His aim, described in the prefaces to several of these works, was to bring Greek philosophy to a Roman audience and to show its relevance to Roman life. His interest in more rarefied theory was limited (though he showed his ability to cope with complex abstractions in *On Fate*): he is above all concerned with the applicability of philosophic principles to life. His letters often show him viewing his own dilemmas in terms derived from ethical theory,[10] and he drew on the wisdom of philosophy to help him endure the most painful loss of his later years, the premature death of his daughter in 46. He describes himself seeking out all the Greek texts on coping with grief and loss, and combining their arguments in a *Consolation* addressed to himself (now lost, though a sixteenth-century forgery was long included in texts of Cicero). Or again, he found it appropriate to view Caesar's dictatorship in terms of a tyranny, the worst form of government possible: a whole series of passages in the *On Duties* (completed after Caesar's death) reflect his outraged detestation of Caesar's self-interested ambition, his indifference to justice or propriety.

Cicero wrote at speed, and admitted that he was not producing original philosophy: 'These writings are mere copies, produced with no heavy labour. I supply only the words, of which I have a rich store' (*Att.* 12.52.3). He makes mistakes, sometimes oversimplifies, and will expand on a theme beyond its deserts if it offers opportunity for rhetorical elaboration; also, he is not always anxious to make the best case possible for those he disapproves of (this applies particularly to the Epicureans). But he is an unfailingly readable, lucid and lively author, who preserves much that we would otherwise not know. Sometimes his work is the earliest source for a given doctrine, often he gives it classic formulation. Even if we knew far more about the original Stoic and Epicurean systems than we do, he would still be a vital source to show the state of discussion in the late Republic, and what aspects of these teachings appealed to or seemed antipathetic to intelligent Romans.

Moreover, his claim that his works are merely copies does not do them full justice. The *On Friendship* includes much that is more relevant to Roman behaviour and standards than Greek: indeed, it sheds important light not only on the place of friendship in political alliances but on its relation to the structures of patronage, for which Greek society offered no true parallel.[11] Similar is the case of *On Duties*, though this is a hastier and less fully considered work than the other major treatises. Addressing his son, a student at Athens, Cicero tries to set out the chief elements of morality as they affect social and public life: he is clearly responding not only to the dictatorship of Caesar but to his perception of a wider problem of degeneracy in civil life. Although he follows the Greek Stoic Panaetius for the general structure of *On Duties* 1 and 2, even there he must have made many adjustments (it is unlikely that Panaetius was writing with a Roman audience in mind); and he is explicit that much of book 3, on the conflict between duty and expediency, represents his own argument, since he had found Panaetius inadequate here. There is much that is high-minded in this work, but much also that reveals a blinkered and class-bound mentality: Cicero often seems to imply that all society's problems will be solved if stricter measures are introduced to enforce the property rights of the rich and restrict debtors. In the past, readers who shared his conservatism looked to Cicero for wisdom: we may not find truth, but we gain much insight into social and moral values.

Similarly, his writings on religion will not help us solve the riddles of the universe, but they shed a flood of light on the diversity of views and conceptions of divinity and religion in educated Roman society, as well as surveying many older theories. In *On the Nature of the Gods* a large realm of intellectual activity and speculation is brilliantly illuminated through Cicero's panoramic and often witty eloquence, although there are many places where arguments are handled too briskly and complex theories given a rough ride by Cicero or his speakers. The first book examines Epicurean theology: one character advocates the Epicurean position, which is then demolished with good-humoured scepticism by Cotta, representing the Academic viewpoint. In book 2 a much fuller account is given of Stoic views by Balbus: Cicero obviously found these much more impressive and even inspiring. Balbus aims to show that the gods exist, that they have shaped the world purposefully and for the sake of man, and that they are concerned with human fate. The modern reader is bound to feel that eloquent description often takes the place of tough argument: in particular, many pages are occupied by an account of the ordered motions of the stars and planets, the wonders of nature, of the animal kingdom (at times recalling a 'Life on Earth' documentary), of the structure and powers of the human body, all of this being part of an attempt to show that the world cannot be a random creation but must be the work of a divine planner (the 'argument from design'). The third and last book (sadly mutilated in transmission) contains Cotta's rebuttal of Balbus' case: especially interesting is the short section on whether divine providence takes account of the destinies of individuals, or only of the larger whole – a fundamental issue related to the whole 'problem of evil'. Cicero concludes ambiguously: at the end of the debate Velleius the Epicurean felt that Cotta's refutation had been convincing, but Cicero himself claims he thought Balbus' position was more persuasive. The powerful influence of this work on early Christianity and Enlightenment thinking forms a key chapter in the history of ideas. More immediately, the *On the Nature of the Gods* makes very clear that in the next generation Virgil would not have expected his readers to adopt a naively literal approach to the gods of the *Aeneid*.

An important part of Cicero's achievement lay in his expansion of the Latin philosophic vocabulary. He found it necessary to invent many terms – especially abstract nouns – as equivalents to the long-developed Greek technical language. (Lucretius too, around the same time, complains of 'the poverty of our native tongue'.) The terms *qualitas, quantitas, essentia* (hence 'quality, quality, essence') are among Cicero's coinages; even the adjective *moralis* ('moral') is his. Less specialized and more wide-ranging than Lucretius, Cicero bequeathed a strong foundation for philosophic diction to the Latin-speaking Middle Ages and beyond. Although not made in this connection, Caesar's handsome tribute to his political enemy does him credit: he declared that Cicero had earned praise beyond any triumphal laurels, for it was more glorious to have expanded the boundaries of Roman genius than those of the Roman Empire (Pliny the Elder, *Natural History* 7.117).

IV

Lucretius' poem *On the Nature of the Universe* was probably known to Cicero: he comments admiringly on the art and inspiration of its author, although it has recently been argued that Cicero refers to earlier poetry and that Lucretius' masterpiece dates from several years later, during the civil wars between Caesar and Pompey.[12] Nothing is known of the author from other sources, for we must surely reject the absurd tale of his madness caused by a love-potion (Christian slander against an Epicurean 'atheist'?). The important thing is that his is one of the greatest poems in the Latin language. He is the poetic prophet of Epicureanism: never has such recalcitrant and unpromising material been handled with such power. Adopting a magniloquent, quasi-epic style which is indebted to Ennius but also to early Greek philosophic poets (especially Empedocles), he expounded the master's teachings in a form far more eloquent than Epicurus' crabbed Greek. It is a long poem – the longest didactic poem from the ancient world. The six-book structure is clear and bold: two books on atomic theory; two on the mind, the soul, sensation and emotion; two on the visible and inhabited world and man's place within it. Each book begins with a long proem, and several of these pay tribute to Epicurus as a heroic saviour-figure, who has brought true revelation to mankind, if they will only heed his message (esp. 1.62–79, 3.1–30, 5.1–54, 6.1–42). If these proems alone, or even the first 150 lines of book 1, had survived, Lucretius' status as a poet of genius would be evident. Only brief samples can be given here:

> Mother of Aeneas' race, delight of men and gods,
> Kindly Venus, who beneath heaven's gliding constellations
> Fill and inhabit the sea where ships pass, the lands where crops grow,
> Since through you it is that every race of living thing
> Is conceived and comes forth to reach the light of the sun:
> You, goddess, you put the winds to flight, the clouds of heaven fly before you
> and your coming; for you the artful earth sends forth delicious flowers,
> for you the waters of ocean laugh
> and placid heaven glows with widespread light.
> . . . and thanks to your power, the wild herds bound across the fertile meadows
> and swim the raging rivers: so captivated by pleasure
> each one follows passionately wherever you choose to lead them.
> (1.1–9 and 14–16)

> And meanwhile cause the savage deeds of war
> to slumber and to sleep across all seas and lands;

for you alone can aid mankind with quiet peace,
since Mars who wields power in arms rules over the savage deeds of war,
and he often takes his repose in your lap,
vanquished by the eternal wound of love,
and gazing upwards with his smooth neck laid back in rest
he feeds his greedy eyes with love, gazing hungrily at you, goddess,
and as he lies there, his breath hangs from your lips.
As he reclines there, goddess, bend over him from above
with your holy body, and pour from your lips words of sweet soft sound,
entreating, glorious lady, the calmness of peace for the Romans.
For in this time of ill fortune for our fatherland, I cannot perform
my task with a mind at ease, nor can the illustrious scion of Memmius
fail to serve the common good in such times of crisis.   (1.29–43)

Here the traditional figure of the goddess of love is transformed into a symbolic entity, representing not only the life force that animates living things, but pleasure, the chief good of Epicureans, and also the charm and beauty which will make Lucretius' own poem a source of pleasure and delight, attracting readers and winning converts. The use of myth to illustrate and enliven philosophic themes is typical of Lucretius: elsewhere he declares that Epicurus' benefactions to mankind have outclassed the deeds of Hercules (5.22–42), and that his own words can claim higher authority than the oracles of Delphi (1.736–9). On occasion he recounts a myth, then denies the validity of the tale (2.600–45, the Magna Mater; 5.396–410, Phaethon's chariot-crash): like Plato, he hijacks poetic fantasies and enriches them with fresh physical or ethical meaning, while rejecting the original premises (e.g. 4.732–43). Still more prominent in the text are the vivid imagery and similes with which he brings to life the physical phenomena he describes.

The poem is also a serious and sustained argument, often polemical: addressing both the Roman Memmius, to whom he dedicates his work, and a wider public, he challenges the reader with stern warnings, demanding interrogations, reiteration and urgent insistence on the importance of his themes. At times the tone is sympathetic and encouraging, guiding the reader along the path to wisdom; elsewhere he is hectoring and sarcastic, directing withering criticism at rival thinkers, dismissing views he declares absurd or self-contradictory, or denouncing negative features of human behaviour: political ambition, greed for wealth, lust and desire. All the techniques of rhetorical polemic are skilfully though not always fairly deployed.[13] Most devastating of all is the central assault on the fear of death (at the end of book 3). The soul's mortality is proved by a series of no fewer than 30 different arguments; the case is further developed in the more eloquent and emotional conclusion to the book.

Death, therefore, is nothing to us, nor does it matter a scrap,
Since it is clear that the nature of the mind is mortal.
And just as in time gone by we felt no discomfort
When the Carthaginians were massing on every front for combat,
When all the world was shaken with the trembling turmoil of war,
Quaking and shuddering beneath heaven's lofty vault,
And none could be sure to which side would pass sovereignty
Over all mankind on land and sea alike;
So too, when we shall exist no more, when there has been dissolution
Of the body and the life-force from which we are composed,
Without any doubt, nothing whatsoever can happen to us
(we shall not exist then), nothing can affect our feelings,
Not even if earth is confounded with sea, and sea with heaven.
(3.830–42)

The whole poem is an exceptionally tough-minded and argumentative performance, which despite its opening address to the ancestress of the Roman race
contains much that defies Roman traditional values. Cicero may have admired
the poetic achievement but will have deeply disapproved of the ethical content.

Although Lucretius presents Epicurus' philosophic teaching as a triumphal
victory over superstition, a liberation of mankind from oppressive beliefs,
the message has its darker side. The poem also stresses not only the narrow
limits of human existence, but the mortality of the world itself (2.1122–74,
5.91–109, 380–95), and its hostility to man. The earth cannot have been
created for humans' benefit (as Stoics claimed), for 'it is too full of faults'
(5.156–234). The narrative of human development and the emergence of
political communities in book 5 is not a simple optimistic tale of progress;
increased resources and technological advancement may enable us to avoid
some of the more terrible dangers that beset primitive man, but they do not
bring happiness and peace of mind. Only acceptance of the limits of human
needs (2.16–53, 5.1379–1435, etc.), and self-discipline founded on Epicurus'
insights, can do that. The opening of the poem celebrates light and life, but
the conclusion paints a horrific picture of destruction and death, in an
extended narrative of the great plague at Athens (as described by Thucydides,
whose account Lucretius adapts and enhances). The ending is one of
darkness and desperation. Is the implication that the Athenians of this time
lacked the wisdom of Epicureanism, which alone would have enabled them
to see their sufferings in a true light? Or is the point that the reader, as part
of his training, needs to confront the worst and view it with open eyes,
strengthened by the doctrines set out earlier in the poem? In either case, it
is strange that the point is not made explicit. But the movement from
creation to destruction also mirrors on a large scale the interplay between
positive and negative aspects of Epicurean teaching throughout the poem:

Lucretius' pessimism about the human condition is often explicit (5.222–7). Despite the simplistic perception of Epicureans as happy hedonists, this is not a cheerful philosophy.

V

It would be an idle exercise to debate whether the poem of Lucretius or the *Georgics* of Virgil is the greater work: what is certain is that they benefit by being read together.[14] Lucretius is the chief model for Virgil's poem, far more important than Hesiod, to whom he pays cursory tribute as founder of the didactic tradition, or the tedious Nicander, from whom he draws his title (*georgica* is Greek for 'books on farming'). Yet there are differences: Virgil's work is much shorter, four books rather than six, and each of them about half the length of a Lucretian book. The subject matter is not strictly philosophic (though the moral worth of country life is prominent): Virgil does not expound a system. The pleasures of Lucretius' poem are chiefly intellectual, whereas in Virgil's one is tempted to dwell more on the aesthetic experience: the beauties of the description of country scenes, of animal and birdlife, the mythical digressions or briefer allusions to other literature, the catalogues of names of Italian townships, vintages, rivers . . . all set out in mellifluous and richly wrought verse.

Virgil affects to be writing a versified handbook for the farmer: book 1 treats the land and weather-signs, book 2 trees and viticulture, book 3 animals (especially horses, cattle, sheep and goats – the unpoetic pig is scarcely mentioned!), and book 4 the keeping of bees. He claims to be composing it for the common countryman, but the poem is also dedicated to the ultra-sophisticated Maecenas, and the didacticism is clearly a pose. Simple farmers would not have turned to the *Georgics* for guidance in their work – many more practical prose guides were available. Nevertheless, the unreality of Virgil's agricultural lore can be exaggerated: although his work admits moralizing, marvels and mythology, there is still a solid core of farming knowledge. Subject and style are sometimes in harmony, sometimes in counterpoint. Virgil teases his reader, who may be inclined to despise these humble topics: 'I can recount much ancient lore of this kind, if you do not recoil and object to learning about these slight matters' (1.176–7). Or else he admits the difficulty only to surmount it: 'I am well aware how large a task it is to vanquish these topics in words and to add this kind of distinction to narrow themes' (3.289–90, cf. 4.6). The treatment is highly selective, but the language and allusions constantly display knowledge of a vast range of past writing, poetry and prose, much of it unconcerned with farming. Aratus and Callimachus are quarried as often as Varro, whose prose manual on farming had appeared some years earlier. Extended digressions on astronomy and on far-off nations with strange climates and customs expand the scope of the poem.

Although often light-hearted, the poem is not frivolous. Central is the celebration of the glories of the land, not only the life of the countryman in general but praise of Italy, its fertility and its landscapes. In part this needs to be seen in its historical context, with the conclusion of civil wars and the prospect of a return to normality, with conscripted soldiers restored to their land and veterans settled. Virgil, writing in the period 37–29 BC, was witnessing a changing situation, and the perspective varies: at the end of book 1 comes a deeply pessimistic, even apocalyptic vision of chaos and disorder resulting from civil war, in which Caesar (Octavian) offers the only hope, and that a slender one, for a better future.[15] In the later parts of the poem, and especially the conclusion, a more positive note is struck (2.170–2, 4.559–66). But the bleakness of outlook at the end of book 1 should not be forgotten:

> this world where right and wrong are overturned; so many wars across the globe, so many faces of wicked crime, where the plough lacks its rightful honour, and the fields grow wild, with the labourers led off to war, and curving sickles are reforged into unyielding swords. On one frontier Euphrates mounts a campaign, on the other Germany. (1.505–9)

Creative country life is the joyful antithesis of destructive war, and not only civil war (though for Virgil and the other poets of his day that has a particular horror); Roman obsession with mutual destruction also weakens the empire as a whole and encourages their most dangerous foreign foes to plan for attack.

On another level, the countryman is a symbolic figure, representative of man as a part of (though also often at odds with) nature. Virgil does not develop this in a full-scale exposition, but we can see that his praise of farming is framed by a larger intellectual scheme from his allusions to the development of society (a Lucretian theme), the decline from the idyllic conditions of the golden age, the 'tough, hard' nature of man (sprung from rocks according to the Greek myth of the flood and its aftermath), which enables him to deal with adversity and combat nature. These are the wars which the country-dweller should be fighting: the military metaphor is persistent (e.g. 1.99, 160, 2.279ff.). Nature often throws obstacles in our path – sterile crops, storms, floods, fire or disease – and there is no room for slackers; persistent effort is needed, as when a man is striving to row a boat upstream (1.197ff.). Virgil's generalizations about the human lot can be as dark as Lucretius' (3.66–8, on old age). But he also promises the countryman rich rewards and well-earned rest and festivity: among the poem's best-known passages are the enthusiastic praise of Italy as a land of plenty, the sympathetic descriptions of rural festivals, and the celebration of the country as a place of refuge, a moral alternative to the ambition and antagonism of city life. These country ways and virtues were the roots of Rome's greatness (2.532ff.); yet we sense a tension between the delight in old Roman virtue and the unease implicit in Virgil's references to the power of Rome today and the cares and conflicts that seem inseparable from the life of the capital.

Often, however, this larger picture is forgotten or masked by visual detail and humorous vignettes. The poet moves readily from mountains and storm winds to smaller-scale aspects of nature. In particular he delights in the mock-heroic treatment of tiny animals. The farmer must beware of the dangers to the grainstore: 'in the cracks the toad will be found, and all the numerous monsters the earth produces: the mighty heap of grain may be devastated by a weevil, or an ant concerned for his impecunious old age' (1.184ff.). The same technique is applied to the tiny community of the bees in book 4: their government and their wars are viewed in human terms (67ff., 153ff., 203ff.). Even the introduction to that section echoes the terminology of an ethnographic writer embarking on a survey of a society (4.4–5). Elsewhere it is simply the fine observation and choice of detail that delights the reader, as when Virgil describes the reactions of animals and birds to impending rain:

> as the storm rises the cranes flee the lower valleys and take to the air, or the young calf gazing skywards sniffs at the breeze with wide-open nostrils; the clear-voiced swallow circles the lake's boundary, and down in the mud the frogs sing their long-familiar complaint. . . . at such times the troublesome raven calls out for the rain in full voice, and struts his solitary path upon the dry sand. (1.374–8, 388–9)

Virgil borrowed from Lucretius many motifs and stylistic devices: the technique of questioning, reassuring and generally engaging with the reader; the setting out of alternative explanations for phenomena; the use of quasi-epic similes. Famous lines in book 2 seem to pay tribute to his predecessor.

> happy the man who has been able to discover the reasons that things happen, and who has trampled beneath his feet all fears and ineluctable destiny and the din of hungry Acheron [one of the rivers of the underworld]. (2.490–2)

But Virgil goes on: 'fortunate too is the man who knows the gods of the countryside . . .', and in some ways the *Georgics* can be seen as a response to Lucretius. Virgil himself had studied with Epicurean teachers at Naples; but he does not thrust any specific doctrine upon the reader, and one feels that his is a more open-minded, exploratory poem (perhaps the motto should be 'There are more things in heaven and earth, Epicurus, than are dreamt of in your philosophy'). On a structural level, one point in particular marks his work as imitation with a difference. Whereas disastrous plague ends Lucretius' poem, Virgil ends not his fourth but his third book with an extended plague-narrative: this is not the poet's last word (and indeed the last book concludes with Aristaeus miraculously recovering his bees after disease has wiped them out).

Otherwise, several strands in the poem are markedly non-Epicurean. First, the patriotic note, however qualified, indicates a deeper concern with politics than Epicurean quietism would allow: the political and military activities of Octavian and others determine the fate of the countryside and the security of Italy (p. 189). Second, the poem makes much of the gods and their generosity to mankind: their 'gifts', natural or supernatural, are a recurring theme. Worship and cult, festival and sacrifice, are presented as essential to the farmer's well-being. Although Virgil's own ideas may have been more sophisticated, the standpoint of his persona is consistent. This contradicts the Lucretian emphasis on the gods' indifference to our condition (Lucr. 6.68–78, etc.). Third, Lucretius ended his fourth book with a vicious assault on passion, especially erotic emotion: these desires destroy peace of mind and should be eradicated or avoided. By contrast Virgil, in an extraordinarily powerful passage of book 3, presents animal and human passion as inescapable but not contemptible: though terrifying and sometimes indeed destructive, love is also a part of nature and a source of awe and wonder (3.209–83). That the bees lack passion is a curiosity, not a reason to emulate them (4.197–202).

A final aspect which cuts against Lucretian practice is the delight in mythology, treated not as the delusions of the ignorant but as a rich store of poetic ornament: sometimes myth provides matter for learned wit, reminding us of the stories associated with different species and places (e.g. 4.150ff., 3.89–94, 152–6); often it is the springboard for imaginative passages that illuminate the themes of the poem (as in the references to the golden age, which country life resembles while still falling short of it). From another point of view, the mythological narrative that concludes the poem can be seen as a training ground for epic. This is not merely hindsight on the part of a reader who knows the *Aeneid*, for Virgil himself writes of his strongly felt ambitions (3 proem). The *Georgics* concludes with a composite myth involving the shepherd-hero Aristaeus and the poet Orpheus, whose bride Eurydice Aristaeus attempted to rape; as she ran from him she was fatally wounded by a venomous snake. The tragic tale of how Orpheus dared to descend to the underworld in an effort to win her back, how even the underworld powers were moved by his song, and released her on conditions, and of how Orpheus failed at the last hurdle, throwing caution to the winds and dooming his love again, is the subject of an exquisitely haunting passage.

> What could he do, where go, his wife twice taken from him?
> What lament would move Death now? What deities hear his song?
> Cold she was voyaging now over the Stygian stream.
> Month after month, they say, for seven months alone
> He wept beneath a crag high up by the lonely waters
> Of Strymon, and under the ice-cold stars poured out his dirge
> That charmed the tigers and made the oak trees follow him.
> As a nightingale he sang that sorrowing under a poplar's
> shade laments the young she has lost, whom a heartless ploughman
> Has noticed and dragged from the nest unfledged; and the nightingale
> Weeps all night, on a branch repeating the piteous song,
> Loading the acres around with the burden of her lament.
> (*Geo.* 4.504–15, tr. C. Day Lewis)

All this, and the subsequent death of Orpheus himself, is mediated through the prophetic figure of Proteus, who relates the tale in order to explain Aristaeus' subsequent misfortunes. Aristaeus, shocked and dismayed, is given a fresh chance, and by obediently following religious ritual regains his prosperity as well as gaining future status as a country divinity. But the reader, ancient or modern, is bound to care more for Orpheus and Eurydice, whose eerie and terrible fate is not erased by Aristaeus' success or the bizarre ritual by which it is achieved. The poem has been much concerned with religious observance and with success in cultivating or preserving one's livelihood; but the concluding part of book 4, by transferring these issues to the more dramatic medium of myth, clouds the picture and suggests that the dilemmas and disasters of human life cannot be explained or solved by Virgil's 'philosophy' (however loosely defined), any more than by Lucretius' Epicureanism. In the end we are left confronting these two opposed destinies, Aristaeus and Orpheus, farmer and poet. It is no coincidence that the remaining eight lines at the close of the poem offer a parallel contrast between Octavian and Virgil, ruler or warrior and poet. But no crudely schematic summing-up can do anything but rough justice to this constantly elusive poem.

VI

Country life is also a frequent subject in Horace, and often represented as conducive to virtuous living, or as a suitable retreat in which to read and think about philosophy. Usually the setting is specific: the estate outside Rome which he was given by Maecenas early in their relationship (the traditional phrase 'Sabine farm' understates its probable scale). Town versus country is a favourite theme. Sometimes he treats the topic in more abstract terms, debating with his friend Fuscus the relative merits of urban and rustic life (*Ep.* 1.10); or he invites a VIP to set aside the cares of government and enjoy a simple meal in his rural retreat (*Odes* 1.20, 2.11, 3.8, etc.). One of the later satires (2.6) celebrates the farm, while also giving a vivid picture of what it is like when he comes to Rome and everybody is badgering him or trying to find out what he knows about high politics: when he pleads complete ignorance, they marvel at his discretion! It is a telling detail that he does not detest *all* aspects of the town: when people enviously comment on his closeness to Maecenas he admits 'I enjoy that, it's sweet to the ears, I admit'. Yet he still longs ruefully for the country: 'when shall I see you again? When will I be allowed to drink draughts of forgetfulness of a care-filled life, either amid ancient books or with sleep and lazy hours? When shall those beans, relatives of Pythagoras, be set before me again?' (Pythagoras believed in transmigration of souls and also advocated vegetarianism, but Horace is jokingly connecting the two doctrines.)

The best part of the poem is the latter half, where he pictures an evening meal with friends on his estate. The discussion turns not to backbiting or trivial gossip but to serious ethical topics: 'whether men are rich through wealth or virtue . . . what is the nature of goodness, and what its highest form'. After this high-minded agenda it is amusing to read the following passage, in which Horace's neighbour Cervius narrates 'old-wives' tales, but to the point'. Cervius' story of the town and country mouse is derived from Aesop's fables but embroidered with Horatian witty detail.[16] The town mouse, a fastidious diner, is polite about his rural host's humble table but asks him if he has never aspired to something more, and quotes debased Epicurean doctrine, encouraging him to seize opportunities while life lasts. (One is reminded of the relationship between Rat and Mole in *The Wind in the Willows*.) The country mouse is induced to join his friend in a raid on a rich man's table, but the inopportune appearance of fierce dogs changes his mind. The fable echoes Horace's own preference for the quiet life, while also bringing his philosophic pretensions down to earth (and spoofing the Epicureanism he takes more seriously elsewhere).

The *Odes* too have their philosophic aspect. Early Greek lyric was full of moralizing sentiments, but by Horace's time the philosophic schools were highly developed: he writes with knowledge of an extensive literature in prose. Epicurus' words are often paraphrased; but so are the sterner precepts of Stoicism. Where everyday morality was concerned the principal schools had much common ground; at the same time Horace does modify his tone and introduce different nuances with different addressees. His meditations on death are more sombre than the 'live for the moment' outlook which we often find in the love elegists. At times the note of foreboding becomes oppressive (2.14), but his best efforts do justice to both the pleasures of the present and the uncertainty of the future, which provides the justification for 'clutching the day' and making the most of what life offers (1.9, 1.11, 3.29, 4.7, etc.)

> Seek not to find what tomorrow holds,
> but count as profit whatever days Fortune grants you;
> and don't spurn love's delights,
> my boy, or dances,
> while sullen grey holds back from your green
> youth. Now is the time for the open air,
> the piazza, and soft sweet nothings as evening falls,
> at an appointed hour . . .   (1.9.13–20)

Satires 2.6, discussed above, is the poem that most clearly anticipates the manner of the later book of *Epistles*, which shows a more sustained concern with ethical themes. The satires mimic the manner of conversation, but the letter form pursues a relationship at a distance. There was precedent for letters on philosophic topics: witness those ascribed to Plato, or the doctrinal letters of Epicurus which still survive. There was precedent also for verse letters in Latin (some of Lucilius' poems, and several of those by Catullus, are epistolary). But it does look as though Horace was the first to combine the two and write about philosophy in versified letters. The experiment is a triumphant success, and *Epistles* 1 is one of his most refined works.[17] The 20 letters vary greatly in length, tone and addressee: at the highest end of the scale there is Maecenas and the future emperor Tiberius; at the bottom there is the poet's own bailiff; in between come various friends, poets and dignitaries, each treated with respect or geniality, sobriety or intimacy, as appropriate. A sense of the appropriate (*decorum*) was important both in ancient ethics and in the theory of letters: style should be suited to both the subject and the writer's relation to the addressee. The avaricious Iccius is handled differently from the distinguished lawyer Torquatus, and Maecenas (who receives three letters) is treated with an affection that does not exclude mild criticism. The addressees are real but the epistolary form is certainly an elegant fiction: the book is carefully shaped as a poetic artefact, and different letters shed light on one another (as in the *Eclogues* or a book of Propertius' elegies).

The *Epistles* deal less with theoretical issues than with everyday problems of good manners, friendship and conflicting interests. One poem recommends another friend, Septimius, to Tiberius, but the focus is all on Horace's anxiety: is he being unduly pushy in approaching the great man? But if he fails to do so, is he failing in his duty to Septimius? (1.9). The self-portrayal is often light-hearted: to Tibullus he jestingly describes himself as 'a sleek hog from Epicurus' herd' (1.4). His Epicureanism is not consistent, however: he insists on his freedom to pick and choose among philosophies, and inconsistency itself is made a motif of the collection. Horace does not present himself as a flawless model: he finds fault with his own progress (or backsliding) as well as that of others (1.8, 1.1 opening). On the whole, he tends to mock or treat with exaggerated reverence the idea of the man who has achieved wisdom, the Stoic *sapiens*; but the possibility of limited moral progress receives a good deal of his attention (already at 1.1.28–32). It is on this basis, not as a sage but as an imperfect teacher who may nevertheless have something to offer, especially to younger and less experienced men, that Horace addresses philosophy to his addressees. The keynote is the opening of the letter to Scaeva: 'listen to what your little friend can teach, though needing guidance himself: it's as though a blind man were showing the way . . .' (1.17.3–4). Since he is writing as a Roman citizen as well as a human being, he deals with the social situations and ambitions of Roman society (as did Cicero in the *On Duties* and *On Friendship*). In particular he writes from experience on how best to handle, or strengthen one's relationship with, one's patrons. Poetic efforts, his own and those of others, are also subjected to ironic scrutiny. Titius is warned against bombast, Celsus against plagiarism (1.3). Horace also humorously dramatizes his own *angst* at the prospect of his work being delivered to Augustus without suitable preparation and tact (1.13). Best of all is the final poem, in which he reproaches the book itself, personified as though it is a bright and pretty slave boy whose eagerness to be put on show and win admirers is morally suspect (1.20).

Augustus is mentioned in passing in this book, but not given a letter of his own. Suetonius tells us that he requested that Horace remedy this omission, and the result was the long first poem of book 2 – an ambitious and elaborate piece, framed by courteous compliments to the monarch.[18] It combines a selective sketch of Latin literary history, a defence of modern poetry against the over-valuation of older writers (also vindicating works written for close reading rather than public/theatrical performance), and a teasing and evasive examination of the role of the poet, including Horace himself, in Augustan society. This is the longest single work by a poet directly engaging with or addressing Augustus (except for Ovid's hopeless self-defence from exile, *Tristia* 2).[19]

Ethics and poetics constantly intertwine in Horace: the poet has a responsibility to himself and to his audience, however elaborately the layers of defensive irony may obscure Horace's convictions. *Epistles* 2.2 and the more elaborate *Art of Poetry* develop these themes in other directions; Pope's *Essay on Criticism* is in the direct line of descent from these poems. In the *Art*, for example, he emphasizes the dangers of recitation sessions and the well-meant flattery they generate: the true friend will also be an honest critic. 'Neither men nor gods nor booksellers permit the existence of mediocre poets' (*Art* 372–3). The humour is self-evident, but Horace's perfectionism is nowhere more serious than when directed at his own work.

VII

As far as we can see, the popularity of Epicureanism in the late Republic was not sustained under the early empire. Stoicism became more prominent, while Platonism was by the third century the most influential school of all. Although Tacitus mentions a number of notable Stoics who carried their principles into politics (and some who failed to live up to them), three major figures dominate the surviving literary evidence: the younger Seneca (whom we have met already as a writer of tragedies), Epictetus, and Marcus Aurelius. They form a striking trio: the first an enormously wealthy courtier, at first adviser but eventually victim of Nero; the second a Greek and an ex-slave, who becomes a teacher of philosophy at Nicopolis in Greek Epirus (with many Romans among his pupils); the third a Stoic on the throne, emperor of the Roman world for 20 years. There is much common ground in their writings, and it is fair to say that the chief interest does not lie in novelty of doctrine, but on the one hand in form and presentation, on the other in the relation of their work to their lives. Critics should be chary of imposing biographical readings on texts, but the invitation to do so is hard to resist when the author himself emphasizes the need for actions to live up to words ('concordet sermo cum vita', wrote Seneca: 'let your speech be in harmony with your life' (*Letters* 75.4)).[20]

Seneca's writings are extensive, mostly in the form of an extended essay on some topic where Stoic teachings can be brought to bear. His three-book work *On Anger* is one of the most significant, full of the black deeds of tyrants and villains (the atrocities of Caligula, whose reign Seneca had lived through, figure prominently). Important in a different way – for the light it sheds on the imperial court and its ideology, on what it was possible and desirable to say to the emperor – is the long work *On Clemency*, addressed to Nero early in his reign. Other works indirectly illuminate Seneca's own problems and preoccupations: he constantly reverts to the topic of death and especially freedom through suicide. Cato, who killed himself at Utica to escape Caesar's rule, is a favourite figure of his.

Few things displease the modern reader more than moralizing, and even students of English literature now seldom read the essays of Bacon or Johnson. As for the ancient world, it is easy to feel that when the moralist tells us that revenge is a bad thing, he is stating the obvious; when he says that death is not a misfortune, he is arguing the obviously false. But to look only at the content risks missing much of the point. Seneca, like many other writers, is using familiar ideas but giving them a fresh sharpness, illustrating them with his own range of examples, modifying the theme to suit his addressee and his times. Formal devices – exclamations, vigorous questions, challenging address to the reader, anecdotes, historical and mythical examples, are all deployed in such a way as to make the reader's experience a startling one: bold paradox, wordplay and striking epigram are rife. In Seneca we find the apotheosis of the pointed style. The effective unit is the paragraph, even the sentence: sustained exposition of an argument is not absent from his work, but it is not his forte. Macaulay complained that reading Seneca was like dining on nothing but anchovy sauce. For this reason many readers will get most pleasure from the *Moral Letters*, written near the end of his career, in which the brevity and informality of the letter form makes it easier to accept the spasmodic, fast-shifting treatment of each subject.

These letters are modelled partly on Cicero's to Atticus, and like those have a single addressee throughout, Seneca's friend Lucilius. But although Lucilius was real enough, the letter form is clearly a fiction: the focus is exclusively on moral themes, and the letters gradually become more detailed and doctrinally complex, until the later ones are like substantial essays. We know that Seneca on retiring from politics had contemplated writing a general work on philosophy: the *Letters* constitute a more satisfying experiment, presenting Stoic teachings as a kind of progressive correspondence course. The topics are wide-ranging, the tone varies from cheerfully encouraging to darkly pessimistic. Seneca had read Horace and takes several hints from his *Epistles*, in particular the technique of instructing while admitting that he is himself only a step or two further along the road to wisdom. Often a letter will begin by replying to a question posed by Lucilius; or Seneca will start from his own location or situation and use the particular as a starting-point for a general moral theme. A colourful passage at the start of letter 56 describes the din and discomfort Seneca is experiencing in temporary lodgings above a bath-house. This leads on to discussion of the capacity of the mind to retain its tranquillity even in the worst of surroundings. A visit to his estate, where he finds everything run down and decrepit, leads on to contemplation of his own advancing years and the need to be satisfied with the achievement of each day (*Letters* 12). Inevitably some themes ring more true or have greater interest than others. A fine instance is letter 7, which includes a powerful appeal to Lucilius to avoid the corruption of crowds, and especially the mob at the gladiatorial games (a recurring source of disgust and horror in the works of Roman intellectuals). Better still is the famous letter on treatment of slaves (47).[21] This extract begins with the imagined voice of a contemptuous slave-owner (not Lucilius himself), and Seneca's efforts to make him see reason.

> 'They are slaves.' No, human beings. 'They are slaves.' No, comrades-in-arms. 'They are slaves.' No, humble friends. 'They are slaves.' No, *fellow*-slaves, if you reflect on fortune's equal power over both sides. . . . Those wretched slaves are not permitted to move their lips even in order to speak: every whisper is curbed by the slash of a cane. Not even involuntary sounds are exempt from beating, such as a cough, a sneeze, a sob. To break the silence with any utterance calls for atonement, and that means severe treatment. All night long they have to stand there, hungry and mute. The consequence is that those who are not allowed to speak in front of their master speak about him behind his back. But there are others, slaves who have not only conversed before their master but with him, whose mouths have not been stitched shut, and they have proved ready to risk their own necks for their master, to divert impending danger onto their own heads. They talked at the dinner-party, but were silent in the torture chamber. And then there is that proverb that has become current, arising from the same arrogance: 'you have as many enemies as you have slaves'. No, we don't *have* enemies, we *make* them so. (47.1, 3–5)

Seneca does not command respect as a man or a politician: he was ambitious, self-interested, accessory or at least complicit to murder, and richer than the basest fat-cats. 'What kind of philosophic doctrines taught him how to amass a fortune of 300 million sesterces?' asks a contemporary (Tac. *Ann.* 13.42, cf. Dio 61.10). While one cannot easily admire his life, we can approve the dignity of his death (vividly recounted by Tacitus).[22] His works had great influence in unexpected quarters, and his principles seemed to some Christians to prove that he was a kindred spirit: 'Seneca is often one of us,' wrote Tertullian. (One of the odder results was the production of a fake series of letters, of startling banality, supposedly exchanged between Seneca and St Paul during the latter's time in Rome. It appears that the forger knew these two men were contemporaries but could think of nothing to make them say to each other.) As important as the influence of his philosophic principles was his impact on literature. Quintilian, 30 years later, is still bemoaning the influence of his work on the young in their rhetorical compositions: in his eyes it encouraged puerile conceits and showy cleverness. He is so conscious of the enticing attractions of Seneca's style that he reserves a special place for him at the very end of his list of prescribed authors (10.1.125–31). Perhaps the most telling phrase in his critique is 'You might wish he had spoken with his own talent, but with someone else's judgement' (130).

Epictetus is a completely different figure. Like Socrates, he did not even write down his thoughts: what we have is the record of his talk and teaching as preserved by Arrian, who heard him in his youth (probably around AD 108) and was deeply impressed. Arrian's own preface makes clear that he sees himself as following the example of Xenophon in the *Recollections of Socrates*. Not all of Arrian's record survives, but we have four books of 'discourses' and, perhaps most influential, the so-called *Manual* or *Handbook*, a short summary of the principles of Stoic teaching which were highlighted by Epictetus. The *Discourses* are repetitive and sometimes drab, but they include much lively dialogue and satirical comment of a kind that the *Handbook* does not. Epictetus evidently played the 'plain man': as Arrian puts it in his preface, these are the kinds of things a man might say offhand to another, and not composed with an eye on posterity. Epictetus did not care to be admired for his style; what mattered was the effect his words had on others. Despite this, there are many eloquent passages.

> Behold now, Caesar seems to provide us with profound peace, there are no wars any more, no battles, no violent brigandage, no piracy, but at any hour we can travel by land, or sail from the rising of the sun to its setting. Can he, then, provide us in any way with peace from fever, from shipwreck, from fire, from earthquake, from lightning? Can he give us peace from love? No, he cannot. From grief? From envy? He cannot, not from a single one of these things. But the teaching of the philosophers promises to give peace from these troubles also. (3.13.9–10)

When he speaks of the freedom of the mind being more important than that of the body, we respond more readily in the knowledge that he has himself been a slave than we would to the high-sounding precepts of aristocratic men of leisure. He does not refrain from outspoken comment on Roman ways, having lived himself as a slave of one of Nero's all-powerful freedmen. 'For the sake of these mighty and dignified offices and honours you kiss the hands of another man's slaves – and are thus the slaves of men who are not free themselves' (4.1.148).

Of fundamental import in his thinking is the distinction between the things in our own power (above all, one's own moral attitude) and those which are not: wealth, health, political power, and the opinions of others, all fall into the latter category. The servants at the door of the emperor's bedchamber may bar you from entering: but if you do not care about entering, you are not really excluded (4.7.19–21). What really counts is to be in control of one's own will and to meet adversity with equanimity. 'Endure and abstain', is his most famous motto. It is a clear-headed and strong-minded ethic of rational choice: the mind can be trained to view externals in the proper light, and a man so trained can face the worst that the world can throw at him. The contrast with the Christian (and especially the Augustinian) emphasis on ineradicable human sin and dependency on God's gift of grace is extremely marked.

Reading Epictetus powerfully influenced the Emperor Marcus Aurelius: he quotes him often, and his own writings often echo his language and thought. Marcus' own book, however, is of a quite different kind. Usually known as the *Meditations*, it is a unique document and a generic hybrid – part spiritual diary, part commonplace book, part training-ground for the author's own mental exercises. It is a short work, divided by later editors into 12 books but covering hardly more than 100 pages. It seems to be the product of his last years (he regularly refers to his old age, though he was only 59 at his death in 180). Internal evidence suggests it was composed at least partly during the extensive campaigns against Germanic tribes that overshadowed his final decade. Written in Greek (still, despite Cicero's efforts, the language of philosophy), it was apparently unknown to contemporary writers and biographers, and seems to be intended for his own eyes alone. This makes it a uniquely intimate and revealing work: we see not how the emperor wanted to be perceived, but what he set himself as his most important goals. Yet the experience of reading it is frustrating: the reflections and self-admonitions are mostly generalized, and we cannot see how they relate to his daily experience. Often he will write down a brief *pensée*, sometimes a more developed argument; elsewhere we find a string of quotations from earlier writers, prose and verse: Euripides, Plato, and of course Epictetus are commonly cited. There are no dates, no record of the day's events, nothing on named individuals, and no hint of his views on military policy or senatorial politics. The exception is the first book, which has a more coherent character: there he sets out the chief debts he owes to relatives and teachers (culminating in the debts to his predecessor, Antoninus Pius, and to the gods).

In the rest of the work, the role of philosophy as self-therapy is plain. Medical metaphors were traditional in this field: Epictetus called the philosopher's lecture-room a hospital (3.23.30). Similarly Marcus writes: 'as doctors have their instruments and scalpels always at hand to meet sudden demands for treatment, so must you have your doctrines ready in order to recognise the divine and human, and to do everything as one mindful of the bond uniting the divine and the human' (3.13). Topics recur, treated now more fully, now concisely: sometimes we have little more than headings, almost shorthand (12.7). The *Meditations* heavily emphasize the need for self-control and self-discipline: anger (esp. 11.18), lust, discontent, envy and other unhealthy emotions must be purged; indignation at what others say and do is pointless. 'The noblest kind of retribution is not to become like your enemy' (6.6). Better understanding of others will lead to greater tolerance. At times the wording does hint at his own circumstances. 'Speak both in the senate and to every man of whatever rank with propriety, without affectation' (8.30). There are some signs of dissatisfaction with his station: 'let no one any longer hear you finding fault with your life in a palace; no, do not even hear yourself' (8.9). The work is permeated with a sense of duty and of many obligations to other men. 'Men have come into the world for the sake of one another. Either instruct them then or put up with them' (8.59). There is also a strongly religious strand, reminiscent of the early Stoic Cleanthes' philosophic hymn to Zeus. Acceptance and affirmation of the cosmic order can prompt a warm enthusiasm: 'Everything is fitting for me, o universe, which fits your purpose. Nothing in your good time is too early or too late for me; everything is fruit for me which your seasons, Nature, bear; from you, in you, and to you all things belong' (4.23).

Thoughts of providence and time often lead him to contemplate the vastness of the universe in comparison with the minuteness of a single human life, and these passages have a sobering yet poetic resonance. A typical reflection is: 'Whatever befalls you was prepared for you beforehand from eternity, and the thread of causation was spinning from everlasting both your existence and this which befalls you' (10.5). 'Flux and change renew the world incessantly, as the unbroken passage of time makes boundless eternity forever young' (6.15). This fatalism does not lead to apathy but to a curious combination of resolution and melancholy. While determined to persevere in his moral efforts, the author is often resigned to their futility: 'Even if you break your heart, they will do just the same' (8.4); 'Who can change men's convictions?' (9.29).

Like Seneca, though without his frenetic morbidity, Marcus regularly recurs to the subject of death and dissolution, often mentioning distinguished examples, sometimes using the metaphor of actors on the world-stage (12.36, and often). Alexander the Great and his stable boy are as one in death; Augustus, Trajan and Hadrian are gone, and he himself will soon follow (6.24, 4.33). 'All is ephemeral, both what remembers and what is remembered' (4.35). Seldom can a monarch have been so unconvinced of the lasting quality of his own achievement. Philosophy in this text does not set high ideals for radical social or political reforms, but provides a moral framework for his own daily conduct and relations with others. It seems that he sometimes finds his associates hard to bear: 'Say to yourself in the early morning: I shall meet today inquisitive, ungrateful, violent, treacherous, envious and uncharitable men' (2.1). But the dominant note is one of patient tolerance, if sometimes world-weary. 'If he goes wrong, instruct him kindly and point out what is being overlooked. If you fail, blame yourself, or better, not even yourself' (10.5).

VIII

To end this chapter we backtrack chronologically to the reigns of Trajan and Hadrian, and shift our gaze from Rome to mainland Greece. The horizon of thought also broadens when we turn from the intense, claustrophobic mentality and the epigrammatic style of Marcus to the ampler and more optimistic Plutarch, writing in Chaeronea in Boeotia, Greek littérateur and priest of Apollo at nearby Delphi. Besides the *Parallel Lives*, the finest biographies of antiquity, he is also the author of a huge number of works of broadly philosophic content, though these vary from the highly technical to the light and entertaining. His works other than the *Lives* are grouped by editors as *Moralia* or *Moral Writings*: this collection includes some spurious items, and omits many lost but genuine works. Even so, the range defies easy summary. The obvious division is into essays and dialogues. Of the former, some are on specific virtues or vices (Bashfulness, Superstition, Exile, Love of Children); sometimes there is scope for comparison with other moralists (both Seneca and Plutarch wrote on anger). Others are polemical: the attack on Herodotus' mean-spiritedness, the critique, as a Platonist, of Epicurean and Stoic views. Some we might call antiquarian: in the *Greek Questions* and *Roman Questions* there is much curious learning gathered about Greek and Roman religion, ritual traditions and relics of the classical past. (This was a typical interest of the period; it can be seen also in the 'guidebook' of Pausanias.) A few are 'declamatory', arguments forcibly put for their own sake, perhaps as showpiece performances (such as the purely academic argument as to whether the Athenians were more distinguished for their achievements in peace or war). Throughout, however, we are aware of a scholarly mind, well-read, well-drilled in the standard techniques of rhetoric, who applies both philosophy and rhetoric to a very wide range of subjects.

A concern with ethics shades on the one hand into politics. Several works offer advice to men in positions of power: Plutarch had a number of distinguished Roman friends (such as Sosius Senecio, twice consul under Trajan, to whom he dedicated the *Lives* and several other works). He would also have known many Greeks in responsible positions serving the imperial government. On the other hand, there is a strong concern with education and hence with literature (a concern that went back, of course, to Plato himself). A very interesting essay examines the proper principles the young should apply in reading, partly with a view to meeting the stern criticism of the poets in Plato's *Republic*.[23]

The other key area, as is natural for a Platonist, is religion. Plutarch is a fascinating source for intellectual paganism of the second century AD. Two important aspects are his devotion to the life and ceremonies of Delphi and his interest in 'demonology' (theories about spirits that mediate between gods and men – the modern connotations of 'demons' are too negative). Another is his fascination with Plato's metaphysics, whether it be problems such as the location and nature of the Forms, or the account of the origins of the world and of the soul in Plato's difficult cosmological dialogue, the *Timaeus*. In these last areas he prefigures the still more spiritual and mystical Platonism of Plotinus in the next century.

Plutarch's most ambitious literary undertakings were dialogues, again in emulation of Plato. Often he represents a conversation between himself and his close friends at Delphi or elsewhere; a notable dialogue discusses the changes in the nature of the oracle and its responses since classical times. The charming *Erotic Dialogue* is an urbane discussion of love, between men and between man and woman, and of the pleasures and perils of the passion. This work is naturally a tribute to Plato's *Symposium*, but although Plutarch cannot match that dramatic masterpiece, his own effort is highly original and amusing, with a vivid background of a semi-scandalous romance. Another major work, by some judged his finest achievement, is the discussion of the nature of Socrates' divine sign or inner voice: what was it, and how should it be explained? Many of his topics, some of his examples and solutions, are traditional (the question about Socrates' sign had been debated by many others[24]); the learning, the breadth of interests and sympathy, the humane good humour, are Plutarch's own.

Perhaps what comes across most clearly in Plutarch's work is that he cares about his subject matter: he *wants* to put his ideas across, wants to do people good, wants to win them to his own point of view – often intelligent, not always predictable, always generous. Vindictiveness or baseness shock him; so do misguided ideas about human nature or the gods. The *On Superstition* strikes a characteristic note, with a well-turned rhetorical effect: he is maintaining that superstitious fears are worse and more damaging than even atheism. Plutarch introduces his own name and personality to stress the urgency of his argument. 'For myself, at any rate, I would rather people said that there is no one called Plutarch and never has been, than that they should say that Plutarch is an unreliable, unstable man, swift to anger, resentful about accidents, who gets bitter over trifles' (170a). He would have had no need to feel misgivings on this score. Perhaps more than with any other moralist of antiquity, we finish reading his books with a sense of a kindly personality, willing not just to urge and upbraid, but to offer friendship and sympathy.

9

Believers

All men need the gods.
Homer, *Odyssey* 3.48

Evil must inevitably haunt human life and prowl about this earth. That is why
a man should make all haste to escape from earth to heaven, and escape means
becoming as like God as possible, and man becomes like God when he becomes
just and pure, with understanding.

Plato, *Theaetetus* 176a–b

I

To isolate a particular selection of texts from antiquity and identify them as
religious literature would be quite impossible. Religion, both the representation of the gods and the rituals, language and practices of mankind,
permeates classical literature. The opening words of the *Iliad* are an invocation of the Muse; the first episodes of that poem involve supplication, a
form of religious appeal, by a priest of Apollo, and the sending of a plague
by that god in anger when his priest's request is spurned. Much lyric poetry
in Greece was composed for performance at a festival or some other sacred
occasion; Latin poets preserved forms and language suited to such events,
even when their imitation was purely literary. No ode of Pindar fails to
make reference to the gods; often they are more prominent than the victor
himself. Oracles are as frequent in Herodotus as in Sophocles. Orators use
arguments from religion; historians, even when they themselves express
reservations, recognize the importance of religious motives in historical
events. Cult practice forms the subject matter of poetry for Callimachus;
rustic religion is nostalgically described by Virgil and Tibullus. Classical
poetry is unthinkable without mythology, and few myths are wholly concerned with the human plane. The list could go on indefinitely.

The omnipresence of religion in literature mirrors its place in ancient society. What is said here must inevitably oversimplify a complex and constantly developing picture. Although we speak of Greek religion, every city-state had its own practices. While the major gods would be worshipped everywhere, they were not equally important in each state. Athena was important at Athens, Apollo at Sparta, Hera at Samos and so on. Often the community's choice of deity is explicable in terms of its location or character: Poseidon the sea-god is prominent in seafaring and coastal towns. Each deity had many aspects and titles; there were also countless minor divinities, some of them worshipped as a group (e.g. the nymphs). As well as gods, there were the heroes, beings who had (generally) been human once, and who were granted worship after death: some of these, like Achilles and Ajax, were famous in poetry, but others were local figures and would be little known outside their own community. A fuller account of ancient religion would certainly need to draw further distinctions, not least between Greece and Rome. Both, however, can be described as societies in which religious practice and ritual play a fundamental part in defining, unifying and celebrating the community. Rites and prayers surrounded not only weddings and funerals, as in our culture, but all the key stages of life: birth, various stages of coming of age, introduction to one's community, and so forth. Libations (a liquid offering to the god) were poured as a Greek soldier set off to battle; prayers, libations and sacrifice preceded every assembly meeting; sacrifices were offered before entering battle; treaties were sanctified by rituals and oaths. Ancient culture did not separate the religious into a special sphere of its own: in particular, political life and religious activity were intertwined. The Greek city's administrative bodies passed sacred laws, laying down regulations for a cult's procedures and sacrifices. They were also responsible for the decision to consult oracles, or to send a sacred delegation. Homicide trials at Athens were conducted in a religious sanctuary. Declaring war at Rome involved ceremonies conducted by a special category of priests, the fetials. At the end of a war, the military triumph was both a political display and a religious ceremonial. Religion was everywhere, and inescapable. Socrates, whatever his accusers claimed, still observed traditional practice: his dying words refer to a pious task that needs to be performed on his behalf. Even Epicurus advised his followers to perform traditional rites and respect oaths sworn in the gods' name, though they should not accept false popular beliefs.[1]

Tradition – what the ancestors did, what had always been done – was of fundamental importance. The old ways had been sanctioned by generations, and were not to be abandoned lightly. This did not exclude innovation and evolution, but changes took place within the traditional framework. Polytheism was an open system, and new deities were frequently added to the list: at the opening of Plato's *Republic* Socrates and his friends are anticipating the novelties at the festival of Bendis, a goddess recently imported from Thrace: these include a torch-race on horseback. But innovation was not undiscriminating: some deities might be too exotic or some cults too disruptive to absorb readily. Examples are the difficulties the Romans found in dealing with the worship of Bacchus or the cult of Cybele.[2]

The religion of Rome took over or reproduced many aspects of Greek religion, most obviously in its mythology. (Thus the Roman god of war, Mars, was assimilated to the Greek Ares.) In modern discussions ancient Greek and Roman religion is sometimes treated as a unity, and labelled paganism. The term has its uses, but caution is needed. The word 'pagan' becomes current in religious contexts at a late date, and is used by Christians against their opponents. The sense in which it is used is debatable: it may mean 'country-dweller', reflecting the swifter growth of Christianity in the big towns. At all events, it is clearly intended as contemptuous, and groups together dismissively all the varied and abundant forms of non-Christian worship. Arguably it should be used only in the later period of interaction and opposition between traditional polytheism and Christianity, which we will treat at the end of this chapter. However, with this reservation, 'pagan' will be used when convenient. Some features of ancient religion are certainly shown in sharp relief when contrasted with the Jewish and Christian tradition.

It was evidently possible for ancient worshippers to conceptualize 'our' religion as opposed to that of other races. For Herodotus, 'common temples and sacrifices of the gods' formed one of the defining elements of 'Greekness' as opposed to other, 'barbarian' peoples (8.144). But what neither the Greek nor the Roman world possessed was a Torah, a set of sacred books like those which the Jews ascribed to Moses (books were used in the Mystery cults, but as we shall see, these were exceptional in a number of ways). Nor did they have anything like a creed or 10 Commandments, an established Church, or even a special group of authoritative spokesmen on religious matters. Priests did not form a loftier hierarchy; although prophets and diviners accompanied generals in the field, they could only advise, not dictate.[3] At Rome, the major religious priesthoods were held mostly by the same families and even the same individuals as those who occupied the major magistracies.[4] Julius Caesar became pontifex maximus, Cicero was proud to be elected to the college of augurs. It follows that 'paganism' was less rigidly defined and more open than Christianity: the antithesis between orthodox belief and heresy is not a classical concept. Paganism did however recognize sacrilege and blasphemous acts, and punished them, as the Athenians punished those who had profaned the Mysteries in 415 BC (Thuc. 6.27–9, 53ff.); but speculative and even scandalous views, even the expression of ideas which verged on the atheistic, only rarely attracted retribution, and usually at times of extreme tension or crisis. Separate groups or sects did exist, notably the Orphics and Pythagoreans, who defined themselves partly by abstaining from the normal rites and in particular from animal sacrifice; they were small minorities, but tolerated as eccentrics, not persecuted.[5]

All of this leads to perhaps the most important generalization about ancient religion, that it is more a matter of acts than beliefs, of ritual rather than dogma.[6] 'The things done' are very prominent in ancient discussions of religion, and many moderns have followed their lead. What mattered was that a citizen should participate in the communal acts of the city, and that the gods should receive their due. The religion of the community celebrates the city's achievements and seeks to ensure its preservation: on another level communal cult acts establish or reinforce the solidarity of the community or specific groups within it, partly by celebrating local traditions. (Hence for instance the founder or past leaders of a state are often worshipped as gods or at least as heroes.) The Romans in particular believed that the gods had favoured them because of their piety, and some outsiders, notably Polybius, were at least convinced that their success was due in part to the social stability generated by this piety.[7] Prayer, thanksgiving, dedications, sacrifice, are gifts to the gods, thanking them for benefits received and seeking their continued favour in the future ('do ut des': I give that you may give). It is assumed that the gods can respond to human appeals, and may be swayed. Plato makes Socrates deride this as turning piety into a kind of trading transaction, but it is clear that the principle is deep-rooted in ancient practice (and not unknown to Christian).[8] It also operated on the level of individual religious devotion, as is shown by the innumerable dedications at shrines in fulfilment of a vow ('ex voto' offerings) – these fulfil a promise to show appropriate gratitude if the god helps the devotee in some endeavour. It is of course possible to overstate the case: although Cicero in one place defines religion as 'cult of the gods', he elsewhere declares that the best worship is the piety of a pure heart.[9] Ritual does not account for everything, and worshippers cannot have approached the altars with wholly vacant minds. But belief is hard to determine, and those whose thoughts on religion we know about are seldom typical.

II

Religion is related to myth but not identical with it, even when cult and myth may concern the same divinity. Many lesser deities have no myths or at least none that enter the mainstream of literature. More important, myths are of very varied types, and few if any embody what the ancients would regard as central religious truths. It was acknowledged that poets invented much of their material: Hesiod and Solon comment on the lies told by bards, and the different literary versions of myths varied so much that it was clear not all of them could be true. The gods' appearance, attributes and to some degree their relationships (though these too could vary) were the essentials, often represented in art; but much of the colourful detail and divine comedy in Homer would be taken by many readers as delightful poetic imagination. Already Homer adapted and even invented stories according to his needs. To draw attention to one's use of a new or unusual version becomes a sophisticated literary technique.[10] Nevertheless, new versions normally remained close to the old in some respects: Pindar even while denying Demeter's cannibalism retains the detail of Pelops' ivory shoulder, which needs the older version to explain it (*Olympian* 1.23ff.).

We may still ask what myths do and how they are used, but must not expect a simple answer: there is no 'key to all mythologies'. Some myths or mythical conceptions seem to explain features of the natural world (storms come because Zeus is angry and hurls thunderbolts); others evidently explain or provide an aetiology for rituals, cult objects (e.g. unusual statues) or taboos. Other myths, particularly those associated with a particular city, said something about the character or defined the priorities of that city. The tradition that Athens was once ruled by Cecrops, a monarch half-man and half-snake, who grew from the soil, is connected with the Athenians' belief that they were 'autochthonous' ('of the land itself'), that they had never migrated to Attica but had always lived there. One category of tales is commonly known as 'charter myths', usually involving some divine edict or action which establishes a practice or institution. The myth of the institution of the Areopagus, the Athenian homicide court, by Athena, as dramatized in Aeschylus, is of this type. Sometimes this might be a justification for conquest. A lion was ravaging the territory of a people in north Africa: in response to a proclamation, the nymph Cyrene slew the lion and was rewarded with the kingdom which subsequently bore her name. This story seems to legitimize Greek colonization of this area.[11] Gods might be claimed as ancestors for families, especially royalty: both the Spartans' royal houses traced their ancestry back to Heracles. Heroic genealogy and mapping of kinship between different peoples often explains or justifies their later relationships (as also in the Bible: the tribes of Israel in Genesis).[12] Thus the Athenians asserted their special status and authority over the Achaean and Ionian peoples by a myth in which an Athenian princess, Creusa, marries Xuthus, and gives birth to Achaeus and Ion, the ancestors of those ethnic groups (Hesiod, fr 10a). Euripides in his *Ion* goes further, making Ion, ancestor of the Ionians, the son of Apollo by Creusa, while Dorus and

Achaeus are given inferior status by being the sons of the mortal Xuthus. As the Athenians themselves were Ionian in descent, this is obviously a form of racial one-upmanship. Changes in myth, as in cultic practice, often reflect socio-political developments. (Thus the effeminacy and decadence of the Trojans in fifth-century literature, though not without background in Homer, are exaggerated as a result of the victory over contemporary Persia.)

Political, racial and civic themes do not exhaust the wealth of Greek mythology. Many of the most famous myths, even if set in particular Greek states, seem to be concerned more with aspects of the human condition. The inevitability of death is the most obvious: yet Odysseus, Heracles, Theseus and others succeeded in returning from the underworld. Odysseus is offered immortality; Heracles eventually becomes a god. There is a recurring interest in exploring the border-area between human and divine, mortality and immortality: but the price paid for crossing the line can be high. Other themes include forbidden sexual acts (incest, bestiality) or horrendous crimes (matricide, infanticide). By describing exceptional figures who violate taboos or cross forbidden boundaries, the storyteller reinforces the need for 'normal' people to accept these limitations. Also recurrent are the stories in which a mortal challenges a god and is struck down or otherwise punished for excess (Pentheus against Dionysus is the most obvious case). The *hubris*-motif, popularly associated with tragedy, permeates many other genres.[13]

The openness and adaptability of paganism, the absence of a creed or prescribed set of beliefs, meant that writers were not bound to abide by any particular rules in dealing with religious themes. Different genres could handle the gods in very different ways, in accordance with their conventions and styles. The menacing Dionysus of the *Bacchae* is quite unlike the buffoonish coward of the *Frogs*, yet these plays were produced within a year of each other and in the same theatre.[14] Genre variation had this effect even in the works of a single poet: Horace's handling of themes such as inspiration or divine intervention is different in the *Epistles* from the *Odes*. In different contexts individual Greeks and Romans might take different views of religion in general and specific doctrines or practices in particular. Varro maintained that there were three kinds of theology, three different ways of talking about the gods: that of the poets, that of the state, and that of the philosophers (Augustine, *City of God* 6.5). The distinction is essentially between mythology, cultic prescriptions, and theoretical discourse. In different types of writing one or other of these would be most prominent, although many authors combine them; none of the three can have an exclusive claim to be dealing with 'real' religion.

There have been many attempts to criticize, explain or defuse mythology: these continue down to our own time, and are not confined to myths of the classical world. From an early stage Greeks (and later Romans) tried to explain myths in other terms. One approach was to rationalize, often by reducing the scale and the improbabilities in the story. Thus Hecataeus rationalized the story that Heracles brought a three-headed dog back from the underworld: more likely it was a monstrous snake 'and it was called the dog of Hades because anyone bitten by it was killed immediately by the venom' (*FGH* 1F27; cf 19). Miracles and supernatural interventions could be explained in naturalistic terms. Similar is the use of physical allegory. Prodicus thought that Demeter in a sense *was* bread (B5); 'most moderns', according to Socrates, identified Athena with intelligence and thought (Plato, *Cratylus* 407a). This approach is first found in Theagenes (sixth century BC). Trying to make credible sense of Homer's tale of the battle of the gods (*Iliad* 21), he argued that the gods represented different elements in conflict with one another: air versus fire, for example.[15] Here etymology came to the reader's aid, as the name Hera can be seen as an anagram for the Greek word for air. Explanations of this kind based on verbal derivation multiplied in the Hellenistic period: the monstrous father god Cronos, who devoured his children, was really Chronos (Time), because Time devours all things! (Cic. *On the Nature of the Gods* 2.64). Varro wrote a long treatise on these philological fantasies. Another resource was moral allegory: myths could be read as offering lessons or sermons on human life. The *Iliad* shows the perils of anger; the *Odyssey* allegorizes the voyage of life; the enchantress Circe represents the temptations of the flesh, which can transform men into beasts.[16] We may smile at these interpretations, but by the Roman period at latest poets were aware of them and sometimes made use of them.[17] But in some authors these reductive readings were carried to ludicrous lengths: for the minor exegete Palaephatus, Medea did not magically rejuvenate an old man in a cauldron, but invented hair-dye and the steam bath![18]

Plato in the *Phaedrus* enjoys himself at the expense of these ingenuities. As Socrates and Phaedrus wander in the countryside outside Athens, Phaedrus asks if this is not the spot from which the north wind, Boreas, was said to have abducted the Princess Orithyia. Socrates replies that the place in question is some distance downstream. Phaedrus asks in surprise whether Socrates really believes in such tales. The reply is a mischievous and suggestive passage.

> I should be doing nothing unusual if I did disbelieve it, in the fashion of the intellectuals; in which case I could do a clever rationalisation and say that it was the North Wind that threw her down on the rocks nearby while she was playing, and that after she'd died people said that she had been carried away by Boreas. . . . But in fact, Phaedrus, I think that accounts of this sort are very charming, but really they are the sort of task that suits an ingenious and

laborious person, one who is not altogether enviable, and here's why – after this performance he next has to set to rights the form of the Hippocentaurs, and after that the Chimaera, and in come flocking a whole host of Gorgons and Pegasuses, and all sorts of unmanageable creatures, strange and miraculous in their natures. If our sceptic is going to expound each and every one of these according to probability, using a rather clumsy kind of ingenuity, he is going to need a great deal of leisure time. As for me, I simply don't have the leisure for that, and the reason, my friend, is this. I cannot yet, as the Delphic maxim has it, *know myself*. And it seems ludicrous to me to investigate matters which are beyond my scope while remaining ignorant of this. (*Phdr.* 229c sqq.)

Ethical self-scrutiny matters more to Socrates than up-to-the-minute intellectual antics.

Criticism of the impropriety or absurdity of myths was more common than attack on ritual or cult practice. The latter can be found, but usually only in the mouths of philosophers. Heraclitus scoffed at some conventional practices: 'men vainly purify themselves of blood-guilt by defiling themselves with blood, as though one who had stepped into mud were to wash with mud . . . and they pray to statues, as if one were to carry on a conversation with people's houses, not recognising the true nature of gods or demi-gods' (B5). Blood sacrifices were condemned not only by the vegetarian Pythagoreans but by Empedocles and Theophrastus; perhaps also, at least implicitly, in some moving lines of Lucretius (2.352–66). The high-minded Plotinus disapproved of those who attended religious festivals only for the fringe benefits of ample food and drink (5.5.11). How one should pray was also raised as a philosophic issue, and naive requests for purely material blessings condemned.[19] It was foolish to represent the gods anthropomorphically, said Xenophanes: 'if cattle and horses had hands, or were able to draw with their hands, then horses would portray gods in the form of horses, and cattle like cattle' (B15, cf 23). Varro appears to have thought that worship in early Rome did not involve statues or other visual representations, and that it was the better for that.[20] For some thinkers, the virtuous soul was more important than ritual action: 'He who has knowledge of the gods worships the gods', wrote Seneca, and 'The good worshipper is the one who imitates those he worships' (*Letters* 95.47, 50).[21] But normally philosophers accepted the traditional religious practice, though sometimes offering a more sophisticated rationale. Thus Stoics accepted divination, but not on the Homeric model, with one-off signals being sent by independent deities to their favourites in response to prayer; rather, the cosmos was seen as one integrated and ordered fabric in which particular phenomena – the weather, shooting stars, the condition of a sacrificial victim – reflected events current or impending in the great structure.[22] Even without such arguments, religion could be seen as acceptable on social grounds: the beliefs of the masses must not be undermined by disturbing novelties, lest morality decay.

III

These generalizations are necessary, but may seem to be taking us too far away from the examination of specific literary works. The complexity of the background does mean that this chapter engages less with particular authors and more with broad historical context and development than the rest of the book; but some texts will still claim our special attention (though these can only be a tiny selection of those which are relevant).

Two examples that illustrate some of the points made so far are the Homeric hymn to Demeter and the account of Romulus in Livy's first book. The 'Homeric' hymns, though ascribed to Homer and composed in a style modelled on epic, are of diverse length, date and origin. The longer, more interesting examples are probably from the seventh and sixth centuries: of these the one to Demeter, a text of some 500 lines, is pre-eminent.[23] Like most Greek hymns, it has an extended narrative element: it tells the story of how Persephone was abducted by Hades, how her mother Demeter searched for her throughout the earth, and how eventually they were reunited, but Persephone having eaten food offered her in the world below was obliged to spend part of the year there, and to become the consort of Hades. All of this, we are told from the start, is by the will of Zeus, the girl's father, though it brings pain and distress to her mother. There are further complexities: during her wanderings, Demeter, disguised as an old woman, comes to the royal court of Celeus, king of Eleusis in Attica, and is permitted to act as nurse to an infant child; she takes steps to give the child immortality through bathing him in fire, but the mother in panic interferes, thus angering the goddess and denying the boy eternal life.

> Ignorant and foolish is the race of mankind, unable to foresee the portion of good or of evil that is to come! For indeed you have committed a ruinous act, beyond all cure, in your folly. Let the oath of the gods, the unappeaseable water of Styx bear witness, I would have made your son immortal and ageless for all time, and granted him deathless honour. But now there is no way for him to elude death and the fates. Yet still will he have deathless honour, because he sat upon my knees and slept in my embrace . . . (256–64)

After her departure the mortal servants hurry to pick up and soothe the child, but he remains inconsolable; 'for now the nurses that held him were of inferior kind' (291). But at the end of the poem the Eleusinians, having built a temple to Demeter, institute the rites which are to become the Eleusinian Mysteries, one of the most famous cults of the ancient world, involving initiation, a revelation of secret truths, and a promise of benefits in this world and the next.

Like several other Homeric hymns, this is a narrative of how the world came to be as it is and how the deities concerned (Demeter and her daughter) obtained their present powers and status. On one level, it explains why summer and winter alternate: winter is the time when Persephone is absent from the world above and Demeter is grieving, so that no crops grow. On another, it gives an aetiology for the Mysteries of Eleusis; we find in the narrative a number of details which anticipate various aspects of the cult. On a third, the main plot enacts a drama of a maiden's coming of age, when a father's decision leads to an uncertain future, and marriage separates her from the mother she loves and unites her with a husband who is unknown and therefore alarming. As often, myth hugely enhances the realistic concerns of life: Demeter's grief is such that she brings devastation to the earth's crops, and Persephone's husband is the most terrifying of all, the lord of the underworld. The internal drama involving the royal child of Eleusis involves sound psychology: Demeter finds consolation for the loss of her child by caring for another's. But through the interaction between goddess and humanity the poem also implies a vision of human life: literal immortality is denied to the son of Celeus through human folly (like the folly of Eve, or of Pandora in opening the fatal box); but there is compensation because the Mysteries of Eleusis will offer comfort and hope to mankind, for initiation is thought to ensure a better fate in the afterlife. 'Blessed among mortal men is he who has seen these things', says the poet; 'but he who has not been admitted to the holy rites and has no part in them can never have a share of the same things in the rotting darkness when dead' (480–2). This summary does not exhaust the poem and cannot do justice to its haunting beauty; but it may give some idea of how myth, cult and belief can be united in an artistic whole.

Romans absorbed and imitated Greek myths, but their originality lay in the narratives about their city's past, which embody their values and their sensibility. Particularly for the early period their history is hard to distinguish from what may well be judged myths. Chronology and genealogy were fluid:[24] for Ennius, Romulus was the grandson of Aeneas, but by the time of Livy and Virgil scholars had calculated that this left 400 years unaccounted for between the fall of Troy and the founding of Rome, so the gap was filled by a series of kings of the interim foundation, Alba Longa. Livy's narrative briefly summarizes a fair number of famous elements: others such as Dionysius and Ovid supply additional detail. Romulus and Remus were sons of Mars by the Vestal Rhea Silvia, but were exposed to die; instead a wolf looked after them until a shepherd found and looked after the children. Eventually they discovered their identity, overthrew the cruel ruler of Alba who had usurped their grandfather's throne, and resolved to found a new city. Bird-signs allocated the supremacy to Romulus (not unambiguously); Remus was to be the junior partner. Mocking the inadequacy of the walls of Rome, Remus leapt over them before they had reached a man's height; in anger Romulus killed him – 'so perish all who assail the walls of Rome!' (in some versions this act is ascribed to a soldier acting on Romulus' orders). Some other episodes of Romulus' career are also notoriously disreputable: the gathering of criminals and refugees to populate his city; the abduction of the Sabine women to provide wives for his citizens. The end of his life was controversial too. After a 40-year reign he died in battle but his body vanished, allegedly in a storm; the Roman people, bereft, invoked their king and father in lamentation, but were soon reassured by the declaration of a man called Julius Proculus that Romulus had appeared to him in a dream and ordered him to report that Rome was destined to world empire; the Romans concluded that he had joined the ranks of the gods (Livy 1.16). Romulus was not, however, worshipped under that name, but identified with the older divinity Quirinus (a figure whose name is connected with Quirites, a term for Roman citizens).[25]

We do not know how old the stories of Romulus and Remus were: some think them almost as old as Rome itself, others trace them back to specific periods in the mid-Republic, connecting the antagonism between the two brothers with the conflict of patricians and plebeians. Some elements are clearly intended to characterize Rome as a nation: the founder's father is Mars, he was raised on the milk of a wolf, he wins the 'supreme prize' by killing the commander-in-chief of opposing forces, he foretells Rome's military successes. But others are more disturbing: the fratricide which so many writers took as a paradigm or symbol of civil war, and the violent means used to obtain women, convey so negative a picture that some have supposed these must be inventions by enemies of Rome. If so, they have been absorbed in the Roman self-image, perhaps to make the nation seem all the more formidable. Even the fratricide can be seen as a precedent for the Roman willingness to sacrifice personal bonds for the public good: comparable are the first Brutus executing his sons for conspiracy against the new Republic, or Horatius slaying his sister because she dared to mourn her fiancé, a member of the enemy side. 'Born not for one's own sake but for the father-land' is a favourite phrase of Cicero's.[26] Livy also mentions, though dismissing, the tradition that Romulus was loved more by the populace than by the senators, and that he might even have been murdered by the senators (there are echoes of the fate of Julius Caesar here – history is anticipated in myth). In general the emphasis of Livy is to stress that Rome's beginnings were special, and that this reflected the workings of divine will or fate (1.4.1, 1.15.6). But Romulus was a potent figure in Roman thought, and an ambivalent one, just as the kingship itself was a symbol both of glorious origins and arbitrary tyranny.[27] Successive political leaders in the late Republic cherished the idea that they were in one way or another new founders, heirs of Romulus;[28] but Octavian's advisors, mindful of the assassination of Caesar, prudently dissuaded him from taking the name of Romulus (Suet. *Aug.* 7). Nevertheless, in adopting the alternative 'Augustus' (the holy one) he was hinting at a parallel with the first monarch, since a line of Ennius had described Romulus as founding Rome 'with holy auspices' (*augusto augurio*) (*Ann.* 469 Warmington). The adaptability of the myth is nicely illustrated by the passages of Virgil which even erase the fratricide: in the golden age of idealized early Rome (soon to be renewed) the poet envisages 'Remus and his brother' ruling together in harmony (*Geo.* 2.533, cf. *Aen.* 1.292).

These two narratives differ in emphasis, partly because of the difference between prose and verse: gods are at home in verse, while prose tends to look at things more from the human standpoint. Both, however, are firmly associated with a specific local community, Eleusis or Rome; both deal with origins and explanations; both explore the boundaries or transition-point between mortality and divinity; both give an idea of the power of the gods and their influence on human affairs. If the hymn is concerned more with the ordering of the cosmos and the historian with political acts, that primarily arises from the nature of the genres, but it is not altogether an unfaithful reflection of the Greek and Roman mentalities.

IV

The deification of Romulus-Quirinus demands further attention. Moderns probably find it easier to imagine a static polytheistic system than one in which new gods who were once men are added to the pantheon; still harder for us to accept is the worship of human beings in their own lifetime, which we meet at least as early as Alexander the Great and frequently in the Roman Empire. Partly this difficulty arises from an exaggerated view of what the term 'god' implies in the classical world. In a polytheistic framework there are many gods of different powers, status and scope; new ones can readily be accommodated. Mythology already told of gods who had been born of mortals and lived on earth before joining the immortals (Heracles, Dionysus). Moreover, abstractions or natural forces can be conceived as divine, because they have an effect on human life: hence the

Sun is a god, but so are Harmony, Memory or Mildew! (Cicero has fun with these ideas in *On the Nature of the Gods*.) We have seen that ancient religion is closely related to the social and political structure of ancient society, and that it has the flexibility to adapt to changes in that society. It was therefore natural for those who made an important impact on an ancient state to be admitted to a place in its religious institutions: this was regularly the case with the founders of cities (hence Romulus), founders of colonies, and sometimes also notable leaders, generals and even athletes. Traditionally these honours, heroic or divine, were posthumous, but this convention was already being eroded by the fourth century BC.[29] Extreme achievement, like that of Alexander or Julius Caesar, earned special honours; but even before Caesar, Greek states had offered divine honours to Roman governors and other dignitaries.[30] Some of them, like Cicero and the Emperor Tiberius, were reluctant to accept these tributes; but they continued to be offered.

The problems are highlighted by the honours granted to Demetrius Poliorcetes, king of Macedon and conqueror or benefactor of Athens, and in particular by a famous hymnic poem of *c.*291 BC, performed at Athens in his honour.[31] Even ancient readers regarded this as sycophantic adulation – Athenaeus is shocked by it. The song addressed him as son of Poseidon and Aphrodite, and contained lines like 'the other gods are far away, or lack ears, or pay no heed to us; but you are present here, not in wood or stone but in reality'. Yet Demetrius' deeds were remarkable, and Macedon's power in the new world of the Hellenistic age was something the Athenians had to come to terms with. The honorific context is important; what mattered was not whether the citizens really believed in Demetrius' divinity, but that the ruler should be given the most abundant honours the city could provide. Similar considerations apply to other examples of ruler-cult. In different contexts scepticism and humour were possible, even normal. An orator could say 'let Alexander be son of Zeus, or Poseidon if he prefers'.[32] Seneca's satire on Claudius' deification has been mentioned before. A witty ruler himself could jest at the assumptions: Vespasian's dying remark was said to have been 'Dear me, I believe I'm turning into a god.'[33]

Divinity was granted, if at all, to figures of exceptional status or achievements. The afterlife for normal people was a shadowy affair. Homer had presented the underworld unforgettably in book 11 of the *Odyssey* (though this episode comes in the narrative of Odysseus, and so is not necessarily endorsed by the bard): a realm of eerie darkness and decay, insubstantial shades, special punishments for certain great sinners. In general the religion of Greece and Rome was focused on this life. The aftermath was defined negatively, and often regarded as wholly uncertain.[34] Plato's myths of the soul's journey after death became ever more elaborate, but are not presented as definitive: indeed, he regularly emphasizes that they are only approximations or guesses at the hoped-for truth (esp. *Phaedo* 114d). Prose authors often use 'if' clauses, and the degree of assurance varies according to author and context: 'if there is any perception in the underworld, as we suppose . . .' (Hyperides 6.43); 'if there is any dwelling place for the spirits of the just; if, as the wise believe, noble souls do not perish with the body . . .' (Tac. *Agric.* 46). When Servius Sulpicius writes to console Cicero on the death of his daughter, he says little of her present condition, only remarking that 'if there is sensation even among the dead, she surely desires that you should not grieve' (*Letters to Friends* 4.5). The Mystery religions were the chief exception: as we have seen, those of Demeter did promise a better life after death for the initiate, and other rites, including those of Bacchus, seem to have given similar assurances. We cannot say how confident initiates felt about this: perhaps it was often regarded as a prudent form of insurance. Naturally, ideas about the soul and life after death were complex and contradictory, and differed in different periods. Even the same person might change his mind: the elderly Cephalus in Plato's *Republic* comments wisely that when people are young they have no thought of death and scoff at the old tales, but when they are frail and failing they begin to brood on their misdeeds and feel anxious lest the tales of retribution in the afterlife may be true after all (*Rep.* 330d–331b). Although Lucretius urged mankind to turn to Epicureanism and be free of the fear of death, Cicero can say that tales of punishment in Hades are not taken seriously.[35] The underworld and its usual inhabitants do figure in Virgil, but this is epic colouring. In the same way five out of Seneca's ten dramas contain extended descriptions of the sufferings of the canonical sinners. Poetic set-pieces are an unsafe guide to popular belief. Even grave-inscriptions have their conventions.[36]

V

Already in ancient times we can detect a fascination with the religions and rituals of the East. Even gods who were not in fact foreign were sometimes regarded as oriental intruders: this is how Dionysus is presented in the *Bacchae*, yet his name already figures in the 'Linear B' tablets of Mycenean times. Sometimes the tendency is to equate foreign deities with Greek equivalents (as Romans identified their own gods with those of Greeks), but in other passages the emphasis is on the foreignness, the novelty and exoticism of the new arrival. This ambiguous attitude to 'foreign' gods has affected much modern discussion: indeed, at various times the importation of 'Eastern' elements or 'Oriental' cults has been blamed for the 'decline' of ancient religion or even of classical civilization! Arguments of this kind are clearly rooted in cultural or racial bias and are ill-supported by the evidence. Greek civilization had been enriched, not corrupted, by contact with the East from the earliest times. Homer's epics include many features which derive from Eastern storytelling. The mutual devotion of Gilgamesh and Enkidu is echoed in the love between Achilles and Patroclus; the distressed appeal of Aphrodite to Zeus in book 5 of the *Iliad* seems to descend from another scene in the Gilgamesh epic, between the goddess Ishtar (a close analogue to Aphrodite) and the sky-god Anu.[37] The festival of the Thracian goddess Bendis is newly established in Athens at the opening of Plato's *Republic*, set in roughly the 420s, and it would be implausible to put the beginnings of 'decline' as far back as the age of Pericles. But for some purposes, and in some contexts, 'foreign' elements might be stressed, for literary frisson or for polemical, sometimes political ends.

A notable case is that of Cybele, the Great Mother of the Gods, at Rome. Her cult, originating in Phrygia (Asia Minor), was the first of the 'oriental' religions to reach Rome. It was imported at a time of crisis, during the second Carthaginian war, in obedience to the Sibylline books, a prophetic compilation which the Romans regularly consulted when in difficulties. A black stone, symbol of the goddess, was brought from Pergamum, and in 204 BC a festival was established in her honour, but it seems that once the Romans had learned more of her cult and the ways of her priests, unease emerged. Roman citizens were strictly forbidden to participate; the priest and priestess who had come from Phrygia were segregated.[38] Special rules, again aimed at separation of different parts of the community, were imposed on the festival. This ban, which continued until the time of the Emperor Claudius, surely arose from the alarm which the Romans felt at the wildness of the music, the ecstatic dancing, above all the self-castration of the priests of the cult, who seem to have commemorated by this act the death and rebirth of Cybele's consort Attis. Roman religion was receptive to new gods and innovations, but Roman morality frowned on disruption of public order or ordered sexual practice.

In this case we have no parallel to the hymn to Demeter, no celebratory foundation-myth of the rites. What we do have is hardly less valuable. Catullus' *Attis* (poem 63) is perhaps the most extraordinary poem in Latin literature. It is a poem which tells how Attis in his madness castrated himself and became a devotee of this cult; but here Attis is not an Asiatic god but a youthful Greek, not a willing consort but a helpless and despairing slave of the dominating goddess. In less than 100 lines, composed in a peculiar metre that seems to have been reserved for verse dealing with this cult, he vividly describes the ecstasy of Attis and his fellow-devotees as they race across land and sea: the pace of the narration and the enthusiasm of Attis'

cries propel the reader forward with almost equal eagerness. Catullus pro-
ceeds to narrate the awakening from madness, the despair of the young man
at what he has done to himself – the poet boldly introduces the feminine
gender to bring out his emasculation. We hear his lamentation for the full
humanity and the life he has sacrificed. Abruptly, the scene shifts to Cybele:
enraged at Attis' recalcitrance, she unleashes the lions which are regularly
associated with her in the cult, and which now drive Attis into the deep
woods of Asia: 'there evermore, for the full span of his life, he remained her
slave'. The poem ends on a note of pious dread:

> Goddess, great goddess Cybele, goddess who rules over Dindymus,
> far from my house, my lady, be all the madness that you send;
> drive others in passionate flight, drive others on in madness.   (91–3)

Interpretation is baffled by this work. The notion that it allegorically presents
some aspect of Catullus' own sexuality is a ludicrous example of the biographical approach taken to extremes; and not many critics nowadays would
resort to the escape route of assuming that he is translating a Greek original
(which would still need explanation in its turn). Indeed, the very fact that this
is a drama involving a foreigner, a Greek, seems crucial: we recall that no
Roman was permitted to become a priest of this cult. By showing how the
power of the cult can drive a civilized youth to self-mutilation, Catullus does
not glorify Cybele but shows her to be an awe-inspiring yet supremely alien
deity; on the other hand, there is no smug self-satisfaction, as if to say 'we
Romans of course know better'. The act of Attis, like the goddess herself, is
both astounding and terrible. That makes it a suitable subject for Catullus,
preoccupied as always with intense and often painful emotions.

The rites of the Magna Mater are as hard for us to fathom as for the
Roman observer, amazed or fascinated. Few of these cults were articulate:
although many brief dedications and thank-offerings do survive, we have no
detailed texts composed by adherents describing or justifying their practices.
Closest to an exception is the account by Apuleius of Lucius' initiation to
the cult and priesthood of Isis (*Met.* xi, p. 155), but that narrative is
couched in a uniquely elaborate literary style and perhaps involves exaggeration and irony. Some support for the lush Apuleian enthusiasm is found
in the sparer comment of Aristotle centuries earlier, who declared that
those undergoing Mysteries should not 'learn' but be affected, 'suffer' or
'experience' (*mathein* vs. *pathein*) (fr. 15).[39] Plutarch, Apuleius' contemporary, goes further, although again we must recognize that a remarkable
experience is being communicated through heightened language and metaphor. At the time of death, he writes, the soul suffers an experience similar
to those who celebrate great initiations.

Wandering astray at the beginning, tiresome walking in circles, some frighten-
ing paths in darkness that lead nowhere; then, immediately before the end
all the terrible things, panic and shivering and sweat and amazement. And
then some wonderful light comes to meet you, pure regions and meadows
are there to greet you, with sounds and dances and solemn, sacred words
and holy views; and there the initiate, perfect by now, set free and loose from
all bondage, walks about crowned with a wreath, celebrating the festival
together with the other sacred and pure people, and he looks down on the
uninitiated, unpurified crowd in this world in mud and fog beneath his
feet. (fr. 178)

It is not clear here how much describes a ritual experience of the living
individual (at Eleusis?) and how much is imaginative embroidery, in the
manner of Platonic myth, of the soul's journey after death; but whichever
application we choose for each point, we can see from this passage how
natural it was for Christian interpreters to see the Mysteries as the closest
approximation in paganism to Christian beliefs.

VI

A different kind of religious tradition is represented by the Jews. Unlike
pagan worshippers, the Jews had not only highly elaborate cults and religious
prohibitions, but a body of sacred texts, above all the Pentateuch, in which
their sacred laws are explained alongside their history. Jewish history in fact
overlapped with Greek at a number of points. Persia was crucial for both,
but the Greeks saw her as a threatening invader and as the archetype of
absolute monarchy, whereas the Jews revered Cyrus the Great for restoring
them from enslavement in Babylon to their own country and allowing them
to continue their own religious practice freely. (Persian religious tolerance is
well-attested.) Yet the Greeks seem to have known little of the Jews before
Alexander and even after that to have paid little attention to them.[40] Jews
spread throughout the Mediterranean (the 'Diaspora' or Dispersal), and
inevitably those dwelling in Greece or Egypt diverged from the ways of
their homeland. Greek being the most widely current language, Jews made
use of it and many would use it in everyday life without frequent recourse
to Hebrew or Aramaic. The great Jewish thinker Philo of Alexandria knew
no Hebrew. There was some adaptation to Greek ways: 'Hellenization'
could become an issue. Jews often adopted Greek names, though sometimes
kept a Hebrew one as well. They were attracted to the gymnasium and the
theatre. Jewish writings in Greek were a natural consequence. Most important were the sacred books themselves, the 'Septuagint' or Greek translation
of the Old Testament, probably begun in Egypt in the third century BC (but

the story of its being commissioned by one of the Ptolemies is a fiction). But there is small evidence that anyone other than Jews or converts read such texts. The first certain quotation by a pagan writer from the Bible is in the book *On the sublime*, ascribed to Longinus (first or second century AD). The author is discussing the magnificent presentation of the gods in Homer, and by way of digression also quotes 'let there be light; and there was light' from the first chapter of Genesis. He refers to the author as 'the lawgiver of the Jews, no ordinary man – for he understood and expressed God's power in accordance with its worth' (9.9). But much of Longinus' work is driven by the need to reply to a book by Caecilius, who was a Jew. Longinus himself may only have dipped into Genesis (the first chapter, at least!), or even derived the quotation from his opponent.

Although the narrative power of the Books of Samuel and Kings can match that of Herodotus, and the historical vision of the biblical authors can also bear the comparison, it does not seem that any affinities arose from direct contact. Classical writers went their own way. Later, the followers of Aristotle seem to have regarded the Jews as Eastern wise men, like the Persian Zoroastrians; Megasthenes compared them with Indian philosophers; another writer bizarrely made Moses the teacher of Orpheus. Fragments survive of a cross-cultural oddity: a version, composed in the second century BC, of the story of Moses from Exodus in the language and form of a Greek tragedy. In this curious hybrid the burning bush and Moses engage in dialogue in tragic trimeters, and later an Egyptian messenger narrates the drowning of Pharaoh's army in the Red Sea.[41]

The Jews were respected, but regarded as odd or antisocial. They were right, in pagan eyes, to revere the ways of their ancestors, but their insistence on one God who would brook no rivals seemed narrow-minded to the Greco-Roman world. Actual hostility is relatively rare, though in Hellenistic Alexandria there was constant conflict between the Greek and Jewish community, which we can follow in the works of Philo and in Roman edicts from Augustus onwards that attempt to control this antagonism. Although the Romans were generally well enough disposed to the Jews, they did not engage with their tradition on an intellectual or cultural level as they did pre-eminently with the Greeks (Virgil's 'Messianic' *Eclogue* 4 may be an exception, although even here Jewish ideas could have been transmitted second hand). Tacitus feels obliged to include an ethnographic description of the Jews before embarking on the Jewish Revolt crushed by Titus; but his account is a startling farrago of misinformation and prejudice (*Hist.* 5.2–10). Romans would have learned much more from the detailed writings of Josephus, the Jewish historian writing self-vindicating works in Greek at the Flavian court. They probably did read his *Jewish War*, but it is hard to imagine many non-Jews studying the far longer *Jewish Antiquities* or the polemics against Apion in which he tries to refute various anti-Jewish allegations going back to the early biblical era.

Unlike the Jews, the Christians were not in a position to present their religion as traditional practice. From the start their claims were of a kind that pagans would find hard to accept: 'we teach Christ crucified, to the Jews a stumbling-block, and to the Greeks foolishness' (Paul, *I Cor.* 1.21). Many pagans would have been receptive to the ethical teachings of Jesus (much is indeed paralleled in ancient popular moralizing); it is the larger claims which they found unacceptable. That God had become man was grotesque enough to those who, following Plato, saw divinity as eternal and unchanging; that God in human form should be subject to the basest of deaths, as a common criminal, was absurd, but still more so was the notion of his resurrection. Critics of Christian teaching also attacked the notion of the resurrection of mankind at the Last Judgement – in bodily form at that. Pagans were quick to discover the uneasy relation between Jewish Scripture and Christian thinking (already in the second century Marcion, who was later branded a heretic, saw the basic incompatibility of Old and New Testament[42]) Infighting and sectarian disputes among the Christians themselves also laid them open to criticism.

Inevitably, the narrative of the early centuries AD has been viewed as the story of the progress or the triumph of Christianity; it might as easily be seen as the tale of its evolution or transformation into something its founder would not have recognized. Although all aspects of early Christianity are the object of heated controversy, it is at least plausible that the 'Jesus movement', as it has been called, was originally restricted to Jews; there are signs of dispute among the Apostles as to whether the mission should be extended to the Gentiles (non-Jewish peoples).[43] Controversial too is the dating of the key Gospel texts which subsequently became 'canonical' (many other versions existed, some of them still extant today but long ago excluded from the charmed circle of the New Testament). It is likely that all four Gospels are the product of the first century, that Mark is the earliest, and that both Matthew and Luke draw on Mark and on other sources. The core of the New Testament, the four Gospels and the 13 epistles of Paul, was established by about 130. Tatian attempted to produce a composite version of the four Gospels as a continuous text *c.*150, which suggests that the four were now central to the tradition. Their interpretation was another matter.

More objective is the task of tracing references to the new sect in classical literature, and the stages by which it gained ground in the Roman Empire.[44] Little can be discerned in pagan authors of the first century AD, and not much more in the second. Tacitus in discussing Jewish history remarks that in Judaea 'under Tiberius all was quiet' (*Hist.* 5.9); no reference to the problems which faced Governor Pilate. Elsewhere he mentions that Nero was said to have used the Christians as scapegoats for the fire at Rome in AD 64 (*Ann.* 15.44). Much more substantial is Pliny's letter from Bithynia to Trajan, asking for advice on how to deal with the Christian phenomenon in the province. Pliny is concerned as to whether Christianity itself is to be regarded as a crime, or only when associated with criminal activity; and he is alarmed by the anonymous denunciations he has received, identifying people as Christians: how far should he take notice of such possibly malicious charges? His inclination is to allow those accused the chance to recant, and to prove it by making sacrifice: if they do so, even if they have been Christians before, he pardons them; but if they stubbornly persist, they are executed ('their obstinacy and intractable doggedness deserved to be punished').[45] But he admits that he has not found evidence of any objectionable behaviour. Trajan's reply is brief but decisive: 'they are not to be hunted down', but if convicted and refusing to renounce their faith, Christians are indeed to be punished. However, anonymous accusations are to carry no weight whatsoever: 'that would be the worst of precedents and out of keeping with the spirit of our age' (Pliny, *Letters* 10.96–7, *c.* AD 110).

To many moderns this explicit religious intolerance will seem appalling; yet it is plain that both men regard themselves as being remarkably generous and the Christians as extraordinarily unreasonable. The clash of mind-set between a determinedly exclusive monotheism and a more open polytheistic society could not be made clearer. Moreover, here for the first time the issue of religion and politics is highlighted: Christians refused to sacrifice to pagan gods in general and the emperor in particular. This exposed them to accusations of disloyalty to the government, and in times of crisis their failure to worship could even be seen as causing misfortune: perhaps the gods were angry at their refusal to pay them due honour.[46] Tertullian complains that whenever disaster strikes, when the Tiber floods, the cry goes up 'The Christians to the lions!' (*Ap.* 40). 'Thanks to the Christians, the drought continues', is a saying quoted by Augustine (*City of God* 2.3). The so-called apologists tried in various ways to deal with these accusations and others, but their arguments were probably more successful with believers.[47] Still, by the late second century Christians were becoming a more familiar name, particularly in the Greek world. Lucian laughs at their superstitious credulity; Galen admires their morality but comments with surprise on their elevation of faith above reason. Around the same time the Platonist Celsus mounted a polemical attack on the sect, provocatively entitled the *True Discourse*. Much of this survives in Origen's massive reply, *Against Celsus*, composed some 70 years later. This is the longest and most intellectually impressive work of early apologetic. In Origen, Christianity had a champion well versed in Greek literature and thought, who could meet pagan opposition on its own terms.[48]

VII

The growth of Christianity cannot easily be quantified, but it is at least clear that by the time of Origen the Christians were a substantial and widespread sect: in the mid-third century the Church in Rome had about 150 officials and the whole Christian community there apparently ran into the thousands.[49] By this date they were found in Rome at all levels of society (although in the late second century polemical writers such as Celsus still maintained that they were predominantly drawn from the ignorant poor). Some Christians probably compromised with the demands of the state: those serving in the army could hardly have avoided involvement in pagan acts of worship. But systematic persecution seems only to have emerged under a few fanatical emperors: Trajan's principle, formulated at a time when they were a tiny minority, must have been widely ignored or allowed to lapse. Even the so-called Great Persecution under Diocletian and Galerius (303–13) probably did not result in a high total of executions: one estimate is 3,500.[50]

On the side of the Christians was their well-integrated Church structure, with its organized hierarchy; but the conversion of the Emperor Constantine in the early fourth century was decisive. His victory at the battle of the Milvian Bridge (AD 312) is a historical fact; how swiftly he ascribed it to the support of the Christian God, and whether his allegiance to that God antedated his victory, are matters of controversy.[51] Discussion of his motives will never end, for the nature of the evidence excludes any certainty. Innumerable positions are possible, depending not only on one's evaluation of the man and his career but on the complex relation between the main sources, Lactantius and two works by Eusebius, all Christian and all distorted by hindsight and enthusiasm for the outcome.[52] What mattered more was Constantine's endorsement of the Church and his powerful support to its funds; he also played a key role, not always welcome to the bishops, in pressing for Church unity and eradication of internal disputes. If Christianity was to be the imperial religion, it should display a united front: this boded ill for the so-called heretics who ventured to dissent from the line laid down by central councils such as the one held at Nicaea in 325 (hence the so-called Nicene Creed). Systematic religious persecution is far more a Christian than a pagan phenomenon.[53]

Constantine's conversion did not lead immediately to attacks on pagan worship, but it certainly encouraged more outspoken condemnation by exultant Christians. Lactantius wrote a gloating essay on the divine retribution which had befallen the would-be persecutors such as Diocletian. Some imperial pronouncements attacking 'superstition' might be ambiguous, but the Emperor Gratian resigned the supreme priesthood and removed financial support from the pagan cults at Rome. The ruling of the Emperor Valentinian that the Altar of Victory should be removed from the Senate House as a pagan idol prompted a vigorous debate between the pagan senator Symmachus and the Christian Bishop Ambrose, in which the Christian prevailed.[54] In 391 Theodosius forbade pagan sacrifices and closed the temples, though his edict was not decisive and he was swiftly ousted in the West. But the precedent was set, and anti-pagan legislation continued to appear.[55] The notion that Christianity succeeded because paganism was dead or dying or had become meaningless is nowadays rightly out of favour:[56] it would be more true to say that Christianity, once dominant, slowly absorbed and replaced the old forms of worship. Yet festivals continued to be conducted, even in the capital itself. Roman religion, like Rome itself, took a long time to decline and fall.

Against this complex background (which becomes many times more complicated when we look beyond the imperial government's immediate concerns to the empire as a whole), it is no surprise that literature reveals countless examples of interaction and influence between Christian and pagan traditions. A handful of instances must suffice. Alongside the more strident apologetic oration of Tertullian we can read the attractive work by Minucius Felix, the *Octavius*, named after the chief speaker, which also defends Christianity and owes something to Tertullian. It is still more indebted, however, to the works of Cicero, especially *On the Nature of the Gods*, which it imitates also in its dialogue form. In this work two believers enjoy a walk by the seaside at Ostia with the pagan Caecilius. The scene-setting is as charming as anything in Plato, including even a description of a game of 'ducks and drakes'. A gesture of obeisance by Caecilius to a statue of a god provides the springboard for a debate on the virtues of Christianity. Caecilius, defending his action, lists many of the stock accusations and suspicions which are held against the new cult; in reply Octavius attacks pagan religion and defends his faith. (The attack on the old gods draws heavily on Cotta's speeches in Cicero.) The dialogue concludes with Caecilius cheerfully conceding defeat and determining to join his friends in the worship of Christ – a harmonious though slightly implausible reaction to Octavius' rhetoric. Not only literary forms but specific images and motifs are adapted to Christian use: the portrait of the Christian martyr as hero, a splendid spectacle for God to admire, has the same note of triumphal masochism as Seneca's presentation of the suicide of Cato, the Stoic martyr, exultant in death.[57]

Elsewhere we find frequent use of pagan sources to criticize paganism, as in the massive defences of Arnobius and his pupil Lactantius.[58] Arnobius praises Christ in terms reminiscent of Lucretius' praise of his saviour-figure, Epicurus (1.38 ~ Lucr. 5.1–21). Lactantius examines the questions posed by Cicero in his philosophic works from a Christian standpoint, and just as Cicero ends the *On the State* with the myth of Scipio's dream, so Lactantius ends his major work with an apocalyptic passage foretelling the end of the world. Looking beyond apologetic and polemic, we can see the same tendency to adapt and transform classical genres and metres. Prudentius used Horatian stanzas for Christian hymns; Methodius wrote a *Symposium* in which a group of young women conversed with the saintly Thecla and sang the praises of virginity. In Jerome's time Virgilian centoes on biblical themes were in vogue. Apollinarius the Younger, we are told, turned the New Testament into Platonic dialogues (Socrates *HE* 3.16)!

It will be clear that most of these cases involve Christian writers adapting or reshaping the classical tradition rather than the reverse: pagans, unless converts themselves, more commonly ignored or despised the new religion. A fascinating case which forms a partial exception is the Emperor Julian, who as a member of the house of Constantine was raised a Christian, though he claimed to have nursed a secret devotion to pagan religion from an early age.[59] Substantial writings from his pen survive: some are public statements and letters, but there is also part of a long work *Against the Galileans*, a polemical but densely argued essay which shows him making full use of the biblical references with which he had been crammed as a youth. He gives many of Celsus' arguments a fresh airing, but writes from greater knowledge. Still more interestingly, he seems to have felt that paganism needed to fight back by adopting some of Christianity's weapons: he aimed at establishing hospices, supporting widows and orphans, and equipping paganism with a hierarchical priesthood. Most famously, his admiration for the Greek classics (above all Homer and Plato) led him to take a strong line on who should be allowed to teach these masterpieces. By an edict of June 362 Christians were debarred from giving instruction about pagan texts: let them expound their Gospels in their churches. Even Ammianus, a pagan and an admirer of Julian, found this distasteful: 'a harsh measure, which should be shrouded in lasting oblivion'.[60] Had Julian lived longer, it is hard to say how much effect his measures would have had. He was not the man to undertake a massive persecution, and his own intellectual versions of pagan 'doctrine', imbued with Neoplatonic mysticism, were unlikely to inspire a popular change of heart. But much can be done by a determined ruler, and his project remains one of the great 'might-have-beens' of history.

Tertullian admitted that few if any came to the Scriptures unless they were Christians already.[61] Literary and linguistic factors are important here:

even Christians could admit that their holy books were offputting to those accustomed to Cicero and Virgil. Lactantius confessed that the cultivated world looked down on Christian simplicity and unsophisticated doctrine; the young Augustine was repelled by his first encounter with the Gospels.[62] We must remember that these comments refer to the old Latin Bible, a crude and often unintelligible text, not to the authoritative version produced by Jerome over two decades at the end of the fourth century (the 'Vulgate'), in its time as important a step forward as the King James version in English. But the contrast between the simplicity of Scripture and the elaborate rhetoric of classical literature became an important theme in the dialogue between pagans and Christians. Origen approves of the straightforward Epictetus rather than the Platonic dialogues, which he says are comprehensible only to an educated elite (*Cels.* 6.1–2). Augustine admits that people brought up on Scripture cannot easily cope with the classical Latin idioms (*On Christian Doctrine* 2.21), and in his own sermons to the people of Hippo he used a much simpler and less allusive style than in the *Confessions.* The debate continued well beyond our period, and its significance extends beyond language. The stylistic aspect reflects key aspects of the Christian teaching (humility, renunciation of wealth) as well as the humble origins of Jesus and his disciples, and, most momentously, the descent of Christ to incarnation as a man.[63]

Tertullian might dismiss pagan culture with a rhetorical question ('what has Athens to do with Jerusalem?'); Jerome could echo this ('what has Horace to do with the psalter, Virgil with the Gospels?'); and the story of his alarming dream, in which he found himself arraigned before Heaven and accused of being 'a Ciceronian, not a Christian', is notorious.[64] But these are rhetorical overstatements, comparable with the comment by the Platonist Numenius, seeking to amalgamate classical and Jewish learning, 'what is Plato but Moses speaking in Attic Greek?'. In practice the earlier Christians found they had to adopt the weapons of classical culture and philosophy in order to defend their faith effectively. Already Paul on the Areopagus could quote Greek poetry in his own cause ('as some of your poets have said . . .', *Acts* 17.28). Even in the later period, quite apart from the genuine attraction many educated Christians felt to pagan literature, the whole educational system of antiquity was based on these texts: it could not be cut away root and branch. Irenaeus, followed by Augustine, argued that Christians might use the ornaments of pagan culture just as the Hebrews had taken spoils from Egypt in the Exodus (*Conf.* 7.15, etc.). A subtler approach was to suggest that educated pagans had come some of the way towards true wisdom, but not yet made the final step – that Christianity completed the task that Plotinus' Platonism had partially accomplished (this is the tenor of the *Confessions*: see esp. 7.13–16, 26–7).

The intertwining of cultures was evident even in the field of religion itself: the Christian Ausonius could write an elegant poem celebrating Roman festivals, nostalgically evoking the world of Tibullus and Ovid (14.6 ed. Green). To see pagans and Christians as opposing forces confronting each other from armed camps is to oversimplify an infinitely varied and complex picture.

VIII

In the fourth century two men of letters, both voluminous writers and distinguished teachers, wrote their autobiographies: one a Greek born and chiefly resident in Antioch, the other a Latin-speaking north African, who subsequently taught in Carthage, Rome and Milan. The Greek, Libanius (314–c.395), was a master of rhetoric and proud of it, a pagan, a friend and posthumous defender of the Apostate Julian. To the end of his life he upheld the standards of Greek education against what he saw as the disturbing growth in the popularity of Latin. The other is of course Augustine, who seemed set for a successful career in the West parallel with Libanius' in the East, but took instead a very different path. He chronicles his disenchantment with rhetoric and his discovery of Christian faith in his masterpiece, the *Confessions*. Both Libanius' *Autobiography* and Augustine's *Confessions* are rich in biographical detail, elegances of style and clever allusion, character-revealing narratives; both are fertile sources of social history (not least regarding the vile behaviour of their students!).

Both works are intriguing in formal terms. Libanius characteristically sets his life in the context of a declamatory thesis: rejecting both the suggestion that he is the most fortunate of men, and the contrary position that he is the most miserable, he undertakes to show the pattern of fortune in his own life, and how good and bad are interwoven in his experience. His vanity is inordinate: 'how could I describe adequately the tears that followed my introductory address, which many had learned by heart before they left? ... The sun did not shine more brightly for Agamemnon the day he captured Troy than it did for me on the day I received this reception' (89). 'I was still in mourning for them when I sustained the injury to my right foot, news of which has reached every city of continent and island' (183). Yet Libanius, though an egoist, a hypochondriac and in his later works more or less permanently disgruntled, is a figure of stature who worked as hard as he could for the benefit of his city and citizens: his protests against municipal corruption, military brutality and social injustice testify to his courage, and he is unusual in ancient times in being a crusader for reform of prison conditions.[65]

The *Confessions* is formally a hybrid: part prayer, part soliloquy, part philosophic polemic, couched in a style full of rhythmical virtuosity and dazzling wordplay: more than any other work in Latin, more even than Apuleius' novel, it can be called a prose poem. Each of these two men is defending his career and shaping his past to give it a meaning and structure; each reveals much deliberately and some things despite himself. But for all Libanius' talent there can be no question which is the more innovative and exhilarating work. The difference is not only one of intellectual edge (though Libanius is no philosopher). The story Libanius tells is one of varied mis-haps and triumphs – illness, bereavement, successful performances, triumph over a series of arrogant Roman governors, and narrow escapes from assault or road accidents. Augustine's narrative is a spiritual odyssey: external events are secondary to the progress of his soul towards its true home, and no outer experience moves him as much as the memory of wrongdoing and the consciousness of sin. The way in which he talks with God is unparalleled in ancient literature: at one point intimate and devoted, at another impas-sioned and self-lacerating. This is not a case of new wine in old bottles: in the *Confessions* we meet something genuinely new in both form and content.

Our knowledge of the facts of his life derives mainly from the *Confessions* themselves, and may be subject to some literary reshaping after the event: the work takes us up to about 389 but was composed eight or ten years later (397–400).[66] The essentials are briefly narrated. Born in 354 in a small north African town, Thagaste, he was educated at Madaurus and Carthage, and became a teacher of rhetoric. At an early stage he was inspired by a reading of Cicero's *Hortensius* (now lost), a powerful exhortation to the study of philosophy. But Augustine was long uncertain which intellectual path to follow. He became a devotee of the Manichean sect, a gloomy religious philosophy based on a stern dualism between powers of good and evil. His mother Monica, a devoted Christian, constantly prayed for his conversion to her faith: she is a key figure in his life (his father died when the young man was 18). His moral life, at least as viewed in retrospect, was self-indulgent. He found himself unwilling or unable to adopt an ascetic life: increasingly he felt guilt and strain over sexuality. For years he lived with a concubine whom he finally sent away, although she had borne him a son, in order to be free to marry a wealthy wife. We know the name of the son, not the mother. Augustine taught at Rome and then at Milan, impress-ing the pagan senator Symmachus and doing his best to impress the Chris-tian Bishop Ambrose. Disillusioned with Manichaeism, he began to study Neoplatonic texts and to absorb the teaching of Plotinus regarding the soul's immortality and its affinity with God. Many of these teachings were at least compatible with and paved the way for his growing commitment to

Christianity, to which he was also attracted by the example of close friends and the stories they told of others (he was impressed by an account of the asceticism of Antony, the founder of desert monasticism).[67] His final conversion he represents as an episode of agony and crisis, brought to an emotional climax by reading a passage from the Apostle Paul which he took as a sign to abandon both fleshly desires and all prospect of marriage and a career. With her son's conversion, Monica's prayers were fulfilled, and her death soon afterwards concludes the narrative section of the *Confessions*. Beyond this, Augustine returned to Africa, was ordained and finally became bishop of Hippo. The post was no sinecure: on one occasion he narrowly avoided assassination by rivals (Possidius, *Life of Aug.* 12.2). The remainder of his life was one of constant activity, instructing, guiding, and above all writing: sermons (over 900 survive!), essays, dialogues, major works of theological speculation, polemics against other sects and numerous letters. More survives from his pen than from any other writer of the ancient world. Isidore of Seville declared that if any man claims to have read all of St Augustine's writings, he is lying.[68] I make no such claim.

The *Confessions* is in 13 books, of which the last four are distinct in character. Three different strands may be distinguished in the earlier part: a hymnic mode, praising and celebrating God in powerfully emotional tones, with constant reminiscences of the Psalms (the work opens with two success- ive psalm-quotations); the autobiographical narrative, also often punctu- ated by passionate exclamations and appeals to God for pardon or clarification; and the more reflective passages on intellectual and theological issues arising from Augustine's experiences. These serve either to explain his own misdeeds, to define the errors of himself or others (especially the Manichaeans), or to expound the true nature of the Christian God or his works as he now understands them. Throughout, the work is artful and carefully designed: the affectation of spontaneity will not deceive the reader. In the last four books the autobiography is suspended (though Augustine himself and his emotions or errors are still sometimes used as illustration). Now philosophic theology is to the fore, and the topics of memory and time versus eternity are explored; there follows an analysis of the opening of Genesis, with rich comment on the richness of Scripture itself – its openness, its profound mystery, its multiplicity of meanings. In a way the first nine books present a more accessible version of the 'theory' of Christian conversion, illustrated by the practical example of Augustine himself, the soul who has wandered from God and must find his way back, by a series of happy chances and accidents as it seems, but in fact thanks to divine grace. In the last four books the theoretical or theological basis is examined in more detail. From another point of view, some parts of the later books are directed against the errors of the Manichees (who frequently criticized the Genesis narrative).

From yet another, Augustine is showing the reader what has taken the place of his earlier sins and misdemeanours: humble yet dedicated pursuit of a deeper understanding of God's precious word.

The most distinguished of modern commentators has condemned the practice of picking out 'purple patches' from Augustine as a betrayal of our duty as readers.[69] It is true that some phrases quoted out of context have become clichés (as with Shakespeare): 'I came to Carthage, and all around me hissed a cauldron of wicked lusts' (3.1). 'Give me continence and chastity, but not yet' (8.17); 'late did I come to love you' (10.38). Yet in a survey of this kind it is hardly possible to avoid mentioning certain high points. Augustine's sharp eye for sin in fallen man finds it even in the selfishness of infants (1.11); his self-reproach over the theft of pears as a boy dwells on the effects of peer pressure, and insists on the special horror of wickedness done *for its own sake* (he did not actually want to eat the pears) (2.9ff.); his amazed examination of audience response at the theatre, gaining pleasure from pain, is a classic formulation of the tragic paradox (3.2–4). Equally acute is the powerful passage on how his friend Alypius became an obsessive devotee of the gladiatorial games (6.13). His psychological shrewdness is unfailing. Constantly he measures other activities against love of God: the death of a beloved friend prompts contemplation of time and the nature of friendship, and of God's role in grief (4.7–15); human judgements and human intelligence are frail unless God is our guide (4.28ff.): 'when our support rests on our own strength, it is infirmity' (31). His increasing hostility to the Manichees makes itself felt in vivid coarseness of language: 'those people whom I should have vomited forth from my overloaded stomach' (7.3); other recurring physical images are those of disease and deformity (7.11 'my swelling conceit'). 'Mental pregnancy' torments him, as he is ready to turn towards Christ yet cannot do so (7.11). 'Fettered by the flesh's morbid impulse and lethal sweetness, I dragged my chain, but was afraid to be free of it' (6.21). He can describe the inexpressible: the mystic experience of oneness with God which he achieves briefly and frustratingly in book 7 (23), and the double experience which he and his mother enjoy together in the moving scene in Ostia, the last conversation which he narrates before she falls ill (9.23–7, esp. 24).

To choose a more extended quotation is hard, when hundreds of passages cry out to be selected. Here is an extract from the passage in which Augustine is struggling to make the final step and accept Christ, impressed as he is with all he has heard about the monastic communities.

The tumult of my heart took me out into the garden where no one could interfere with the burning struggle with myself in which I was engaged, until the matter could be settled. You [God] knew, but I did not, what the outcome would be. But my madness with myself was part of the process of recovering health, and in the agony of death I was coming to life. I was aware how ill I was, unaware how well I was soon to be. So I went out into the garden. Alypius followed me step by step. Although he was present, I felt no intrusion on my solitude. How could he abandon me in such a state? We sat down as far as we could from the buildings. I was deeply disturbed in spirit, angry with indignation and distress that I was not entering into my pact and covenant with you, my God, when all my bones were crying out that I should enter into it and were exalting it to heaven with praises. But to reach that destination one does not use ships or chariots or feet. It was not even necessary to go the distance I had come from the house to where we were sitting. The one necessary condition, which meant not only going but at once arriving there, was to have the will to go – provided only that the will was strong and unqualified, not the turning and twisting first this way, then that, of a will half-wounded, struggling with one part rising up and the other part falling down. (8.19, tr. Chadwick)

The resources of rhetoric are applied to new purposes: the paradoxes of the Old Testament on God and the Gospels on Christ are given fresh edge. 'He who for us is life itself descended here and endured our death and slew it by the abundance of his life' (4.19); 'Always you were with me, mercifully chastising me, touching with bitterness all my wicked pleasures. . . . You "fashion pain to be a lesson"; you "strike to heal"; you bring death upon us so that we should not die apart from you' (2.4). So too with the figure of *prosopopoiia* ('impersonation'), which we have met in Cicero (p. 95). At the moment of crisis in his conversion at Milan, he is still held back by his sexuality:

Vain trifles and the triviality of the empty-headed, my old loves, held me back. They tugged at the garment of my flesh and whispered 'Are you getting rid of us?' And 'from this moment we shall never be with you again, not for ever and ever.' . . . Meanwhile the overwhelming force of habit was saying to me: 'Do you think you can live without them?' (8.26)

But in the next section a counter-force is introduced, also through personi-fication: 'For from that direction where I had set my face and towards which I was afraid to move, there appeared the dignified and chaste Lady Continence, serene and cheerful without coquetry, enticing me in an honourable manner to come and not to hesitate. To receive and embrace me she stretched out pious hands . . .' (27). The choice between Virtue and Vice had been dramatized long before; the saving figure of a divine power, Isis, was unforgettably introduced by Apuleius at the climax of his novel; but Augustine's use of this technique is set within an extended narrative of mental distress that is totally compelling: the discovery of underlying models in Plotinus does nothing to diminish the power with which he recaptures and enhances this supremely significant experience.

IX

The other work which demands attention, and with which we conclude, is the *City of God*, a 'great and arduous task' in the author's own words: it runs to 22 books and was composed over a period of 13 years (413–26).[70] Augustine was 59 when he began it, 72 when he completed it. It may be viewed as the third part of a triptych with Plato's *Republic* and Cicero's *On the State*. Each author in his own way is examining the ideal society: but Plato wavers between maintaining that his state could be realized if certain highly implausible conditions were met, and declaring it to be a utopian ideal, perhaps laid up in heaven; Cicero sees the ideal as having existed in Rome's historical past, viewed through rose-tinted spectacles. Augustine, however, can see the ideal society only as the kingdom of Heaven, contrasted throughout with the empires of this world, above all the domination of Rome. The city of God will be realized at the end of the world, in the Last Judgement; but meanwhile individuals can live as citizens of that better state even in this world, though they are 'strangers' or aliens, out of place.

In 410 the forces of Alaric the Goth had seized control of Rome. Politically this was less significant than it might seem: emperors had not been resident in Rome for generations, and Alaric, a Christian himself, was bent on increasing his own influence, not on wanton destruction and plunder. But the symbolic impact of an invader's entry within Rome's walls should not be underestimated. Jerome's letters attest to his dismay at the news.[71] It appears that some pagans maintained that the Christians were to blame: the abandonment of the old gods had led to the gods abandoning them. Augustine in his late *Retractations* (a work in which he reviews all his own writings) mentions the need to respond to these mistaken complaints; but the concept of the two cities, and many of the other themes of the work, were well-established in his thought, and although the sack of Rome must have provided an added stimulus, there were other motives which impelled him to compose this work. Few will read it from end to end, but it contains much of what is typical of the mature Augustine, and few if any of his works have had such influence. (It is said to be the most frequently copied of all Christian Latin texts.)

The argument is carefully articulated (though admitting many a digression): five books responding to those who worship the old gods hoping for felicity on earth, five more on those who do so because they hope for happiness after death; there follow 12 on the theme of the Two Cities: four on their origins, four on their unfolding histories in the past; and four on their ultimate destiny.[72] Livy and Sallust are major sources for Rome, the narratives of the Old Testament for the historical process preparing for the City of God. It is fascinating to see him engaging with the pagan classics: the dark outlook of Sallust, the imperial assurance of Virgil, are turned to new uses, as Augustine seeks to show that Rome, and all other earthly empires, was driven by a lust for power. Yet the Roman Empire is not simply a domain of evil: in some ways it has helped to pave the way for the kingdom of heaven. Divine providence promoted the successes and the conversion of Constantine (5.25). Parts of the work engage with the arguments of polytheistic thinkers in general (as on the topics of astrology and predestination) and particularly the leading philosophers (Platonists on demons, Stoics on the suppression of the emotions), confronting their teaching with Christian doctrine and thought. Other parts re-evaluate heroes of history and myth: Regulus, Scipio, Cato. The story of Romulus' fratricide of Remus (a struggle for earthly power resulting in an evil crime) is brought into relation with that of Cain and Abel, where Abel, the virtuous victim, is seen as representative of the heavenly city (15.5). Elsewhere he is dismissive of Roman beliefs that Romulus was a god: the mistaken deification of the founder is contrasted with the true divinity of Christ. Throughout he draws on classical Latin literature and thought, long assimilated and deeply pondered, but examines it with unsparing criticism as an outsider, a citizen of a different world. No writer presents so clearly and in such detail the Christian vision of history as subordinate to the all-embracing providence of God, whose kingdom will endure forever while earthly powers pass away. It is a majestic conception even to the non-believer, and its historical importance is beyond question.

In his own recollection, it was the contrast between the ruins of the pagan monuments and the new life of Christian worship on the same site that prompted Edward Gibbon to undertake his great History: 'It was at Rome, on the 15th of October, 1764, as I sat musing amidst the ruins of the Capitol, while the barefooted friars were singing vespers in the Temple of Jupiter, that the idea of writing the decline and fall of the city first started to my mind.'[73] The disintegration of empire has a perennial fascination: it is significant that Gibbon's masterpiece is perhaps the one work on the ancient world of which every educated person has heard. Classical literature as described in the present book begins and ends with the fall of a city. The sack of Troy, a great city and heart of a kingdom, is foreshadowed throughout the *Iliad*. The fall of a city is a concept deep-rooted in the ancient consciousness.[74] At the time of the sack of Carthage, Scipio and Polybius looked on, and the Roman commander wept, quoting Homer, and fearing that the same fate might one day befall Rome the conqueror.[75] Imagination foresees the passing of a civilization; memory or written record preserves that past society's achievements, including the writings in which the beliefs, the dreams and the follies of innumerable individuals are vividly brought back to life. Classical studies are sometimes dismissed as anachronistic or irrelevant – a strange complaint, when the pages of these writers engage constantly with themes of life and death, pain and joy, disaster and survival, war, aggression and imperialism, ambitions achieved and ideals corrupted, self-discipline and self-sacrifice, political success and rejection of the world, freedom of speech and oppression of thought.

To contemplate the literature of the past is not to accept it uncritically. If we study the literature of the Greek and Roman world, we should neither idolize the glory that was Greece nor despise antiquity as a primitive era that lacked the advantages of fast food and mobile phones. To reject the past is to abandon all prospect of understanding what has shaped our own present and therefore what we are. To ignore the literature of the past is to deny ourselves – to lose some of what gives meaning and value to our lives. The literature of the classical world is not the whole of that past, but it does form an important part of it. I hope that this book has done something to show how diverse, how sophisticated, and how challenging this literature remains.

Appendix 1

Translations of Four Longer Passages

These four passages are not only of great interest in themselves, but are chosen to show something of the range of classical literature. Four genres are represented: epic, philosophic dialogue, erotic elegy and history; both the first and the fourth passages show the importance of speechmaking and the value of speeches as a means of highlighting the themes which concern the writer. These are presented with minimal comments, but they are referred to at various points in the main text of the book.

1 Homer, *Iliad* 24.471–551

In this passage (already referred to on p. 23), Achilles, grief-stricken by the death of Patroclus, is astounded by the sudden appearance of the haggard figure of Priam, King of Troy, who has come in person late at night through the Greek lines to plead for the return of Hector's corpse. It powerfully illustrates the importance of speeches, pity and the bond between father and son in the *Iliad*.

> The old man drew near to the house in which Achilles dear to Zeus was sitting. He found him there within, and his companions seated apart from him. Two only were with him, the hero Automedon and Alcimus, Ares' offspring, busy with their tasks. Achilles himself had only just stopped eating and drinking; the table still stood by his side. Unseen by them all, great Priam entered, and standing close by he seized Achilles' knees with his hands, and kissed the terrible manslaying hands that had slain so many of his own sons. As when strong frenzy comes upon a man, who kills another in his own land then finds his way to a different country, entering the house of a rich man, and those who see him gaze and marvel, so Achilles marvelled, when he saw godlike Priam. The others marvelled too, and glanced at one another. Then Priam spoke to him in supplication.

'Remember your father, godlike Achilles, for he is a man of my years, on the grim threshold of old age. And now, I would suppose, his neighbours persecute him, and there is no one close at hand to ward off assault and harm. But even in this state he still rejoices in his heart when he hears news of you, and every day that goes by, he hopes and prays to see his beloved son returning from Troy. But what of me? I am altogether wretched, for I fathered the best sons in all of broad Troy, and not one of them, I tell you, is left alive. Fifty sons I had once, when the Achaeans first came. Nineteen were born of the same woman's womb, while the rest were mothered by women of my household. There are many of these whose limbs raging Ares has loosened in death. Yet there was one who still remained for me, who alone defended our city; and he is the one whom you slew just the other day, as he fought to protect his homeland – Hector. For his sake I am here by the ships of the Achaeans, to ransom him from you. I bring a massive store of treasure. Reverence the gods, Achilles, and pity me, remembering your own father; yet I am still more pitiable. I have endured such things as no mortal on this earth has endured, drawing to my lips the hands of the man who has slain my son.'

These were his words, and in Achilles he roused a deep longing to weep for his own father. Clasping the old man's hand, he gently pushed him away. Then the two men were lost in memories, as the one wept floods of tears for Hector slayer of men, collapsing in a heap before Achilles' feet, while Achilles wept for his own father, and again at times for Patroclus. Their lamentation filled the house. But when godlike Achilles had had his fill of weeping, and the deep longing had passed from his wits and his frame, at once he rose from his seat and lifted up the old man by the hand, pitying his white head and white old beard. Then he spoke, addressing him with winged words.

'Poor wretch, you have indeed taken many hardships to heart. How did you dare to come alone to the ships of the Achaeans, to come face to face with a man who has killed many of your fine sons? Truly your heart has the strength of iron. But come now, sit down upon this chair, and we shall let these sorrows rest in our hearts, for all the grief we feel. For nothing is gained by chilly lamentation. For this is the destiny the gods have woven for wretched mortals – to live in misery; but they themselves are free of care. There are two jars that stand on the threshold of Zeus, full of gifts that he bestows – bad in one, good in the other. And when Zeus who delights in thunder gives a man some mixture of the two, that man sometimes meets with ill fortune, sometimes with good. But when he gives only from the jar of sorrows, he makes that man desolate, and dreadful hunger drives him across the divine earth, and he wanders without honour from either gods or men.

Think of this. The gods gave fine gifts to Peleus from the day he was born. He excelled all mankind in prosperity and wealth, and was lord over the Myrmidons, and to him, mortal though he was, the gods gave a divine consort. But even to him god brought misfortune, for he had no strong stock of fine sons growing up in his halls, but fathered only one son, and that one doomed to a death long before his time. Nor am I caring for my father now in his old age, since far indeed from my homeland I sit here in Troy, bringing trouble to you and your children. And as for you, old sir, we have heard that you were fortunate in time gone by. In all the realm that is north of Lesbos, seat of Makar, and all that is bounded by Phrygia and the vast Hellespont, in all these lands they say you were supreme in wealth and in your sons. But since those who dwell in heaven have brought this misfortune upon you, and ever around your city there is conflict and slaughter of men, endure, and do not grieve incessantly in your heart. For you cannot achieve anything through grief for your son, nor will you raise him up again. Before that you may suffer still another evil.'

2 Plato, *Republic*, Book 7, 514a–518b

This elaborate allegory forms part of Plato's account of the difference between the ignorance or false opinions of the ordinary man, and the knowledge of the philosopher who has contemplated true being and understood the importance of the forms, including the ultimate form of the good. It will be obvious that much of the dramatic detail of the imaginary situation is introduced in order to shed satirical and critical light on the attitude of society to intellectuals in general and Socrates in particular (note the prediction that the ignorant prisoners will try to kill the man who attempts to set them free). Formally, the passage consists of Socrates discoursing with brief reactions from Glaucon. Earlier in the dialogue, and especially in book 1, Socrates' companions engage in lively debate and challenge the main speaker's assumptions; the rather perfunctory contributions made by the interlocutor in this extract are typical of Plato's later style.

'Next', I said, 'consider the following comparison to illustrate our natural condition as to education and the lack of it. Imagine a number of men who live in a sort of underground cave; there is a long entrance open to the light across the whole width of the cave; and these men have been imprisoned there from childhood, their limbs and their necks fettered so that they are motionless, and can look only forward, their chains preventing them from turning their heads around. Imagine that there is a fire burning further up the cave behind them, and a path running between the prisoners and the fire and above them, along which a wall has been constructed, just like the constructions of showmen who put on exhibitions of puppets – the wall masks the men, and above it they put on their shows.'

'I am imagining it all,' he answered.

'And now visualize along the length of this wall a number of men carrying equipment of all sorts, big enough to show above the wall, and statues of men, and images of other living things too, made of stone or wood or all sorts of material; and presumably some of the bearers are speaking, others silent.'

'A strange comparison to make,' he said, 'and strange prisoners.'

'They are like ourselves,' I said. 'Now first, do you suppose that such men could ever have seen anything of themselves or one another apart from the shadows cast by the fire upon the wall of the cavern facing them?'

'How could they, if they were forced to keep their heads motionless all through their lives?'

'And the same goes for the objects being carried past them?'

'Obviously.'

'Suppose they are able to talk to each other; don't you think they would believe the things they saw and identified were the true reality?

'Inevitably.'

'And what if there were an echo from the wall opposite them? When any of the passers-by spoke, don't you think they would believe the utterance was made by the shadow passing before them?'

'I certainly do.'

'Such men, then, would believe true reality to be no other than the shadows of the objects.'

'That is inescapable.'

'Imagine now,' I continued, 'what would be involved if one of them were released from this bondage and healed from the delusion it involves. If one of them was set free and suddenly forced to stand up and move his head from side to side and walk and look in the direction of the fire, he would find all of these actions painful and because of the bright glow of the light he would be unable to see those things of which he had formerly seen the shadows. What do you think he would say, then, if you told him that in the past he had seen illusions, but now that he was closer to reality and turned towards real objects, he was seeing more truly? And what if you showed him each item as it went by and questioned him, making him tell you what it was? Don't you think he would be at a loss, and would think what he saw before was more real than what you were pointing out to him now?'

'Much more.'

'And then if you forced him to look towards the light itself, wouldn't that make his eyes hurt and make him flinch and run away, turning back to what he could see before, and think those things truly clearer than what you were showing him?'

'Indeed.'

'But suppose someone were to drag him away by force, along the rough, steep path to the entrance, and not let go of him until he had been forced out to the sunlight – surely he would be in pain and angry at this treatment, and when he reached the light, his eyes would be filled with the bright glare and he would not be able to see even one of the things we call "real".'

'Certainly not all at once.'

'I suppose he would need to acclimatize himself, in order to be able to see the upper world. First he might look most easily at the shadows there, and next he might look at the reflections of men and other things in water, and only later their actual selves. And after those he would gaze at the heavenly bodies and heaven itself during the night hours, observing the light of the stars and the moon; that would be easier for him than the sun and its light by day.'

'Clearly.'

'Last of all, I assume, he would be able to look at the sun, not its images reflected in water or in some other medium, but the sun itself in itself, in its own sphere, and to perceive its nature.'

'That is necessarily true.'

'And after that he would deduce that this is the force which produces the seasons and the cycle of the year, which presides over all that is visible, and is in some way the cause of all the things that they had seen back in the cave.'

'That would evidently be the next step.'

'Well then; when he remembers his previous existence, and what passed for wisdom there, and thinks of his fellow-prisoners, don't you think he will congratulate himself on his change of state, and pity them?'

'He certainly will.'

'Perhaps in that earlier time there were honours and credit gained amongst them and prizes for the man who had the sharpest eye for what was being carried past, and who remembered most accurately what commonly came first and what next and what in combination, and on this basis was most skilled at predicting what would come along next. Do you suppose he would now feel any desire for those rewards, or envy for those who are honoured in that company of captives, those who lord it over them? Or will he rather feel as Homer did, and wish with all his heart "to be a serf and work the land in service to a man of little property",[1] and endure any form of misfortune, rather than remain in that state of delusion and live as the captives do?'

'That is my belief: he would be willing to endure anything than live on those terms.'

'Now consider this,' I said. 'If such a man were to descend into the cave again and take up his old seat, would he not find his eyes clouded with darkness, if he came in suddenly from the sunlight?'

'Absolutely.'

'So if he were obliged to join in the competition with those who had been permanently imprisoned, and try to distinguish which shadow was which, while he was still unable to see, before his eyes had adjusted (and no small time would be needed for re-adjustment), would he not cause great hilarity? Wouldn't they say of him that because he had gone up and out he had come back with his eyesight ruined, and so it was not worth even trying to make the ascent? And if they were able to get their hands on anyone trying to release them and lead them up to the light, they would even kill him, wouldn't they?'

'Definitely.'

'Now is the time, my dear Glaucon, to apply this whole image to what we were discussing before – comparing the realm which is revealed through sight to the dungeon of the cave; the light of the fire in the cave is comparable with the power of the sun. And if you make the ascent and the vision of the upper world correspond to the soul's ascent to the realm of the intelligible, you will not be far from my own guess, since that is what you want to hear. But God (presumably) knows if this is true or not. This at any rate is how my fancies appear to me: in the realm of knowing, the form of goodness is the last of all and only gradually discerned; but once seen it demands that we acknowledge it responsible for all that is right and beautiful in all things, giving birth to light in the visible world and itself the sovereign provider of truth and intelligence in the world perceived by thought; and that anyone who is to act wisely in private or public life must behold this sight.'

'I share your belief,' he said, 'at least as far as I can.'

'Well then, go on to consider this too: you should not be surprised if those who journey to that realm are reluctant to engage in human affairs, but their souls are always impelled upwards and wish to spend time in the world of thought. This reaction is natural, if our comparison holds in this respect as well.'

'Natural indeed.'

'Moreover, do you think it surprising if one who is returning from divine contemplation to the affairs of men cuts a poor figure there, and seems altogether comical while he is still blinking and not yet adapted to the darkness that surrounds us, supposing that he is forced to participate in contests in the law courts or elsewhere, where the prizes are the mere shadows of justice or the objects by which the shadows are cast, and to take part in disputes about the understanding of these objects held by those who have never seen justice itself?'

'Not at all surprising.'

'But a man of good sense,' I went on, 'would recall that there are two ways in which the sight can be disturbed, springing from two causes – when one passes from light into darkness and from darkness into light. And recognizing that the same holds true of the soul, when he sees a soul confused and unable to see, he would not laugh unthinkingly, but would examine whether it has come from a brighter life, and is plunged in darkness and not adjusted to the change, or whether it has come from greater ignorance into a lighter realm and is overwhelmed by the more dazzling light there. He would count the latter fortunate in its experience and its life, but pity the former; and if he chose to laugh, his laughter would not itself be laughable – as would the mockery directed at a soul that has descended from above.'

'What you say is judicious indeed,' he replied.

3 Propertius, Book 2, Poem 15

This is one of the many poems Propertius devotes to the subject of his mistress Cynthia, and what their relationship means to him. Erotic enthusiasm is here combined with imagery of light and dark, suggesting life and death;

at a late stage in a striking passage the poet deplores the losses in the recent civil wars and comes close to condemning the victory of Actium, which established Augustus' power. The concentration of elegy on an alternative lifestyle to the traditional civic and military career is especially clear in this poem.

O how happy I am! O night that was bright for me! And you,
    my couch, made rich by my darling's presence!
How many words we exchanged with the lamp placed by our side;
    and what a tussle followed when the light was gone!
For now she wrestled with me, her breasts bared,
    and now her dress got in the way, and she forced me to wait.
When my eyes were closed in sleep, she opened them
    with her lips, and said to me 'Are you so down, then, lazybones?'
How often we embraced, in how many positions!
    How my kisses lingered on your lips!
It gives no pleasure to spoil passion by working blind;
    as you must know, the eyes lead the advance in lovemaking.
Paris himself, they say, died of love when he saw Spartan Helen naked,
    as she rose to leave Menelaus' chamber.
Endymion, so they tell, was naked when he won Phoebus' sister,
    and lay beside a naked goddess.
But if you insist on sleeping in your clothes,
    then your dress will be torn and you will feel my hands upon you.
Indeed, if anger drives me further,
    you will even have to show your mother bruised arms.
The time has not yet come when drooping breasts bar you from play;
    leave those who feel ashamed of childbearing to worry on that score.

While the fates allow us, let us give our eyes excess of love.
    The long night comes for you, and no day will return.
If only you would let us be bound in chains as we hug one another,
    so that no day could ever part us!
Well-matched doves should be your model in love,
    male and female, perfect union.
He who seeks a limit to maddened passion is deluded;
    true passion knows not how to be confined.
Sooner will the earth deceive the ploughman with fake produce,
    sooner will the sun-god drive black horses,
and rivers start calling their waters back to the source,
    leaving the fish parched in a dried-up eddy –
sooner all this, than I can shift my sorrowful love to another;
    hers I shall be while I live, hers when I die.
But if she is willing to share with me nights like this one,
    then even a year of life will be long.
If she grants me many such nights, I shall become immortal:
    in a single night a man can even be a god!

If all men desired to follow this track in life,
    and to lie with their limbs overwhelmed by wine,
then there would be no cruel steel, no ships of war,
    and Actium's sea would not be tossing our bones;
nor would Rome, so many times assailed by triumphs over her own,
    have grown weary of letting down her hair in mourning.
My descendants can justly praise this life of mine;
    no gods have been offended by my carousals.

Do not spurn the fruits of life, while the light lasts!
    If you give me all your kisses, your gifts will still be too few.
We are like leaves that have dropped from dried-up garlands –
    you see them scattered, floating aimlessly in the punchbowl.
So with us, breathing mightily now in our love;
    perhaps tomorrow will bring the closing line to our fate.

4 Tacitus, *Annals* 4.34–5 (AD 25).

This episode occurs in the reign of the Emperor Tiberius ('Caesar' in the first paragraph). Sejanus is the emperor's most important adviser, then at the height of his power. In the preceding passage Tacitus has allowed himself some important comments on the problems of historical writing in his own time, contrasting the good fortune of historians under the Republic. He now dramatizes these issues in the speech and fate of Cremutius.

In the consulship of Cornelius Cossus and Asinius Agrippa, Cremutius Cordus was summoned to trial, but on an unfamiliar charge, now heard for the first time: it was said that he had published a history, praised Marcus Brutus, and called Gaius Cassius the last of the Romans.[2] Prosecuting were Satrius Secundus and Pinarius Natta, members of Sejanus' entourage. That proved damaging to the defendant, as did Caesar's stern expression as he listened to the defence undertaken by Cremutius, who saw clearly that death was inevitable. It was along these lines.

'My words, senators, are called to account; such is my innocence in deeds. But those words were not directed against the emperor or his father, who are protected by the law of treason: rather, I am alleged to have praised Brutus and Cassius, whose deeds many authors have commemorated, and never without respect. Titus Livius, whose fame places him in the first rank of historians on grounds of eloquence and impartiality, lavished such praise on Gnaeus Pompeius that Augustus called him a "Pompey-ite"; but this never damaged their friendship. When mentioning Scipio, Afranius, and these same men Cassius and Brutus in his *History*, he nowhere calls them criminals or parricides, their customary titles today, but often speaks of them as of distinguished citizens. The writings of Asinius Pollio hand down to us an unexceptional account of these men; Messalla Corvinus regularly described Cassius as "my commander"; and both these men flourished, wealthy and enjoying high office. When Cicero wrote a book praising Cato to the skies, what did Caesar the dictator do? He replied in a written oration, just as if he were putting his case before a jury. Antony's letters, Brutus's public speeches, are full of slanders against Augustus, false I admit, but still extremely vicious; the poetry of Bibaculus and Catullus is packed with abuse of the Caesars; yet the divine Julius and the divine Augustus endured and ignored these insults. It would be hard to say whether their conduct showed more magnanimity or good judgement. If scorned, such comments wither away; but if one shows indignation, they seem to be acknowledged.

'I need not refer to the Greeks, among whom not only liberty but licence went unpunished; or if someone took note of it, he retaliated in kind, words against words. But to publish opinions concerning those whom death has freed from hatred or favour has always been admissible and immune from criticism. Are Cassius and Brutus campaigning and in possession of the field of Philippi today? Am I supposed to be inflaming the mob to civil war by the power of oratory? Didn't they die seventy years ago? Men know of them by their statues, which even the victor did not destroy; and in the same way, they retain a share of remembrance in the writers of history. Posterity repays to every man his due distinction; if the guilty verdict is brought in, there will be others to remember not only Cassius and Brutus, but me as well.'

Cordus then left the senate and ended his life by self-starvation. The senators ordered his books burned by the junior magistrates; but they survived, hidden and later published. Hence we can take pleasure in deriding the stupidity of those who suppose that a future age's memory can be wiped out by power in the present. On the contrary, when talent is persecuted, its influence is enhanced; and foreign kings, or anyone else who emulates their barbaric behaviour, achieve only dishonour for themselves and renown for their victims.

Appendix 2

Timeline

This table includes only the main writers and a selection of the most notable public events mentioned in the text of the book. Many dates, especially in the earlier centuries, are very approximate. Fuller chronological tables are available in a number of reference works, notably the volumes of the revised *Cambridge Ancient History*, and in E. J. Bickerman, *Chronology of the Ancient World* (2nd edn, 1980), esp. 167–218.

Events	Literary and cultural phenomena
BC	
	776: traditional date of first celebration of Olympic Games
753: traditional date for founding of Rome	
	c.750: first evidence of use of Greek alphabet in inscriptions
	c.700?: *Iliad*, followed by *Odyssey*
	c.700–670?: Hesiod
	c.650: Archilochus active
	c.600: Alcaeus and Sappho active
	585: Thales, first of Presocratic thinkers, predicts an eclipse
560–46: Croesus king of Lydia until conquered by Cyrus the Great of Persia	Anacreon and Ibycus active 540s–30s and later
c.550–527: Pisistratus tyrant in Athens	
c.535–522: Polycrates tyrant of Samos	

Events	Literary and cultural phenomena
	Dramatic festival instituted at Athens, at uncertain date (?530s?)
510: overthrow of Hippias, son of Pisistratus of Athens 508: proto-democratic reforms by Cleisthenes of Athens	c.515–at least 470s: Simonides active c.500: Heraclitus of Ephesus active
490: Darius of Persia attacks Greece; battle of Marathon	c.495–c.450: Pindar and Bacchylides active
480–79: Xerxes' invasion of Greece repelled by Greek alliance; establishment of 'Delian League' against Persia	Empedocles active (d. 432) Parmenides active (visited Athens c.450) 472: Aeschylus, Persians
	468: first production of Sophocles
462: radical democracy established Mid-century: pre-eminence of Athens under leadership of Pericles; extensive building programme (Parthenon, etc.)	458: Aeschylus, Oresteia trilogy 456: death of Aeschylus 455: first production of Euripides
431–404: Peloponnesian War (Athens vs. Sparta) 430–29: plague at Athens; death of Pericles	440s–20s: Herodotus writing 430s?: Protagoras visits Athens 427: Gorgias visits Athens 425: Aristophanes' first surviving play
415–13: Athenian expedition to Sicily ends in disaster	431–c.397: Thucydides writing
411: attempted coup at Athens	411: death of orator Antiphon late 400s and early 300s: orator Lysias active
404: defeat of Athens, with loss of empire; temporary government by '30 Tyrants', soon overthrown	406: deaths of Euripides and Sophocles 405: Aristophanes, Frogs
401–399: Xenophon on mercenary expedition to Asia Minor	399: execution of Socrates; subsequent growth of 'Socratic literature', especially by Plato (active till death in 347) and Xenophon.

Events	Literary and cultural phenomena
377: second Athenian League established	
	Isocrates active as writer and orator until his death in 338
359–336: Philip II king of Macedon; conquers Greece in 338 (battle of Chaeronea)	340s: Demosthenes, already active in forensic cases, becomes prominent in Athenian politics
336: Alexander succeeds to throne of Macedon after Philip's assassination	
	335: Aristotle founds his school at Athens (the Lyceum)
334: Alexander's expedition against Persia: victories over Darius III, 334, 333 followed by further wars in the East	
	330: Demosthenes' speech *On the Crown*
323: death of Alexander and division of his conquests	322: deaths of Aristotle and Demosthenes
	317: Menander, *Angry Old Man*
	307: Epicurus founds his school
	300: Zeno founds Stoic school
297–72: campaigns of Pyrrhus of Epirus in Italy	
	270s–50s: Callimachus, Theocritus, Apollonius, Herodas and others writing, mainly in Alexandria
264–41: first war between Rome and Carthage	
	c.240: at Rome, Livius Andronicus composes the first known Latin works modelled on Greek, including a translation of the *Odyssey*
218–202: second war between Rome and Carthage (the 'Hannibalic' war)	
	200: Plautus' first datable play, *Stichus*
	191: Plautus, *Pseudolus*
172–68: last of three wars between Rome and Macedonia, ending in battle of Pydna.	169: Death of Ennius
	167: Polybius brought to Rome

Events	Literary and cultural phenomena
	166–59: Terence producing plays
149–6: third Punic war; destruction of Carthage	
146: sack of Corinth; Greece becomes subject to Rome	
	130s–20s: Lucilius writing satires; associates with Scipio Aemilianus and Laelius
	*c.*100: Meleager, epigrammatist, compiles *Garland*, original core of Greek Anthology
	81: Cicero's first surviving speech; thereafter he is increasingly prominent until his death in 43
	70: Cicero, *Verrine speeches*
63: consulship of Cicero; conspiracy of Catiline crushed.	
60: alliance formed between Caesar, Pompey and Crassus ('first triumvirate')	
58–7: Cicero exiled	
58–49: Julius Caesar in Gaul (55–4 in Britain)	50s: Catullus writing
	56: Cicero, *Defence of Caelius*
	55 or ?49: Lucretius' poem published
	52: Cicero, *Defence of Milo*
49: Caesar crosses Rubicon; civil war.	
48: battle of Pharsalus; death of Pompey in Egypt	
46: suicide of Cato the Younger at Utica (north Africa)	46–4: Politically inactive, Cicero writes many philosophic works
47–44: dictatorship of Caesar; he is murdered on 15 March 44	
43: 'second triumvirate' formed (Antony, Octavian, Lepidus); elimination of opponents, including Cicero	44–3: Cicero, *Philippics* against Antony
	Between 46 and 35: Sallust, *Catiline* and *Jugurtha*
	Before *c.*40: Gallus' love elegies

Events	Literary and cultural phenomena
30s: increasing tension between Antony and Octavian leads to civil war; battle of Actium 31	c.38: Virgil, *Eclogues*
	c.31: Horace, *Epodes*
30: deaths of Antony and Cleopatra	29: Virgil, *Georgics* completed
27: Octavian granted title 'Augustus'; holds supreme power until his death in AD14	Elegies of Propertius and Tibullus begin to appear Livy's *History* begins to appear in instalments
	23: Horace, *Odes* books 1–3 published
	c.20: first works of Ovid 19: death of Virgil; *Aeneid* published posthumously 19: Horace, *Epistles* i
	8: deaths of Maecenas and Horace
AD	8: exile of Ovid; *Metamorphoses* largely complete, *Fasti* incomplete at this point
	9–12: Ovid, *Tristia*; *Letters from Pontus* are later
14 Accession of Tiberius	17: death of Ovid at Tomi
31: downfall of Tiberius' minister Sejanus	
	30: Velleius Paterculus' *History*
	54: Seneca, *Apocolocyntosis* ('Pumpkinification')
64: fire at Rome; Nero treats the Christians as scapegoats 65: purge by Nero; deaths of Lucan, Petronius, Seneca the Younger	60s: Persius, Lucan, Petronius active c.63: Seneca, *Letters*
69: year of the four emperors	67: Josephus deserts to Rome, subsequently writes works on Jewish history there

Events	Literary and cultural phenomena
70: fall of Jerusalem ends Jewish Revolt against Rome; destruction of the temple	
79: eruption of Vesuvius destroys Pompeii and Herculaneum	
	80: Martial celebrates construction of the Colosseum
	81–96: chief period of Statius' literary activity; Martial, epigrams.
	90s: Epictetus teaching in Nicopolis; heard by Arrian
	c.95: Quintilian, *Education of an Orator*
	98: Tacitus, *Agricola*, *Germania*
	99–109: Pliny, *Letters*, periodically published
	100: Pliny, *Panegyric*
Under Trajan (98–117): Roman Empire reaches its largest extent.	c.108: Tacitus, *Histories*
	c.100–120: Plutarch's most productive period
	c. 110: Pliny governor of Bithynia (*Letters*, book 10, mainly from this period)
	c.116: Tacitus completing the *Annals*
	c.120: Suetonius, *Lives of the Caesars*
	120s (and later): Arrian active
	c.150: Pausanias, *Description of Greece*
	150–80: Lucian active
	158 or 159: Apuleius, *Apology*, *Metamorphoses* undatable, but probably later
	170–80: Marcus Aurelius, *Meditations*
	c.175–80: Celsus, *On the True Doctrine*
	late 2nd and early 3rd century: Tertullian active
212: Caracalla grants citizenship to all those under Roman rule	
	c.224: Dio Cassius, *Roman History*
235–84: military anarchy	
	c.249: Origen, *Against Celsus*

Events	Literary and cultural phenomena
	269/70: death of Plotinus; his writings
284: division of the empire by	subsequently published by Porphyry
Diocletian	(c. 300)
303–5: 'great' persecution of Christians	
312: battle of the Milvian Bridge;	
Constantine proclaims himself Christian	
	c.317: Lactantius, *On the Deaths of the*
325: Council of Nicaea	*Persecutors*
362–3: Julian invades Parthia and dies	
on campaign	
374: Ambrose becomes Bishop of	
Milan	
	380–c.391: Ammianus composes his
384: dispute over removal of pagan	*History* in Rome
Altar of Victory from the Senate House	382: Jerome begins his work on the
in Rome	Latin Bible (the 'Vulgate'), completed
	c.405
	386: Conversion of Augustine
	395: Augustine becomes bishop of
	Hippo
	c.397–400: Augustine, *Confessions*
410: sack of Rome by Alaric the	
Visigoth	
	413–26: Augustine composing
	City of God
	430: death of Augustine

Appendix 3

List of Roman Emperors

All dates are AD after Augustus. Some who are neither mentioned in this book nor of great historical importance in themselves are omitted. Their full names and titles are not given, but only those by which they are most commonly referred to. For complete lists see e.g. E. Bickerman, *Chronology of the Ancient World* (2nd edn, 1980).

49–44 BC:	Julius Caesar dictator
31 BC–AD 14:	Augustus (his supremacy more clearly official from 27 BC)
14–37:	Tiberius
37–41:	Caligula (Gaius)
41–54:	Claudius
54–68:	Nero
68–9:	Galba
69 ('year of the four emperors'):	Otho
69:	Vitellius
69–79:	Vespasian
79–81:	Titus
81–96:	Domitian
96–8:	Nerva
97–117:	Trajan
117–38:	Hadrian
138–61:	Antoninus Pius
161–80:	Marcus Aurelius (with Lucius Verus 161–9)
177–92:	Commodus
193:	Pertinax
193:	Didius Julianus
193–211:	Septimius Severus

211–17:	Caracalla
217–18:	Macrinus
218–22:	Elagabalus
222–35:	Alexander Severus
235–84:	a long series of short-lived emperors, many of them usurpers. In 284 Diocletian establishes a system whereby the Western and Eastern halves of the empire each have a separate ruler (known as Augustus) and a deputy (Caesar). The Caesar sometimes succeeded to the Augustus role.

285–305: Maximian (West)

284–305: Diocletian (East)

293–306: Constantius I (Augustus from 305)

293–311: Galerius (Augustus from 305)

305–7: Severus (Augustus from 306)

305–13: Maximin Daia

306–8: Constantine I (as Caesar)

306–12: Maxentius usurper in Italy

308–11: Domitius Alexander usurper in Africa

308–24: Licinius

308–37: Constantine I joint emperor with Licinius until 324, thereafter rules alone

324–37: Constantine I

337–40: Constantine II

337–61: Constantius II

337–50: Constans

350–3: Magnentius attempts to usurp rule

353–61: Constantius II sole ruler of East and West, supported by Gallus (351–4) and Julian (355–61)

361–3: Julian sole ruler

363–4: Jovian sole ruler

364–75: Valentinian I

364–78: Valens

375–83: Gratian

379–95: Theodosius I

375–92: Valentinian II

392–4: Eugenius

394–5: Theodosius sole ruler of East and West

395–423: Honorius

395–408: Arcadius

408–50: Theodosius II

Appendix 4

Major Greek and Roman Gods

Since these are the divinities most frequently referred to in Greek and Latin poetry, it may be convenient for the reader to be able to see at a glance the conventional equivalents. It should be remembered that this is not just a matter of translating: in many cases gods of the Roman tradition are brought into line with the Greek deities and have some of their acts ascribed to them, while retaining much of their Roman character or significance (thus Mars is important for Romans as the father of Romulus, a relationship irrelevant to the Greek Ares). There were of course other Roman gods for whom no Greek equivalent was found, e.g. Janus, Terminus; and some Roman deities can be seen to resemble Greek gods without being fully identified with them (as Faunus has similarities to Pan).

Greek names	Roman names
Zeus	Jupiter
Hera	Juno
Demeter	Ceres
Poseidon	Neptune
Apollo	Apollo (the name Phoebus is also used by both Greeks and Romans)
Artemis	Diana
Hephaestus	Vulcan
Ares	Mars
Aphrodite	Venus
Athena	Minerva (also often called 'Pallas' by both)
Hermes	Mercury
Dionysus	Bacchus (though this name is also used in Greek)
Hades	Pluto or Dis ('Pluto' is also found in Greek, though more rarely)
Persephone	Proserpina
Heracles	Hercules

Notes

Preface

1 For this anecdote, see H. Lloyd-Jones, *Blood for the Ghosts* (1982), 200–1.

Introduction

1 Quintilian, 12.2.30; Horace, *Epistles* 2.1.156–7.
2 See further D. A. Russell, in D. West and T. Woodman (eds), *Creative Imitation and Latin Literature* (1979), 1–16.
3 Hor., *Epistles* 2.1.50–9, with Brink's notes; Prop., 4.1.64.
4 On the debate on silent reading, see A. K. Gavrilov and M. Burnyeat, in *CQ* 47 (1997), 56–73, 74–6.
5 Provoked by plagiarism, Galen went so far as to write a work *On My Own Books.* See also Cicero, *Letters to Atticus* 3.12.2; *On the Orator* 1.94. Horace, *Epistles* 1.20, plays with the notion of the book escaping from the author's control.
6 *Recollections of Socrates,* 4.2.10.
7 L. Casson, *Libraries in the Ancient World* (2001).
8 Catullus, 95, cf. Hor., *Epistles* 2.1.269–70.
9 C. H. Roberts and T. C. Skeat, *The Birth of the Codex* (1983).
10 A. S. Hollis, *Callimachus. Hecale* (1990), 37–40.
11 O. Skutsch, *The Annals of Q. Ennius* (1985), 26, is sceptical.
12 L. D. Reynolds and N. G. Wilson, *Scribes and Scholars* (3rd edn, 1991), 127.
13 Petrarch, *ad Familiares* [*To Friends*], 24.3, cf. 4 (16 June 1345), reprinted in F. E. Harrison (ed.), *Millennium, a Latin Reader* AD *374–1374* (1968), nos 49–50.
14 *JRS* 69 (1979), 125–55, re-edited by E. Courtney, *The Fragmentary Latin Poets* (1992), 259–68.
15 T. J. Luce, *Livy* (1977), 3–24; Augustine, *Letter to Firmus* (*Ep.* 1.A1 Divjak).
16 Ancient quotation, Plato, *Rep.* 380a; combined with papyrus find as Aeschylus F 154a Radt (translation in Aeschylus, Loeb edn, F77 + 277).

Chapter I Epic

1   H. Bloom, *The Anxiety of Influence* (1973). See also W. Jackson Bate, *The Burden of the Past in English. Poetry* (1971).

2   A. Cameron, *Callimachus and His Critics* (1995), 273–4.

3   Aristotle, *Rhetoric* 1375b30; M. L. West, *The Hesiodic Catalogue of Women* (1985), 10–11; P. A. Brunt, Loeb *Arrian* i (1976), appendix 4.

4   Rutherford, *Homer* (1996), 9–20, gives a fuller account with much bibliography. Adam Parry's introduction to the collected papers of M. Parry, *The Making of Homeric Verse* (1971), ix–lxii, gives a history of the debate.

5   Isocrates, 4.159; E. Hall, *Inventing the Barbarian* (1989), 164, etc.

6   J. Griffin, *Homer on Life and Death* (1980), 188–90.

7   A. Parry, *The Language of Achilles and Other Essays* (1989), 1–7; J. Griffin, *JHS* 106 (1986), 36–57.

8   On the history of the figure Odysseus/Ulysses, see W. B. Stanford, *The Ulysses Theme* (1963).

9   For an illuminating discussion of the ethos–pathos distinction, see C. Gill, *CQ* 34 (1984), 149–66.

10   West, *Hesiodic Catalogue*; R. L. Fowler, *PCPS* 44 (1998), 1–19.

11   M. Davies, *The Epic Cycle* (1987), gives a brief account.

12   The raw material was assembled by J. F. Carspecken, *Yale Classical Studies* 13 (1952), 33–143. More subtle treatments in G. O. Hutchinson, *Hellenistic Poetry* (1988), ch. 3; R. Hunter, *The Argonautica of Apollonius: Literary Studies* (1993).

13   G. O. Hutchinson, *Hellenistic Poetry* (1988), 87–97; A. Köhnken, in T. D. Papanghelis and A. Rengakos (eds), *A Companion to Apollonius Rhodius* (2001), 73–92.

14   M. Crump, *The Epyllion from Theocritus to Ovid* (1931) (very out of date); K. Gutzwiller, *Studies in the Hellenistic Epyllion* (1981); C. J. Fordyce, *Catullus. A Commentary* (1961), 272–6.

15   The fragments of Ennius are translated in the Loeb volume *Remains of Old Latin* I, ed. E. H. Warmington. The commentary on the Latin text of the *Annals* by O. Skutsch (1985) is definitive; for a fine introduction, see A. Gratwick, in *CHCL* ii.60–76 = paperback version ii.1.60–76.

16   Ovid, *Tristia* 2.259, 424.

17   P. Hardie, *Virgil's Aeneid, Cosmos and Imperium* (1986).

18   D. Feeney, *The Gods in Epic* (1991), ch. 4, has a rich discussion of these matters.

19   A. Parry, 'The Two Voices of Virgil's *Aeneid*', orig, 1963, in *The Language of Achilles . . .* , 78–96 (seminal). See also R. O. A. M. Lyne, *Further Voices in Virgil's Aeneid* (1987); P. Hardie, *Virgil* (*G & R*, new surveys, 28, 1998), esp. 94–101.

20   On the so-called 'Oration to the Saints', see R. Lane Fox, *Pagans and Christians* (1986), ch. 12, esp. 647–52.

21   *On Poetry and Poets* (1957), 53–71, 121–31.

22 K. Reinhardt, *Tradition und Geist* (1960), 16–36, esp. 25.

23 C. and M. Martindale, *Shakespeare and the Uses of Antiquity* (1990), ch. 2; J. Bate, *Shakespeare and Ovid* (1993).

24 *Amores* 3.6.17–18, *Tristia* 2.64, etc. See F. Graf, 'Myth in Ovid', in Hardie (ed.), *Cambridge Companion to Ovid* (2002), 108–121.

25 D. Quint, *Epic and Empire* (1993).

26 See Petronius, 118–24; this surely reacts to Lucan's poem, as argued e.g. by Walsh, *The Roman Novel* (1970), 50ff.

27 D. C. Feeney, *The Gods in Epic* (1991), 301–12; but contrast G. O. Hutchinson, *Latin Literature from Seneca to Juvenal* (1993), e.g. 71–2, 289–94.

Chapter 2 Drama

1 R. Rehm, *Greek Tragic Theater* (1992); P. E. Easterling (ed.), *Cambridge Companion to Greek Tragedy* (1997); E. Csapo and W. Slater, *The Context of Greek Drama* (1995).

2 Recent treatments of the topics covered in this paragraph include P. A. Cartledge, in Easterling, *Companion* 1ff.; C. B. R. Pelling, in his *Greek Tragedy and the Historian* (1997), 213–35, and many of the other contributions to that volume, esp. R. Parker, 143–60.

3 The topic attracts heated views. For a characteristically judicious introduction to the issues, see P. E. Easterling, in *Companion*, 36–53.

4 W. Burkert, *Greek Roman and Byzantine Studies* 7 (1966), 87–121, at p. 121, repr. in Burkert's *Savage Energies* (2001), 21.

5 Arist., *Poetics*: see esp. S. Halliwell, *Aristotle's Poetics* (1986); A. Rorty (ed.), *Essays on Aristotle's Poetics* (1992). Also E. Hall, in M. Silk (ed.), *Tragedy and the Tragic* (1996), 295–309.

6 Easterling, 'From Repertoire to Canon', in *Cambridge Companion to Greek. Tragedy* (1997), 211–27, discusses the processes of selection.

7 R. Buxton, *Persuasion in Greek Tragedy* (1982).

8 B. Knox, *The Heroic Temper* (1964), esp. chs 1–2 .

9 Soph., *Ajax* prologue; *Niobe* F 441A Radt. See R. Parker, in C. Pelling (ed.), *Greek Tragedy and the Historian* (1997), 143–60, and in J. Griffin (ed.), *Sophocles Revisited* (1999), 11–30.

10 M. Silk and J. P. Stern, *Nietzsche on Tragedy* (1981).

11 P. T. Stevens, *JHS* 76 (1956), 87–94, with reservations, e.g. by M. Lefkowitz, *Lives of the Greek Poets* (1981), ch. 9.

12 C. Collard, *G & R* 22 (1975), 58–71 = *Greek Tragedy* (eds I. McAuslan and P. Walcot, *G & R Studies* 2, 1993), 153–66; M. Lloyd, *The Agon in Euripides* (1992).

13 Full references, e.g. in W. K. C. Guthrie, *History of Greek Philosophy* iii (1969), 126–9, 151–9, 161, 226–34, 241, etc.

14 E. Hall, in Easterling, *Companion*, 93–126.

15 E. R. Dodds' commentary on the play remains a classic (1943, 2nd edn, 1960), as is R. P. Winnington-Ingram, *Euripides and Dionysus* (1948), recently reissued

with a foreword by P. E. Easterling. For more recent work, see C. Segal, *Dionysiac Poetics and Euripides' Bacchae* (1982; revised edn, 1997), esp. the afterword at 349–93; and an important series of papers by A. Henrichs on Dionysus, bacchants, etc.: e.g. *HSCP* 88 (1984), 205–40.

16 Soph., F314–317 Radt (tr. in Loeb, Sophocles vol. 3); T. Harrison, *The Trackers of Oxyrhynchus* (Faber, 1990).

17 E. Hall, 'Ithyphallic Men Behaving Badly; or, Satyr-Drama as Gendered Tragic Ending', in *Parchments of Gender*, ed. M. Wyke (1998), 14–37.

18 For different approaches, see A. W. Gomme, *More Essays on Greek History and Literature* (1937), 70–91; G. de Ste Croix, *The Origins of the Peloponnesian War* (1972), appendix 29; C. Pelling, *Literary Texts and the Greek Historian* (1999), chs 7–8; M. Silk, *Aristophanes and the Definition of Comedy* (2000), ch. 7.

19 I borrow the phrase from E. Segal, in a *TLS* review of Silk's book.

20 Valuable cautions by E. Csapo, in M. Depew and D. Obbink (eds), *Matrices of Genre* (2000), 115–33.

21 K. J. Dover, *Aristophanic Comedy* (1972), ch. 3, esp. 31–41; other aspects discussed in S. Halliwell, *CQ* 41 (1991), 279–96.

22 Eupolis, *Taxiarchs* F 268, 269, 272, 274 K-A.

23 *The World of Athens* (JACT, 1984), 318; author not identified: P. Jones?

24 P. Rau, *Paratragodia* (1967); M. Silk, *Aristophanes . . .* , ch. 2.

25 T.11 Koerte = Plut. *Mor.*347F.

26 Horace, *Art of Poetry*, 189–90, with C. O. Brink's commentary.

27 Menander, *Twice-deceiver*, 18–30, 102–12, and Plautus, *Bacchides*, 494–562; E. W. Handley, *Menander and Plautus: A Study in Comparison* (1968); D. Bain, in *Creative Imitation and Latin Literature*, eds D. West and T. Woodman (1979), 17–34.

28 *Epistles*, 2.1.170ff., 182ff.

29 Gripus, in *Rudens*, 1249ff, see R. Hunter, *The New Comedy of Greece and Rome* (1985), ch. 6.

30 H. D. Jocelyn, *The Tragedies of Ennius* (1967), introd. (advanced); A. S. Gratwick, in *CHCL* ii. 77–84.

31 *Selected Essays* (3rd edn, 1951), 68.

32 Discussion in J. Bate's edn (1995), esp. 29–36; cf. his *Shakespeare and Ovid* (1993), 100–17.

Chapter 3 Rhetoric

1 P. Shorey, *TAPA* 40 (1908), 185.

2 *Iliad* 3.204–24; simile, 16.384–93; scene on shield, 18.497–508. Odysseus as speaker, *Od.* 11.333–4, 373–6, 17.513–21, 19.203, etc.

3 Hdt. 7.7ff., esp. 10.1; Cambyses' court, 3.31–6.

4 A. H. M. Jones, *Athenian Democracy* (1957); M. H. Hansen, *The Athenian Democracy in the Age of Demosthenes* (1991).

5   D. M. MacDowell, *Gorgias, Helen* (text, translation, commentary) (1982).

6   Seneca the Elder, *Suasoria* 3; Juvenal 1.15–7. S. F. Bonner, *Roman Declamation* (1949).

7   D. A. Russell, 'Rhetoric and Criticism', *G & R* 14 (1967), 130–44; A. E. Douglas' introduction to his edn of Cicero's *Brutus* (1966), xxv–lii.

8   I. Worthington (ed.), *Demosthenes, Statesman and Orator* (2000).

9   E. Hall, *Bulletin of the Institute of Classical Studies* 40 (1995), 39–85; S. Halliwell, in *Greek Tragedy and the Historian*, ed. C. Pelling (1997), 121–42.

10 Eur., *Hipp.* 899–1101, *Trojan Women*, 860–1059.

11 C. Macleod, 'Thucydides and Tragedy', *Collected Essays* (1983), 140–58.

12 G. Wills, *Lincoln at Gettysberg: The Words That Remade America* (1992).

13 S. Halliwell, in *Persuasion*, ed. I. Worthington (1994), 222–43.

14 *Phaedrus* 230, 246–7, 253c–6d; see further Rutherford, *The Art of Plato* (1995), ch. 9.

15 Important discussions assembled in A. O. Rorty (ed.), *Essays on Aristotle's Rhetoric* (1996).

16 E. Gruen, *Studies in Greek Culture and Roman Policy* (1990), 171–4.

17 Biographies of Cicero are numerous: see esp. E. Rawson, *Cicero: A Portrait* (1973). D. R. Shackleton Bailey's translations of the whole correspondence are outstanding: originally in Penguin, they are now available in the revised Loebs.

18 Brutus to Atticus, *Letters to M. Brutus* 1.17; Seneca, *On the Brevity of Life* 5.1.

19 The classic statement of this case was by T. Mommsen, *History of Rome* (1856): iv.159, 572ff. in the Everyman translation (1901). In response, see e.g. T. P. Wiseman, *Historiography and Imagination* (1994), 86–9.

20 Shackleton Bailey, *Cicero, Letters to Atticus* i (1965), introduction, esp. 57–9; J. P. V. D. Balsdon, 'Cicero the Man' in *Cicero*, ed. T. A. Dorey (1965), 171–214.

21 For a model analysis of a passage from another speech, see R. G. M. Nisbet, *Collected Papers on Latin Literature* (1995), 362–80.

22 Sen., *Controversiae* 1, preface 6; 10, preface 6–7.

23 Syme, *Tacitus* (1958), ch. 25, with appendices 26–7.

24 Pliny's speech is in vol. 2 of the Loeb of his works. The others are translated and analysed by C. E. V. Nixon and B. S. Rodgers, *In Praise of Later Roman Emperors* (1994).

25 Quintilian has been outstandingly edited, with rich annotation, by D. A. Russell in the Loeb Library (2001), completely superseding the older edition in that series. G. Kennedy, *Quintilian* (1969); M. L. Clarke and M. Winterbottom, in T. A. Dorey (ed.), *Empire and Aftermath* (1975).

26 G. Bowersock, *Greek Sophists in the Roman Empire* (1969); G. Anderson, *The Second Sophistic* (1993); S. Swain, *Hellenism and Empire* (1996).

27 Translated by V. J. C. Hunink, in S. J. Harrison et al., *Apuleius, Rhetorical Works* (2001).

28 M. Edwards et al. (eds), *Apologetics in the Roman Empire: Pagans, Jews and Christians* (1999).

29 M. L. Clarke, *Rhetoric at Rome* (1953, revised 1996), ch. 14.

Chapter 4 History, Biography and Fiction

1 Hdt. 1.24. Ultra-sceptical treatment by D. Fehling, *Herodotus and His 'Sources'* (1989), 21–4; contrast W. K. Pritchett, *The Liar School of Herodotus* (1993), 16–25.

2 *Die Fragmente der griechischer Historiker* (1923–), incomplete at Jacoby's death and recently resumed by a team of scholars.

3 J. Gould, *Herodotus* (1989), is a brilliant overview; see also D. Lateiner, *The Historical Method of Herodotus* (1989); R. Thomas, *Herodotus in Context: Ethnography, Science and the Art of Persuasion* (2000). A Cambridge Companion to Herodotus is imminent. Two essays of fundamental importance are O. Murray, 'Herodotus and Oral History', now revised in N. Luraghi (ed.) *The Historian's Craft in the Age of Herodotus* (2001), and R. L. Fowler, 'Herodotus and his Predecessors', *JHS* 116 (1996), 62–87. The revised Penguin by J. Marincola is the best modern version, with much additional material; excellent too is the World's Classics version, tr. R. Waterfield, with notes etc. by C. Dewald.

4 Thucydides: W. R. Connor, *Thucydides* (1984), S. Hornblower, *Thucydides* (1987); an English version of H. P. Stahl's important 1966 monograph appeared in 2003. The Penguin badly needs replacing; a new World's Classics by Simon Hornblower is promised and eagerly awaited. Meanwhile there is a version in the Hackett library by S. Lattimore (1998), and a de luxe version, with extensive maps and appendices, by R. B. Strassler, *The Landmark Thucydides* (The Free Press, 1996), incorporating the translation by R. Crawley.

5 On Xenophon, see G. L. Cawkwell's introductions to the revised Penguin versions of the *Hellenica* ('A History of my Times') and the *Anabasis* ('The Persian expedition'). A forthcoming volume of essays on the *Anabasis* edited by R. Lane Fox will break new ground.

6 A. Momigliano, *The Development of Greek Biography* (1971, revised edn 1993)

7 M. A. Flower, *Theopompus of Chios* (1994).

8 O. Murray, *Classical Quarterly* 22 (1972), 200–13.

9 U. Wilcken, *Alexander the Great* (Eng. tr. 1932), is a classic; A. B. Bosworth, *Conquest and Empire* (1988), is the standard modern account.

10 F. W. Walbank, *Polybius* (1972); the same scholar gives a shorter sketch in the Penguin selection, and a brief essay in *Latin Historians* (1962).

11 See Walbank, *Polybius*, 88–9.

12 For a masterly survey of the evidence for these lost sources, E. Badian in *Latin Historians*, ed. T. A. Dorey (1966), 1–38. On Livy himself, see P. G. Walsh in the same volume, 115–42, and his *Livy: His Historical Aims and Methods* (1961. More recent studies include T. J. Luce, *Livy: The Composition of His History* (1977); J. D. Chaplin, *Livy's Exemplary History* (2000).

13 E.g. Rutilius on Scaurus: see Badian, in *Latin Historians*, 23–5.

14 Livy's sources: Walsh, *Livy*, ch. 5, gives a brief account; for vastly more detail on the annalistic tradition, S. P. Oakley, *Commentary on Livy Books VI–X*, vol. 1 (1997), 21–108.

15   Cicero to Lucceius, *Letters to Friends* 5.12. The letter has been much discussed: see N. Rudd in T. Woodman and J. Powell (eds), *Author and Audience in Latin Literature* (1992), 18–32.

16   On Sallust generally, G. M. Paul, in *Latin Historians* (1966), 85–114; D. C. Earl, *The Political Thought of Sallust* (1961).

17   K. Welsh and A. Powell (eds), *Julius Caesar as Artful Reporter* (1998).

18   T. Rajak, *Josephus* (1984), esp. chs 4 and 8. Two 'collaborators', Polybius and Josephus, are compared by F. W. Walbank, *Polybius, Rome and the Hellenistic World* (2002), 258–76, an illuminating essay.

19   A. J. Woodman, in *Empire and Aftermath*, ed. T. A. Dorey (1975), 1–25, and other studies listed in Kraus and Woodman, *Latin Historians* (1997), 82–4, 86.

20   Claudius' speech has long been known: *ILS* 212, compared with Tac. *Ann.* 11.24. For the Tiberian document, the recently discovered Senatus Consultum de Pisone patre, see M. Griffin, *JRS* 87 (1997), 249–63.

21   R. Syme, *Tacitus* (1958), a landmark work but complex and not for the beginner: the essential critique is the review-discussion by A. N. Sherwin-White, *JRS* 49 (1959), 140ff. More accessible than Syme: R. Martin, *Tacitus* (1981); R. Mellor, *Tacitus* (1993). A. J. Woodman, *Tacitus Reviewed* (1998), is in many ways the most stimulating work since Syme.

22   J. Matthews, *The Roman Empire of Ammianus* (1987), is very long but very rich: see esp. chs 1–2, 6–8, 18. For a short and excellent account by the same author, see the essay on Ammianus in T. J. Luce (ed.), *Ancient Writers: Greece and Rome* (1982), vol. 2, 1117–38. The Penguin is admirable but abridged.

23   Ammianus' obituary of Constantius: 21.16; of Julian: 25.4.

24   17.1.14.

25   E.g. 17.11.2ff., 24.2.16–17, 24.4.5, 24.6.7 and 14.

26   Matthews, 274–7, on eunuchs.

27   *Alexander* 1, cf. A. J. Gossage, in T. A. Dorey (ed.), *Latin Biography* (1967), 58ff., with nn. 34–42.

28   A. Wallace-Hadrill, *Suetonius* (1984). The Penguin version should be avoided; better is the translation by C. Edwards in the World's Classics.

29   D. A. Russell, *Plutarch* (1973); C. Pelling, *Plutarch and History* (2002), with many important papers: note 'Truth and Fiction in Plutarch's *Lives*', 143–70.

30   In general, see E. Gabba, 'True History and False History in Classical Antiquity', *JRS* 71 (1981), 50–2; C. Gill and T. P. Wiseman (eds), *Lies and Fiction in the Ancient World* (1993), esp. the essays by Wiseman and Morgan.

31   J. S. Romm, *The Edges of the Earth in Ancient Thought* (1992).

32   Fehling, *Herodotus and His 'Sources'* (1989). For criticisms, see J. Gould, *Herodotus* (1989), 136–7; Pritchett, cited above; K. J. Dover, in *Modus Operandi* (Fest. G. Rickman), eds M. Austin et al. (*BICS* Suppl. 71, 1998), 219–25.

33   T. P. Wiseman, *Clio's Cosmetics* (1979); A. J. Woodman, *Rhetoric in Classical Historiography* (1988) – controversial; Pelling 'Truth and Fiction', cited above.

34   Polyb. 10.21, Lucian *How To Write History*, e.g. 7–12.

35   Suda s.v.; A. Grafton, *Forgers and Critics* (1990), ch. 1.

36   Diodorus 5.41–6.

37 Various passages from 4.6 onwards, concluding in 7.3. See D. Gera, *Xenophon's Cyropaedia* (1993), 192–245.

38 S. Stephens and J. Winkler, *Ancient Greek Novels: The Fragments* (1995), 94.

39 All of these, and other related works, are translated in B. P. Reardon (ed.), *Collected Ancient Greek Novels* (1989).

40 B. Perry, *The Ancient Romances* (1967) 5, cf. 98. For more recent discussion of the readership and context of these works, see S. Swain, *Hellenism and Empire* (1996), ch. 4, with ample bibliography (104n.9 on readers).

41 Stephens and Winkler, 101–72; Reardon, 775–82.

42 Stephens and Winkler, 358ff.; Reardon, 816–18.

43 Stephens and Winkler, 340, 190; Reardon, 783–97.

44 Stephens and Winkler, 194–5; Reardon, 788.

45 E. Auerbach, *Mimesis*, ch. 2. A detailed study by B. Boyce, *The Language of the Freedmen in Petronius' Cena Trimalchionis* (1991).

46 Translated in Reardon's collection, 589–618. Comparison between the texts, e.g. by Walsh, *The Roman Novel*, 146–9.

47 Julian, *Epistle* 89.301b Bidez (vol. 2.326 Loeb); Macrobius, *Commentary on the Dream of Scipio* 1.2.7–8.

Chapter 5 Erotic Literature

1 For Greek lyric, elegiac and iambic poetry the most thorough editions with translations are the Loeb volumes: Greek lyric by D. A. Campbell, iambic and elegiac by D. Gerber. M. L. West's compact translation of the fragmentary authors (World's Classics 1993) is by a world expert but gives very slender annotation. More helpful though less complete is A. W. Miller, *Greek Lyric* (Hackett 1996), which also has extensive selections from Pindar and Bacchylides.

2 Originally published by R. Merkelbach and M. L. West, *ZPE* 14 (1974), 97ff. Discussion by A. P. Burnett, *Three Archaic Poets* (1983), 83–97.

3 A. Cavarzere et al. (eds), *Iambic Ideas* (2001).

4 Semonides 7 West; H. Lloyd-Jones, *Females of the Species* (1974).

5 J. Gould, *JHS* 100 (1980), 38–59 = Gould, *Myth, Ritual, Memory and Exchange* (2001) 112–57, and R. Just, *Women in Athenian Law and Life* (1989), are important contributions on Athens, S. Treggiari, *Roman Marriage* (1991), on Rome.

6 D. Halperin, *One Hundred Years of Homosexuality* (1990), esp. ch. 1.

7 K. J. Dover, *Greek Homosexuality* (1978), which strongly influenced Foucault.

8 Aeschylus, *Myrmidons*, part of a lost trilogy: see frr. 135–7 Radt (Loeb edn. frr. 64–6). Thucydides 6.54–9.

9 P. Brown, *The Body and Society* (1988).

10 Women's writing: J. M. Snyder, *The Woman and the Lyre* (1990). Sappho: see two collections of essays edited by Ellen Greene, *Reading Sappho. Contemporary Approaches*, and *Rereading Sappho. Reception and Transmission* (1996).

11 I take the opening words here to be part of what the departing girl is saying, but they may possibly be Sappho's own reaction.

12 O. Murray, *Sympotica* (1992).

13 R. Hunter, *Plato's Symposium* (2004).

14 W. M. Ellis, *Alcibiades* (1989), D. Gribble, *Alcibiades and Athens* (1999), ch. 4.

15 Many authors are discussed by P. M. Fraser, *Ptolemaic Alexandria* (1972), 553–617, but this book requires considerable Greek. The same is true of D. H. Garrison, *Mild Frenzy* (1978), K. Gutzwiller, *Poetic Garlands: Hellenistic Epigrams in Context* (1998).

16 Text and translation by C. Austin and G. Bastianini, *Posidippi Pellaei quae Supersunt Omnia* (Milan 2002).

17 A. Cameron, *The Greek Anthology* (1993), discusses the processes of compilation. (advanced). Select translations, often very free, in Penguin (*The Greek Anthology*, ed. P. Jay, 1973).

18 The lamp as witness: Meleager *AP*. 5.8. Lovers outside the door: Call. Epigram 63 Pf. = *AP*.5.23, Ascl. ibid. 145. Eros as truant: Meleager *AP* 5.177.

19 *SH* 401; bolder text in Page, *GLP* 120; C. M. Bowra, *Greek Poetry and Life* (1936), 325ff = *Problems in Greek Poetry*, 151ff.; Snyder, *The Woman and the Lyre*, 86–97, with cautious translation on 93.

20 Theocritus: A. W. Bulloch in *CHCL* i, 576–86; G. O. Hutchinson, *Hellenistic Poetry* (1988), ch. 4. Translations by R. Wells (Penguin, 1988) and by A. Verity, with introduction by R. Hunter (2002).

21 F. Graf, *Magic in the Ancient World* (1997, Fr. original 1994), esp. 175–85.

22 Virgil *Eclogue* 2; compared in detail with Theocritus by I. Du Quesnay, in *Creative Imitation and Latin Literature*, eds D. West and T. Woodman (1979), 35–69. For Ovid's treatment see *Met*. 13.738–897.

23 A good book on Catullus is still needed: one by J. H. Gaisser is expected from Blackwell. T. P. Wiseman, *Catullus and His World* (1985), is readable and rich on the historical background.

24 J. Griffin, *Latin Poets and Roman Life* (1984), ch. 1. See also J. P. V. D. Balsdon, *Romans and Aliens* (1979).

25 Cic. *Att*. 15.11.

26 R. MacMullen, *Changes in the Roman Empire* (1990) 177–89.

27 For the type of poem, compare e.g. Simias 1 Gow-Page (*AP* 7.203), on a dead partridge. G. Williams, *Tradition and Originality in Roman Poetry* (1968), 185–94, for other examples of Catullus' procedure.

28 Callimachus epigram 25 Pfeiffer = *AP* 5.6; Catullus 70.

29 Tom Stoppard's play, *The Invention of Love* (1997), captivatingly explores this and other aspects of classical studies of erotic literature.

30 *JRS* 69 (1979), 125–55, re-edited by E. Courtney *The Fragmentary Latin Poets* (1992) 259–68.

31 Older handbook by G. Luck, *The Latin Love Elegy* (1959, revised 1969), retains some value. More recent approaches: P. Veyne, *Latin Erotic Elegy* (Eng. tr. 1988; Fr. original 1983); M. Wyke, *The Roman Mistress* (2002): her ch. 5 surveys 'gender and scholarship on love elegy'.

32 The new book by M. Skole, *Reading Sulpicia: Commentaries 1476–1990* (2002), surveys the history of interpretation, shedding light only indirectly on the actual poems.

33 Williams, *Tradition and Originality in Roman Poetry*, 526–42.

34 I. Du Quesnay in *Ovid*, ed. J. W. Binns (1974), 1–45, is a very useful introduction.

35 J. N. Adams, *The Latin Sexual Vocabulary* (1982), 118–38; more broadly A. Richlin, *The Garden of Priapus* (2nd edn, 1992); A. Corbeill, *Controlling Laughter* (1996), chs 3–4, esp. 154–9.

36 *PMG* 976. Sometimes ascribed to Sappho, but not before Arsenius in *c*.1500: to suppose he had any evidence for this is wishful thinking.

Chapter 6 Literature and Power

1 K. J. Dover, 'The Freedom of the Intellectual in Greek Society', in Dover, *The Greeks and Their Legacy* (1988), 135–58; on Rome, R. MacMullen, *Enemies of the Roman Order* (1966); F. H. Cramer, *Journal of the History of Ideas* 6 (1945), 157–96.

2 *Annals* 3.65, accepting the traditional interpretation despite the arguments of Woodman ad loc; cf. 4.33 and 35 (see appendix 1.4).

3 Nisbet and Hubbard on Horace, *Odes* i.12.50.

4 For an outline of the world of Greek lyric, see E. L. Bowie in *Oxford History of the Classical World*, eds Boardman et al. (1986), 99–112. More detail in D. Gerber (ed.), *A Companion to the Greek Lyric Poets* (1997); on the authors and texts, G. O. Hutchinson, *Greek Lyric Poetry: A Commentary on Selected Larger Pieces* (2001).

5 H. V. Canter, *American Journal of Philology* 54 (1933), 201ff.

6 D. Boedeker and D. Sider (eds), *The New Simonides. Contexts of Praise and Desire* (2001).

7 F. Nisetich provides a valuable introduction and the best translation (*Pindar's Victory Odes*, 1980). See also H. Lloyd-Jones, 'Pindar', in *Academic Papers* i (1990), 57–79, and W. H. Race's excellent Loeb edition (1997).

8 Partial exceptions include *Py.* 1.75–7, *Isthm.* 2.6ff.

9 E. L. Bundy, *Studia Pindarica* (1962). An important counterblast was the paper by H. Lloyd-Jones, *JHS* 93 (1973) 109–37 = *Academic Papers* i (1990), 110–54. Pindar is restored to his rich historical context in a forthcoming work by Simon Hornblower.

10 Pind. fr. 76; Ar. *Acharnians* 637, cf. *Knights* 1329.

11 Arist. *Rhetoric* 1398a.

12 *Rhet.* 1405b 23–8 = *PMG* 515.

13 Onesicritus, *FGH* 134 T8 = Plut. *Alexander* 46.

14 Suet. *Aug.* 89, cf. Hor. *Ep.*ii.1.229ff.

15 On Callimachus, see A. Bulloch, in *CHCL* i.549–70; Hutchinson, *Hellenistic Poetry* (1988), ch. 2; more advanced are Fraser, *Ptolemaic Alexandria* (1972), ch. 11 (very detailed, and out of date on a number of important points); A. Cameron, *Callimachus and His Critics* (1995).

16 Timon, *SH* 786. The rendering is disputed: 'scribblers' is another possibility for 'inmates'. See A. Cameron, *Callimachus and His Critics* (1995), 31.

17 J. B. Burton, *Theocritus' Urban Mimes* (1995).

18 Hutchinson, *Hellenistic Poetry* (1988), 39.

19 Plut. *Is. et Os.* 360c.

20 A. Dalzell, *Phoenix* 10 (1956), 151–62; J. Griffin, in *Caesar Augustus* (1984), 189–218; P. White, *Promised Verse* (1993), with review by D. Feeney, *Bryn Mawr Classical Review* (online journal; 1994).

21 Important review of Syme by A. Momigliano, *JRS* 30 (1940), 75–80; see also F. Millar on Syme, *JRS* 71 (1981), 144–52; K. Raaflaub and M. Toher (eds) *Between Republic and Empire* (1990); *La Révolution romaine après Ronald Syme*, Fondation Hardt Entretiens 46 (2000).

22 E. Rawson, *Intellectual Life in the Late Roman Republic* (1985), ch. 16.

23 R. Jenkyns, *Virgil's Experience* (2000), is good on these themes; for other aspects see the works cited by P. Hardie, *Virgil* (*G & R* new surveys 28, 1998), ch. 2.

24 On the *Georgics*, see works cited in notes 14–15 to ch. 8, and p. 340.

25 Catullus' poem 13 exploits the convention. See also Nisbet and Hubbard on *Odes* i.20.

26 P. A. Brunt, *The Fall of the Roman Republic* (1988), ch. 7, arguing against the cynicism of Syme and others.

27 S. Commager, *The Odes of Horace. A Critical Study* (1962), ch. 4.

28 P. White, *Promised Verse* (1993), 266–8.

29 Fraser, *Ptolemaic Alexandria* (1972), 311–12.

30 Older view: L. P. Wilkinson, *Ovid Recalled* (1955), chs 9–10. Rehabilitations: E. J. Kenney, *PCPS* 11 (1965), 37–49; R. J. Dickinson in *Ovid*, ed. J. Binns (1974), 154–90; G. Williams, *Banished Voices* (1994). R. Syme, *History in Ovid* (1979), did much to reawaken historians' interest in Ovid. More recent work is accessible through *The Cambridge Companion to Ovid*, ed. P. Hardie (2002).

31 Suet. *Tib.* 45, Tac. *Dial.* 3. See further MacMullen, *Enemies of the Roman Order* (1966), chs 1–2; S. Bartsch, *Actors in the Audience* (1994), ch. 3.

32 The edition of the *Apoc.* by P. T. Eden includes translation. See further M. Coffey, *Roman Satire* (1976), ch. 9.

33 K. Coleman, 'The Emperor Domitian and Literature', *Aufstieg und Niedergang* ii.32.5 (1986), 3087–3115, and 'Latin Literature after AD 96', *American Journal of Ancient History* 15 (1999), 19–39.

34 The new Loeb edition by D. R. Shackleton Bailey (2003) will now be the standard text and translation; it includes an essay by K. Coleman on recent literary study of the work. See esp. A. Hardie, *Statius and the Silvae* (1983); also D. Vessey in *CHCL* ii, a lively treatment (pp. 561–72).

35 R. Syme, *Tacitus* (1958), 95–7.

36 On Symmachus and Claudian, see the essays by J. Matthews and A. Cameron in J. W. Binns (ed.), *Latin Literature of the Fourth Century* (1974).

Chapter 7 Aspects of Wit

1 J. N. Bremmer, in Bremmer and G. Roodenberg, *A Cultural History of Humour* (Cambridge 1997), 11–28.

2 Macr. 2.1–7; 2.3 for Cicero, 2.4 for Augustus.

3   M. A. Grant, *Ancient Theories of the Laughable: The Greek Rhetoricians and Cicero* (1924); R. Janko, *Aristotle on Comedy* (1984), esp. 161–7: see Arist. *Rh.* i.11, iii.11; Demetr. 128–72; Cic. *On the Orator* 2.235–90, *Orator* 87–90, Qu. vi.3.

4   Callimachus, Epigram 43 Pfeiffer =*AP* 12.134.

5   K. J. Dover, *Theocritus, Select Idylls* (1971), lxvii; F. Cairns, *Tibullus* (1979), 7–17; H. Lloyd-Jones, 'A Hellenistic Miscellany', in *Academic Papers* ii (1990), 231–49.

6   In what follows I owe much, as elsewhere, to P. J. Parsons: see esp. his superb overview 'Identities in Diversity', in A. W. Bulloch et al. (eds), *Images and Ideology: Self-definition in the Hellenistic World* (1993), 152–70, with the response by A. Henrichs, 171–95.

7   It was already felt at the end of the fifth century: Choerilus F 2 Bernabé = *SH* 317. For parallels, see Nisbet and Hubbard on Hor., *Odes* i.26.10.

8   See esp. R. Pfeiffer, *Ausgewählte Schriften* (1960), 154ff., 160ff.; *History of Classical Scholarship*, i (1968), 87ff., 133f., etc.

9   Though recent studies of an Athenian inscription, *SEG* 32.118, a list of donors, suggest he did visit Athens.

10   See R. Queneau et al. (eds), *Oulipo Laboratory: Texts from the Bibliotheque Oulipienne* (1996).

11   A. S. Hollis, *Callimachus Hecale* (1990), 339–40.

12   M. L. West, *Hesiod Theogony* (1966), 158–9.

13   P. J. Parsons, *ZPE* 25 (1977), 1–50.

14   *SH* 259; cf. E. Livrea, *ZPE* 34 (1979), 37, summarized at *SH*, pp. 114–15.

15   *FGH* 442.

16   E.g. T26 and 89 Pf.

17   Reputation: e.g. Qu.10.1.58. Influence: W. Wimmel, *Kallimachos in Rom* (*Hermes Einzelschrift* 16, 1966).

18   The need for a good modern study of Propertius is as great as for Catullus. M. Hubbard, *Propertius* (1974), is not adequate. H. P. Stahl, *Propertius: 'Love' and 'War': Individual and State under Augustus* (1985), is thorough but one-sided.

19   A. Wallace-Hadrill, in *Homo Viator*, Fest. J. Bramble, eds M. Whitby et al. (1987), 221–30; D. Feeney, in *Poetry and Propaganda in the Age of Augustus*, ed. A. Powell (1992), 1–25; G. Herbert-Brown, *Ovid and the Fasti* (1994), ch. 1.

20   A. Barchiesi, *The Poet and the Prince* (Eng. tr. 1997; Ital. original 1993).

21   J. McKeown, *PCPS* 25 (1979), 71–84; E. Fantham, *HSCP* 87 (1983), 185–216.

22   *Met.* 7.484; 4.607, 673.

23   *Met.* 15.4ff, 479–81. Contrast Cic., *On the State* 2.29, Livy 1.18. Ovid's knowledge of Livy's first book is evident from his version of the Tarquinius story in the *Fasti*.

24   Useful material on comparanda between Greek and Roman epigram in J. P. Sullivan, *Martial: The Unexpected Classic* (1991), 322–7.

25   R. G. M. Nisbet, *Cicero, In Pisonem* (1961), appendix on invective (pp. 192–7).

26   On puns on names, see Corbeill, *Controlling Laughter* (1996), ch. 2.

27   *Against Piso* 1, Macrobius 2.3.5, Cicero, *Letters to Quintus* 2.3.2, *Defence of Caelius* 32, 36.

28   Catullus 16; Ovid, *Tristia* 1.9.59, 2.353ff.; Martial 1.4.8. Cf. Sullivan, *Martial*, ch. 2.

29   N. M. Kay on Mart. 11.29.

30   L. Watson, in *Homage to Horace*, ed. S. J. Harrison (1995), 188–202.

31   The fragments of these are translated in L. Watson, *Arae: The Curse Poetry of Antiquity* (1991), 223–9.

32   See M. Coffey, *Roman Satire* (1976), ch. 2; J. Powell, in *Homo Viator*, eds Whitby et al. (1987), 253–8.

33   Gratwick, in *CHCL* ii.162–71, an excellent account. See also Coffey, *Roman Satire*, ch. 4.

34   On the politics of the satires, I. Du Quesnay in *Poetry and Politics in the Age of Augustus*, ed. T. Woodman and D. West (1984), 19–58.

35   Cf. Dryden, *A Discourse Concerning Satire* (1693), repr. e.g. in J. Dryden, *Of Dramatic Poesy and Other Essays*, ed. G. Watson, vol. 2 (1962), 71–155.

36   W. S. Anderson, *Essays on Roman Satire* (1982), 293–361.

37   R. Jenkyns, *Three Classical Poets* (1982), ch. 3, has much of interest. On the levels of style, see J. Powell, in *Aspects of the Language of Latin Poetry*, eds J. N. Adams and R. Mayer (1999), 311–34.

38   E. Gowers, *The Loaded Table* (1993), esp. chs 1 and 3. On the dinner-party theme, see also N. Rudd, *The Satires of Horace* (1966), ch. 7; on food, J. Davidson, *Courtesans and Fishcakes* (1997), P. Garnsey, *Food and Society in Classical Antiquity* (1999).

39   S. Braund, *Beyond Anger* (1988), though primarily applying this title to poems 7–9.

40   W. Jackson Bate, *Samuel Johnson* (1978), ch. 17.

41   C. Robinson, *Lucian and His Influence in Europe* (1979); J. Hall, *Lucian's Satire* (1981); C. P. Jones, *Culture and Society in Lucian* (1986). Selection by P. Turner in Penguin.

42   In the traditional numeration of Lucian's works, those referred to are: nos 58, 7, 45, 48, 33.

43   *Twice Accused*, 33–4, *Prometheus in Words*, 7. See e.g. Robinson, 8–20.

Chapter 8 Thinkers

1   R. B. Rutherford, *The Meditations of Marcus Aurelius, a Study* (1989), 66–76, e.g. Plato, *Gorgias*, 484–5; Tac., *Agr.* 4.3; Suet., *Nero* 52.1; Epictetus 1.26.5. For the other side, however (philosophers receiving high civic recognition), see C. Habicht, *Athen in Hellenistischer Zeit: gesammelte Aufsätze* (1994), 231–47 ('Hellenistic Athens and Her Philosophers').

2   Cic., *On the Nature of the Gods* 1.79; Juvenal 2; Lucian, *Philosophers for Sale*.

3   See further E. R. Curtius, *European Literature and the Latin Middle Ages* (1953), ch. 11.

4   A. D. Nock, *Conversion* (1933), ch. 11.

5   Rutherford, *Meditations of Marcus Aurelius*, 22 n.61.

6   There is an excellent commentary on *Republic* 10, with translation, by S. Halliwell (1988). J. Powell's tr. and comm. (*Cicero On Friendship, and The Dream of Scipio*, 1990) is the best introduction to Cicero's imitation.

7   J. Dillon, *The Middle Platonists* (1977), 1–11; *The Heirs of Plato* (2003).

8   Cic., *Letters to Atticus* 13. 19.3–4, *Letters to Quintus* 3.5.1.

9   R. Lane Fox, *PCPS* 42 (1996), 127–70.

10 See esp. *Att.* 9.4: more in Rutherford, *Meditations of Marcus Aurelius*, ch. 2, esp. 69 n.75.

11 P. A. Brunt, *Fall of the Roman Republic* (1988), ch. 7.

12 *Letters to Quintus* 2.10.3 (54 BC), G. O. Hutchinson, *CQ* 51 (2001), 150–62.

13 C. J. Classen, *TAPA* 99 (1968), 77–118 = *Probleme der Lukrezforschung*, ed. Classen (1986), 331–73.

14 C. Bailey, 'Virgil and Lucretius', *Proc. of Classical Assoc.* 28 (1931), 21–39; W. Liebeschuetz, 'The Cycle of Growth and Decay in L and V', *Proc. of Vergilian Soc.* 7 (1967–8), 30–41, repr. in *Virgil in a Cultural Tradition*, eds Cardwell and Hamilton (Nottingham 1986); P. Hardie, *Virgil's Aeneid: Cosmos and Imperium* (1986),157ff.; M. Gale, *Virgil on the Nature of Things* (2000).

15 R. O. A. M. Lyne, in *Quality and Pleasure in Latin Poetry*, eds D. West and T. Woodman (1974), 47–66.

16 Aesop 245 Chambry; D. West, in *Quality and Pleasure* . . . (cited above), 67–80.

17 C. Macleod, *Collected Essays* (1983), 280–91 (masterly).

18 Standard discussions in G. Williams, *Tradition and Originality in Roman Poetry* (1968), 71–6; C. O. Brink, *Horace on Poetry*, vol. 3 (1982), 464–87, 523–72.

19 A. Barchiesi, *Speaking Volumes* (2001), ch. 4.

20 Parallels in Rutherford, *Meditations of Marcus Aurelius*, 39–43.

21 Cf. M. Griffin, *Seneca: A Philosopher in Politics* (1976), ch. 8.

22 For Tacitus' account, see *Annals* 15.60–65. On Seneca's life, see M. Griffin, in *Seneca*, ed. C. D. N. Costa (1974), 1ff.; on his death, and the philosophic context, Griffin, *G & R* 33 (1986), 64–77, 192–202, on suicide.

23 *Mor.* 14dff.: tr. in *Classical Literary Criticism*, eds Russell and Winterbottom (1989).

24 Pease on Cic., *On Divination* 1.122.

Chapter 9 Believers

1   J. M. Rist, *Epicurus* (1972), ch. 8; Pease on Cicero, *On the Nature of the Gods* 1.85, 123.

2   M. Beard, J. North and S. Price, *Religions of Rome* i: *A History* (1998) [henceforth BNP], 91–6, 96–8.

3   R. Parker, in *War and Violence in Ancient Greece*, ed. H. Van Wees (2000), 299–313.

4   BNP, 27–30, 103–4.

5 Burkert, *Greek Religion*, 296–304, and in B. F. Meyer and E. P. Saunders (eds), *Jewish and Christian Self-Definition* iii (1982), 1–22; R. Parker, 'Early Orphism', in A. Powell (ed.), *The Greek World* (1995), 483–510.

6 Strong statements of this position in L. Bruit Zaidman and P. Schmitt Pantel, *Religion in the Ancient Greek City* (Eng. tr. 1992), 27; S. Price, *Religions of the Ancient Greeks* (1999), 3, 183. My formulation is meant to allow a place for beliefs: see also T. Harrison, *Divinity and History* (2001), 20, who promises a further study.

7 *SIG* 601 (193 BC), 611.23ff. (189); Polybius 6.56; Pease on Cic., *On the Nature of the Gods* 2.7–8.

8 C. Gill, N. Postlethwaite, R. Seaford (eds), *Reciprocity in Ancient Greece* (1998).

9 *On the Nature of the Gods* 2.8 and 71.

10 T. C. W. Stinton, *Collected Papers on Greek Tragedy* (1990), 454–92.

11 Acesander of Cyrene, *FGH* 469 F4 = schol. Ap. Rhod. 2.498.

12 Genesis 49; cf. 4.17–24, 10.1–32, 35.23ff.: see further M. L. West, *The Hesiodic Catalogue of Women* (1985), ch. 1.

13 The standard work is N. Fisher, *Hybris: A Study in the Values of Honour and Shame in Ancient Greece* (1992), who makes very clear that the traditional rendering of the term as 'pride' is inadequate.

14 Cf. D. Feeney, *Literature and Religion at Rome* (1998), e.g. 14–19.

15 Pfeiffer, *History of Classical Scholarship* i (1968), 9ff.; Pease on Cic., *On the Nature of the Gods* 2.63ff.

16 Horace, *Epistles* 1.2 for the Homeric interpetations; see further F. Buffière, *Les mythes d'Homère et la pensée grecque* (1956); on pseudo-Heraclitus, *Homeric Allegories*, see D. A. Russell, in G. Boys-Stone (ed.), *Metaphor, Allegory and the Classical Tradition* (2003), 217–34.

17 D. Feeney, *The Gods in Epic* (1991), ch. 2, etc.

18 Palaephatus 43; see J. Stern, in *From Myth to Reason?*, ed. R. Buxton (1999), 215–22.

19 Rutherford, *The Meditations of Marcus Aurelius* (1989), 190.

20 Aug. *City of God* 4.9, cf 31; 6.10.

21 R. Parker, *Miasma* (1983), ch 10; cf. 252–4 on conscience.

22 Cf. Cic. *On Divination* 1.64ff., 70, 125f.; *On the Nature of the Gods* 1.27; Virg., *Geo.* 4.220–7.

23 R. Parker, *G & R* 38 (1991), 1–17.

24 J. Bremmer and N. M. Horsfall, *Roman Myth and Mythography* (*Bulletin of the Institute of Classical Studies* Suppl. 52, 1987), 25–48 (Bremmer); T. P. Wiseman, *Remus: A Roman Myth* (1995); T. J. Cornell, *The Beginnings of Rome* (1995), ch. 3, esp. 60–3, 70–5.

25 Pease on Cic. *On the Nature of the Gods* 2.62.

26 J. Griffin, *Latin Poets and Roman Life* (1985), 178–80.

27 E. Rawson, *JRS* 64 (1974), 148–59 = Rawson, *Roman Culture and Society* (1991), 169–88.

28 S. Weinstock, *Divus Iulius* (1971), ch. 9.

29 The forthcoming book by B. Currie, *Pindar and Hero Cult*, argues that the practice begins considerably earlier.

30 G. Bowersock, *Augustus and the Greek World* (1965), ch. 9 and app. 1; BNP, 145ff.

31 J. U. Powell, *Collectanea Alexandrina* (1925), 173–4; R. Parker, *Athenian Religion: A History* (1996), 258–64.

32 Demosthenes, quoted in Hyperides, *Dem.* col. 31; A. B. Bosworth, *Conquest and Empire* (1988), 283.

33 Suet., *Vesp.* 23, doubted by B. Levick, *Vespasian* (1999), 197.

34 K. J. Dover, *Greek Popular Morality* (1975), 61ff.; J. D. Mikalson, *Athenian Popular Religion* (1983), ch. 10; J. N. Bremmer, *The Rise and Fall of the Afterlife* (2002).

35 *Tusc.* 1.36–7, 48, 111; P. A. Brunt in *Philosophia Togata* i, eds M. Griffin and J. Barnes (1989), 180.

36 R. Lattimore, *Themes in Greek and Latin Epitaphs* (Illinois Stud. In Lang. and Lit. 28, 1942).

37 W. Burkert, *The Orientalizing Revolution: Near Eastern Influence on Greek Culture in the Early Archaic Age* (1992), 96–9; M. L. West, *The East Face of Helicon* (1997), 335–47, 361–2.

38 BNP, 96–8.

39 W. Burkert, *Ancient Mystery Cults* (1987): see p. 69 for the quotations from Aristotle and Plutarch.

40 A. Momigliano, in M. I. Finley (ed.), *The Legacy of Greece: A New Appraisal* 325–46; E. Bickerman, *The Jews in the Greek Age* (1988).

41 Text only in *TGF* i. 288–301 (no.128). Full treatment, including translation, in H. Jacobson, *The Exagoge of Ezekiel* (1983).

42 BNP, 309; E. C. Blackman, *Marcion and His Influence* (1948).

43 Tension visible in *Acts* 10–11. See further e.g. K. Hopkins, *A World Full of Gods* (1999), ch. 3.

44 For a recent survey that tries to look beyond the traditional antithesis, see M. Goodman, *The Roman World 44 BC–AD 180* (1997), chs 29–31.

45 On their obstinacy cf. Mayor on Tert., *Ap.* 27, 50.

46 G. de Ste Croix, *Past and Present* 26 (1963), 6–38, repr. in M. I. Finley (ed.), *Aspects of Ancient Society* (1974), 210–49.

47 M. Edwards and others (ed.), *Apologetics in the Roman Empire. Pagans, Jews and Christians* (1999).

48 H. Chadwick, *Origen Contra Celsum* (Cambridge 1953, revised 1985); also his *Early Christian Thought and the Classical Tradition* (1966).

49 BNP, 267, cf. 375–6.

50 Liebeschuetz, *Continuity and Change*, 246ff., citing Frend.

51 BNP, 366.

52 Eusebius, *Church History* 9.9 (composed *c*.313?); Lactantius, *Deaths of the Persecutors* 44 (*c*.314–6?); Eusebius, *Life of Constantine* 1.29 (much later, well after Constantine's death). See A. H. M. Jones, *Constantine and the Conversion of Europe* (1948); Lane Fox, *Pagans and Christians* (1986), ch. 12, esp. 610–27; A. Cameron, in M. Edwards and S. Swain (eds), *Portraits: The Biographical in the Literature of the Empire* (1997), 245–74.

53 G. de Ste Croix, *The Class Struggle in the Ancient Greek World* (1981), 448–52, esp. Ammianus 27.3.12–13, etc.

54 For a sourcebook containing most of the relevant material from Symmachus, Ambrose and Prudentius, see B. Croke and J. Harries (eds), *Religious Conflict in Fourth-century Rome* (1982).

55 BNP, 374–5.

56 On the vitality of paganism, see esp. J. Geffcken, *The Last Days of Greco-Roman Paganism* (revised tr. by S. MacCormack, 1978; orig. 1920), R. MacMullen, *Paganism in the Roman Empire* (1981); R. Lane Fox, *Pagans and Christians* (1986), esp. part 1.

57 Minuc. 37.1–6 ~ Sen. *On Providence* 2.7–12.

58 Liebeschuetz, *Continuity and Change*, 252–77.

59 On Julian, besides the classic treatment in Gibbon, *Decline and Fall*, chs 22–3, see esp. G. W. Bowersock, *Julian the Apostate* (1978), and R. Smith, *Julian's Gods* (1995), esp. chs 1, 2, 7; also H. Chadwick, *The Church in Ancient Society* (2001), 295–313.

60 Julian, *Epistle* 61a Bidez (36 in Loeb vol. 3); *Theodosian Code* 13.3.5; Ammianus 22.10.7.

61 Tert. *de testim. animae* 1.4.

62 Lact. *Div.Inst.* 5.1.15–18; Aug. *Conf.* 3.9; Jerome *Ep.* 53.10. But for a contrary view, see Tatian, *Oration to the Greeks*, 29.

63 E. Auerbach, *Literary Language and the Reading Public* (1965, Gmn. original 1958), ch. 1, esp. 36–53.

64 Tert. *de praescriptione* 7; Jer. *Ep.* 22.29–30, cf. R. Marcus in *Latin Literature of the Fourth Century*, ed. J. Binns (1974), 5–6.

65 A. F. Norman, introduction to the Loeb Libanius i, gives a sympathetic survey.

66 See Brown, *Augustine of Hippo* (1967), ch. 16 and passim.

67 Probably the *Life* by Athanasius in a Latin version. Cf. C. White, *Early Christian Lives* (Penguin, 1998).

68 *PL* 83.1109, echoing Augustine himself on Varro (*City of God* 6.2).

69 J. J. O'Donnell, intro to his comm. on the *Confessions* (1992), vol. 1, xix.

70 The Loeb edn has useful introductions; see also Brown, *Augustine of Hippo*, chs 26–7; G. O'Daly, *Augustine's City of God: A Reader's Guide* (1999).

71 *Ep.* 123, 127–8, 125 (125 and 127 are in Loeb selection).

72 For comments by Augustine on the overall structure see 1.36, 2.2, 3.1, 4.1–2, 6 preface, 11.1, 18.1, 19.1.

73 *Memoirs* (1796), 160, World's Classics version.

74 G. M. Paul, *Phoenix* 36 (1982), 144–55.

75 Polybius 39.5–6; J. Hornblower, *Hieronymus of Cardia* (1981), 104–5.

Appendix I: Translations of Four Longer Passages

1 A quotation from Homer, *Odyssey* 11.489–91, where Achilles speaks in these terms to Odysseus of his miserable condition among the dead (see p. 26).

2 These men were the most famous of the assassins of Julius Caesar (44 BC).

Further Reading

Throughout I have tried to cite works which are either completely or largely accessible to those without knowledge of Latin and Greek. Works which are particularly suitable as an introduction to an area or author are asterisked. Many other items could of course be cited, but these should be enough to guide the reader on most areas discussed in this book.

General Works of Reference

First and foremost comes the invaluable *Oxford Classical Dictionary* (3rd edn, eds S. Hornblower and A. J. Spawforth, 1996): this version completely supersedes the earlier editions of 1949 and 1970. There are entries, with rich bibliographies, on all authors mentioned in this book (and many more), as well as numerous thematic entries. I do not refer to this elsewhere because citations would become too frequent, but I cannot stress too strongly my debt to this work. Under the same editorship is the *Oxford Companion to Classical Civilization* (1998): this is an abridgement of the *OCD* which includes pictures and maps, but omits bibliographies and the more detailed references to sources. Another useful work is M. C. Howatson (ed.), *The Oxford Companion to Classical Literature* (1989), which gives abundant help in identifying classical names and myths.

The following two titles are also useful: E. J. Bickerman, *Chronology of the Ancient World* (2nd edn, 1980), and G. W. Bowersock, P. Brown and O. Grabar (eds), *Late Antiquity: A Guide to the Postclassical World* (1999; an abridged version, *Interpreting Late Antiquity* (2001), has been published).

Atlases: the monumental work is R. J. A. Talbert (ed.), *Barrington Atlas of the Greek and Roman World* (2000), but its price is as high as its quality. Cheaper alternatives are N. G. L. Hammond, *Atlas of the Greek and Roman World in Antiquity* (1982; paperback 1992), and R. J. A. Talbert, *Atlas of Classical History* (1985).

Other notable reference works that give reliable help in the areas they cover are C. J. Rowe and M. Schofield (eds), *Cambridge History of Greek and Roman Political Thought* (2000), P. France (ed.), *The Oxford Guide to Literature in English Translation*

(2000), J. Boardman (ed.), *The Oxford History of Classical Art* (1993), and J. Davidson Reid (ed.), *The Oxford Guide to Classical Mythology in the Arts 1300–1990s* (1993).

Other Histories of Classical Literature

CHCL (= *Cambridge History of Classical Literature*), vol.1 (Greek Literature), eds P. E. Easterling and B. Knox (1985), and vol. 2 (Latin Literature), eds E. J. Kenney and W. V. Clausen (1982). Many contributors and of uneven quality; at its best very good.

O. Taplin (ed.), *Literature in the Greek and Roman Worlds* (2000), contains attractive essays focusing on audience and performance. J. Boardman, J. Griffin and O. Murray (eds), *The Oxford History of the Classical World* (1982), covers literature, history, art and thought, and has excellent illustrations.

Of single-author works, the best on Greek are by Germans, the best on Latin by an Italian: fortunately all are translated. I refer to A. Lesky, *A History of Greek Literature* (Eng. tr. 1966), now rather dated but very clear and fair-minded; A. Dihle, *A History of Greek Literature from Homer to the Hellenistic Period* (Eng. tr. 1994), compressed but highly intelligent; G. B. Conte, *Latin Literature: A History* (1994), informative and judicious. Briefer single-author works include S. Braund, *Latin Literature* (2002), emphasizing literary theory; P. Levi, *The Pelican History of Greek Literature* (1985); S. Said and M. Trédé, *A Short History of Greek Literature* (Eng. tr. 1999; Fr. original 1990).

More specific works on particular aspects: D. A. Campbell, *The Golden Lyre* (1983); M. Fantuzzi-R. Hunter, *Muse e modelli: la poesia ellenistica da Alessandro magno ad Augusto* (2002, Eng. tr. imminent); J. Griffin, *Latin Poets and Roman Life* (1985), mainly on Augustan poetry; E. Fantham, *Roman Literary Culture from Cicero to Apuleius* (1996); N. Horsfall, *The Culture of the Roman Plebs* (2003); D. A. Russell (ed.), *Antonine Literature* (1990), esp. the editor's opening essay; S. Swain, *Hellenism and Empire: Language, Classicism and Power in the Greek World* AD *50–250* (1996); A. Dihle, *Greek and Latin Literature of the Roman Empire from Augustus to Justinian* (Eng. tr. 1994).

Some 'Classics' of the Classics

E. Gibbon, *The Decline and Fall of the Roman Empire* (1776–88), is still a work of rich insight, quite apart from its enormous literary merit: the best selection is the excellent Penguin abridgement by David Womersley (2000), which includes many famous chapters (though not ch. 37 on the rise of monasticism).

J. Burckhardt, *The Greeks and Greek Civilization* (ed. O. Murray, 1998), provides selections from a great historian's lectures, and is one of the founding documents of cultural history. E. R. Dodds, *The Greeks and the Irrational* (1951), is a work which every student should read: its learning and perception still inspire, even though many particular propositions have been refuted.

E. R. Curtius, *European Literature and the Latin Middle Ages* (Eng. tr. 1953), and E. Auerbach, *Mimesis: The Representation of Reality in Western Literature* (1946; Eng. tr. by W. Trask, 1953), are inexhaustible. The latter starts with a chapter on Homer which has been much criticized, but the whole book is a treasure-house of critical insights.

Italo Calvino, *Why Read the Classics?* (tr. M. McLaughlin, 1999; Ital. original 1991), contains memorable essays on major authors.

Translations

The most wide-ranging series is the Loeb Classical Library, which for almost a century has published compact hard-cover volumes with text and facing translation. This includes almost all authors cited in this book, but the series is uneven. Early volumes were mostly unambitious, plain prose and few if any notes; a few ventured into verse, disastrously for the most part (though B. B. Rogers' rendering of Aristophanes into a style modelled on Gilbert and Sullivan is worth noting). Some of the older versions of major authors have been updated (Homer, Virgil among them); others have been completely replaced (Sophocles, Euripides, Aristophanes, Propertius, Quintilian). In general the rule is that the more recent the Loeb, the better it is likely to be: in some cases this is the best edition for both amateurs and scholars to use (e.g. Manilius, Quintilian, Arrian).

The other series which can be strongly recommended are the Penguin Classics and the Oxford World's Classics: these normally offer good and idiomatic versions, with informative introductions and notes. Both series have some gaps and some weaker volumes (the Penguin Catullus is very poor). Hackett's Library performs a similar service, although their range is less wide. I mention a few other translations below and in the notes, where the Loeb or Penguin are not helpful.

Anthologies: A. Poole and J. Maule (eds), *The Oxford Book of Classical Verse in Translation* (1995); R. Stoneman (ed.), *Daphne into Laurel: Translations of Classical Poetry from Chaucer to the Present* (1982). An excellent series of Penguin 'Poets in Translation' was inaugurated by G. Steiner (ed.), *Homer in English* (1996), and volumes have appeared on Catullus, Virgil, Horace, Ovid, Seneca, Martial and Juvenal. It is sad that the series has been discontinued.

Further Reading Relevant to Particular Chapters

Introduction

Ancient history: probably the best introductory books, scholarly but stimulating, are the Fontana History of the Ancient World, esp. O. Murray and J. K. Davies on Early and Classical Greece, F. W. Walbank on the Hellenistic World, and A. Cameron on late antiquity. Longer and more detailed are the Routledge series: see esp. the volumes by R. Osborne (early Greece), S. Hornblower (479–323 BC), and T. J. Cornell (early Rome). The massive volumes of the *Cambridge Ancient History* (2nd edn), a work by many hands, provides expert guidance and huge bibliographies across the full range from Mycenae to the beginning of the Middle Ages: coverage of literature is variable, but there are some fine essays on culture, religion and social contexts.

A selection of other titles: A. Andrewes, *Greek Society* (Penguin edn, 1971); P. Cartledge, *The Greeks* (1993); M. I. Finley, *The World of Odysseus* (2nd edn, 1978), *The Use and Abuse of History* (1971), and *Economy and Society in Ancient Greece* (1981); A. R. Burn, *Persia and the Greeks* (revised edn by D. M. Lewis, 1984); J. P. V. D. Balsdon, *Life and Letters in Ancient Rome* (1969), *Roman Women* (1962), and *Romans and Aliens* (1979); P. A. Brunt, *Social Conflicts in the Roman Republic* (1971); F. Millar and E. Segal (eds), *Caesar Augustus* (1984); G. K. Galinsky, *Augustan Culture* (1996); Z. Yavetz, *Plebs and Princeps* (1969); P. Veyne, *Bread and Circuses* (Eng. tr. 1990; longer Fr. original 1976); P.Garnsey and R. Saller, *The Roman Empire: Economy, Society and Culture* (1987); P. Garnsey and C. Humfress, *The Evolution of Late Antiquity* (2001).

For the ancient theorists on their own literature, see D. A. Russell and M. Winterbottom (eds), *Ancient Literary Criticism* (1972), a valuable sourcebook; the abridged version, *Classical Literary Criticism* (1989), includes four key texts: Aristotle's *Poetics*, Horace's *Art of Poetry*, Tacitus' *Dialogue on Orators*, and Longinus' *On the Sublime*.

On genre, D. A. Russell, *Criticism in Antiquity* (1981), ch. 10; A. Fowler, *Forms of Literature* (1982), very wide horizons; also S. J. Harrison, *Forms of Appropriation: Generic Enrichment in Vergil and Horace* (forthcoming).

On literary cross-reference, see S. Hinds, *Allusion and Intertext* (1998), esp. chs 1–2; D. Fowler, *Roman Constructions* (2000), 115–37; L. Edmunds, *Intertextuality and the Reading of Roman Poetry* (2001). For other aspects of literary theory and the classics, see D. P. and P. G. Fowler, *OCD* s.v. 'literary theory and classical studies'; S. J. Harrison (ed.), *Texts, Ideas and the Classics* (2001); *M. Heath, *Interpreting Classical Literature* (2003).

On literacy, varying views in W. V. Harris, *Ancient Literacy* (1989); R. Thomas, *Literacy and Orality in Ancient Greece* (1992); A. K. Bowman and G. Woolf (eds), *Literacy and Power in the Ancient World* (1994).

On the textual traditions, above all *L. D. Reynolds and N. G. Wilson, *Scribes and Scholars* (3rd edn, 1991). See also Reynolds' introduction to L. D. Reynolds (ed.), *Texts and Transmission: A Survey of the Latin Classics* (1983); M. L. West, *Textual Criticism and Editorial Technique* (1973); E. G. Turner, *Greek Papyri* (1968, revised 1980); E. G. Turner, *Greek Manuscripts of the Ancient World*, 2nd edn revised by P. J. Parsons (*BICS* Suppl. 46, 1987).

On the classical heritage, two very different but equally rich works are *G. Highet, *The Classical Tradition. Greek and Roman Influences on Western Literature* (Oxford 1949), and R. R. Bolgar, *The Classical Heritage and Its Beneficiaries: From the Carolingian Age to the End of the Renaissance* (1954).

On modern scholarship, besides Reynolds and Wilson, cited above, see U. von Wilamowitz, *History of Classical Scholarship* (Eng. tr. 1981), a stimulating if opinionated overview (originally published in German, 1921); R. Pfeiffer, *History of Classical Scholarship* i (1968), on the ancient world, and ii (1976), from Erasmus to the Victorians, are masterly, but advanced.

Chapter 1 Epic

C. M. Bowra, *From Virgil to Milton* (1945); *J. Griffin, *Homer on Life and Death* (1980); R. B. Rutherford, *Homer* (*G & R* new surveys 26, 1996); *W. A. Camps, *An Introduction to Virgil's Aeneid* (1969: elementary but useful); *P. Hardie, *Virgil* (*G & R* new surveys 28, 1998); R. Thomas, *Virgil and the Augustan Reception* (2001); L. P. Wilkinson, *Ovid Recalled* (1955), remains a sympathetic study of its subject; more up-to-date is P. Hardie (ed.), *Cambridge Companion to Ovid* (2001); E. Fantham, *Ovid's Metamorphoses* (2004). D. C. Feeney, *The Gods in Epic* (1991), especially good on Ovid and Lucan; M. P. O. Morford, *The Poet Lucan* (1967), mainly on his rhetoric; W. R. Johnson, *Momentary Monsters* (1987), is a short, vigorous essay on Lucan; see also P. Hardie, *The Epic Successors of Virgil* (1993), and, in *CHCL*, J. C. Bramble on Lucan, and D. Vessey's chapter on other Latin epic.

Chapter 2 Drama

CHCL i (the sections on tragedy and comedy are all excellent, and reprinted as a separate paperback). *O. Taplin, *Greek Tragedy in Action* (1978), stimulating introduction; A. H. Sommerstein, *Greek Drama and Dramatists* (2000), combines basic factual data with a selection of translated passages; *P. E. Easterling (ed.), *Cambridge Companion to Greek Tragedy* (1997), one of the best in this series so far, has excellent essays and very full bibliography; also S. Goldhill, *Reading Greek Tragedy* (1987); J. Winkler and F. Zeitlin (eds), *Nothing to do with Dionysos?* (1990) (uneven); C. Pelling (ed.), *Greek Tragedy and the Historian* (1997); *E. Csapo and W. Slater, *The Context of Greek Drama* (1995), is a valuable sourcebook. J. Mossman (ed.), *Oxford Readings in Euripides* (2003), collects some influential essays; similar volumes are planned for Aeschylus and Sophocles.

Comedy: *K. J. Dover, *Aristophanic Comedy* (1972); M. Silk, *Aristophanes and the Nature of Comedy* (2001); on the fragmentary Greek comedies, D. Harvey and J. Wilkins (eds), *The Rivals of Aristophanes: Studies in Athenian Old Comedy* (2000) (advanced); *R. L. Hunter, *The New Comedy of Greece and Rome* (1985); G. E. Duckworth, *The Nature of Roman Comedy* (1971); T. S. Eliot, 'Shakespeare and the Stoicism of Seneca' and 'Seneca and Elizabethan Tragedy', both repr. in his *Selected Essays* (1932; 3rd edn, 1951); C. J. Herington, in *Essays in Classical Literature*, ed. N. Rudd (1972), 169–219; and the same author's chapter on Seneca in *CHCL* ii.

Chapter 3 Rhetoric

Standard handbooks are G. Kennedy, *The Art of Persuasion in Greece* (1963); *The Art of Rhetoric in the Roman World* (1972); see also I Worthington (ed.), *Persuasion. Greek Rhetoric in Action* (1994); S. Usher, *Greek Oratory, Tradition and Originality* (1999); *M. L. Clarke, *Rhetoric at Rome* (1953, revised by D. Berry, 1996); D. A.

Russell, 'Rhetoric and Criticism', *G & R,* 14 (1967), 130–44; S. F. Bonner, *Roman Declamation* (1949); S. F. Bonner, *Education in Ancient Rome* (1977).

Selections from the Greek speeches include W. R. Connor, *Greek Orations* (1966); C. Carey, *Trials from Classical Athens* (1997). A complete series of translations is in progress from Austin, Texas: so far, note esp. S. Todd, *Lysias* (1999).

An excellent translation of a number of Cicero's best speeches is *Cicero: Defence Speeches* (World's Classics); a larger selection in various Penguin volumes. For Cicero's life, see *E. Rawson, *Cicero. A Portrait* (1973); D. L. Stockton, *Cicero, A Political Biography* (1971); *C. Habicht, *Cicero the Politician* (1990).

Chapter 4 History, Biography and Fiction

General: *A. Momigliano, 'History and Biography', in *The Legacy of Greece: A New Appraisal* (ed. M. I. Finley, 1981), 155–84; see also his *The Classical Foundations of Modern Historiography* (1990), posthumous and no annotation, but resting on deep knowledge of the whole field: still more penetrating are the specific studies in his *Studies in Historiography* (1969), and *Essays in Ancient and Modern Historiography* (1977); *The Development of Greek Biography* (1971). See further S. Hornblower (ed.), *Greek Historiography* (1994), esp. the editor's contributions; *J. Marincola, *Greek Historians* (*G & R* new surveys 31, 2001); *C. S. Kraus and A. J. Woodman, *Latin Historians* (*G & R* new surveys 27, 1997). T. A. Dorey (ed.), *Latin Historians* (1962): oddly, this includes the Greek Polybius.

For studies of particular writers see the notes to ch. 4.

On later developments, see Momigliano, *Essays*... (1977) on 'Pagan and Christian Historiography' and on Ammianus Marcellinus; D. Rohrbacher, *The Historians of Late Antiquity* (2002).

Fiction: *T. Hägg. *The Novel in Antiquity* (1983) – wide horizons, excellent illustrations; *E. L. Bowie in *CHCL,* i, 683–99 (paperback, i.4.123–39), reprinted in S. Swain (ed.), *Oxford Readings in the Greek Novel* (1999), 39–59; *P. G. Walsh, *The Roman Novel* (1970); *M. Coffey, *Roman Satire* (1976), ch. 10, discusses Petronius; E. Courtney, *A Companion to Petronius* (2000). On Apuleius, besides Walsh, see esp. J. J. Winkler, *Auctor & Actor* (1985); also S. J. Harrison, *Apuleius: A Latin Sophist* (2000); various papers on both Petronius and Apuleius in S. J. Harrison (ed.), *Oxford Readings in the Roman Novel* (1999).

Chapter 5 Erotic Literature

General themes and background: *G. Clarke, *Women in the Ancient World* (G & R, new surveys, 21, 1989); K. J. Dover, *Greek Homosexuality* (1978) – fundamental, though quite detailed; J. Winkler, *The Constraints of Desire* (1990); D. M. Halperin, *One Hundred Years of Homosexuality* (1990); J. Davidson, *Courtesans and Fishcakes* (1998); P. Brown, *The Body and Society* (1988). Interesting essays collected in D. M. Halperin, J. J. Winkler, F. Zeitlin (eds), *Before Sexuality* (1990), and M. C. Nussbaum and J. Sihvola (eds), *The Sleep of Reason* (2002). On Latin poetry, see R. O. A. M. Lyne, *The Latin Love Poets* (1980), with useful chapters on social history, but his discussion of the poets is one-sided; P. Veyne, *Roman Erotic Elegy* (1988); M. Wyke, *The Roman Mistress* (2002).

Women's writing: *J. M. Snyder, *The Woman and the Lyre* (1990). For translations see e.g. Josephine Balmer, *Classical Women Poets* (Bloodaxe Books, 1996).

There are numerous sourcebooks: note especially M. Lefkowitz and M. Fant, *Women's Life in Greece and Rome* (1982, revised 1992); T. K. Hubbard, *Homosexuality in Greece and Rome: A Sourcebook of Basic Documents* (2003).

For translations of Greek lyric poetry which include the newer material, there are two useful books. M. L. West, *Greek Lyric Poetry* (Oxford, World's Classics 1993), is by a world expert but gives very slender annotation. More helpful though less complete is A. W. Miller, *Greek Lyric* (Hackett 1996), which also has extensive selections from Pindar and Bacchylides.

Chapter 6 Literature and Power

On the early Greek lyric poets in this context, see A. Podlecki, *The Early Greek Poets and Their Times* (1984); many relevant observations also in O. Murray, *Early Greece* (1980). B. K. Gold, *Literary Patronage in Greece and Rome* (1987) cites much older work and brings the story down to the Augustan age. That period has been much studied: see e.g. G. Williams, *Tradition and Originality in Roman Poetry* (1968), esp. ch. 2, 'The Poet and the Community', and ch. 6, 'The Poetry of Institutions'; *J. Griffin, on Augustus and the poets, in *Caesar Augustus*, eds F. Millar and E. Segal (1983), 188–218; P. White, *Promised Verse* (1993). P. Zanker, *The Power of Images in the Age of Augustus* (Eng. tr., 1988), discusses the relevant art and architecture and relates it to the poetry. For later developments, see E. Fantham (cited in the section on other histories of classical literature (p. 334)); A. Hardie, *Statius and the Silvae* (1983), valuable not only on Statius but on the wider history of patronage; R. MacMullen, *Enemies of the Roman Order* (1966).

Chapter 7 Aspects of Wit

Parody: J. P. Cèbe, *La caricature et la parodie dans le monde romain antique des origines à Juvenal* (1966); M. Silk, *Aristophanes and the Definition of Comedy* (2000), ch. 2.

Hellenistic literature: *A. W. Bulloch provides a helpful survey of the main figures in *CHCL*, i. See also H. Lloyd-Jones, 'A Hellenistic Miscellany', *Academic Papers*, ii (1990); G. O. Hutchinson, *Hellenistic Poetry* (1988), esp. on Callimachus; P. J. Parsons, in A. W. Bulloch et al. (eds), *Images of Ideology* (1993).

On the 'pointed' style, W. C. Summers, *Select Letters of Seneca* (1910), xv–xli; P. Plass, *Wit and the Writing of History* (1988). Martial: J. P. Sullivan, *Martial, the Unexpected Classic* (1991).

Satire: E. Fraenkel, *Horace* (1957), a very important work, but assuming knowledge of Latin; *N. Rudd, *The Satires of Horace* (1966); *M. Coffey, *Roman

Satire (1976), excellent on literary history though not detailed on particular poems; S. H. Braund, *Roman Verse Satire* (*G & R*, new surveys, 23, 1992). G. Highet, *Juvenal the Satirist* (1954), is uncritically biographical but useful on Juvenal's influence. Lucian: C. Robinson, *Lucian and His Influence in Europe* (1974).

Translations: for Callimachus, see the version by F. Nisetich (Oxford 2000), with full notes (the Loeb is now very out of date). More translations of Hellenistic literature are needed. For Lucilius, see E. H. Warmington, *Remains of Old Latin*, vol. 3 (Loeb).

Chapter 8 Thinkers

C. Gill, *Greek Thought* (*G & R*, new surveys, 25, 1995); *T. Irwin, *Classical Thought* (1989), is more concerned with Greek than Latin. On the Roman side, see *M. L. Clarke, *The Roman Mind* (1956); similar though more up-to-date, *M. P. O. Morford, *The Roman Philosophers* (2002).

More specific studies: G. E. R. Lloyd, *Magic, Reason and Experience* (1979), esp. ch. 4; R. Buxton (ed.), *From Myth to Reason?* (1999), esp. the editor's introduction; *E. Hussey, *The Presocratics* (1972). On the sophists and Socrates, see W. K. C. Guthrie, *History of Greek Philosophy*, vol. 3 (1969) – later volumes are less stimulating. On Socrates, *C. C. W. Taylor, *Socrates* (1998); more advanced is G. Vlastos, *Socrates, Ironist and Moral Philosopher* (1991. On Plato, e.g. R. Kraut (ed.), *The Cambridge Companion to Plato* (1992); R. B. Rutherford, *The Art of Plato* (1995). For Roman thinkers, M. Griffin and J. Barnes (eds), *Philosophia Togata: Essays on Philosophy and Roman Society* (1989), esp. M. Griffin, 'Philosophy, Politics and Politicians at Rome', and P. A. Brunt, 'Philosophy and Religion in the Late Republic'; M. Griffin, *CAH*, ix (1994), ch. 18, 'The Intellectual Developments of the Ciceronian Age'; E. Rawson, *Intellectual Life in the Late Roman Republic* (1985); P. MacKendrick, *The Philosophical Works of Cicero* (1989), has its uses, but reads more like the materials for a book than a book.

Lucretius: the revised Loeb (M. Smith) is helpfully annotated, as is the version by A. Melville in the Oxford World's Classics; see also *D. A. West, *The Imagery and Poetry of Lucretius* (1969). K. Volk, *The Poetics of Latin Didactic* (2002), covers Lucretius, Virgil's *Georgics*, Ovid's *Ars Amatoria*.

On Virgil's *Georgics*, the standard book is still *L. P. Wilkinson, *The Georgics of Virgil* (1969) – the same scholar is the author of the admirable Penguin translation. See also the relevant section in Hardie, *Virgil* (*G & R* survey). The most recent full-scale study, M. Gale, *Virgil on the Nature of Things* (2000), gives access to earlier work and is valuable for the detailed comparisons with Lucretius.

Horace, *Epistles*: N. Rudd's translation (Penguin) combines Horace's *Satires* and *Epistles* and Persius.

Imperial Stoicism: C. D. N. Costa (ed.), *Seneca* (1974), esp. the essays by M. Griffin on his life, and *D. A. Russell on his *Letters*; *P. Veyne, *Seneca* (1997); *A. A. Long, *Epictetus* (2001). On Marcus Aurelius, P. A. Brunt, 'Marcus Aurelius in His *Meditations*', *JRS*, 64 (1974), 1–20; P. Hadot, *The Inner Citadel* (1998);

see also P. Hadot, *Philosophy as a Way of Life: Spiritual Exercises from Socrates to Foucault* (1995).

On Plutarch, *D. A. Russell, *Plutarch* (1973), is outstanding; excellent selections from the *Moral Essays* in both Penguin and World's Classics, with little overlap.

Translations: the works that survive intact are available in many versions. As for the more fragmentary authors, on the Presocratics see the Penguin volumes, *Early Greek Philosophy* and *The Greek Sophists*, or the World's Classics, *The First Philosophers*; on Hellenistic thinkers, A. A. Long and D. Sedley, *The Hellenistic Philosophers* (1987), vol. 1, or B. Inwood, *Hellenistic Philosophy; Introductory Readings* (1988).

Chapter 9 Believers

The unquestioned master of the study of early Greek religion is W. Burkert, whose *Greek Religion* (1985) is long but constantly illuminating. Many approaches are surveyed by *J. Bremmer, *Greek Religion* (*G & R*, new surveys, 24, 1994); the companion volume by *J. North, *Roman Religion* (*G & R*, new surveys, 30, 2000), is also helpful and serves partly as a guide into Beard-North-Price (below). On Greek religion generally, see also R. Buxton (ed.), *Oxford Readings in Greek Religion* (2000); *S. Price, *Religions of the Ancient Greeks* (1999). For Rome, J. H. W. G. Liebeschuetz, *Continuity and Change in Roman Religion* (1979); D. C. Feeney, *Literature and Religion at Rome* (1998); M. Beard, J. North, S. Price, *Religions at Rome* (1998), vol. 1, a history, and vol. 2, a sourcebook in translation. See also S. Price and E. Kearns (eds), *The Oxford Dictionary of Classical Myth and Religion* (2003).

Myth: W. Burkert, *Structure and History in Greek Mythology* (1979), ch. 1; F. Graf, *Greek Mythology* (1987, Eng. tr., 1993); Bremmer (see last paragraph), ch. 5; *R. Buxton, *Imaginary Greece: The Contexts of Mythology* (1994) (excellent).

The Jews and classical literature: A. Momigliano, in *The Legacy of Greece, A New Appraisal*, ed. M. I. Finley (1981), 325–46; E. Bickerman, *The Jews in the Greek Age* (1988); T. Rajak (ed.), *The Jews among Pagans and Christians in the Roman Empire* (1997); R. Lane Fox, *The Unauthorised Version* (1991), and note esp. ch. 11.

Paganism/Christianity: Gibbon, *Decline and Fall*, esp. chs 15–16; A. Momigliano (ed.), *The Conflict of Paganism and Christianity in the Fourth Century* (1963), esp. the essays by Momigliano and Jones; *E. R. Dodds, *Pagan and Christian in an Age of Anxiety* (1964); *P. Brown, *The World of Late Antiquity* (1971); R. MacMullen, *Paganism in the Roman Empire* (1981); R. Lane Fox, *Pagans and Christians* (1986), esp. part 1; K. Hopkins, *A World Full of Gods* (1999), has much of interest, though his time-travel narratives may not appeal to all. For a short history of early Christianity, see H. Chadwick, *The Early Church* (Penguin 1967); a larger treatment by the same author, *The Church in Ancient Society: From Galilee to Gregory the Great* (2001). J. Binns (ed.), *Latin Literature of the Fourth Century AD* (1974).

Augustine: P. Brown, *Augustine of Hippo* (1967, revised 2000: inspiring), supplemented by his *Religion and Society in the Age of St Augustine* (1971); *H. Chadwick,

Augustine (1986); G. Clark, *Augustine, Confessions* (1993); G. O'Daly, *Augustine's City of God* (1999) – advanced.

Translations: H. Isbell, *The Last Poets of Imperial Rome* (Penguin 1971); C. White, *Early Christian Latin Poetry* (1999). Some works by Tertullian and Augustine are available in Loeb; for fuller coverage of the Christian prose works one has to turn to older versions, in particular the multi-volume Library of the Ante-Nicene and Post-Nicene Fathers. For further guidance, see the bibliography in Chadwick, *The Church in Ancient Society* (above).

Index

This index is selective, and concentrates principally on names of authors or other major figures. It includes only the most prominent names referred to in the summaries of particular works, or in quotations. Entries are also provided for a number of technical terms. A few thematic entries have been added, but these are not intended to be exhaustive. Where a writer is frequently mentioned, the principal discussions are indicated in bold.